LOVE IS A SWEET CHAIN

LOVE IS A SWEET CHAIN

DESIRE, AUTONOMY, AND FRIENDSHIP IN LIBERAL POLITICAL THEORY

JAMES R. MARTEL

ROUTLEDGE

NEW YORK   LONDON

Published in 2001 by
Routledge
29 West 35th Street
New York, NY 10001

Published in Great Britain by
Routledge
11 New Fetter Lane
London EC4P 4EE

Routledge is an imprint of the Taylor & Francis Group.

Printed in the United States of America on acid-free paper.

Library of Congress Cataloging-in-Publication Data
Martel, James R.
     Love is a sweet chain : desire, autonomy, and friendship in liberal political theory / by
James R. Martel.
     p. cm.
     Includes bibliographical references and index.
     ISBN 0-415-92856-7 — ISBN 0-415-92883-4 (pbk.)
     1. Liberalism. 2. Love. I. Title.

JC574 .M39 2001
320'.01—dc21
                                                                        00-062817
1 0   9   8   7   6   5   4   3   2   1

FOR MY PARENTS

CONTENTS

Acknowledgments

I would like to thank a great many people who made this book possible: First and foremost to my family: Carlos, with all my love, as well as Rudie, Ralph, Huguette, Django, Shalini, Nina, Kathryn, Erica, Elic, and Lisa. I would also like to thank Nasser Hussain, who is a true friend was possible, even as he helped me learn how to critique such concepts. I thank all of the great teachers that I have had who inspired me and helped me fall in love with political theory: Michael Rogin, Shannon Stimson, Hanna Pitkin, Tom Laqueur, Norman Jacobson, and in particular Wendy Brown, Jane Lewis, and Janice Wells. I want to thank several members of the Amherst College faculty: Austin Sarat, Thomas Dumm, Pavel Machala, and my good friend Javier Corrales, as well as Alec Irwin, Martha Umphrey, Barry O'Connell, and Janet Gyatso. Thanks to Joyce Seltzer for much advice and years of support and friendship. Thanks to Judith Butler, and the faculty and staff of the rhetoric department at Berkeley. And thanks to Eric Nelson, as well as Nicole Ellis, for their excellent work as editors, as well as everyone else at Routledge. I also want to thank many friends, teachers, students, and colleagues for support and advice: Nate Teske and Tom Burke for many, many reasons, Beverly Crawford for years of sponsorship and friendship. Thanks to Susan Silbey for her interventions on my behalf. Thanks to my many wonderful students including Nadia Latif, Vanessa Legagneur, Jon Prokup, Anthony Smith, Flori Fischetti, Katie Dowd, Susannah Black, Steve Seelbach, Annie Kao, Gergana Yankova, Samantha Alves, Eric Roman, Melvin Rogers, Melissa Rodes, Anush Kapadia, Sanjay Pinto, Divya Rajamaran, and David Berman, as well as my new students in rhetoric. Thanks to Michael Sherman for many years of support and encouragment. Thanks also to the following people: Jeanne Failevic, Albert Cohen, Morris Kaplan, Jane Taylorson, Judith Foster, Maxine Fredericksen, David Niedorf, Lynne Gordon, Vicki Farrington, Nick Biziouris, Jackie Stevens, Sultana Hussain, Kateri Carmola, Laura Harrington, Aaron Belkin, Elizabeth Armstrong, Duncan Cranmer, Joan Cocks, Mark Andrejevic, Christopher Clay, Lisa Clampett, Alyson Cole, Joan Tronto, Vida Prater, Michael Kimmel, Elaine Thomas, Kathy Moon, Christine Trost, Ricardo Muñoz-Martin, Donnett Flash, Marcus Kurtz, Paul Thomas, Ed Stettner, Carole Spencer, and many, many others.

INTRODUCTION:
THE PROBLEM OF LOVE

LOVE IS A SWEET CHAIN

In his play *The Discovery of the New World* [*La Découverte de Nouveau Monde*], Jean-Jacques Rousseau muses on the mixed blessings of love. This play is set in the Americas and begins on the eve of Columbus's invasion with a vague foreboding on the part of the Americans that catastrophe will strike them. It does indeed with the arrival of the Spanish ships. The chief of the Americans, who Rousseau refers to as "Cacique" (i.e., chief), fears that the Spaniards will defeat him militarily. As it happens, it is not military weakness that threatens the Americans, but love. Cacique is betrayed by Carime, a young woman who loves him and is jealous that he loves only his wife, Digize. Carime tells a Spanish soldier where Cacique is hiding and he is captured. Subsequently, the Americans are enslaved. When Columbus learns of Cacique's great love for Digize he decides to retain him as leader of the conquered Americans. Everyone is now "happy," united in their appreciation for love. Together they say:

> There is no savage heart when it comes to love. And those who engage in it share other pleasures from its sweet chains.[1]

The Discovery of the New World suggests that the existence of love doomed the state of nature in America; it was a scorned woman who betrayed the Americans. And yet losing this freedom is not entirely unrewarded; it was also the love for a woman that united the Americans and Spaniards in the end. Love is a "sweet chain" which makes the Americans willing to be enslaved by the Spanish. When Columbus plants the Spanish flag on American soil, he says, "Lose your liberty, but gain, without complaint, a more precious yoke."[2] For Rousseau, love unites not only persons, but also entire nations; it causes us to give up a natural freedom for a brave new world of danger and promise. It is both a betrayal of the self and our *telos,* developing us toward a higher, social perfection.

The questions which Rousseau leaves us with at the end of the play are "What kind of collectivity can we form given the tragic origins of our bonds?"

1

"Can a new sort of freedom be developed out of the loss of the old?" "What have we gained and what have we lost?"

In this book, I want to ask similar questions. Understanding love as a political and philosophical construction, I want to look at the relationship between love and democracy. Does love necessarily compromise and enslave us? Is it necessary for or does it preclude the possibility of a democratic polity?[3] Rousseau's play affords us a glimpse of the presupposed, naturalized, and prepolitical sphere which underlies our conceptions of self and society. He shows us that the realm of love is one of inequality, hierarchy, conquest, and even genocide as much as it is one of unity and relationship. Although he seems to breezily accept the inevitability of love, he implicitly holds out the question "must it be this way?" Can we, should we, do without love? But if so, what, if anything, would hold us together?

THE MANY NAMES OF LOVE

Love is generally thought of as an emotion, a state of surrender, something that we write songs about, but rarely is it linked in common parlance to questions of politics. Indeed, the term "politics of love" sounds funny to one's ears, seeking to link two unrelatable terms. And yet, the relationship between love and politics is quite well established. Politics is after all the study of human arrangements, how we treat and deal with each other, and love, in all of its romantic, filial, paternal, and social senses, is concerned with precisely the same thing. A study of the role of love in political theory reveals that it is quite difficult to parse these two seemingly separate notions apart.

In Western philosophy the idea of love has long served as a way to link human beings to one another and also to the divine. Love transposes us from our ordinary lives. It gets us to think beyond ourselves; it causes us to sacrifice ourselves for others and generally to act as we would otherwise not act. Perhaps for this reason, philosophy has long sought to enlist (and produce) love, to draw upon it as the basis for the kinds of transformations that it enables. The love of the polis, the requirement of ethics, philosophy itself (the love of knowledge) are all predicated on a relationship with love.

When so enlisted, love becomes not just a tool for but the basis of the political orders that it helps to engender. Love connects and transcends distinctions such as private and public, individual and community, heaven and earth, and in so doing becomes part of the fabric, the "nature" behind ourselves and our actions. To treat love as a historical concept enables us to examine ourselves and our society at a most profound level, to visit the intimate and often violent realm that is presupposed by the political itself.

The English word "love" covers a great terrain which in both Greek and Latin was separated into quite a few subcategories with vastly different connotations. Among other terms, the Greeks distinguished between *eros, storge, philia,* and *agape.* These terms might be translated respectively as erotic love, affection or "care," friendship, and finally, the love of God. Of these, the terms *eros* and *philia* were of most interest to classical Greek philosophy, whereas *agape* is a term most associated with the Greek of the New Testament, especially the Gospel according to John. Common to all of these terms is a notion of human relationships that are constituted in the context of and the search for the divine. Critically, the question of love becomes one of boundaries: If love always relates us to ourselves and to one another on the basis of that which cannot be seen, how much is love our own? How do we gain a sense of our own autonomy and agency from such an external source? What kind of ethics, what kind of politics stem from such a conception?

We find many different answers to these questions across the span of classical and early Christian philosophy. Yet it is remarkable to note the persistency of the question of human agency as well as the continual reproduction of a particular political vision in which identity, law, and community are always produced in reference to some external and "higher" standard. With some important exceptions, particularly among the Romans, love, the "glue" which holds us together, simultaneously calls our agency and even our very being into question.

Whereas in early Christian doctrine the various Greek ideas of love form a ladder from lower (least Godly, most human) to higher (most Godly, least human), for Plato the "lowest" term, *eros,* was in fact the most important category of all. This would seem to suggest that Plato has given (as Anders Nygren will complain many centuries later) human experience and agency a central position. To some extent this is the case. And yet it becomes fairly clear that Plato appropriates *eros* not for its own sake but to enlist it in the quest for higher, better truths.

In *The Symposium, eros* is shown to be the basis for the polis, for all political virtues, and even for the pursuit of philosophy itself. As Diotima tells Socrates:

> Some men are pregnant in respect to their bodies...and turn more to women, and are lovers in that way, providing in all future time, as they suppose, immortality and happiness for themselves, through getting children. Others are pregnant in respect to their soul.... What then so pertains? Practical wisdom and the rest of virtue....[T]he greatest and most beautiful kind of practical wisdom...is that concerned with the right ordering of cities and households, for which the name is temperance and justice.[4]

Here we see how something as "base" as *eros* can serve as the basis for politics and virtue. Diotima's name means "God-fearing." She is a woman who uses metaphors of pregnancy and the body to construct a social hierarchy. She describes love as a great continuum binding us together, permitting us to have a political order and relating us *from lowest to highest* according to our relationship to truth. What medieval Christian scholars will later call the "ladder of being" is in a sense already present in the notion of *eros*.

Diotima further tells us that *eros* is not itself a divine. Rather it is the desire for God, for perfection; *eros* is a lack. Through *eros,* human beings are constituted by something that they don't have, by their incompleteness. With *eros* we intuit and desire something higher and better than ourselves.

Politically speaking, the lack implicit in *eros* is the very thing which produces differences among human beings. In the face of our collective lacking, we differentiate ourselves according to what we are "pregnant" with, what level of lacking we achieve. But even as some of us may reach higher than others, we are all partaking of the same quest, in *eros* itself. *Eros* is thus responsible both for our communality (our collective lacking) as well as our differences, our relative higherness and lowerness. In either case, what is valued, what is "true," is never here among us but always "there" in the heavens, invisible and ultimately unreachable. This understanding of love sets a pattern that will be reproduced in Western philosophical systems for the next two and a half millennia. Even when the definitions of love change, as we will see from *eros,* to *agape,* and later yet to a highly secularized concept, the basic pattern persists. It persists even to the present day, despite several spirited and important attempts to root it out. With this understanding of love, we remain defined by a lack. Our sense of self and community is both founded upon and undermined by this profound inadequacy.

LOVE AFTER PLATO

Let me now trace, however briefly, a few ways in which what will emerge as the doctrine of love has been shaped and reshaped, struggled against and reproduced in a line from Plato to the contemporary period. There have been many challenges to the doctrine of love, including during Socrates' own time. In *The Symposium,* among the many stories which seem to support Socrates' position on love, there is one that stands out as arguing an entirely different line. This is Aristophanes' strange tale of love, whereby human beings were once "round, with back and sides forming a circle . . . [they] had four arms and an equal number of legs, and two faces exactly alike on a cylindrical neck."[5] Such beings were absolutely content and fulfilled. In their self-love, power, and hubris, they "set upon the gods." For this crime, Zeus punished them by slicing them in half. Each half now spends its life searching for its lost other. In this tale, love is a punishment, a conquest.

As I read it, this story, from one of Socrates' most vociferous critics, offers a radically different notion of love, implicitly attacking the doctrine of *eros*. True, love remains defined as a lack in this discourse, but it is not a lack of the divine; rather it is a lack of a terrestrial wholeness. What we lack is what *we once had*, and perhaps what we could have again. For Aristophanes, the lack is not constituted as a permanent state, but rather is historically produced, a result of having been conquered by heaven. Humans become colonized by an idea of the divine, their love becomes not a source of wholeness but of enslavement to their new masters.

Aristophanes offers us an alternative genealogy for love and also an alternative notion of what love "might have been"; a subcurrent in the Western history of the notion of love, which I am going to argue persists as much as Platonic love to the present day and which offers a vastly different ethics and a different politics. This love is more democratic. It reinforces rather than disenfranchises human beings. It does not insist on hierarchies (as revealed by the fact that these four-legged humans did not care much for the Gods' height and power). It does not submit us to external and invisible judgments that are not part of the political (and human) realm.[6] In this tale, heaven comes down to earth to impose an order based on its own worship, an order that we have been stuck with ever since; Aristophanes' tale strikes a discordant note in a banquet otherwise in harmony. His idea of love is and remains a minority view, at odds with and subversive to the powerful doctrine of *eros*.

At first glance, Aristotle's preference for *philia* over *eros* may seem to ally him more with Aristophanes than Plato. *Philia* is a relational, terrestrial love, the love between friends. Seemingly it is by definition a more democratic love. Indeed, as I will show further, contemporary thinkers such as Arendt and Derrida are attracted to Aristotle's notion of *philia politike*, a political friendship that promises a genuine democratic polity. And, as we will see, Derrida goes on to suggest that Aristotle himself is wistful for just such a democratic friendship himself.

Derrida suggests that Aristotle participates in an "immense rumor," a subversive democratic dreaming that persists even among some of the most ardent defenders and reproducers of the doctrine of love, including Aristotle himself.[7] Yet, if it is true that Aristotle seeks to value the humanistic, democratic, self-regarding perspective, he also roots this perspective in the context of the external, of nature and the divine. In this way he reproduces a struggle at the heart of Western philosophy.

Despite his participation in the "immense rumor," the doctrine of love is very much present in Aristotle and seems to be stronger than his subversive tendencies. *Philia*, although secular and focused on human relationships, reveals itself to presuppose the same hierarchies and externalized judgments as can be found in *eros* itself.[8] For Aristotle, the notion of *philia* contains many different levels. Friendship among equals, among those "who are good, and similar in their goodness," he calls "perfect"[9] and equates them to "two friends, one soul."[10]

For Aristotle, a perfect friendship is one in which each friend wishes to give to the other more than he receives. This suggests a model for a truly ethical notion of friendship and community, a political friendship (*philia politike*), Yet this friendship is built upon a hierarchy; such "equal" friends do not exist in a vacuum; they are able to treat each other only as ends because of the entire edifice of dissimilar and imperfect "friendships" they stand upon.

There are many unequal friendships which are just as important for Aristotle's notion of community; those between father and son, husband and wife, or between a master and his subordinates. The idea of friendship contains not just different categories, but also a ranking of these categories from lowest to highest. The "lower friends" take care of material needs and create a realm where the perfect friend can afford to be "self-less."[11]

For Aristotle, the lower friends will necessarily outnumber the "equal friends." He tells us, "that [perfect] friendships are rare is natural, because men of this kind are few."[12] But such friendships are few not only by "nature," but also by virtue of the requirement of the social apparatus which produces and enables them. Such friendship is perfect only in relationship to imperfection, autonomous only in relationship to non-autonomy.

In Aristotle's political vision, we see the ways in which our personal insufficiency and need for one another creates a political ordering that binds us together. Friendship, like other forms of love, equates and resolves, even as it presupposes and requires difference. Aristotle tells us that lesser friendships, despite their inequality, are rendered just and equivalent through the quality of friendship itself:

> In all of these friendships between persons of different standings the affection must be proportionate: i.e. the better person must be loved more than he loves, and so must the more useful.... For when the affection is proportionate to merit the result is a kind of equality which of course is considered to be characteristic of friendship.[13]

Ultimately friendship can even transcend the greatest of social divides for Aristotle: that between master and slave, as when he writes, "friendship [by the master] to him as a slave is impossible, although as a human being it is possible."[14]

Thus, for all of his differences from a system rooted in *eros*, Aristotle reproduces the essential questions that we have already seen with Plato. For Aristotle as well, selves are produced, judged, and ranked according to external criteria—in this case, according to an idea of "nature" which reproduces itself and insinuates itself into the most intimate fabric connecting a society together.

THE TWO COMMANDMENTS

Early Christian thought inherits and struggles with this legacy of Platonic and Aristotelian notions of love. For Saint Augustine, despite its very otherworldly orientation, *eros* remains bounded by its finiteness, by its very lacking.[15] *Eros* thus contains the tendency for terrestrial "corruption," for self-love at the expense of Christian demands for piety. Yet rather than abandon it altogether, Augustine combines *eros* with *agape,* the "highest" love that comes only from God. In so doing, he forms them into the concept of *caritas* (or, as many Christian scholars refer to it, the "*caritas* synthesis"), which implies far more than its English cognate of "charity."

In *The City of God,* Saint Augustine conceives of a politics that situates itself in the context of *agape,* a love that is constituted not by lacking but by having. *Agape* is juxtaposed as the "answer" to *eros*'s inadequacy and tendency toward corruption. The problem for Saint Augustine though is that this having is not "ours" but God's. What can we do with a love that is not exactly our own?

This question becomes paramount to the quest at the heart of much of Christian scholarship from Saint Augustine onward, the desire to unify the two "great" commandments of "love thy God" and "love thy neighbor." Can we love our neighbor with a love that belongs to God? How can two such different kinds of love be made into one? How can a human politics be based upon or folded into a divine one? Saint Augustine, in his own attempt to answer this question, writes:

> In [the two commandments] man finds three beings to love, namely, God, himself and his fellow man, and knows that he is not wrong in loving himself so long as he loves God. As a result, he must help his neighbor (whom he is obliged to love as himself) to love God.[16]

In allowing for self-love, so long as it is contained within *agape,* Saint Augustine renders *eros* as the earthly mirror and recipient of *agape.* In order to ensure that man can follow *both* commandments, *agape* is required for the first commandment and *eros* for the second. The duty to one's fellow human beings, which might not otherwise follow out of an ecstatic and self-effacing love for God, becomes possible when properly submitted under God's love. When filled with *agape,* the human-based love of *eros* leads not to hubris but to the embodiment of God's love on the earth. For Saint Augustine, the political salience of love would not be possible without *eros.*[17]

The merger of *eros* and *agape* into the concept of *caritas,* continued and improved upon by thinkers like Saint Thomas Aquinas, has been the basis of enormous controversy in Christian academic contexts. Thinkers ranging from

Anders Nygren to Denis de Rougemont have attacked the *caritas* synthesis as preserving the grounds of human corruption, sin, and hubris. *Eros* in this view is too earthly and pagan, endangering the devotion to God himself. As with Saint Augustine, these thinkers focus on the relationship between the two great commandments in making their critique. As Nygren puts it:

> In the commandment: "Thou shalt love thy neighbor as thyself," Augustine had actually held that a commandment of self-love was implied—even if it did not need to be expressly stated by a separate commandment, in view of man's natural inclination in that direction. Luther, on the contrary, asserts that the Commandment of Love involves the rejection and condemnation of all self-love whatsoever.[18]

Nygren acknowledges that Augustine, Aquinas, and medieval Catholic doctrine in general have formally shed the explicit hierarchicalism of classical Greek thought, but he claims that in the end they simply reproduce it in a new guise. He argues that the problem with such early Catholic doctrine is that, given the ongoing presence of *eros*, "grace makes it possible to win blessedness, but merit must win it."[19] In other words, grace serves as the prerequisite for the possibility of salvation, but it is still entirely up to us to actually achieve it. Grace thus becomes merely a means to an end—salvation rather than an end in itself. A true *agape*, divorced from its connections to *eros*, does not presume to distinguish between sinner and saved. It relies entirely upon God's grace and wisdom to be redeemed. For Nygren, we must place ourselves entirely within the context of God's love, filling ourselves wholly with it.

But does a turn to a pure *agape* resolve the problems of love and hierarchy any better than the *caritas* synthesis? In *The Nature of Love,* Irving Singer suggests that Luther, always the hero of Nygren's system, reproduces the difficulties of Platonic love even after explicitly rejecting *eros*. Singer argues that in submitting human will so utterly to *agape*, Luther risks reducing ourselves to nothing at all; we become beings that are not capable of our own moral agency, the very concern that motivated Saint Augustine to conceive of the *caritas* synthesis in the first place.[20] According to Singer, Luther's "reduction" of human agency calls into question the possibility of having a position from which we can love God at all (and hence also of loving one's neighbor as oneself).[21] Once again we ask, can we love with a love that is not our own?

Singer further argues that this "emptying" of the self has a peculiar effect; in filling us up with God's love, Luther produces, in his own words, "a divine man, who is one cake with Him [God]."[22] In essence, he makes us all part of God ourselves.

For Singer, in a final irony, Luther ends up reproducing the very same kinds of hierarchies and "ladders" of early Catholicism that he sought to overturn. As we have seen, Luther (and Nygren) resists the idea that grace should be merely the means for human beings to come to their own salvation. But clearly, even in Luther, there must remain some concept of "higher" and "lower" among us according to our relationship to the divine. Despite his strong denunciation of *caritas,* Luther has preserved the central core of Greek thought even as he objects to it. His thinking, as with Saints Augustine and Aquinas, remains firmly rooted in the concept of Platonic transcendentalism.[23] As Singer puts it:

> In effect, Luther parodies the caritas circuit: an up and down movement remains, but human beings can participate in it only as they become the hollow men through whom the sacred fluid runs. Drawing on their major symbols, Nygren characterizes Luther versus caritas as the downward tube versus the upward ladder. But in both cases the ultimate symbol is a ring or elliptical chain, love beginning and ending with God, all other points being way stations or intermediaries in the closed trajectory.[24]

Julia Kristeva, in her own analysis of *agape* and the relationship between the two great commandments, reinforces Singer's arguments, albeit in an entirely different context. In *Tales of Love,* she describes *agape* as a killing of the self:

> Circumscribed within the unique experience of the Son with a capital S, this killing of my own body in order for Me to be equal to the Father is by the same stroke removed from fantasy, which belongs to me alone and grabs me in my immeasurable pleasures and losses. On the contrary, the passion of the cross, raised to the level of *universal narrative,* is the vanishing point of fantasy—its unloading into a universality that, on the one hand, forbids me to take myself for Christ (it short-circuits fantasy), and on the other, introducing into the pre-conscious the idealizing necessity of one's own death, at once favors my leap into the name of the Father.[25]

For Kristeva, as for Singer, *agape* produces a subject who is "hollowed out," colonized by the divine and given over to universal "fantasies." For Kristeva, this is an act of masochism whereby we give up our own power. A "Me" is created in the act of burning away the sinful body. By this act of self-annihilation, one becomes (as seen with Luther) "equal" to the Father (God).[26]

Kristeva reveals how for Paul, the commandment to "love thy neighbor as thyself" is predicated on the notion that human beings are not in a position to make judgments about who they can and cannot love. Instead, we must love (as God does) sinners and the faithful alike. Yet for Kristeva there *is* a judgment preserved, and a hierarchy established even in the face of the "equality" which proceeds from *agape*'s coming down to earth. This judgment is preserved in what she calls "Johannine love" (i.e., *agape*).[27] Kristeva describes a "slippage" between the meritless, divine love in heaven and the de facto divisions produced by the fact that not all of us will receive and enucleate ourselves as a "Me," as a being infused only with *agape*. [28]

In this sense, Kristeva reiterates Singer's position that the move toward *agape* does not radically change from its roots in Plato's own treatment of *eros*, subsuming a potentially disruptive earthly passion in the name of a higher, better truth. As Kristeva herself puts it, "Possibly what is outlined here is a sublime Platonic Eros, a celestial Eros lacking his burden of carnal lust."[29] Even when it is so unburdened, eros has not lost its character. Always in the service of a transcendental truth, *eros, philia, caritas,* and *agape* share a common tendency to hollow us out, filling us with a new identity, as a series of "Me"s who are bound together and whose differences are presupposed. Different iterations of love lead back, always to the same Athens and the same Rome.

Recent (and even not-so-recent) scholarship has been deeply critical of Nygren's arguments, claiming that he greatly overstates the difference between the *caritas* synthesis and subsequent notions of love to be found in Luther and Calvin.[30] Even Calvin himself does not truly dismiss all human agency, but rather struggles with it. In both Luther and Calvin the human perspective remains constituted, if not by *eros,* then still by the expectation of *agape,* by the desire to be filled with the divine. Whether we accept Nygren's position or not, for my own purposes we can see that either as *caritas* synthesis, or pure *agape,* the core of the doctrine of love remains: The notion of human inadequacy, the need to be filled with the divine, and an ordering of human beings are retained regardless of which name love takes on.

Where then might we find a basis for love that is more democratic, more concerned with human lives and politics? Or, to ask the question that Rousseau implicitly raises, should we, could we, do away with love altogether?

HANNAH ARENDT: POLITICS VS. LOVE?

Throughout her life and her writings, Hannah Arendt evinces a tremendous ambivalence toward the concept of love. In her earliest writings, eventually published as *Love and Saint Augustine,* she directly confronts the problem that existing notions of love pose for politics. In this book, Arendt pursues the same lines of questioning that we have already seen with Saint Augustine himself: the question of human agency, the relationship between the two great commandments. If God's love within us is not exactly "us," and if in order to access this love we have to forget or even hate ourselves, what kind of subjects do we become?[31] How can the love of God serve as the foundation for politics when it seems to remove the possibility of politics altogether?

10

For Arendt, Saint Augustine's answer is to see God as our "Creator" (by con-figuring us as God's "creatures"). In so configuring God, Augustine argues that although not "exactly" God, we are yet related to him, by this act of creation, so that the God who "circulates within us" is also the source of and thus somehow part of us.

But such an understanding of our relationship to God still does not satisfy Arendt, who is looking for an idea of love that is explicitly political. Augustine's notion of politics is constituted as a *dilectionis ordo,* a "well-ordered" love. Arendt tells us that the Greek terms *eros, storge,* and *agape* roughly correspond to the Latin *amor, dilectio,* and *caritas.*[32] As with their Greek counterparts, in Christian thought a hierarchy is created whereby *amor,* the love of the body, is lowest; *dilectio,* the love of the neighbor (as the self), is intermediary; and *caritas,* the love for and of God, is the highest.[33] The *dilectionis ordo* determines the politics that come out of the doctrine of love.

Arendt tells us that the very ordering inherent in this system makes our *dilectio,* the basis of terrestrial politics, derivative and lesser.[34] By putting God at the top of our political process, we are left inadequate in terms of having our own legitimate right to make judgments.

It is at this point that Arendt begins to pull away from a strict accounting of Augustine and begins to engage in her own theorizing within the context of Augustinian philosophy, to envision a love that has the ethical possibilities of *caritas* without the reduction of human love (and the political realm it spawns) to a secondary and derivative force.

To do this, Arendt turns to Saint Augustine's notion of memory (which becomes the basis of her idea of narrative) as a way for human beings to literally re-collect themselves personally and collectively into an ethical and political community:[35]

> By recalling a past that is prior to all possibilities of earthly, mundane experi-ence, man who was created and did not make himself finds the utmost limit of his own past—his own "whence."[36]

The focus on memory makes the act of God's creation "mine," that is to say belonging to the self and not to God alone. This act of remembering is also the basis of her cherished notion of natality. The memory of our creation is repro-duced in each of us by the fact of our birth. As beings born into the world, "once called into existence, human life cannot turn into nothingness."[37] In other words, there is not only the possibility, but even the demand for action, for our own responsibility in this world given by the fact of our birth.

For Arendt, the idea of God as Creator resolves a problem that the Greeks had with time. For the Greeks, time is a way for finite beings to conceive of the "all at once-ness" of Being.[38] Implicitly time itself and the human perspective it contains are denigrated (reminiscent of her complaint about the fate of love in Saint Augustine's hands when he remains overly "Greek"). The idea of God as Creator has a different and more promising orientation toward time. The notion of God as our Creator gives us a "before," a definite moment from which the world is produced.[39] As such, time becomes redefined as a position between "being and non-being," a perspective that gives legitimacy to the human condition on its own terms.[40] We become "bounded by eternity" on two ends, and in this in-betweenness we constitute a narrative that is held and contained by the act of creation, by our birth, and by our own memory.[41] Time becomes "ours," and with it comes a position for human authenticity, our own substance and our own valid perspective.

Accordingly, Arendt determines that Saint Augustine's philosophy (when interpreted in this way) does not create a contradiction between politics and theology but rather the latter serves as the necessary ground for the former. Revisiting Saint Augustine's question about the two great commandments, Arendt writes that "In self-denying love, I deny the other person as well as myself but I do not forget him."[42] For Arendt, this denial of our self and others "dissolves" our mutual dependence, replacing it with a mutual love (*diligere invicem*), which does not forget, but incorporates our terrestrial history together.[43] She concludes:

> Although we can meet the other only because both of us belong to the human race [in our history together, in the terrestrial and political "before" that contains our life] it is only in the individual's isolation in God's presence that he becomes our neighbor [in terms of the "before" of God as our Creator]. By virtue of this isolation in God's presence, the other is lifted out of the self-evident dependence in which all people live with each other, and then our connection with him is subject to the explicit obligation of kinship.[44]

For Arendt, our neighbor only becomes our "brother" as a result of freeing us from one another and rediscovering each other through our common origin, the memory of our creation by God.

In *Love and Saint Augustine* we see the roots of so much of the theory that Arendt comes to embrace in her later writing. The idea of natality, of narrative, of memory, and of "reality" are all present here as well as her understanding of time that is reproduced in later works such as *Between Past and Future* and *The Human Condition*. And yet the "resolution" that she finds with Saint Augustine still does not seem to fully satisfy her but rather propels her toward further inquiry. In Saint Augustine, Arendt sought a way to render a political realm possible without resorting to the sort of nihilism and relativism that might otherwise follow from the full embrace of human subjectivity. The idea of God as Creator represents an ethical envelope within which to contain and bind human agency.

And yet throughout the book Arendt struggles repeatedly with the question of self-denial that she finds in Augustine even when the denied self is not forgotten. Augustine's resolution may make logical sense, but it does not necessarily answer her complaint entirely. Ultimately, it still makes human life and politics derivative in a way that seems to make her uncomfortable. Augustine gives with one hand (the idea of memory) and takes away with the other (this memory is only "ours" insofar as we are "God's"). The idea of mutual recognition and collective narrative that makes the world real for us may have been born in an engagement with Augustinian theory but needs to find its expression elsewhere.

In *The Human Condition,* written much later in her life, Arendt seems to have turned against the concept of love altogether. Here she calls love "antipolitical" and says that it "destroys the in-between which relates us to and separates us from one another."[45] This seems to be directly contradictory to what she said in *Love and Saint Augustine,* where love in fact serves as the *basis* for our in-betweenness (serving as it does to dissolve the mutual dependence that forms in its absence). Arendt goes on to argue that love transgresses our boundaries and denies us the possibility of freedom, of action and of speech, that serves as the basis of politics.

To better establish her argument, we must be clear which notion of "love" Arendt is evoking here. In *Love and Saint Augustine* she reminds us that whereas the ancients had a plethora of terms for love, we have one or at most two.[46] Thus in *The Human Condition,* "love" might mean several very different things. It might seem here that she is talking of *amor,* the "basest" of loves, the love of the body, sexual love, selfish love. But Arendt herself seems to warn us against this interpretation:

> The common prejudice that love is as common as "romance" may be due to the fact that we all learned about it first through poetry. But the poets fool us; they are the only ones to whom love is not only a crucial but an indispensable experience, which entitles them to mistake it for a universal one.[47]

For Arendt, the love she speaks of here is rarer than *amor,* not basic but something "higher."

Arendt also writes that such love is "unconcerned to the point of total unworldliness" with our particularities, reminiscent of the indifference of *agape.*[48] She writes that we could never have the power to forgive (and therefore to judge) if love was the basis of our politics. In other words, such a love does not allow human beings to make up their minds on their own—its indifference to our respective qualities disqualifies it from political considerations.[49] Seemingly, Arendt's position has changed.[50]

What then happens to love for Arendt? Does she abandon it entirely? Curiously, of the various notions of love discussed in *Love and Saint Augustine,*

Arendt never mentions *philia*. As we have seen, *philia* is a term especially dear to Aristotle, with connotations of an explicitly political and even democratic notion of friendship. It might seem as if *philia* is a better cognate for *dilectio*, the "egalitarian" or "next to" notion of love that Augustine uses. But Arendt translates *dilectio* into the Greek term *storge*, which has connotations of familial affection. Her choice of *storge* may reveal her ongoing link to Heidegger in terms of the latter's attention to this term. But at the same time, it might be a sign of her dissatisfaction with Saint Augustine's notions of love that she considers his politics to remain rooted in what for her is a "private" or social notion of love. *Philia*, with its explicitly political and *public* orientation, must come from a different source.

In searching for a contrast to love in *The Human Condition*, Arendt comes up with the notion of respect:

> Respect, not unlike the Aristotelian *philia politike*, is a kind of "friendship" without intimacy and without closeness; it is a regard for the person from the distance which the space of the world puts between us, and this regard is independent of qualities which we may admire or of achievements which we may highly esteem.[51]

Here the indifference of *agape* is reinterpreted in a way that reinforces rather than undermines human judgments. Each of us comes to a position that is not given to us by God, but is simply "ours." In so arguing, Arendt may be attempting to rescue Aristotle from the clutches of his Christian Aristotelian interpreters who locate his notion of friendship in the context of "higher" love. *Philia*, once shorn of its prior connections, emerges in its new guise as respect. As such, it seems to accord us a position in society which is ours and ours alone and which relates us, as love does not, to one another (i.e., the commandment to "love thy neighbor" can finally be met on its own terms). Whereas love tends to annihilate the self as well as the other, respect is rooted in our respective "hereness," in our physical presence in the world.

But in so turning "back" to Aristotle, has Arendt abandoned Christian love in general and Augustine in particular? And if so, what of her own critique of Greek philosophy implicit in her initial alliance with Augustine? The strange similarity to *agape* that we find in the concept of respect suggests a less than complete abandonment of love. We see other evidence as well in *The Human Condition* that Arendt is reluctant to do away with Christian love altogether. For Arendt, the one "miracle" that human beings are capable of performing is action, a self-insertion into the monotonous regularity of existence. This is a miracle because "left to ourselves" we might never act at all.[52] To be able to conceive of action, we require a sense of something beyond us, of faith and hope, two qualities "which Greek antiquity ignored altogether."[53] By evoking these clearly Christian notions, Arendt summons back Augustinian doctrine and in particular the figure of Jesus of Nazareth as a representation of the possibility of newness, of strangeness, and of unpredictability, which is the prerequisite of action.[54] In this sense, her notion of action denies but does not forget its rootedness in Augustinian notions of love.

What we are left with is Arendt's ambivalence toward both Greek and Christian ideas of love. Augustinian love seems to preserve the possibility of escaping from *telos,* from the "already is" and the sameness of the Greek idea of the eternal. For Arendt, freedom can only be found by not knowing the future, through the real experience of time. But in terms of that "real time" that we occupy, such love does not go far enough; it has its own tendency toward sameness, it too fails to make sufficient distinctions. And Christian love itself does not deliver an explicitly political vision, as the Greeks do for Arendt. In looking for a love that neither co-opts nor excludes politics, Arendt must look beyond both Aristotle and Augustine.

THERE IS NO FRIEND...

Arendt is not the only one who sees in Aristotle's notion of *philia politike* a vision worth pursuing despite the perils and complications of love. In *Politics of Friendship,* Jacques Derrida considers a fragment attributed to Aristotle, the phrase "O my friends, there is no friend."[55] This fragment is attributed to Aristotle by Montaigne, among others, and constitutes part of the "immense rumor" that Derrida sees as running through Western philosophy, an alternative genealogy of love and friendship. Derrida reads this phrase as a lament, an awareness of the promise and also the impossibility of friendship in the world.

Derrida's ambivalence toward the notion of friendship in Aristotle is even more pronounced than Arendt's. Unlike Arendt, Derrida directly acknowledges that Aristotelian friendship is not the purely public entity that it seems to be. He sees that it is built on a subterranean network of inequality. For Aristotle, both love and friendship, which Derrida collectively calls "lovence" (*aimance*), are bound up with the family and hence with the notion of *physis,* of nature and hierarchy and the *telos* of human society.[56] As we have seen, even among social "equals," friendship makes us different, makes us higher or lower from one another. Such friendship makes us not neighbors but brothers. And for Derrida, brotherhood or "consanguinity" is a troubling basis for any kind of democratic polity, containing within its construction troubling questions of exclusion and ranking and blood.[57] And yet Derrida writes that "something trembles" in Aristotle's natural hierarchies and notions of brotherhood.[58]

What "trembles" is the possibility of turning the social dissymmetries that are present in fraternal friendship into another kind dissymmetry. Derrida searches for a responsible dissymmetry which finally realizes Aristotle's dictum that a friend loves more than he (or even she) is loved without simultaneously requiring that other, lesser friends (wives, slaves, etc.) love him more than he loves them.

As Derrida writes:

> "Good friendship" supposes disproportion. It demands a certain rupture in reciprocity or equality, as well as the interruption of all fusion or confusion between you and me. By the same token, it signifies a divorce with love, albeit self-love. [59]

Thus, in the same manner as Arendt, Derrida looks for a love that does not seek to merge us but to keep us separate. Part of the dream of love to make us all the same (equal), filled up from without (and therefore also *un*equal), is cast aside. Derrida seeks a "divorce" from love—the self-love that seeks to turn all otherness into a sameness, the love that smothers and enchains.

In seeking out such a friendship, Derrida turns to Nietzsche, who, in his own reading of Aristotle's fragment, writes:

> *Perhaps* to each of us *will come* the more joyful hour when we exclaim "Friend, there are no friends!" Thus said the dying sage. "Foes, there are no foes," Say I, the living fool. [60]

In contrast to Aristotle (the dying sage), Nietzsche, the living fool, offers a new possibility, a new "perhaps" which suggests that in order to be friends, we must first be foes. In order to realize the democratic dreams of friendship, the possibility of *philia politike*, we need to divorce ourselves from the love which binds it. We must create a new spatial arrangement, a new distance from one another given not by love but by enmity. Such a distance will not make us the same, and it will not preclude other kinds of relationships, other kinds of love. The living fool, who eschews divine wisdom, chooses life itself with all of its surprises, its hatreds and maybe its friendships as well, as the basis for an alternative vision.

For Derrida, this relationship remains at the level of the "perhaps," an immense rumor, but one very much worth pursuing, for it promises the realization of what we have been searching for in vain within the doctrine of love itself.

Derrida goes on to ask, "Is such a friendship still Greek? Yes and no...the future still chimes with *philia* but is already no longer Greek." [61] Yet at the same time Greek culture for Derrida is not some totalizing unity, not the oneness that Plato seems to offer us. For Derrida, as we find in his reading of Aristotle, beneath the surface of love as a doctrine lie multiple possibilities. Derrida's use of the term "divorce" is instructive. It suggests that what we must do is not annihilate love but overcome it; we must not pretend that we never had love, never had the democratic dreams that it spawned in us. We must seek not to start over but to respond, as Nietzsche does, to the promise in love itself.

Derrida asks, in a different, more direct form, the question that Rousseau seems to ask us, however obliquely, in *The Discovery of the New World:* Can we have a love that is not rooted in nature, in the divine, in family and kinship and murder? As Derrida puts it:

> Why would the friend be *like* a brother? Let us dream of a friendship which goes beyond the proximity of the congeneric double, beyond parenthood, the most as well as the least natural of parenthoods, when it leaves its signature, from the outset, on the name as on a double mirror of such a couple. Let us ask ourselves what would then be the politics of such a "beyond the principle of fraternity."
> Would this still deserve the name "politics"? [62]

Can we have a politics without love? What is the alternative? Is there another notion of love, perhaps already present within the doctrine itself, which might resist or realize the subversive possibility within the Platonic, which might better serve us in our search for a *philia politike,* a democratic love?

In this book I would like to think about these questions in two senses. First, to think about the consequences of remaining inscribed by love as it is received and constituted by Plato. Secondly, to think about a politics that is not caught up with the doctrine of love and fraternity, a politics based on a different kind of love.

To look at love in this way, I want to contrast the troubling and contentious modern conception of love as inherited from these classical and early Christian predecessors on the one hand with the alternative genealogy, the "immense rumor" of love stretching back to Aristophanes and forward to the present time, on the other. As I've suggested, the alternative can be found even in those thinkers who remain inscribed within the bonds of love; my choice of authors is predicated on this concept. Each of the authors that I deal with in the next four chapters, namely John Locke, Jean-Jacques Rousseau, Ralph Waldo Emerson, and Henry David Thoreau, grapples with even as he reproduces the doctrine of love. This is true even with Locke, who I argue is the thinker who best articulates the modern incarnation of love, making it the basis of our contemporary lives. In the final chapter, I argue that Thomas Hobbes offers us a different path, a rupture with love more in line with what Arendt and Derrida are seeking.

THE SECULARIZATION OF LOVE

The thinkers that I focus on in this book describe and encounter love in its modern and secular guise. Given love's explicitly religious origins, we must become aware of how and why it evolves into a formally secular doctrine and with what consequences. Here we turn to the modern notions of self and community, rooted in the political and theological battles in seventeenth- and eighteenth-century England. After the epistemological chaos of the civil war period and its aftermath (including Hobbes's challenge), John Locke reinvents love by turning back to classical and early Christian doctrines. He does this in part because of his own Puritan background, but also because of his indebtedness to Richard Hooker, a Christian Aristotelian thinker who Locke invariably referred to as "the Judicious Hooker."[63] Hooker was himself influenced by Jean Calvin, Saint Thomas Aquinas, and also of course by Aristotle himself.

In his *Of the Laws of Ecclesiastical Polity*, Hooker laid out a notion of politics that Locke cites and incorporates repeatedly in his *Two Treatises on Government*. We see in the Preface to *Ecclesiastical Polity* evidence of what Hooker's ideal community might look like:

> Far more comfort it were for us . . . to labour under the same yoke, as men that look for the same eternal reward of their labours, to be joined with you *in bands of indissoluble love* and amity, *to live as if our persons being many our souls were but one,* rather than in such dismembered sort to spend our few and wretched days in a tedious prosecuting of wearisome contentions. (emphasis added)[64]

Here we have a vision of a society that very much approximates an Aristotelian vision of the city wherein both individual interests and collectivity can coexist unproblematically. And in his idea that many persons share one soul, we see an approximation of Aristotle's notion of *philia* wherein we find the formula "two friends, one soul."[65] For Hooker, as for Aristotle, our diversity—which stems from our respective abilities to know higher truths—can be reconciled in a common relationship to God, who is the master of us all. Under God's rule, we are both equal and unequal, united by "bands of indissoluble love."

For Hooker, love serves a political purpose in that it ensures that the necessary hierarchies that he sees as essential for a just order be allowed to function without rancor or interference. Because error and misinterpretation of Christ's words are rampant, Hooker looks to Protestant clergymen (like Calvin) to lead their flock in the correct direction. Some questions, he writes, "are so familiar and plain, that truth from falsehood, and good from evil, is most easily discerned in them, even by men of no deep capacity."[66] But other denser matters require the "Offices of Christian men" to "be a light to direct others."[67] Hooker goes on to say:

> There are but two ways whereby Spirit leadeth men into all truth; the one extraordinary, the other common; the one belonging but unto some few, the other extending itself unto all that are of God; *the one that which we call by a special divine excellence Revelation, the other Reason.* (emphasis added)[68]

We have already seen that for Hooker, many easier questions of faith and politics can readily be answered by the many. We all have access to "common" reason. But such reason, to retain its validity, must coexist with revelation, so that this more limited relationship to the truth can be bolstered by direct and higher insight.

This sentiment echos Aristotle's own notion that even a slave has some reasoning faculties, but that his limited capacity to reason must be bolstered by his master's:

> It is clear therefore that it is the master who ought to be the cause of . . . virtue in the slave. . . . Hence they are wrong who would deny all reason to slaves.[69]

They are "wrong" because the slave does have reason—that reason just happens to principally reside with the master. The master and the slave can be said to share one reason ("two friends, one soul") and are thereby joined through the bonds of *philia*.

We can see in Locke a very fair approximation of this system; he too sees it as possible to coexist as one and yet be many, and he too sees us as bound by bonds of love. Locke, in paraphrasing Hooker in the *Second Treatise*, writes:

> This *equality* of Men by Nature, the Judicious *Hooker* looks upon as so evident in it self, and beyond all question that he makes it the Foundation of that Obligation *to mutual Love amongst men, on which he Builds the Duties they owe one another,* and from whence he derives the great Maxims of *Justice* and *Charity*.[70] (emphasis added)

For Locke, our mutuality is guaranteed by the fact that we are all God's property:

> For Men being all the Workmanship of one Omnipotent, and infinitely wise Maker; All the Servants of one Sovereign Master, sent into the World by his order and about his business, they are his Property, whose Workmanship they are, made to last during his, not one anothers Pleasure.[71]

We work, not for ourselves but for God, and we hold one another accountable, not to our own law but God's. This notion of God's dominion over us reproduces the notion of *agape* that we have already seen with Saint Augustine or Luther or Hooker; it fills us and gives us to ourselves. Here again, our love, that which binds and organizes us, is not our own.

As I will argue further, an entire generation of Locke scholars ranging from Richard Ashcraft to Kirstie McClure have championed Locke's religious intentions as being precisely what makes him not only a moral but even a progressive and democratic thinker. But, as I will argue in the next chapter, while this reading of Locke may be an improvement on C. B. MacPherson's reading of him as an advocate of naked greed, by reproducing the ancient doctrine of love, Locke brings with it all of the questioning of human agency, the notion of the self as hollowed out and not valid on its own. The reintroduction of the doctrine of love brings with it all of the demands for hierarchy, all of the conflict that we find in earlier philosophy. Locke's vision is perhaps communitarian, but it is not progressive, nor is it as democratic as it promises to be.

As I will argue further in the next chapter, given his own secularizing tendencies, if anything, Locke's notion of love is *more* problematical than earlier versions. One major difference between Locke and Hooker is that while for Hooker the ongoing possibility of revelation serves to unite and ensure our mutual love, filling us with *agape,* for Locke, the age of revelations is over and we only have "common" reason left by which to discern higher truths.[72] In the absence of revelation, Locke has an epistemological crisis on his hands: We must continue to organize ourselves according to higher truths, we must remain loyal to God, our true master, but at the same time it is not clear what that master now demands of us. We remain, as ever, constituted by a lack, waiting to be filled, but now the promise of the *caritas* synthesis to meet that need is sundered by the end of revelation and the turn to non-messianic time.

Secularizing the doctrine of love might appear to resolve some of the problems that we have seen with *eros* and *agape,* making our love wholly "ours" as is the case with Hobbes. But although secularizing the doctrine of love, Locke preserves its religious basis. Rather than welcoming the turn to human time, Locke seeks to reproduce eternal laws as best he can. If anything, as I will try to establish further in this book, to overly secularize the doctrine of love threatens to eliminate its most democratic and promising aspects. It is precisely the belief in the equality of souls, in the absolute worth of each individual because of our relationship to God, that gives any meaning to the democratic qualities that can be found in Locke. Otherwise C. B. MacPherson might have been right about him after all.

Once secularized, love retains its double-edgedness, offering both community and freedom, equality and hierarchy, but in a way that is much more in tension. With Locke, our lacking becomes more pronounced and, even worse, unresolvable. The religious basis for resolution, whereby all differences are "dissolved" in the divine, is removed. And yet our need for hierarchy, for a *dilectionis ordo,* is as great as ever.

LOVE AFTER LOCKE: THE DEVELOPMENT OF A LIBERAL SUBJECT

Although Locke begins our journey down the road of reviving and then secularizing love, it is really with Kant that secularized love reaches its apogee. In his own revisiting of the problem of *agape* and *eros*, of human agency and the relationship between the two great commandments, Kant attempts to restore balance to the epistemological chasm opened up in part by Locke himself (a chasm that Kant glimpsed particularly in the work of one of the most radical of English empiricists, David Hume). Kant reproduces a version of Saint Augustine's *caritas* synthesis, only instead of having a relationship between "us" and "God" we create a relationship between our "sensible" and "intelligible" selves. For Kant, as for Saint Augustine, morality is produced by the adjudication between these two realms.[73] For Kant, we have no "acquaintance" with the intelligible world or even our "higher" self. It exists only as "a 'something' that remains over when I have excluded from the grounds determining my will everything that belongs to the world of sense."[74] The complaint that we find with Saint Augustine and later Christian thought seems to be resolved—we are not "losing ourselves" or being "hollowed out" to be filled with God's *agape*. Instead we are being "filled" with ourselves, with our own a priori notion of a free will. As such moral agents, we are in conflict neither with ourselves nor with one another—we are capable, as Aristotle hoped for in his idea of perfect friendship, of treating each other as ends and not as means. And God's silence is no longer a problem. It becomes an opportunity for us to come to the law on our own, to become ethically and politically "mature."[75]

But Kant, for all his radical thinking, remains inscribed within the doctrine of love itself. As with Locke, Kant's secularizing preserves the essential core of Christian and classical doctrines. In *Rethinking Generosity*, Romand Coles suggests that this process of "self hollowing" and its resultant achievement of "neighborliness" are not as successful as Kant would have us believe. He writes that

> Kant must reimagine, in the absence of a foundational generous God, an *intertwining* of giving and receiving between self and otherness that can secure the subject's stable, lawgiving sovereignty. However, this otherness (and receptivity itself) must be purged of the disruptiveness contingency brought into sharp focus by Hume. It must be thinned out to the point of absence and yet present at the same time: a functional presence-absence for the sovereign subject and its transcendent story. Like Hegel's master, Kant's sovereign subject requires an otherness which is not really otherness and thus it must be narrated through equivocations in which it is slipped in and out of being in order to fulfill the functional requirements of sovereignty.[76]

In other words, Kant has succeeded neither in establishing a firm sense of self nor in creating an ethical basis whereby these "selves" can interact. Rather than having human beings artfully straddle the divide between the terrestrial and the divine, Kant (not unlike Locke) gets us suspended in between. The "true" self is indiscernible (like God) but is also "us." The "otherness which is not really an otherness" is our relationship between our "higher" and "lower" selves, a relationship which simultaneously produces a uniformity and a hierarchy between our "true" and "necessary" selves. This relationship in turn becomes reproduced in our relationship to other people, who are also "others who are not really others," reproducing in a sense the very kinds of simultaneous equality and inequality that we find with Locke, with Hooker, and with Aristotle.

In *Politics of Friendship*, Derrida addresses the ways in which Kant considers the question of love and friendship. As Derrida tells us, Kant (like Arendt) holds love in suspicion as an "ardour" that might violate the reciprocity between persons.[77] Kant tells us that "even the best of friends should not make themselves too familiar with each other," and argues that distance and respect are the bases of friendship.[78] Whereas love "can be regarded as an attraction," respect is a "repulsion."[79] Derrida argues that in turning to language of natural "forces,"

> Kant introduces into the continuum of a tradition, which is nonetheless confirmed by him, a principle of *rupture* or *interruption* that can no longer be easily reconciled with the values of proximity, presence, gathering together, and communal familiarity which dominate the traditional culture of friendship.[80]

In other words, Kant has preserved at the heart of his ethical vision of friendship an unstable and even dangerous love. Without this love, however dangerous it may be, Kant shows no reason why friends should not become infinitely distant. Rather than eliminate or replace "natural law" or love itself with a self-posited ethical concept of respect, Kant has presupposed and preserved love with all of its dangers, hierarchies, and "ardours" at the heart of his secular system.

Secularized love appears to offer so much initially, but then we find ourselves facing its other, nastier side. Who, for example, could be more inoffensive than John Stuart Mill, champion of egalitarianism and tolerance? In *On Liberty* he calls for widespread recognition of rights and not only the need to tolerate but even to *appreciate* social and ideological diversity. But upon closer analysis we see that Mill's agenda is not only the empowerment of separate persons but also the production of a social mechanism whereby "truths" may be discovered. Only by having a diversity of ideas both true and untrue (as well as those in between) can the truth become known to us.

The problem with this notion is that as "true" truths emerge out of the social dialectic, they eclipse the right and ability of people to hold on to "false" truths. Since having an autonomous notion for Mill is the basis of our individuality and our freedom, it seems as if freedom itself is at stake in the narrowing of opinion. Our self-reliance, our conviction in our right and ability to decide something for ourselves, becomes compromised by this secularization of *agape,* this truth which descends to earth and colonizes us.

Mill is aware of the conflict between truth seeking and the democratic principle which underlies it. He writes: "But though this gradual narrowing of the bounds of diversity of opinion is necessary...we are not therefore obliged to conclude that all its consequences must be beneficial."[81]

And despite his egalitarianism, Mill tells us:

> Persons of genius, it is true, are, and are always likely to be a small minority; but in order to have them, it is necessary to preserve the soil in which they grow. Genius can only breathe freely in an *atmosphere* of freedom. Persons of genius are...more individual than any other people.[82]

Mill never questions the need for or existence of higher truth nor for the necessarily hierarchical social relationships that emerge from such a conception. For Mill, one of the chief benefits of tolerance is that it allows the great thinkers to "grow" out of the "soil," the arena of divergent opinions inherent in the masses, dependent upon but ultimately transcending this lowly basis.[83] What should self-empowered but lesser individuals do with our own truth-seeking capacity then? Mill answers:

> The honor and glory of the average man is that he is capable of following that initiative, that he can respond internally to wise and noble things, and be led to them with his eyes open.[84]

This is almost a perfect mirroring of Hooker's ecclesiastical polity. To be fair (and Mill makes this point repeatedly so that we don't misunderstand him), he is not calling for a blind following. Instead, the "average man" must use his own relative (and lesser) reason to put himself under the auspices of the great. But this is exactly what Hooker, and Aristotle as well, calls for. For those thinkers, the point of giving reason to the lesser members of society is to prevent false prophets and false claimants to greatness in general, but otherwise it is a largely derivative and vicarious faculty.

Although even with Mill we *are* "freely" choosing to follow a better person's lead, we lose the "right" to be wrong, or the right to decide what is right for ourselves, without reference to an eternal and external truth. Ultimately out of the soil of free thinking comes the necessary expectation that a "reasonable" person will think this and not that. Once again, ours is not to reason on our own, but always in reference to, in search of some higher, better truth.

In making these claims about modern and secularized notions of love, I am also making claims about the more specific albeit broad and deeply nuanced category of liberalism that has come to be the main vehicle whereby love is secularized. Through thinkers ranging from Locke, to Kant, and more recently Rawls, liberal theory has reformulated love into something almost unrecognizable from its earlier roots. But many of the basic tenets of liberalism, for better or worse, are derived from a relationship to older doctrines. The focus on the individual, for example, is a reflection of the idea of *agape* and the individual worth of each person in the eyes of God. We are taken out of our communal ties and loved and judged alone. We are filled up not from terrestrial ties, but from divine ones (even when the divine takes on a new, secular guise as the state).

The idea that these individuals are all fundamentally equal is related to this idea as well. The requirement that liberal persons treat one another according to certain "inalienable" rights is related to the concern that we have seen for equating the two "great" commandments, "to love God" and "to love thy neighbor." And as we shall see, the more nefarious aspects of liberalism have a similar genesis in the religious roots of the doctrine of love.

Although not all of the figures that I treat in this book are incontestably liberal in the way that Locke is, I yet consider them, with the clear exception of Hobbes, to be liberals insofar as they contribute to and remain inscribed within a secularized notion of love.

RETHINKING LOVE

Why should all of this matter to us today, when even Mill has recently become a figure from a century twice removed? Looking at the history of love, from its Greek, to early Christian, to its secular incarnations, offers us a sense of a trajectory, a way to see a process of naturalization whereby love becomes increasingly hard to recognize, increasingly part of the background, unchangeable and eternal. To think of love as a process, a product of history, makes us more aware of how it continues to operate in our lives to this day.

To look at liberalism's relationship to love helps us think about certain questions that are pertinent to our own sense of agency, selfhood, and community. Liberalism promises that it is indifferent to human difference, at least so far as structural and economic differences are concerned. It promises that all de facto inequality is a temporary and vestigial side effect. But the doctrine of love suggests otherwise—that inequality is produced along with equality, that the two cannot be separated. Liberalism promises a notion of identity that is wholly and only "ours." But as is evidenced in the contemporary culture wars, in debates over gender, sexuality, and the family, in the endless "individual versus communitarian" question, in the myriad unsettled and unsettling questions that we pose to ourselves, we see a great deal of anxiety and confusion over identity.

Perhaps the clearest voices to see the effects of love in contemporary life are those of feminist and queer theorists who specifically question the role of gender and sexuality as it is constituted by liberalism, those thinkers who focus upon the way the doctrine of love becomes literalized in our most intimate relations. One such thinker, Leo Bersani, makes a persuasive claim that the failure to think critically about how identity is produced in terms of sexuality leads to the reproduction of the very categories that feminist and queer theory was born in protest to. He writes:

> [U]nless we define how the sexual specificity of being queer... gives to queers a special aptitude for making that challenge [to conventional notions of sex and gender], we are likely to come up with a remarkably familiar, and merely liberal, version of it.[85]

Bersani insists that queerness threatens to lose any meaning at all, so long as it is considered exclusively in terms of a rights-based, liberal discourse. So long as it remains a derivative identity, it will also remain "filled up" with what it has always been.

In her own writing, Wendy Brown cautions us that

> the hollowness of liberalism's universalist promise, then, inheres not only in its depoliticization of invidious social powers... but in its emergence out of and sustenance of female difference and subordination. Feminism, operating with unreconstructed liberal discourse is therefore trapped. . . . [T]he trap consists in working with formulations of personhood, citizenship, and politics that themselves contain women's subordination, that can indeed be extended to women... but are not thereby emancipated from their masculinism by virtue of such extension.[86]

In other words, liberalism's reproduction of gender roles is not wholly and only synonymous with gender itself. Rather, Brown tells us, gender differences are reflective of a need to produce "free" or "unencumbered" subjects by simultaneously producing "unfree" or "encumbered" subjects:

> Insofar as this formulation of liberty *requires* the existence of encumbered beings, the social activity of those without liberty, it can never be fully universalized. . . . In this regard, liberalism would seem to tacitly sustain rather than break with the explicit belief of the ancient citizens of Athens: some must be slaves so that others might be free.[87]

Some women may be very successful, and some people of color might be rich, but *someone* is going to have to sacrifice themselves; differences are going to be produced no matter what. As Aristotle has already shown us, we cannot have perfect friendships without imperfect ones. We can't have friendship without slavery: "O my friends, there is no friend."

In very different ways, Bersani and Brown are alluding to the danger of asking for "rights" from liberalism. The dispersal of such rights tends to reinforce difference rather than to democratize liberalism. This, I want to suggest, is indicative of the ongoing presence in liberalism of the doctrine of love. Love promises us inclusion, equality, community. Liberalism incorporates those values and promises them too, as "rights." But what is the price of accepting this *"agape"* of universal rights? We become hollowed out, subject to sovereignty, colonized. As such, we give ourselves over to a system of thought that makes distinctions, that requires and produces difference. Hierarchies are endemic to liberalism in part because our identities are not "given" by what we are but rather are received and constituted by a relationship to the external, in this case to the state and our received civic identities. We still have the same kinds of "oscillating" identities that we found with Kant, never stable, always formed in reference to something else.[88] To paraphrase Kristeva, there is a "slippage" between our universalist pretensions and the particularities of our condition, between *agape* that does not discriminate, and the very discriminating judgment that separates the sinner and the saved.

As I've already argued, to see love as leading us in this direction does not mean that love should be annihilated—as if it could be. As we've seen, love contains a promise as well as a peril, an "immense rumor" that suggests a hope or a dream for a different kind of love. Without the doctrine of love, we might not have the dream of democracy at all. The question therefore is not so much can we live without love, but can we rethink our relationship to it? Can we have a "civil" divorce?

This book seeks to engage in this rethinking in part by revisiting important thinkers who map out a trajectory of love and engaging with some of their contemporary interpreters. Understanding the role of love in liberal theory helps to challenge the idea that relationships (and by extension love) are a "problem" in liberalism that needs to (or can) be worked out without fundamentally rethinking the concept of relationship, of love and friendship, itself. Many contemporary thinkers who have returned to the foundational texts of liberalism to seek out answers to the ongoing dissatisfaction with liberalism tend, if not to replicate, then at least to not fully escape the issues that they address.

Specifically, I am referring to two loose camps of thinkers that I will concern myself with. The first camp is composed of moderate and liberal thinkers like George Kateb, Judith Shklar, Richard Ashcraft, and others. Such thinkers insist that the democratic promise of liberalism is already present in liberal doctrine; the essential soundness of the liberal subject is already given. Such thinkers argue that the problem we face in liberal society stems from a fundamental misunderstanding of the intent of the founders of liberalism, who are much more progressive than we have previously understood. To return to those foundational texts is to see how liberalism offers a profoundly democratic and just system, specifically in terms of how we are to relate to one another.

My argument against this group is that they only get liberalism half right. As I've already argued, liberalism isn't as bad as some people say it is; C. B. MacPherson is not exactly right. But liberal "rights" exist only in the abstract, in the celestial heights of equality (or concretely only for those who are privileged by the system) and they presuppose their opposites.

The second camp is composed of more "anti-foundationalist" thinkers like Stanley Cavell, Richard Rorty, Tracy Strong, Richard Flathman, and others, who make a more complex argument. Not all of these thinkers are liberals, but insofar as they treat and refer to thinkers whom I consider to be liberals, I choose to engage with them. These thinkers tend to grant the troubles of liberalism, yet point out that the very instability of this subject leads to the possibility of a multiple, ironic, and detached self—a basis for a truly progressive subjectivity that can coexist with other selves without threat.

My argument with this camp is tempered by a great deal of agreement. Yet I feel that irony and detachment are possible avenues to democratic friendship only when actual inequality is not presupposed and "background" to existing social relations. As we will see, for example, with Cavell's analysis of neighborliness or "nextness" as a model of self that allows for both autonomy and community, such a conception does not preclude a prior and generally unseen ordering. The notion of neighborliness (with its clear ties to the commandment to "love thy neighbor") is revealed to be, like Aristotle's *philia,* a democratic dream that for now at least is built on an edifice of hierarchy and lack. It is not that there is no other possibility for *philia*—Cavell himself perfectly articulates the "perhaps"—but we must not be premature in seeking to emulate these models of friendship or neighborliness. Where questions of love are involved, it is always worth searching for the inequalities that are produced along with the equalities.

I believe that an appreciation for how love has worked its way into liberalism helps to dispel the notion that relationships in liberal theory need to be discovered or resolved; the problem is exactly that there is a very resolved, very functional notion of relationship already in place in liberal theory and practice. It is this relationship itself that needs to be examined and rethought.

I divide this book into five further chapters to pursue this line of argument. First, I will look at Locke, who as I've suggested is a kind of refounder of love in a new liberal guise. I will describe how Locke reproduces the dilemma between *eros* and *agape.* On the one hand, he is an empiricist, insisting on a human-based, sensory discovery of meaning and truth. On the other hand, for Locke the "real" truth lies in heaven, in natural law, and is invisible to the senses. This epistemological tension is reflected in a political tension between the self-regarding equality of his empiricism and the hierarchical "ladders" produced by his ontology. Whereas for Hooker there is only one standard of judgment (God's), for Locke there are two and the question "Who shall be Judge?" is one of the more complex and taxing issues in his system of thought.

As I will be arguing, both Locke's epistemology and politics fall between two stools—the demands and outcomes of Christian Aristotelianism, and the hopes and expectations of modern secular empiricism, receiving the worst of both worlds. Like Hooker, Locke arranges us hierarchically, but like Hobbes he insists on our equality and equal potential to reason. Like Hooker, Locke merges our identities to achieve a common goal, but, like Hobbes, he promises us our own autonomy, making this merger a problem. Locke's social hierarchies are not absolute and unquestionable, but socially constructed. As we will see, those on the lower rungs of Locke's social ladders are not, like Hooker's subjects, happily giving themselves over to a higher power, but rather they are giving up their own chance at "higherness" to promote the reason and freedom of their superiors. It is hence an unstable and often unhappy doctrine. In Locke we find that the alluring promise and troubles of contemporary liberalism are already in place.

The other thinkers that I deal with have this legacy to work out for themselves. Rousseau in particular offers us a vision of how painful and complicated love can be as a force in politics. Rousseau, despite his linkages to Lockean epistemology, was particularly dissatisfied with the tableau of liberal subjectivity. He constantly juxtaposes love and freedom as two opposites, but inevitably throughout his work the one turns into the other. In fleeing from the suffocating embrace of love, he discovers and retreats from the loneliness of his ideal of freedom. In seeking to merge entirely with the social, he discovers how it is built upon an unseen network of intimate, contentious relationships where there can never be harmony and where he feels threatened. For all his brilliance and optimism, Rousseau never resolves this tension. As his play suggests, he shows us that love is not only a bond, but a bondage.

Emerson, in seeking to reestablish and resolve the liberal subject in America, takes the notion of love to its metaphysical conclusion; he looks to the transcendent heights to leave the troubled social body behind. There, messy connections with other people can no longer affect the self, and love itself (at least in its terrestrial forms) can be forgotten. Whereas Emerson, despite great reservations, really believes that the sacrifices and hierarchies of love are effectively transcended by realizing our oneness and unity in a higher realm, his student Thoreau, a man who was more drawn to the world and its troubles, sees that this attempt is a failure. Thoreau, who seeks a true and pure love above all, cannot escape the construction of love and its cruel demands and, in his own suffering, reveals the dilemma of love to us, his readers.

With all of these thinkers, I suggest that their struggles and despair serve as a warning to contemporary readers against seeking to resolve the problem of love as it is constituted and then reconstituted. Rousseau and Thoreau, who explicitly name and problematize the darker sides of love's embrace, serve as witnesses to the prices that must be paid for friendship and "equality." In different ways, they delineate the promise and shining vision that love inspires in them, and then show how and why that vision cannot be achieved without a radical reconceptualization of love and friendship.

Finally, I come to the perhaps surprising conclusion that Thomas Hobbes, who is so associated with hatred and fear, comes much closer to offering us a way to understand and rethink the nature of love. I find in Hobbes a vision of politics that offers something to Arendt and Derrida's search for *philia politike.*

Through his valuation of the body and his emphasis on our common mortality, Hobbes offers us something that we all share but is also unique to each of us, creating the kind of spatial relationship that is consistent with Arendt's notion of respect (and hence *philia politike*). Whereas in the doctrine of love the act of discovering the "truth" tends to be solipsistic (since the truth is not ours but God's and each of us has our own path to discerning it), truth for Hobbes can only be produced through social engagement, through speech, and through relationship.

In this sense, Hobbes partakes in a tradition that might be called "realist," linking him to figures such as Ovid and Lucretius, valuing humanity and its perspectives in its own right. But there is a way in which I think Hobbes departs from and improves upon on these thinkers, exactly by participating in the "immense rumor" that we find with Aristotle, by rethinking rather than rejecting love, by being and by not being "Greek." Hobbes threads a path between Platonic mystery and realist literalism. In this way he avoids both totalizing sameness as well as nihilism and relativism. As I will argue, Hobbes does this chiefly through his understanding of God.[89] For him, unlike for many other "realists," God is not absent but he is utterly unknowable. This present but silent God serves as a check on the hubris and nihilism that might otherwise constitute or threaten a "realist" position. It also serves as a check on external yardsticks that Platonists might resort to. For Hobbes, unlike Locke, God's unknowability does not lead to crisis. For Hobbes, God's silence affords us the space and responsibility for self-creation, but it also contains our endeavors. For Hobbes, the only things that we *do* know that God has given us are our bodies, our ability to speak, and our mortality. These things become building blocks for Hobbes, to be reverenced and held in dignity, the basis of a political community. They may derive from God, but they remain, as far as we are concerned, wholly ours, already filled up.

In this and other ways, I believe that Hobbes anticipates some of the insights of contemporary Continental philosophers such as Nietzsche who, while rejecting eternal and knowable truths, also distance themselves from nihilism and relativism. Given the hopeless choice that Rousseau seems to present us between an enslaving, smothering love on the one hand or the isolation and nihilism of its absence, Hobbes takes a different route, one which may deliver him from both.

I am not trying to suggest that Hobbes and Hobbes alone figured something out that no one else could; as we will see, Hobbes does not produce a perfect model of *philia politike* either; he must engage in conversation, in the "immense rumor," with other figures, including Arendt and Derrida. Yet Hobbes is an important figure in this story because he came at the dawn of liberalism, and lived during a period of time when, as Christopher Hill tells us, the world was "turned upside down."[90] Hobbes was a right person at a right time. He was able to take advantage of an epistemological rupture, to think outside of classical notions of love and politics. And he offers us something else, too, that rarest of things which the early moderns did so well: a fully developed, completely articulated notion of subjectivity, the kinds of building blocks that are always required as a basis for rethinking political relationships. If Locke has founded the persons that we have become, Hobbes offers an alternative subjectivity, an alternative genealogy, another kind of love. He does not turn his back on Western philosophy, on the rumor that sustains it, but rather his philosophy is produced from within it and in response to it.

But Hobbes's understanding of love and politics was not to be the direction or fate of liberal theory. Most of this book is spent considering the first implication of Derrida's question: the consequences of living and being organized by the politics of love. What does it mean to live in this way? Who do we become when we surrender to love's embrace? How does love reconstitute itself? What does it look like from the inside? Before we seek a divorce from it, we must first know what it means to live and struggle with the doctrine of love.

LOCKE'S REASONABLE
SUBJECT

1. THE ORIGINS OF LOCKEAN PHILOSOPHY

Given their common vocabulary of natural right, contract, sovereignty, and reason, one might infer that Hobbes and Locke are united in a common project. Indeed, this reading of Hobbes as a "proto-liberal" and of Locke as the culmination of liberalism can be found in scholars from many ideological camps ranging from C. B. MacPherson and Alisdair MacIntyre to Leo Strauss.[1] Other scholars such as Kirstie McClure and John Dunn argue that Hobbes and Locke are quite different and that it is Hobbes who suffers in the comparison. McClure writes:

> For Hobbes, Hume, and Rousseau, the natural condition of humankind principally referred to its worldly characteristics, or behavior as observed or inferred by human agents; Locke's account of natural humanity had as its central reference the created condition of the species. Where they, in other words, emphasized what they found to be the actual or descriptive characteristics of the species—its physical passions, worldly desires and material interests—he began with an image of humanity as it was divinely constructed within and in relation to a larger created cosmos.[2]

For McClure, Locke's abandonment of Hobbes's harsh manner of accounting everything according to some petty and self-interested calculation is the source of his morality and what allows Locke to be more than simply a thinker of mere self-interest. This reading of Locke is also what attracts Richard Ashcraft, who insists that Locke's notions of property are *not* to be read (as C. B. MacPherson does) as a doctrine of selfishness but rather as a genuine concern for collective moral principles. Ashcraft tells us:

> To consider Locke's position on the relationship of labor to property divorced from its theological underpinnings is not only a serious interpretive mistake...it also misrepresents through omission a crucial dimension of the political radicalism that [the *Two Treatises*] expresses.[3]

Ashcraft argues that for Locke a meaningful sense of community is given to us only by the fact that we are all God's "workmanship."[4] For both Ashcraft and

McClure, it is Locke and not Hobbes who offers us a hope for genuine democracy and community, if only we can come to see the genuine and radical promise in his doctrines.

For Ashcraft, Locke's religious convictions overlap with more secular concerns. He argues that for both philosophical and political reasons, Locke (like many Whig theorists) was quite sympathetic to the radical politics of the Levellers who preceded him by some thirty years. As Ashcraft points out, the Whigs, although chiefly a party of wealthy and often landed men, were in alliance with artisans and tradesmen and the rising urban bourgeoisie. This was the same constituency of the Levellers themselves.[5] At the same time, the Whigs echoed the Levellers' position on rationality and property.[6] Like the Levellers, Whig rhetoric defended existing property rights and arrangements even as it advocated an idea of rationality that makes all men equal.[7]

The question of whether Locke had any sympathy for the Levellers and just how radical the Levellers were themselves continues to be a source of much scholarly debate. For the first question, Locke's (and Anthony Ashley Cooper Shaftesbury's) association with the Leveller John Wildman is cited.[8] Ashcraft himself acknowledges that while there is no direct evidence that Locke read Leveller texts, in his tone, style, and language he demonstrates a discernible link.[9]

As for the radicalism of the Levellers (which would therefore suggest the "radicalism" of Locke himself), Ashcraft argues that MacPherson makes too much of the Levellers' exclusion of servants and beggars from their post-Putney declarations about universal manhood suffrage.[10] MacPherson's position is that the term "servant" could be extended to virtually the entire working class. Ashcraft argues on the contrary that this exclusion was most likely the result of some political bargaining and not to be inferred as the Levellers' "true" position.[11] And furthermore, he argues, the category "servant" was widely considered to be only a temporary one or at least limited in nature, certainly excluding vast numbers of workers.[12] Somewhat against this vein, Christopher Hill argues for taking the Levellers at their (published) word, saying that they were not for universal manhood suffrage but sought it only for "men of small property, the artisan, yeoman and husbandman majority of the population"—in other words, for their own constituency.[13] Hill argues that at most the Levellers (who after all, Ashcraft himself concedes, were "defenders of property") sought the doubling of suffrage, not the quadrupling that universal manhood suffrage would offer.[14] Yet whoever is right, at the very least we can clearly see that the "two-class" model that MacPherson subscribes to, wherein the "rich" oppress the "poor," is not an accurate description of Locke's times, nor of the period between the English civil war and the Glorious Revolution.

Ashcraft argues that the *Two Treatises of Government*, while not calling for a radical redistribution of property, nonetheless offers a vision of society whereby both landowners and non-landowners can be accounted for and given their due. For Locke, as we have seen, the point of owning property is to improve it, not for one's own self but for the greater good of the community, and ultimately for God himself.[15] Ashcraft quotes Locke as arguing that:

> therefore he that encloses land and has a greater plenty of the conveniences of life from ten acres, than he could have from a hundred left to nature, may truly be said to give ninety acres to mankind.[16]

He surmises that:

> Locke is plainly not interested in *individual motivations* for property development; rather, what concerns him are the moral and social uses to which property (and labor) can be put.[17]

Clearly, Locke was opposed to the kind of wealthy, leisured landowners who constituted the basis of Tory power. Ashcraft tells us that Locke's attitude toward such landowners was "decidedly negative,"[18] while "[o]n the contrary, Locke's general attitude toward manual labor...was overwhelmingly positive."[19] Ashcraft even points out that Locke sought to have landowners and men of leisure spend some number of hours every day physically toiling to gain the virtue of manual labor.[20]

Is Locke then truly a champion of the downtrodden and the lower laborer even at the expense of the landed aristocrat? Is he a misunderstood radical democrat, wrongly charged with being an apologist for greed and wealth? We must be clear in distinguishing a critique of C. B. MacPherson, which Ashcraft accomplishes quite handily, from any kind of larger testament to Locke's democratic credentials. I agree with Ashcraft that there can be no doubt that Locke's commitment to community, his belief in our common rationality and implicit respect for individuality in all of its guises, is genuine and important. These commitments, I agree, stem from his religious beliefs, in the notion that we all have souls and that we are all God's "workmanship." It is important to recognize this fact not only because it paints Locke in a more favorable light, but also because it points to the promise that is in love, even as it condemns us to hierarchy and sacrifice. The promise of democracy is present in Locke, but remains so deeply compromised that we must look elsewhere for its fulfillment.

Any appreciation that Locke has for the rights and reasonableness of the lower classes (however plural they might be) must be understood within the context of a larger organizing principle that presupposes and requires these differences as organized by the doctrine of love. For Locke, the connection between classes (and, I will argue, gender and family relations as well) amounts to a social division of labor devoted to reproducing God's love on earth. As I will argue, this goes well beyond a "two-class" model whereby the poor toil for the rich to give them wealth and leisure. Locke offers a highly integrated conception of society whereby divisions of class and gender serve to embody and control desires and passions, enabling those who are privileged in the hierarchy to achieve their fullest reasonableness for the sake of the collective whole. In secularizing the doctrine of love, Locke makes it the blueprint of the social and political order of liberalism. Much of this chapter is devoted to detailing the organization of this social vision.

Thus I agree with Ashcraft in terms of his seeing all labor (that of rich, poor, and in-between) as being organized according to higher moral and social issues, but disagree as to the *sort* of moral and social constructions that Locke submits us to. It is not that Locke is amoral but rather that his moral system functions much as Aristotle's does. Those in "lower" positions benefit vicariously; they are rewarded for their subordination by the industry and Godliness of the world created by their masters.

In political terms, therefore, I think that the prospective Whig allies (those artisans and tradesmen) might have done well to take a closer look at what they were being offered. Locke's work in the *Second Treatise* does banish primogeniture and the absolute right of the noble born. But these "improvements" come at a price for those newly enfranchised persons. An absolute hierarchy becomes replaced with a relative one, and the townsmen, yeomen farmers, and artisans come into the alliance above most people but below the landed gentry themselves.

For Locke there is a great chain of reason stretching from the highest to the lowest member of society. As he puts it:

> A day labourer in a country village has commonly but a small pittance of knowledge because his ideas and notions have been confined to the narrow bounds of a poor conversation and employment; the low mechanic of a country town does somewhat outdo him: porters and cobblers of great cities surpass them.[21]

Sure enough, there is no absolute "cutoff" between the "rational" rich and the "irrational" working classes, and there are lots of classes in between. But just because rationality can be found at all levels of the social hierarchy does not mean that it can be found in equal measures. And just because the lower classes are blessed with some rationality does not mean that Locke thinks that they should not be subservient to those who have more. It may be true that Locke loosens the bonds of hierarchy quite dramatically compared to Filmer or even Hooker, but the point is that hierarchies are still required. To paraphrase Carole Pateman, it is not so much a matter of whether the landed gentry are absolute rulers but whether they are rulers at all.[22]

And, as we will see further, given the need for reason to substitute for the loss of revelation, given that Locke sees that rationality is very hard to maintain and very easy to lose, the hierarchical system he posits is not temporary but permanent. As Locke's fear of the depravity of the rich implies, his notion of rationality requires a permanently hierarchical relationship, rather than a tutelary system with a long-term progressive outcome.

Locke's religious influences

Although I have argued that Locke "revives" the doctrine of love, such a statement needs to be qualified by a recognition that, aside from ruptures such as that offered by Hobbes and other seventeenth-century English figures, love, as a force for organizing politics, was never really absent. But Locke does something that no other thinker did, at least not to the same degree—he revises and reformulates the doctrine of love to meet the needs of a modern and necessarily more secular political order. But this secularization, as I hope to show further, derives itself almost entirely from Locke's own roots in a particular theological discourse.

There are several strands of religious influence on Locke, some of which appear to be contradictory. John Dunn makes much of Locke's Puritan upbringing. While Dunn concurs that Puritan clergy might have been "shocked" by Locke's departures from orthodoxy, he nonetheless sees a strong Puritan influence in his tenets, however secularized.[23] Dunn suggests that the restraint that Locke demonstrates in calling for a restricted notion of liberty and his commensurate curbing of the privileges and powers of the landowning classes (including himself and his own patrons) stems from this Puritan background.[24] Dunn writes that "It should not be difficult . . . to make out why Locke did not become a gay and careless libertine."[25]

Like Ashcraft, Dunn argues that Locke's understanding of labor cannot be comprehended without reference to the idea that we are all God's "workmanship," and furthermore likens this relationship to labor to the Calvinist notion of a calling. And yet Dunn concedes, much more forcefully than Ashcraft, that this idea of the calling does not translate into a truly egalitarian political order:

> In social terms the dominant characteristic of the calling was its egalitarianism. This was not, it is true a *secular* egalitarianism. It involved no proposals for the destruction of terrestrial hierarchies.[26]

If indeed Locke is so heavily influenced by Puritan doctrine, it might seem curious that another principle influence is Richard Hooker, a man highly associated with Anglican orthodoxy and the attack against Puritan doctrines.[27] Samuel Parker, the nemesis of the Puritans, approvingly cites Hooker himself when he makes his arguments against unorthodox thought.[28] But the Puritans had their own reasons for appreciating Hooker's views.

Unlike Parker, Hooker's argument against Puritanism is not so much to renounce the centrality of scripture but to include its interpretation in the context of a variety of other sources of truth.[29] Hooker himself grew up in a Calvinist environment and came to defend the Church of England late and with great respect for his foes in the Puritan reformist movement.[30] And he praised Calvin himself as just the sort of religious leader that humanity required. Perhaps most important of all is Hooker's promotion of reason (which Parker denounces), a notion dear to the Whigs' hearts. It is Hooker, as we have already seen, who presents us with a vision of how reason and revelation can coexist nicely, "the one extraordinary, the other common."[31]

With Hooker, we find a rearticulation of the *caritas* synthesis that we have seen earlier with Saints Augustine and Aquinas. Revelation is like *agape,* the truth of God that comes down to us and fills us. Reason is like *eros,* human but constituted in relationship to divine truth. With Hooker, as with Saint Augustine, *eros* and *agape,* reason and revelation, are coordinated, producing in their wake the basis for a political community.

Hooker's own version of the *caritas* synthesis nicely serves the Whig agenda. Hooker promotes certain political and philosophical liberties without a concomitant denunciation of Scripture and the rights of natural law. He promotes human reason without conflicting with or superseding divine truths. He promotes the idea of widespread reason, but allows for property and social hierarchy to remain intact. All of this serves the Whig position of pursuing a more egalitarian vision of society, without contravening the bases of that society: property, natural law, and God.

As Michael Walzer tells us in *The Revolution of the Saints,* Hooker offers the Whigs a much more decentralized notion of a politics lived in accordance with higher truths than the Puritans' own roots in Calvinist doctrine:

> In contrast with the Catholic view, repeated by Hooker at the very end of the sixteenth century, which found room in its theory of natural law for the imaginative investigations and crafty adaptations of human reason, Calvinists reconstructed the theory as a tight and authoritative system of "Thou shalt" and "Thou shalt not."[32]

Thus, however ironic it might seem, Hooker, for all his Anglican orthodoxy, suits Locke quite well. Again, we must be careful to avoid the tendency to replicate Nygren's strict distinction between the pure *agape* of Calvin and the *caritas* synthesis of Saint Augustine.[33] Although from a strict Puritan perspective Hooker, and by extension Saint Augustine himself, may seem dangerously "Catholic," the real issue that made Catholicism itself unattractive was not *caritas* per se but papistry. On this issue Hooker was as stern a critic as any Puritan hardliner. When it came to matters of political pragmatism, Locke and the Whigs in general were hardly orthodox Puritans, and so any lesser doctrinal differences could be overlooked.

It is in his political agenda that Hooker is perhaps most useful for Locke. By making revelation rather than state rule central to his "ecclesiastical polity," Hooker enables Locke to envision a Godly society that is not absolutely concomitant with the prerogatives of state power. As for the secular state itself, Hooker argues (and Locke quotes him frequently to the effect) that "[t]o live by one Man's Will, became the cause of all Mens misery."[34] Locke also cites Hooker as offering support for his idea of legislative supremacy.[35] And Hooker provides justification for Locke's reconciliation of property and "self-interest" with Godliness.[36]

In so doing, Hooker offers Locke a platform by which to coordinate human law and action with the divine. As Locke will do himself, Hooker distinguishes between "natural" and "positive" law, between those laws that we cannot but follow and those that are "merely human" whereby we can do as we please (and Hooker even comes up with a "mixed" category that is simultaneously "our own" and "God's" will).[37]

But these political doctrines do not come without a price. This seemingly democratic and humanistic tendency in Hooker has to be understood as being part and parcel of that other crucial doctrine that Locke takes from Hooker, the idea of love itself. Hooker takes his idea of love straight out of Christian Aristotelian (or in this case more specifically Aquinian) dogma, arguing that we are incomplete by ourselves and all of our endeavors after happiness and fulfillment can only come from God himself (God being the only being that requires no external perfection as part of his nature).[38] For Hooker, love is the name of the process whereby we are brought to our perfection via our fulfillment in and through God.[39] Although we are united under a common bond, within that commonality we are also ordered by it.

In considering the "mutual Love amongst men, on which [Hooker] Builds the Duties they owe one another," Locke preserves love as the basis of his new secular order.[40] Early in the *Second Treatise* he quotes Hooker as writing: "The like natural inducement, hath brought Men to know that it is no less their duty, to Love others than themselves, for seeing those things which are equal, must needs all have one measure."[41] Here we see a vision of society that seems quite communitarian, even egalitarian. But the next time Locke quotes Hooker we see that the challenge to love others is rendered difficult by the failures of human nature: The "Laws which have been hitherto mentioned [the Laws of Nature], do bind Men absolutely, even as they are Men . . . [t]o supply those Defects and Imperfections which are in us, as living singly and solely by our selves, we are naturally induced to seek Communion and Fellowship with others."[42] Here we can already see signs of how love can both presuppose and "solve" our differences. Despite our differences, despite the fact that some of us are better than others, we seek out one another due to our God-given propensity to love each other. Once together, love smoothes over our differences and joins us into a whole that is better than its parts.

The withdrawing of miracles

As I have already argued, Locke's key distinction from Hooker is that he does not hold to the ongoing possibility of revelation. As he tells us in *A Discourse on Miracles,* there has been a "withdrawing of miracles"; the age of revelation is over.[43] It might appear as if this alteration would only enhance the democratic potential in Hooker, keeping reason, that "common" and lower tendency, and removing the higher and external standard of judgment which organizes us into hierarchies. There is indeed a greater democratic potential in Locke than in Hooker, but it is one that is as much thwarted as it is aided by Locke's secularizing tendencies.

In the absence of revelation, Locke's task is to reconcile reason without revelation as best he can. One text where he makes this attempt is *A Discourse on Miracles*. He begins this essay by mimicking language we see also in Hobbes's *Leviathan,* arguing that "it is unavoidable that that should be a miracle to one, which is not so to another."[44] But Hobbes's argument that the appearance of a miracle is in and of itself no proof of sanctity is set up by Locke only to be refuted. Ultimately, Locke makes the exact opposite argument, stating that God only performs miracles which are by their nature perceivable as being "true" by any reasonable person. There can thus be no doubt that one must not only obey but also believe in God and God's laws as they are presented to us via revelation. The upshot of this is that for Locke reason does seem to have the capacity not only to recognize a miracle, but also to know and perhaps even approximate the higher truths contained by them.[45] As Locke puts it elsewhere:

> God, I believe, speaks differently from Men, because he speaks with more Truth, more Certainty: but when he vouchsafes to speak to Men, I do not think he speaks differently from them, in crossing the Rules of language in use amongst them.[46]

In considering how to have a just political order in a time without miracles, Locke clearly cannot make reason exactly equivalent to revelation, but it must fill in the breach, become clearer and better developed.[47] In so doing, while still allowing that reason is "common" to all of us, Locke also begins to make distinctions about abilities to reason and hence elevates something that we might call "higher reason" above the rest. As for the rest of society, those who only have a lower version of reason, Locke offers them faith. In *The Reasonableness of Christianity* he writes:

The greatest part of mankind want leisure or capacity for demonstration, nor can carry a train of proofs.... [H]earing plain commands, is the sure and only course to bring them to obedience and practice. *The greatest part cannot know, and therefore they must believe.* And I ask, whether one coming from heaven in the power of God, in full and clear evidence and demonstration of miracles, giving plain and direct rules of morality and obedience, be not likelier to enlighten the bulk of mankind...than by reasoning with them from general notions and principles of human reason?[48] (emphasis added)

This passage suggests that reason might actually be lost on the lower classes. Their faith serves to ensure their continued obedience not only to God's law but to those who best discern it on earth. Thus Hooker's ecclesiastical community is roughly preserved in its new semi-secular guise.

But elsewhere in this same essay, Locke acknowledges that reason on its own—even the reason of the greatest thinkers—is not enough. Without revelation (particularly in terms of Christ), Locke tells us that reason leads us into "a wild wood of uncertainty...an endless maze."[49]

And therein lies the problem: While reasonable men *are* able to know a miracle when they see it, they can do so only because God has vouchsafed to have his miracle occur in a way that they can understand. It is still up to God to reveal the truth, and reason remains a largely passive faculty. The truth is not being discovered from the ground up, but is revealed from heaven down. Reason is not a truth-making faculty as it is for Hobbes; for Locke, reason can only derive truth from a higher source. This is why God's silence becomes such a problem for Locke. While revelation might remain present in Scripture, it still needs to be interpreted—a heavily contentious issue in Locke's time. Where Hooker calls for revelation as a living part of a community, an active connection to higher truth, Locke is left with memory and nostalgia, an inadequate ability to know what he must know.

I interpret Locke's frequently posed question "Who shall be judge?" to reveal an epistemological crisis over the loss of revelation.[50] We can make good guesses on earth, but ultimately we are all accountable to our true "owner" in whose name we act, God himself. Reason is merely a substitute for revelation, and an inadequate one at that. It is a derivative faculty, suited to interpret and receive but not to find or preserve divine truths. Reason must be passive because it is not wholly ours; we receive reason, as we receive love, from God.

What serves so well for Hooker, the loosening of absolute secular power in the name of giving over to divine power, has a different connotation for Locke. Like Hooker, Locke sees the realm of human freedom as being enabled only by a strict duty to God. But if that duty is difficult to discern, then human freedom becomes more dangerous, more susceptible to corruption. *Eros* is enabled in the *caritas* synthesis because it is linked to *agape,* but in an age without revelation, *agape* is less certain, and *eros* is left to its own devices, returned to its own lacking. As we have seen, Locke too holds onto a *caritas* synthesis, but in this case its component parts have unraveled; we remain ready to be filled, but we are not.

There are consequences for the political vision produced by such an unraveled *caritas* synthesis. Like Hooker, Locke seeks to impose a hierarchy on his subjects, to create a division of labor that serves to promote a society which organizes itself according to God's judgments. But if that judgment is uncertain, the justification for the hierarchy is also uncertain. For Hooker, the possibility of revelation means that there is an absolute and unquestionable step between the ecclesiastical leader and his community. We see this with Aristotle as well in his doctrine of "natural slaves." With this absolute difference, those in subordinate positions can fully trust and merge with those above them. With Locke, however, all we get is social relativism; since even the highest person is quite possibly wrong and even the lowest person might just be right (however deeply unlikely the latter event might be for Locke), the demands that Locke puts on his subjects serve to endlessly threaten resentment, rupture, and uncertainty.

The realm of the senses

It may well be the case that Locke's interest in empiricism is a response to this epistomolgical crisis. Empiricism suggests the possibility of rethinking truth altogether. With its promise of looking to the world for signs of God's order, empiricism might seem to resolve the gap between divine and terrestrial truths.[51] And yet, in Locke's case, such a conceptualization simply reproduces the epistemological crisis that spawned it.

Empiricism itself is nothing new; Aristotle himself embraces it, as does Epicurus. In the Christian era, with the notion of *agape,* comes a commensurate concern that human reason might interfere with or even replace divine truths with truths of our own. As we have seen, the *caritas* synthesis suggests the coordination of reason and revelation, but "heresies" such as Socinianism suggest that the matter is not easily settled. Socinianism promoted reason as being in and of itself capable of discerning and knowing natural law. Locke himself was accused of advocating Socinianism, a charge he vigorously denied.[52]

The question of empiricism therefore carried fairly high stakes—to argue that "common" reason is capable of discerning truths on its own is to suggest, as the Digger leader Gerrard Winstanley does, that no one is inherently more Godly or truth knowing than any one else.[53]

During the reign of Charles II, questions of reason and innate truths were highly charged political issues directly related to the religious battles that still dominated England. One of the greatest opponents to Puritan Dissenters on the issue of empiricism was the aforementioned Anglican clergyman Samuel Parker. Parker, in denouncing empiricism, argued that reason is not particularly widespread and certainly not capable of deducing divine truths on its own. For Parker we remain utterly dependent upon revelation, Scripture, church, and state to show us how we must live.[54] Against him were arrayed figures ranging from John Owen to Robert Ferguson, who argued that reason was common to all of us and furthermore that it not only could be but had to be involved in discerning truths.

Locke steps into this tangle with his own epistemological arguments. Like so many of his contemporaries, he argues against the idea of innate truths. In his *Essay on Human Understanding*, Locke distinguishes between innate truths and "self-evident" truths.[55] An innate truth is "stamped upon the mind of man...which the soul receives in its first being."[56] A self-evident truth, on the other hand, is simply "obvious" and easily recognized by reason. Self-evident truths are no less true than innate ones, and we are no less compelled to follow them, but when we do, we come to it of our own accord, individually and collectively, thus preserving more of a position for human agency and freedom than a strictly innatist viewpoint might allow for.[57]

In taking his positions on empiricism, Locke echoes but also dissents from some of his main empirical influences, Hobbes himself and also Pierre Gassendi (disagreeing more radically with the former than the latter). For Locke, unlike Hobbes, truths are not wholly determined by our actual experience of natural objects around us. Locke recognizes a distinction between abstract concepts and the material objects which we discern via our senses. Whereas for Hobbes such abstract ideas are produced only by "decaying sense" and imagination, for Locke they point to a series of "higher faculties" which are not entirely in the thrall of sensory data after all.[58] Although Locke is careful to avoid making an absolute separation between abstract thought and the direct experience of objects (because to do so overmuch would be to undermine the sensory basis of empiricism itself), he is much more likely even than Gassendi to embrace abstraction *qua* abstraction rather than as the final product of a chain of sensory-based understanding.[59]

Michael Ayers, in his consideration of Locke's empiricism, argues that given this tension between sensory imput and higher faculties, this idea that Locke is an empiricist needs to be qualified:

> It may not always be helpful to look on Locke as an "empiricist" but his doctrine that experience supplies the materials of thought does involve a thoroughgoing and consistent experiential or imagist theory of thought.[60]

Ernst Cassirer more or less echoes this sentiment when he tells us:

Without doubt Locke took an important step forward and first blazed the trail for empirical investigation. But he stopped half way and recoiled before the most difficult problem. For where the higher functions of mind—those of comparing, distinguishing, judging and willing—are concerned, Locke suddenly proves unfaithful to his genetic method. He is content merely to enumerate these faculties and leave them as fundamental powers of the mind without tracing them to their source.... Locke successfully attacked innate ideas but he permitted the prejudice regarding innate operations of the mind to survive.[61]

Locke's retaining of higher, abstract qualities of the mind, while not making him an innatist, does not necessarily qualify him as a pure empiricist either. For Locke, while we receive the world through our senses, we are designed by God so as to be able to understand him; our higher faculties therefore are disposed to be able to receive and recognize higher truths than a stricter empiricism would suggest (where we have to figure everything out for ourselves). For Locke, we are custom made to recognize and respond to natural law; this is at best a quasi empiricism.

In seeking to understand the peculiarities of Locke's empiricism, it might be worth turning once again to Hooker's influence upon him. In *Ecclesiastical Polity*, Hooker offers his own view of empiricism:

In the matter of knowledge there is between the angels of God and the children of men this difference:—angels already have full and complete knowledge in the highest degree that can imparted to them; men, if we view them in their spring are at first without understanding or knowledge at all. Nevertheless, from this utter vacuity, *they grow by degrees,* till they come at length to be even as the angels themselves are.... The soul of *man* being therefore *at the first as a book wherein nothing is, and yet all things may be imprinted.*[62]

In Hooker's own empiricism, we see many commonalities to Locke. They use similar metaphors (Locke uses the notion of blank paper as well as the idea of us being an "empty cabinet" waiting to be filled).[63] In Hooker too, we see an earlier echo of Locke's insistence that reason does not know something all at once but must learn in degrees.[64] Hooker goes on to write (as Locke will echo) that children possess only the most basic kind of reasoning skills and that "[e]ducation and instruction are the means, the one by use, the other by precept, to make our natural faculty of reason both the better and the sooner able to judge rightly between truth and error, good and evil," an idea, as we will see, that Locke takes up as a central component of his own project.[65]

Most importantly of all, however, Locke reflects Hooker's belief that reason does not exist for its own sake but in order to bring us out of ourselves and toward God. In the *Essay* Locke argues once again that reason itself does not contain or produce truth; to believe otherwise would be to believe that truths are "in the understanding, and not to be understood."[66]

Here, Locke's attack on innate truth is another reiteration of his subscription to a kind of *caritas* synthesis via Hooker. To suggest that a truth is innate is to suggest either that we are already imbued with full knowledge (a position too close to the hubris of *eros* alone, or Socinianism) or are merely vessels of God's truth (i.e., pure *agape*). Locke wants to carve out, as Hooker does, a zone of human endeavoring after truth that exists between heaven and earth.

Yet, once again, Locke's language is never as sanguine or forceful as Hooker's. Hooker fully expects that we will come to become "as angels," a book upon which "all things may be imprinted." This is possible because of the role of revelation and scriptural interpretation that serves as the anchor for Hooker's vision. Hooker smoothly reconciles *eros* to *agape*, thanks to the possibility of communication between the divine and the mortal. But Locke's empiricism does not permit such an easy relationship. Because the truths that our higher faculties are meant to receive are unclear, the relationship between these higher faculties and our sensory imputs is also problematized, hence the epistemological crisis.

Rather than resolve the ambivalence between divine truths and reason, Locke's empiricism reproduces the conflict, preserving that ambivalence at the heart of his epistemology. In Locke's secularization of Hooker, the *caritas* synthesis unravels. *Eros* is left without *agape*, reason without revelation, sense without certainty. The attempt to substitute for this loss is by definition inadequate, hopeless. This tension is preserved and manifested throughout Locke's work, simultaneously promising and undermining the democratic principles to which he subscribes.

2. REASON AND SOCIETY

These theological and philosophical concerns are reflected in Locke's political vision as well. Even in the *Essay*, a text devoted to epistemological questions, Locke reveals some of the political dimensions of his conceptualization of reason. He frequently cites the example of "children, idiots, savages, and illiterate people," whom he calls "a great part of mankind" (and elsewhere "at least one half of mankind"), to prove that there are no innate truths because such persons cannot give a universal assent to things that they cannot understand.[67] Such persons do not have any inkling of natural law, yet at the same time, Locke does not consider them to be incapable of reason. In *Of the Conduct of the Understanding* Locke writes that "every man carries about him a touchstone [i.e., reason itself], if he will make use of it, to distinguish substantial gold from superficial glitterings, truth from appearances."[68] If we have whole categories of reasoning individuals who yet have no sense of higher truths themselves and who rely on faith and the guidance of their betters, what is the political salience of reason? Is there any value, any democratic potential inherent in Locke's insistence that each of us has reason?

To answer such questions, we must look more closely at the ways in which Locke has constructed reason itself.

According to Locke, reason is "the faculty of deducing unknown truths from principles or propositions that are already known."[69] This is a simple enough assertion and yet, having the capacity to reason is not the same as reasoning itself. In the *Conduct,* Locke writes of reason that

> We are born with faculties and powers capable almost of anything...but it is only the exercise of those powers which gives us ability and skill in anything and leads us towards perfection.... As it is in the body, so it is in the mind: practice makes it what it is.[70]

From this passage we learn that reason is more akin to a muscle than a sensory organ. It does not passively accept stimuli but needs exercising in order to develop (here Locke is making the same argument that Hooker did). Locke warns us against thinking that "[I]t be reasonable to suppose and talk of faculties as distinct beings that can act."[71] To become a reasoning individual requires practice and discipline. Reason is a behavior that can be learned and improved upon—and it is also one that we can lose the habit of.

Thus Locke held that "[the obtaining of reason in those who don't have the background or training for it] will not be done without industry and application...and therefore, very seldom done."[72] And further:

> The Americans are not all born with worse understandings than the Europeans, though we see none of them have such reaches in the arts and sciences. And among the children of a poor countryman, *the lucky chance of education,* and getting into the world, gives one infinitely the superiority in parts over the rest, who continuing at home had continued also just of the same size with his brethren.[73] (emphasis added)

To obtain reason one must have the "the lucky chance of education" or simply belong to the right class (since "knowledge and science in general is the business only of those who are at ease and leisure").[74] There is a big discrepancy between the potential for reason and its full realization, with significant political consequences.

There are scholars of Locke who argue that he simply dismisses the subservient members of society. Uday Singh Mehta, for example, makes the claim that the social underlings are deemed "irrational" and therefore not really members of society at all.[75] Peter Schouls, in a similar vein, points to language whereby

Locke calls those who have quit reason "wild beast, or noxious brute with whom Mankind can have neither Society nor Security."[76] He writes that

> Locke holds a human being to be *essentially* different from nature. Hence Locke characterizes those who fail to achieve any degree of mastery [i.e., rationality] as non human: they have destroyed their own humanity by refusing to develop the rational potential which naturally characterizes the newborn child.[77]

While Schouls's category of the "irrational" is smaller than Mehta's, I believe that in either case, this point is overstated. For Locke the potential to be rational is always present, it is the birthright of every human being, and even if quit it can be regained—although more in theory than in practice.[78] As we have seen, there is a kind of continuum of reason from the most reasonable to the least. No one is "unreasonable" in an absolute sense, but that does not mean that reason does not presuppose and indeed require social hierarchy in order to function. We still need to understand why this is so.

Appetite and indifference

The failure to reason, then, is not from a congenital lack of some capacity but rather from the presence of some obstacle to the ability to reason more than one already does. For Locke that obstacle is the privileging of (or excessive exposure to) the immediate over the mediate.[79] He holds that the exercise of reason is impossible when the subject is too caught up in the present and consumed with desire and the need for immediate satisfaction. For Locke, reason (and hence human freedom) is only possible if desire can be controlled:

> [The mind has] a power to suspend the execution and satisfaction of any of its desires and so all, one after the other is at liberty to consider the objects of them, examine them on all sides and weigh them with others. In this lies the liberty man has. We tend to engage too soon before due examination. To prevent this, we have a power to suspend the prosecution of this or that desire. This seems to be at the source of all liberty; in this seems to consist that which is (as I think improperly called) free will.[80]

Locke calls this power to suspend the "execution and satisfaction" of desire "indifferency."[81] Not indifferency as in "I don't care," but rather meaning that one is able to temporarily suspend one's desires and to make a decision based on rational weighing of the relative good and evil of each potential choice:

> Indifferency. First, he must not be in love with any opinion, or wish it to be true till he knows it to be so; and then he will not need to wish it . . . nor [will he have] a desire that it should have the place and force of truth, and yet nothing is more frequent than this.[82]

If one is so thoroughly invested in a particular outcome, one cannot make an objective choice. In order to be able to suspend desire, one must have a certain reserve to draw on. Poverty, illness, and other afflictions make choices much more limited. In order to be able to afford indifference, then, one's basic needs must largely be met. As Locke puts it, "the first step in our endeavors after happiness being to get wholly out of the confines of misery, and to feel no part of it, the will can be at leisure for nothing else."[83]

Locke did not, however, believe that appetite should be entirely suppressed or destroyed; indeed, he felt that we did so at our peril. In *Some Thoughts concerning Education,* he wrote, "the [importance in terms of appetites]...lies not in the having or not having appetites, *but in the power to govern and deny ourselves in them.*" (emphasis added)[84] For Locke, appetite is a vital aspect of human mastery because without it no action would be taken at all. He writes: "It seems plain to me that the principle of all virtue and excellency lies in a power of denying ourselves the satisfaction of our own desires where reason does not authorize them."[85]

Locke's appreciation for appetite thus goes beyond seeing it as a necessary evil. Calling desire the "spring of action," he argues that there are some desires which are directly involved in achieving mastery (what Peter Schouls calls Locke's "master passions").[86] These passions stem from a desire for mastery itself.

Locke is consistently ambivalent in terms of how reason should engage with desire. Should reason fail to engage with desire, especially in its "master" forms, it becomes impotent, without direction:

> [T]ill [a man] hungers or thirsts after righteousness, till he *feels an uneasiness* in the want of it, his *will* will not be determined to any action in pursuit of this confessed greater good.[87]

But at the same time, this engagement with desire can be perilous:

> On the other side, let a drunkard see that his health decays, his estate wastes; discredit and diseases and the want of all things, even of his beloved drink...yet...the habitual thirst after his cups at the usual time, drives him to the tavern.... It is not want of viewing the greater good: for he sees and acknowledges it, and in the intervals of his drinking house.[88]

Desire can therefore overwhelm reason as much as it supports it. This is true not only for desires themselves, but also in terms of their physical manifestations. The poorer classes are not the only ones subject to being overwhelmed by desire. In the quote cited above, we can see that wealth, the very thing which "liberates" the upper classes, can itself constitute a threat in that it is too a manifestation and source of desire. The drunkard, who had estates, who has access to reason ("he sees and acknowledges it"), has yet succumbed to the desire whose conquest led him to higher good in the first place. In so doing, he has fallen from having the command of full reason into a state that Locke calls "depravity."

In his own lifetime, Locke saw to his dismay that the threat of depravity was very real. In the *Conduct,* he paints this portrait of a depraved individual:

> A country gentleman who, leaving Latin and learning in the university removes thence to his mansion house, and associates with neighbors of the same strain, who relish nothing but hunting and a bottle: with those alone he spends his time, with those alone he converses and can away with no company whose discourse grows beyond what claret and dissoluteness inspire.[89]

This is clearly a characterization of the Tory gentry, a critique of what he saw as the unjustified accumulation of wealth that brings no moral or social benefit. This is precisely what John Dunn refers to when he quotes Locke as arguing:

> But this at least is worth the consideration of those who call themselves gentlemen, that, however they may think, credit, respect, power and authority the concomitant of their birth and fortune, yet they will find these things still carried away from them by men of lower condition who surpass them in knowledge.[90]

For Locke, there are lures particular to the very rich. He speaks of "fantastical uneasiness (as itch after honour, power or riches etc.)."[91] These "itches" can themselves create "a constant succession of uneasinesses," which drown out the cries for mastery.[92] The rich are never out of the woods, never free from the threat posed by the very passions whose mastery has led them to their own reasonableness.

By looking at reason as an engagement with desire, as a reconciliation with its own state of lacking, we can begin to see how for Locke, Hooker's (and Aristotle's) doctrine of love has become embodied in a new, secular form. As a secular version of *eros,* a lacking in its own right, reason is not without its passions. Reason must remain engaged with love, with need and desire, in order to fulfill its function. Because, like *eros* itself, reason is a mixture of poverty and plenty when it comes to truth, we see it as a balancing act. Like *eros* itself, reason is an adjudication between the body and the truth, between earthly desires and eternal love. Locke has rearticulated the Christian Aristotelian vision as an interior mental faculty which is then to be reproduced as a blueprint for the organization of society itself.

How to build a reasonable subject

In considering how a person comes to reason, Locke writes:

> [T]here are some Men's constitutions of body and mind so vigourous and well framed by nature, that they need not much assistance from others; but by the

strength of their natural genius, they are, from their cradles carried towards what is excellent; and by the privilege of their happy constitutions are able to do wonders. But examples of this kind are few.[93]

Some of us may be fully reasonable by virtue of sheer character alone. For the rest of us (the vast majority; for political purposes we might as well say all of us), reason must be produced and constructed one person at a time.

For Locke, these questions of teaching a subject how to negotiate a relationship with desire, with necessity, and with other persons is the province of education. By "education" Locke means much more than a narrow focus on schooling, but rather the teaching of reason itself.[94] Because reason is so central, education becomes a matter of making us "who we are":

> I think I may say that, of all the men we meet with, nine parts of ten are what they are, good or evil, useful or not, by their education.[95]

For Locke, education was a matter of national urgency, shoring up the future lords of England against the dangers of depravity and collapse:

> the welfare and prosperity of the nation so much depends on [education] that I would have every one lay it seriously to heart; and...set his helping hand to promote every where the training of youth.[96]

Locke sees two extremes to be especially avoided in education, commensurate with the kind of balancing with desire that constitutes reason itself. On the one hand, Locke worries that the young (rich) boy will be led to depravity by the surfeit of unmediated sensual pleasures that are available to him:

> He that has not a mastery over his inclinations, he that knows not how to resist the importunity of present pleasure or pain, for the sake of what reason tells him is fit to be done, wants the true principle of virtue and industry, and is in danger of never being good for anything.[97]

Locke considers this sort of lack of control "contrary to unguided nature" and therefore entirely a product of a venal education.[98]

On the other hand, Locke fears that in repressing desires too much, one would strangle all that is autonomous in the child and create a docile, overdependent failure. After all, it might be recalled that Locke held that "without desire there can be no industry" and that:

> If the mind be curbed, and humbled too much in children, if their spirits be abased and broken much by too strict a hand over them, they lose all their vigour and industry and are in a worse state than the former.... [D]ejected minds, timorous and tame, and low spirits, are hardly ever to be raised, and very seldom attain to anything.[99]

Locke calls these two extremes "the Scylla and Charybdis which on the one hand, or the other ruin all that miscarry."[100] The proper balance between these two extremes, he felt, was the key to creating an autonomous, upright, and reasonable subject:

> He that has found a way, how to keep up a child's spirit, easy, active and free; and yet, at the same time, to restrain him from many things he has a mind to, and to draw him to things that are uneasy to him; he, I say, that knows how to reconcile these seeming contradictions, has, in my opinion, the true secret of education.[101]

How can reason be produced out of this difficult balancing act between plenty and poverty? Locke begins *Some Thoughts Concerning Education* logically enough by focusing on the body and its desires as the initial site from which to build up a reasonable subject. He believed that education must begin at birth, so that the body can be trained to be a proper vehicle for the reasonable mind; it must be developed so that it can withstand temptation and necessity. He calls for "due care being had to keep the body in strength and vigour, so that it may be able to obey and execute the orders of the mind."[102] Too much softness and comfort leads to spoiling the child with the attendant risk of depravity. The children of the upper classes must be protected from, even as they are enabled by, their wealth.[103]

Unlike the poorer members of society, however, who are truly living lives of squalor, Locke balances his calls for hardness in educating young weathy boys with a concern that all the essential needs of a child be met:

> I say not this, as if children were not to be indulged in anything, or that I expected they should in hanging sleeves have the reason and conduct of counsellors. I consider them as children, who must be tenderly used, who must play and have playthings.[104]

We can see, in Locke's training of the body, a forerunner for his training of the mind itself. The mind, like the body, must be trained to do without, for "as the strength of the body lies chiefly in being able to endure hardships, so also does that of the mind."[105] Yet the mind too must not be starved of that which it needs to spur it forward.

In order to reach a state of indifference, the mind must learn from the body how to suspend desire. Having a more immediate relationship with its own needs, the body "teaches" the mind how to engage with and yet resist temptation. The body "embodies" the needs and desires that are to be struggled with, serving as a site of harnessing and conquest.

As I will argue, this relationship serves as a template for the entire social apparatus that constitutes reason. Education is not simply a matter of instilling reason in one child; for Locke, left to our own devices, few of us would develop our full potential to reason. We need help, and a good deal of it; an entire social apparatus must be constituted to reproduce externally the internal dynamic and teachings of the mind/body relationship. The endeavor to produce reason creates what might be called an *erotic* community, or perhaps a community of reason. The relationship between body and mind is reproduced in society through the relationship between those who gain full reason and those who support them, giving up their own chance to reason in the process. These supporters, these other bodies, embody and mediate the more reasonable subject's desire for him but also, like his own body, teach him the rudiments of how to grapple with desire for himself, to keep him engaged with desire (as he must be) without being overwhelmed by it. This entire apparatus is required and justified by the doctrine of love. Without the resolution of *agape*, other, more prosaic arrangements must be made.

To better understand this sytem, we must look at the mechanics of this community of reason. What does it mean to live in a society organized by love? What happens when the *caritas* synthesis unravels? Let us examine three relationships that are critical to Locke's system, to show how this theoretical model works in particular cases, beginning with class.

3. The Community of Reason

A. Class

In order to understand how class and property relationships might be constituted by love, we must return once again to Locke's understanding of how human beings are related to God. As we have seen, for Locke all of the material relations of property and class stem from the fact of God's ownership of us. Yet, in addition to being God's property, Locke sees that we all also have a "property in our own person." In the *Second Treatise,* he writes this often-quoted passage:

> [E]very Man has a Property in his own Person. This no Body has any Right to but himself. . . . Whatsoever then he removes out of the State that Nature hath provided, and left it in, he hath mixed his Labour with and joined to it something that is his own and thereby makes it his property.[106]

Here, once again, we see evidence of Locke's version of *caritas*—our self-ownership must coexist with God's ownership of us. Of course, there should be no real conflict in this overlapping concept of ownership. The true "me" is an agent for God, taming and controlling ourselves and the world in his name. This is why we are not free to do as we please (it gives us no "license," to use Locke's term) but are only free to follow the dictates of natural law. We are "really" ourselves only when we submit our own desires and loves to the love of God.

But as we have seen, Locke recognizes that to proclaim this dual ownership over ourselves is no guarantee that we will indeed behave in accordance with God's interest in us. Locke's ongoing concern with the depravity of the rich and his concerns with the unruliness and disorder of the lower classes all stem from a fear that given too much self-control, we will violate the true purpose of our property.

Accordingly, Locke conceives of property and property relations as a way to reaffirm the "bands of indissoluble love," which hold us to God, as well as to ourselves, and to one another. In subsequent passages in "Of Property," he suggests that those persons who do not make good use of their internal property (those who demonstrate faulty or lesser reasoning) should not be rewarded with external property either. He writes that "[God] gave [the world] to the use of the Industrious and Rational, (and *Labour* was to be *his* Title to it) not the Fancy or Covetousness of the Quarrelsom and Contentious."[107]

By extending the analogy of dual ownership a bit further, Locke even seems to suggest that reasonable people can not only extend their properly controlled boundaries into the material world, but possibly even into the "property" in another ("quarrelsom") person as well. He writes:

> Thus the Grass my Horse has bit, *the Turfs my servant has cut,* the Ore I have digg'd in any place where I have a right to them in common with others become my Property, without the assignation or consent of any body. *The Labour that was mine,* removing them out of that common state they were in hath fixed my Property in them.[108] (emphasis added)

In the same way that God's "ownership" of us overlaps with our self-ownership, it is also possible that to some degree the master can "own" the servant, at least in a limited sense, which does not preclude the servant also "owning" himself. Even though by Locke's own arguments the servant's labor ought to give him the right of ownership, his labor is located within the rubric of the master's subjectivity ("the Labour that was mine").[109] The servant is reduced in some sense to a supporter of the master's person (and of course his reason). Here we see, in a new iteration, Hooker's idea that we can be "one soul" but many persons (or also Aristotle's notion of friends being "two friends, one soul"); the servant retains his own reason, his own property in his own person, but under the rubric of serving a higher purpose it becomes possible to overlap and interweave these subjectivities, even without fully collapsing them.

Thus the question of the relationship between master and servant goes well beyond one marked by one-sided toil. The simultaneous owning and not owning of selves inherent in this relationship, which reflects the way God owns and doesn't own us, offers both access and safety, allowing the master to safely engage with his desires—they are mediated through the servant's body. But there is a price to be paid for this mediation as well. The servant, in mediating the master's desire for him, has access, as Hegel tells us, to the desires themselves in a way that the master doesn't. This helps protect the master but it also isolates him from the source of his reason.[110] In many ways, the master's relationship to his own desires is always screened via the bodies, lives, and examples of his servants and others in his retinue. The servant has something to offer the master but also poses a serious and ongoing threat to his autonomy.

The lessons of labor

What do the workers have to teach the masters in Locke's system? I've been speaking of servants so far because this is the first and earliest class relationship that Locke addresses, but at this point it is worth taking Ashcraft and others seriously and looking at Locke's relationship to the working class in general, which is a far larger portion of the population. Although necessarily less intimate, and not part of the landed household, a gamut of workers, mainly manual, illiterate, and uneducated, nonetheless play a role for Locke in fostering reason that similarly goes far beyond the material plenty that they accumulate for their social betters.

All members of the working classes, in their very engagement with labor, present a model that the master himself can emulate, albeit in a very limited way. In his *Commonplace Book,* Locke argues that manual labor is the proper project not only of the working poor but also, in a different way, for the rich:

> [The overly idle rich man] becomes a useless member of the commonwealth in that mature age which should make him most serviceable, whilst the sober and working artisan and the frugal laborious country man performs his part well, and cheerfully goes on in his business to a vigorous old age.[111]

He argues initially that ideally everyone would spend six hours a day at mental labor and six at physical. He reconsiders this, however, since too much toil is clearly more of a danger than an asset for the would-be (fully) rational subject:

> If this distribution of the twelve hours seem not fair *nor sufficiently to keep up the distinction that ought to be in the ranks of men,* let us change it a little. Let the gentleman and scholar employ nine of the twelve on his mind . . . and the other three in some honest labor, and the man of manual labor nine in work and three in knowledge.[112] (emphasis added)

For Locke, the chief virtue of such a system would be that

> The populace, well instructed in their duty, and removed from the implicit faith their ignorance submits them in to others, would not be so easy to be blown into tumults and popular commotions by the breath and artifice of

designing or discontented grandees. To conclude, this is certain, that if the labour of the world were rightly directed and distributed there would be more knowledge, peace, health and plenty in it than now there is. And mankind be much more happy than now it is.[113]

In Locke's view, then, all members of society have something to gain from the self-discipline implicit in labor. We see here an attempt by Locke to prevent the masters from being completely cut off from desire and need, as well as its disciplining functions altogether. To allow the workers to completely mediate their access risks a turn to depravity.

As we have seen, Ashcraft cites Locke's call for the rich to engage in manual labor when he claims that Locke's attitude toward manual labor is "overwhelmingly positive."[114] He portrays this as a sign that Locke believed in an essential social harmony between the "contributing" classes, both rich and poor, as if the richer could bond with their workers over this shared experience. And indeed, there is something to this claim.[115] But for Locke the rich are not meant to labor in order to share the experience of the workers simply for the sake of communion across class lines, but rather in order to contribute to the overall project of keeping themselves and their desires in check. In so doing they are in fact keeping the all-important hierarchy working, so that their dabbling in work only reinforces rather than reduces social difference.

Through the surpluses they generate, through their example and their own self-discipline via labor, the workers and servants, in all of their variety, do have a crucial and ongoing role in ensuring that the discipline they receive is reproduced in society as a whole. They are central to the maintenance of the social apparatus, to the upkeep of reason, but as with Aristotle, they benefit mainly in vicarious ways. Labor is their contribution to reason, the best use that they can make of whatever reasonableness they possess. While it might be true, as Ashcraft implies, that Locke admires and respects these workers, such admiration must be understood in the context of the social hierarchies that such a vision of labor presupposes.

The dangerous worker

If Locke demonstrates anxiety about the collision between God and our own self-ownership, the question of overlapping ownership constituted by class is even more fraught with peril. In this case, he is dealing with not one but two fallible creatures, with the chances of disruption and depravity exponentially increased. Locke recognizes that the persons involved in class relationships may not equally appreciate their union, especially when the benefits do not accrue equally (and when natural justification for this arrangement becomes increasingly intangible). He insists on a language of contract and rent to ensure that the servant or worker is voluntarily engaged in this operation, hence preserving a sense of separateness even amid this highly intimate relationship.

Even while evincing a strong appreciation for why the workers are necessary and integral to the achievement of self-mastery for the rich (and thereby for everyone in the community), Locke also sees them as a terrible, permanent source of danger. Fearing that the workers of his day were becoming increasingly ill-disciplined, Locke at one point wrote a letter to a parliamentary commission on unemployment and poverty. Here he suggests the creation of "work schools" in which labor is both "taught" and actually performed by poor children as well as by able-bodied working-class adults who otherwise refuse to work. In pondering on the source of social ills in the England of his day, Locke prefaces this argument by writing:

> If the causes of this evil [i.e., the growing number of unemployed poor] be looked into, we humbly conceive it will be found to have proceeded neither from scarcity of provisions, nor from want of employment for the poor, since the goodness of God has blessed these times with plenty.... The growth of the poor must therefore have some other cause; and it can be nothing else but the relaxation of discipline, and corruption of manners: virtue and industry being as constant companions on the one side as vice and idleness are on the other.[116]

In this and other writings, Locke urges Parliament to force the poor to work for the sake of every member of society (and, as a way to create discipline, advises punishments ranging from whippings to having one's ears cut off to being sent to penal colonies). He sees the breakdown of the work ethic as a "spreading evil," threatening not only the discipline of the workers themselves but the elite that they support:

> The laborer's share [of the national income] being seldom more than a bare subsistence, never allows that body of men, time, or opportunity to raise their thoughts above that, or struggle with the richer for theirs (as one common interest) unless when some common and great distress, uniting them in one universal ferment, makes them forget respect and emboldens them to carve to their wants with armed force and then sometimes they break in upon the rich, and sweep all like a deluge.[117]

But even if the servants and workers *are* relatively self-disciplined, Locke is concerned that their presence and example, as crucial as it is for the ongoing maintenance of reason, would still somehow undermine or damage the ability of their masters to reason, presenting a real dilemma. This issue seems particularly troubling for Locke in considering the relationship between a master and his servants, who, after all, live among the master's family. Despite his claim that the servant's membership in the master's household "gives the master but a temporary power over him and no greater than what is contained in the contract between them,"[118] we see nonetheless that for Locke there is a high price to be paid for living in such proximity with servants, particularly when it comes to matters of education.

For Locke, servants pose a constant threat to young minds, because, having less reason, they are especially sensual, unmediated people and therefore serve as a visible temptation and a bad example.

The servant, seeing the harsh methods that Locke advocates be used in child rearing, and not understanding the long-term purposes of such activity, is prone to sabotage the educational process by spoiling and otherwise tempting the young boy away from his course of study. For example, in warning against the influence of strong drink, Locke writes:

> In this case it is, that servants are most narrowly to be watched and most severely to be reprehended when they transgress. Those mean sort of people placing a great part of their happiness in strong drink, are always forward to make court to my young master, by offering him that which they love best themselves; and finding themselves made merry by it, they foolishly think it will do the child no harm. ... There [is] nothing that lays a surer foundation of mischief, both to body and mind, than children's being used to small drink: especially to drink in private with servants.[119]

Note that Locke's language does not paint the servant as being malicious, but as simply unable to comprehend the potential that the young master is being groomed toward achieving. Locke urges that, if possible, children are to be prevented from talking to servants at all, especially "the meaner sort," because "the contagion of these ill precedents ... horribly infects children,"[120] and furthermore:

> [boys] frequently learn, from unbred or debauched servants, such language, untowardly tricks and vices, as otherwise they possibly would be ignorant of all their lives.[121]

Like the epistemological crisis that spawned it, Locke's notion of class evinces a great degree of instability. His system depends entirely upon relationships that simultaneously threaten it; a disruption in the division of labor would be a disruption of reason itself, a catastrophic undoing of our duty to God and to ourselves. It might seem peculiar then that Locke's "remedy" for this danger is to give the workers more rather than less autonomy; unlike Aristotle, for example, Locke will never call another human being a "tool." In part this is a testament to Locke's real devotion to the proposition that each of us is blessed with the "touchstone" of reason; even with the dangers posed by lower-class resentment, Locke holds steadfast to this view. But the idea that each of us has our own personhood, our own potential to reason, also allows Locke to avoid reifying a potentially hostile relationship as being irreparably joined. Although basing his thought on a model of "two friends, one soul," Locke yet insists on sufficient distance to protect the master from angry servants and hostile workers (and presumably to protect the workers from cruel and depraved masters as well). In the face of indeterminacy present in the unraveling of *caritas*, Locke's "bands of indissoluble love" must be quite a bit looser than Hooker's. Only, as we have seen, this loosening is not as democratic as it at first appears.

B. Gender

Let me now shift attention to another important relationship in Locke's system that is just as integral to and just as dangerous for the maintenance of reason: that between men and women. Although he concedes that Queens Mary and Elizabeth were themselves reasoning persons, and although he inherently includes women in his idea that all human beings are endowed with the ability to reason, Locke yet holds that women have "different [i.e., worse] understandings" than men.[122] For him, gender is just as important a tool as class in maintaining reason and the community which sustains it. Women, in terms of their relationship to men as mothers and as wives, although certainly threatening to male autonomy, still play an essential part in maintaining their husbands on the path toward mastery, a part very similar to that played by the working classes.[123]

Love often manifests itself in highly abstract ways for Locke, but in the case of gender we can see its operations quite clearly, perhaps most explicitly in his understanding of the first lovers, Adam and Eve. Literally Adam's rib, Eve epitomizes how you can have two bodies with one soul, how one person can own and yet not own another.[124]

As with so much else, this first relationship is constituted by a mixture of democratic tendencies and hierarchical requirements typical of Locke's unraveled *caritas* synthesis. On the one hand, he suggests that Eve is held below Adam only because of her role in the fall:

> though as a helper in the Temptation as well as a Partner in the Transgression, Eve was laid below [Adam], and so he had *accidentally* a superiority over her, for her greater punishment.[125] (emphasis added)

Locke's use of the term "accidentally" implies that things could have been otherwise, that Eve's potential, while real, was simply not realized.[126] On the other hand, Locke also seems to see Eve's subjugation to Adam as "natural" and preordained, as when he writes against Filmer that God's grant

> gives not, that I see, any Authority to Adam over Eve, or to men over their wives but only foretells what should be the woman's lot. How by his providence

he would order it so that she should be subject to her husband, as we see that generally the Laws of Mankind and custom of Nations has ordered it so; and there is, I grant, a Foundation in Nature for it.[127]

The curse that falls upon Eve as a result of her transgression, the basis of Adam's dominion over her combines these "accidental" and "natural" features.

We see this duality throughout Locke's treatment of women. In "Of Paternal Power," he famously argues that "the mother too has her share with the father," in terms of having power over their children.[128] This might suggest that Locke is willing to entrust mothers, just as he does fathers, with the creation of reasonable, and autonomous offspring. Yet he makes this argument to refute Filmer's claim that fatherhood is akin to kingship. When not enlisting motherhood to make such claims, Locke's views shift quite dramatically.

For Locke, there are two very different roles in parenting, those that regard nurturing and those that regard education and inheritance, the two building blocks of instilling reason. When it comes to the latter, Locke is quite explicit that he is interested in the role of fathers alone. He writes, "the first part then of Paternal Power, or rather Duty, which is education belong so to the father."[129]

As for inheritance, Locke writes:

> There is another power *ordinarily in the father*, whereby he has a tie on the obedience of his children.... And this is the power to bestow their estates on those, who please them best.[130] (emphasis added)

When we look closer at what Locke is offering mothers by replacing paternal power with parental power, we see a role that is supportive of rather than constitutive of rationality in their (male) offspring. In those passages in which Locke specifically discusses "parental power," his language is one of duty and obligation rather than power per se, such as when he states:

> The power then, that parents have over their children arises from that duty which is incumbent on them—to take care of their offspring during the imperfect state of childhood.[131]

In making his arguments against Filmer, Locke wants to downplay the political importance of family (or, more accurately, the explicit linkage between fatherhood and kingship). In claiming that parental power should replace paternal power, he is not exalting the status of mothers but rather denigrating the status of fathers *qua* kings by clearly associating fatherhood with motherhood (by pointing to its "merely" biological aspects).

Accordingly, Locke points out that a father's role in parenting is a product of what he calls "the bare act of begetting."[132] If anything, the father is at a disadvantage with the mother, who has "an equal share; if not the greater as nourishing the child a long time in her body out of her own substance."[133]

A father's power, then, does not stem only or even mostly from begetting (even though to some extent Locke sees Adam as having a power over Eve since he "begot" her); in fact, Locke offers that a foster father has as much power over a child as a natural father and should be considered no differently.[134] It is not literal fatherhood (in its biological sense) which creates the special relationship between a father and a son. For Locke, fatherhood is more than biology and less than kingship. Shorn of its these extremes, we see that fatherhood for Locke should be concerned above all with maintaining and transmitting reason across generational lines, something mothers have little or nothing to do with.

What can mothers then do? What is their role in building reason? Although Locke doesn't say much on this point, one might infer from his theory of education that, because the father's role in education is largely one of guidance and must therefore be relatively stern, it is in part up to the mother to embody and represent to the son the desires and needs that are necessary to urge him on toward self-mastery. As we've seen, Locke tells us that "I say not this, as if children were not to be indulged in anything."[135]

While both parents must help a son achieve a balance between arid autonomy and sensuous dependence, as the less rational and more passionate parent, the mother is a logical choice for ensuring that her son has any passions at all. Locke actually bemoans the emotional distance between a son and his father, but grants that this is somewhat inevitable given the father's stern and necessary task.

At the same time, a keen worry of Locke which he *does* explicitly write about is that mothers will overly coddle their sons, rendering them effeminate and depraved. As with servants, we see that for Locke mothers too don't fully "understand" the difficulties and dangers of raising a rational son. The mothers "may think this [i.e., the techniques of education and punishment] a little too hard." And so Locke offers "a general and certain observation for the women to consider:... that most children's constitutions are either spoiled or at least harmed by cockering and tenderness."[136] Locke fears that a (male) child's natural inclination to grow strong and hardy is eclipsed by what he sees as the preening, social orientation of contemporary mothers:

> [Women] should be afraid to put nature out of her way...and yet I have seen so many instances receiving great harm from strait-lacing that I cannot but conclude there are other creatures, as well as monkeys, who little wiser than they, destroy their young by senseless fondness and too much embracing.[137]

In general then, Locke sees that mothers, although obviously necessary, interfere with his plans to educate the young. After putting out his manifesto for creating hardened bodies for children, he writes:

> How fond mothers are like to receive this doctrine, is not hard to foresee. What can it be less than to murder their tender babes, to use them thus? What? Put

their feet in cold water in frost and snow when all one can do is little enough to keep them warm![138]

Locke worries that mothers will respond to their babies' cries, which he depicts as "cries for mastery," and to overindulge this will lead to "that effeminacy of spirit which is to be prevented or cured."[139] Indulgence, sensuality, spoiling, weakness, and the like are all the forerunners of depravity. Perhaps one reason that Locke doesn't completely dismiss the education of (wealthy) girls out of hand is that they need to know enough to be able to see the wisdom in deferring to their future husbands' authority when it comes to questions of child rearing.

Perhaps even more important (and dangerous) for Locke's system than mothers is the role of wives. For Locke, mothers at least have the check of fathers to ensure that the pampering of sons will not go overboard. It is quite another thing when a young man is out on his own, without his father's oversight. Here, Locke cites the Bible, urging the young man to "leave mother and father and cleave to the wife."[140] And yet this advice does not come without concerns of its own.

Even more than the mother, Locke sees the wife as having a grave responsibility to handle her husband's passions in a responsible way. Concerned about the dangers of lust and sexuality as a major source of depravity, Locke writes:

> adultery, incest and sodomy [are] sins which I suppose have their principal aggravation [in that] they cross the main intention of nature, which willeth the increase of mankind and the continuation of the species in the highest perfection and the distinction of families, with *the security of the marriage-bed* as necessary thereunto.[141] (emphasis added).

For Locke, wives, necessity-bound and sensual as he finds them to be, still make the best guardians against the husband's sexual depravity. The marriage bed, a place where sensuality is mediated by the bonds of respectability and the task of procreation, offers, like the worker's labor, a chance for a safely mediated relationship with desire. As with the earlier discussion of class and discipline, we see here a parallel structure in Locke's understanding of gender and sexuality: Internally within the subject, desire must be maintained and yet controlled in order to compel the subject toward mastery without veering off toward depravity. Externally, the wife allows this same relationship to occur: She serves as a source for and even the embodiment of desire, yet, through her own chastity and subjugation, she ensures that the husband keeps his own sexual desires in check. And her subjugation is in turn made possible by his patriarchal command of her.[142]

By disciplining and dominating her, even as she controls and disciplines herself, the young (and even not-so-young) husband receives further training and support in the complex handling of desire. The wife plays a central role in maintaining the husband's autonomy, simultaneously motivating him and keeping him in check, embodying desire as well as its overcoming. Her chaste body becomes another object to place between a subject and his desires, along with the worker's laboring body and the subject's own carefully disciplined body.

The important role of chastity for Locke in holding a young man to the course of reason cannot be understated. In *Some Thoughts Concerning Education*, for example, he notes how as venerable an institution as the British navy can, without the mitigating presence of a wife's chastity, sink into depravity, in this case homosexuality. He writes:

> What has been talked of some late actions at sea of a kind unknown to our ancestors, gives me occasion to say, that debauchery sinks the courage of men, and when dissoluteness has eaten out the sense of true honour, bravery seldom stays long after it.[143]

The very kind of debauchery and effeminacy threatened by the ill discipline of wives and mothers is even more present in their absence. Clearly, the wife is a critical factor in regulating her husband's management of his various and sundry passions. In this regard, it might be argued that Locke sees that chastity is for wives what labor is for the working classes, another way to build up reason. A woman's ability to reason must, like a (male) worker's ability, be channeled into this all-important institution in order to fulfill her function in the social hierarchy. And as with the laborer, the wife has something to teach her husband as well. Not only must the wife be chaste, but with her help the husband as well.

In light of this, we can see why Eve is so problematical for Locke as a model of womanhood. Her "crime" is twofold in a sense—in acting autonomously as she does, she violates her special bond with Adam; here his own "rib" is betraying him. She epitomizes the dangers of the epistemological crisis that we have fallen into in the absence of God's ongoing direction. Eve fails at the duty that Locke seeks in all wives—chastity. Unable to contain her own sensuality and her own curiosity, not only does she condemn herself to punishment, but perhaps worse yet, from Locke's perspective, she drags down Adam's autonomy and his freedom in the process. Eve shows the dangers of reasonable subjects being betrayed by those who serve them—a warning to all women, but also to all men, that depravity is only one bite of an apple away.

C. Fatherhood

The final relationship to examine is that between a father and son, which, while sharing many features with class and gender, is also unique in Locke's philosophy. In many ways, for Locke the father is the only real ally a son will ever have in his life. As with other relationships, the interests, properties, and even personhoods of father and son overlap, but in this case Locke feels that the overlap is less threatening in that what the father owns today, the son will own tomorrow.

Because of the bond of inheritance, their subjectivities are merged in a way that mimics, but is very different from, the other relationships we have examined. In this case, the promotion of reason leads to no threat, and no resentment. Once shorn of its biological and kingly associations, fatherhood is at the centerpiece of Locke's vision of a community of reason. In this sense we have a paradox in that Locke's arguments against Filmer establish that it is impossible to have freedom within the bounds of patriarchy. Yet it seems as if it is just as impossible to have freedom *without* patriarchy either.

On some level, Locke considers the relationship between fathers and (matured) sons to be formally equal and non-intimate. He writes:

> The father's empire then ceases and he can from thence forwards no more dispose of the liberty of his son, than that of any other man.[144]

And yet there is a level of intimacy that is maintained in the relationship between fathers and sons even when the son has left the house. For Locke, of all the persons that the son will rely on and come into contact with in order to achieve his own self-mastery, the only real friends a man will ever have are his mother and father:

> I imagine everyone will judge it reasonable that their children, when little should look upon their parents as their lords... and that when they come to riper years, they should look on them *as their best, as their only sure friends; and as such, love and reverence them.*[145] (emphasis added)

While mothers are also "friends," as we've seen, the nature and degree of the son's trust in her must be limited by her relative lack of rationality. It is the father that the son can both love (as he can his mother) and fully trust (as he cannot with his mother).

To ensure this friendship, Locke recommends that a father gradually wean his son from a relationship marked by total dependency to one of greater equality. Ultimately for Locke it is far more important that a son love his father than that he fear him, especially as the child gets older:

> Fear and love ought to give you the first power over [your children's] minds and love and friendship in riper years to hold it; for the time must come when they will be past the rod and correction and then, if the love of you make them not obedient and dutiful...I ask what hold will you have to turn them to [virtue]?[146]

The fear (and its distancing quality) is not forgotten but incorporated into the gradual transformation of the boy into a man. In general, Locke counsels the father to treat the son as what he is: a peer in training. He tells the father to open his books to the son and not treat him as if he were "guarding a secret of state from a spy or an enemy." Such behavior lacks the "marks of kindness" which a father owes to his son.[147] In return, the son will develop "a perpetual obligation of honoring [his] parents."[148] What was once a duty, a function of biology, has given way to a relationship marked by respect and friendship, held through voluntary rather than obligatory linkages.[149]

For Locke, this "friendship" goes well beyond a pleasant familial relationship. Cultivating such a friendship is crucial for Locke because it allows the father to continue to manage and even mediate his son's desires (to help the son to help himself) during the young man's early years of independence. For Locke, the period of time after the son leaves the father's house is a particularly hazardous one. As we have already seen, the wife has to play a big role in keeping the newly independent son's desires in check. But she herself is hardly a bearer of full reason. The father (whether biological or not) must not forsake this responsibility. A father of a newly independent son would be foolish to let the untested son live in the world without his guidance, for:

> to put them [the sons] out of their parent's view... when they think themselves too much men to be governed by others, and yet have not prudence and experience enough to govern themselves: what is it but to expose them to all the greatest dangers of their whole life, when they have the least sense and guard against them.[150]

At the same time, an overly interfering father would clearly be problematic as well, since Locke argues that a father must respect his son's newly established boundaries:

> be sure you advise only as a friend of more experience; but with your advice mingle nothing of command or authority, nor more than you would to your equal or a stranger.[151]

The father must tread carefully, to make the son feel that he is fully autonomous and fully reasoning, when in fact he is not. The son is still not ready to make decisions on his own and needs his father's guidance. We see here, as we will see further in *Émile,* that it does not matter if the son is actually autonomous so long as he thinks that he is. Even if he can't actually rely on his own judgments yet, it would be lethal to his freedom if he knew that he still depended upon his father's judgments. Autonomy is as much a product of the community of reason as anything else.

Inheritance and reason

For Locke, the most important mechanism by which a father can guide his son even after he has left the house is the institution of inheritance. The instant a young man inherits his father's property, he is de facto subscribing to the social contract that created the society that he lives in.[152]

This consent, however, is just the beginning of how inheritance binds the son and enables him to come to reason. Locke also sees the promise of future property as a sort of check on the son's present-day behavior, arguing that "this is no small tye on the obedience of children."[153] This has both a negative and a positive sense. For Locke the father has a tremendous disciplinary power inherent in the threat to withhold property. If a son is not capable of full reason, he should not be trusted with a father's estates.[154] Yet ultimately Locke realizes that the power of a father to control his son via inheritance has some limitations, as when he writes:

> Indeed, fear of having a scanty portion, if they [the son] displease you may make them slaves to your estate, but they will be never the less ill and wicked in private.[155]

In the end, inheritance can only be effective in bringing a son to reason if he has already received a good education. A depraved son will hardly become rational simply because he stands to inherit (or not inherit) his father's estates.

More important still perhaps, through inheritance the son is offered a future promise of bounty to suspend his short-term tendency toward more immediate pleasures. Mediated by time (the lag between the son's achieving maturity and the death or retirement of his father), the property of the father becomes a safely distant lure to keep the young man on his upward path without itself constituting the grounds for temptation and depravity. The father's property is the son's property once removed. It is "safe" wealth and will only be his when he is reasonable enough to be able to resist its temptations himself. In this way the father, at least in the son's first years of autonomy, adds his own body (or his own property, which in many ways is the same thing) to those bodies which we have already seen, mediating and helping the son so as to bring him to his own reason.

4. Faith, Autonomy, and the Community of Reason

We can see the community of reason as a series of bodies standing between the would-be reasoning subject and his own needs and desires. Some of these relationships are explicitly hierarchical. Others, such as the father-son relationship, are of a different order. But what finally does it deliver? What is produced here? Locke's answer is that the community of reason produces autonomy, self-mastery, reason, and an equitable basis for political community. The community of reason is Locke's best answer to the question "Who Shall be Judge?" But does this system actually create freedom or equality, for any of its members? Is it or could it be a democratic polity?

Maybe the best way to begin to answer this question is by looking at those others (fathers excepted) who sacrifice their own chance at mastery for this man's sake. Since, as we have seen, the development of reason is not chiefly a matter of native ability but rather is the production of careful education, training, discipline, and the social division of labor itself, those more reasoning persons are not absolutely "better" than anyone else. Under different circumstances, these subordinates presumably could have been the ones whose potential to reason was developed, just so long as *someone* sacrifices himself to someone else.[156] As this is the case, do these subordinates receive anything besides vicarious freedom for their self-sacrifice?

One might argue that even if hierarchy is required in Locke's own lifetime, it might eventually become unnecessary. If we can't all be free today, maybe one day we can all be free together, as reason develops to a greater and greater extent and spreads itself, like the wealth it produces, downward. Yet as we have seen, hierarchy in Locke's system is not simply an unfortunate side effect. Nor is it some atavistic behavior to be overcome. Hierarchy is absolutely essential to the perpetuation of the system; it is not simply a matter of producing a surplus but also a question of the mediation of desire itself. This system cannot serve as a kind of tutelary democracy, where reason is spread from top to bottom. Because reason is not a thing one has or doesn't have, but constitutes a lifelong and perilous interaction with desire and need, it must constantly produce and be reproduced by the social division of labor within the community. As with *eros* itself, reason is a permanent state of lacking. As I will argue further, this is not to say that Locke's notion of equality is disingenuous or even categorically empty, but only that it must remain a largely abstract concept in Locke's system.

But what of the privileged person himself? What of the recipient of all of this labor, chastity, and fatherly guidance? Is he at least autonomous? How does he reconcile the problem of overlapping ownership with his own notion of self-ownership? We have seen how compromised Locke's notion of personhood is, especially given that Locke holds out the promise of autonomy. Besides owning himself, the privileged subject is also "owned" by God; he shares property with his father; he "owns" and yet does not own those who labor for him (including his wife). The various disciplines in the community of reason involve a great deal of control and manipulation, on the servants' part, on the mother's part, on the wife's part, and of course on the father's part. If we see the son as a field, it is these other bodies and not the son who is initially responsible for planting and harvesting. Who then owns the product of the land?[157]

Furthermore, what does it mean to say that the son has his "own" reason, and hence his autonomy? How does the son come to reason *on his own* when he in fact learns to reason by following the lead of his father and the standards of his community? This question reproduces a larger epistemological one: How do we as a society come to "judge" on our own when all of our wisdom is predicated on following the word of our "true father," God?

The question of autonomous thought would not be a real problem for Locke if reason simply meant "thinking on one's own." If we could just think whatever we wanted, then autonomy might indeed be "natural." But here we see how Locke's insistence on subjecting us all to higher law interferes with the production of autonomy which is so vital to him. The son cannot think any old thing, he must learn to *reason*—that is to say, he must discern natural law. And Locke tells us that "[t]he floating of other Mens Opinions in our brains makes us not a jot more knowing, though they happen to be true."[158]

Thus even if the father is "right" and models rightful thinking to his offspring, the son will learn nothing from simply absorbing his father's truths. For Locke, reason becomes merely "opinion" when viewed from an external perspective; if I discern the correct decision, then I am using my own reason, but once I vocalize this to others it cannot be other than opinion as far as they are concerned. To maintain self-mastery Locke's subjects must think things out on their own, via their own reason. Causing the child to follow his father's reason suggests the danger that he will fall into the permanent and undesirable habit of obeying the whims of others, even as "safe" an other as the father.[159] And worse yet, the path to reason is forged by an enormous number of helpmates, not all of whom, like the father himself, have the boy's best interest at heart.

Throughout his work, Locke equivocates on the issue of where autonomy comes from. Sometimes our autonomy is "natural" and already given, as when Locke writes:

> *Plain and rough nature, left to itself* is much better than an artificial ungracefulness, and such studies ways of being ill fashioned.[160] (emphasis added)

Other times autonomy is learned, as we have seen when he tells us that ninetenths of "what we are" is a product of education. Sometimes Locke even equivocates in the same sentence, as when he writes:

> Every man must some time or other *be trusted to himself* and his own conduct; and he that is a good, a virtuous and able man *must be made so within*. And therefore, what he is to receive from education, what is to sway and influence his life, must be something put into him betimes; *habits woven in to the very principles of his nature.*[161] (emphasis added)

Although he must be "trusted to himself," this "self" is produced through "habits woven into the very principle of his nature." The son must develop the habit of following the "reasonable" lead of his father or other elders, the habit of following opinion. Here habit serves as a stand-in or substitute for authenticity, a *second* nature for the subject that stands for or becomes his original, "authentic" nature itself. The son must be filled with externally received truths.

Given these questions, given the epistemological crisis which produces them, is it possible to "own" oneself at all? Can we have control of the property in our own persons? Is there an authentic self at the heart of Locke's system? Here we come to a central difficulty. In the unraveling of *caritas,* we find that reason without revelation, like *eros* without *agape,* is left seeking to discover what is no longer present; the epistemological crisis is endlessly reproduced in Locke's philosophy and with it comes a question of substance and selfhood. Do the human faculties of judgment have any validity on their own in such a vision? Can we value ourselves as ourselves? Can we find a democratic possibility in Locke after all?

Reason on its own promises a great deal: autonomy, equality, democracy, the valuation of human beings *qua* human beings. But reason does not, as we see, deliver these things, because it remains, like *eros,* constituted as a lack. Reason cannot revel in its own autonomy because the doctrine of love does not recognize the value of that autonomy. That autonomy is always constituted in terms of something else, something higher and better and absent. We remain in "an endless maze," waiting to be delivered.

In the *caritas* synthesis, without *agape, eros* is nothing at all, just human hubris, signifying nothing. Similarly, without revelation as an ongoing and central component of human judgment and society, reason turns us to our own devices, which are by definition inadequate. We are no longer "filled" with God, yet we are still hollowed out, in expectation of that filling. We remain suspended between the desire for our own substance and the "truth" that is above us, and in so doing fall between epistemological stools.[162]

The Self and the Savior

Locke's own best and only answer to the question of where the son gets his autonomy from can be found in the *First Treatise,* where he argues that fathers should not take too much credit for how they make their sons. That credit, he claims, belongs more properly to God. Talking rather forcefully against a father who might take too much pride in his own son, Locke writes:

> If any one thinks himself an Artist at this, let him number up the parts of his Childs Body which he hath made, tell me their Uses and Operations, and when the living and rational Soul began to inhabit this curious structure, when Sense began, and how this Engine which he has framed Thinks and Reasons.[163]

Locke suggests that the reason of the son is a gift from God and not anything that the father has made. While this seems to go against so much of his theory of education (it is nine-tenths of "what he is"), it makes perfect sense that Locke would advance such a view. By positing the reason of a son as being God-given and explicitly leaving the father out of the picture, he seems to have carved out a space for autonomous, self-owning sons after all; the son's "ownness" stems (as in the case of all of us) from the fact of God's ownership of all of us, permitting us to be both one soul and many persons. Here *agape* returns as a kind of refilling of the empty chalice that is our selves. God's ownership of us, rather than complicating things, resolves them, brings them all into line. Out of the complex interwoven fabric of a mutually dependent society, God's ownership rescues each of us and gives us to ourselves, even as we give ourselves to him.

In seeking to reconcile divine and human identities, Locke has a special role to play for Jesus, who, having both natures, reconciles the *caritas* synthesis in a way no one else can. Locke adds to the mix of bodies that help mediate a subject's desire a further and ultimate body, that of Jesus Christ himself:

> To these I must add one advantage more by Jesus Christ and that is the promise of assistance. *If we do what we can,* he will give us his spirit to help us to do what, and how we should.... If a wise man knows how to prevail on his child, to bring him to what he desires, can we suspect, that the Sprit and wisdom of God should fail in it...?... If any one needs go beyond himself...To a man under the difficulties of his nature, beset with temptation, and hedged in with custom; 'tis no small encouragement to set himself seriously on the courses of virtue, and practice of true religion, *that is he from a sure hand, and an almighty arm, promised assistance to support and carry him through.*[164] (emphasis added)

The final labor, the final "work of the hands" and "labor of the body," is Jesus's. He is the final guide for us. All troubling questions of ownership and autonomy are finally resolved. Even if revelation is no longer an active part of political life, the example and living presence of Jesus serve to link our struggles with desire to a higher purpose. With Jesus as the ultimate body mediating desires for the son, lending him a "sure hand" and "an almighty arm," the possibility of truth, of Godliness, of authenticity are present after all. Within the context of Jesus's love, earthly questions of relationship and duty all seem to fall into place.

As with Hooker, it is the belief in higher truths that sustains the politics of Locke's system. Ultimately, Locke's liberalism is based on this faith. He believes fundamentally that there *is* an authentic core to us, a center from which we can approach the truth, even if we don't actually see it or find it. Only that center is not really "ours" at all but rather stems from God's presence in us.

It is therefore on this most religious level that Locke's system works best. The ongoing presence of Jesus, the fact of God's presence in us, serves to reconcile *eros* and *agape,* reason and revelation, despite the latter's absence. It is Locke's religious convictions, his basis in Hooker, that makes his system work at all.

But what is the political salience of such a system, particularly as it becomes increasingly secularized? Although on the most abstract level Locke's faith in

God's presence gives us substance and gives us to ourselves, this does not in and of itself resolve the epistemological crisis when it comes to matters of politics. If reason were perfect (i.e., if it were revelation) then the conflict between what is "God-given" about us and our ability to "find it out for ourselves" would be resolved—our reason would simply reconnect us to our original truth. But reason is not perfect; even the teachings of Jesus must be interpreted, and might be interpreted wrongly without religiously inspired teachers telling us what they mean.

Locke might have chosen to reproduce Hooker's ecclesiastical polity as a way to reconcile his problems, but he chooses not to. In part this might be because he does not believe that any claimant to such authority will be genuine in an age without revelation; he is a far more secular thinker, as we have seen. But perhaps even more importantly, for all his hierarchicalism, Locke is also more democratic than Hooker. Although he structures his system to receive a higher truth, he necessarily locates such a reception in a much more populist, wider venue than Hooker does. He struggles mightily to make reason valid on its own terms. The part of Locke that I find most attractive is the part of him that appears to accept the loss of revelation as an opportunity for the freedom of the human community to find its way on its own. Indeed, even with his discussion of Jesus, Locke says that the subject must "do what he can" himself. Although nostalgic for the patriarchy of the Hebrew judges, Locke evinces a whiff of rebelliousness against all fathers—something we can easily see in his own role in the Glorious Revolution.

But as we have also seen, the acceptance of the end of revelation does not lessen Locke's faith, nor does his rebelliousness lessen his reliance on patriarchy. We are able to "do what we can," not on our own terms, but only in relation to God or Jesus or our father. Locke cannot, as Hobbes did, find an authentic position for the subject, because Locke's authenticity can only be revealed from above, by a (now) silent deity.[165] Our filledness, our unity in God, does not translate into a democratic polity here on earth.

As a principal architect of the modern self, Locke betrays not despair but only some anxiety about the future, about the "spreading contagion" of depravity and the boundaries of the self that he has created. His faith is all that is best and worst about his system. Locke's faith in God and God's earthly corollary, love, becomes the faith of all liberalism. Even when racked with doubt and even when increasingly secular, this faith stands as the underpinning of the entire system and cannot and perhaps should not be removed. Without love and faith, we would have a naked power system after all—just dominating bodies, piling up resources for no real purpose. Without love and faith, we would have what C. B. MacPherson attributes (wrongly) to Hobbes and to Locke himself—relativism and purposeless power. Within the confines of liberalism as it is received from Locke, such an ugly vision seems to be the only alternative to love itself.

Thus every liberal after Locke, who remains inscribed within his logic and his epistemology, labors to love love. They will try to love the other even as they fear her (and hope that the other will love them in turn). To love one another is a way to love God and to love and discover ourselves. Despite the apparent differences among us, despite clear lines of "better" and "worse," despite resentment, danger, and threat, the liberal thinker knows that we must love each other or else we will face the end of community, the death of spirit, and the collapse of the liberal order. Bolstered by his faith and his love, Locke's subject works for him, it does what he asks of it. It is for his heirs to live with and to suffer from the shifting, unbounded, and non-autonomous selves that he has described and handed down.

3

JEAN-JACQUES ROUSSEAU:
THE TRANSPARENCY OF
PATRIARCHY

1. ROUSSEAU AND THE MODERN SELF

When Tracy Strong writes that Rousseau is "in ways that others around and before him were not, *modern*,"[1] he means that Rousseau is a herald of the self that we have become; he is a self that is independent even as it is multiple and therefore connected with others. Strong reads Rousseau's *Confessions* as a confession of the complexity of the self, the denial of one privileged perspective from which the author can speak "down" to the masses.

Strong spends some time distinguishing Rousseau's notion of personhood and nature from Locke's. He writes that for Locke "nature" is a term that is constantly in flux:

> For Locke humans have no naturally existing definition, no natural characteristics, but they have natural activities and thus make nature part of themselves.[2]

For Strong, Locke's idea of nature serves as a way to delineate and mark off human substance; nature is that which is outside of us, that with which we interact. Our relationship with nature is complicated, as we have already seen, by questions of boundaries and ownership, inherently complicating our own sense of self. For Rousseau, on the other hand, the idea of nature must be something that we give to ourselves:

> [A]ny exploration [of how we might rethink what we are, what we might become] must come from the abstraction of oneself to one's self, because that self is of the world we are seeking to re-form.[3]

The Rousseauvian subject is meant to be "denatured" in order to return to some original possibility:

> Thus Rousseau explicitly denies that he is looking for "the man in the child." He seeks instead to think of that "which he was before becoming a man," that is, that which is not human. It is important to realize here that this accomplishment has its dark parallel in the procession of human history traced in the

71

Second Discourse. There, in a circle, humans are returned to a second state of nature, a state in which they are nothing, but in which their nothingness is now completely exterior. The problem for Rousseau, one might say, was to retain the original nothingness as an interior quality of the human itself.[4]

We have already seen that Locke has a problem with substance and authenticity; he insists on self-ownership but does not provide the epistemological grounds for such a self to exist. Rousseau, according to this argument, gives us back to ourselves by accepting our lack of absolute self-ownership and locating us instead in a sense of self which is a product of our own devising.

Strong argues that in this way, Rousseau offers a different perspective on what democracy might look like. Unlike Rawlsian (read Lockean) liberalism, where we must bracket ourselves from one another, place "veils of ignorance" and boundaries to set one of us off from the rest, Rousseau offers us a transparent notion of self that is more akin, in Strong's opinion, to the views of Tocqueville, Whitman, and, more recently, George Kateb. In this "less liberal" vision,

> What if the self were not "thin" in Rawls' world but transparent, nothing? Such a self would . . . not be defined by that which it was not. Such a self would not be Hegelian, that is, its nature would not be premised on recognition by an other. As in Rousseau, such a self could then not ever hold an other in domination, not be subject to an other. The other is me.[5]

For Strong, in this vision, "I see, as I see myself, every other person as myself. This is not identity but equality and possibility."[6]

Strong writes that Rousseau's notion of democratic transparency is particularly useful because it is so historically rooted in a given community. For Rousseau, unlike Locke, we submit ourselves not to universal wills but to general ones:

> [Rousseau] shares with Tocqueville (and Kateb and Whitman) the notion that seeing oneself, the egalitarian (or democratic) individual sees all persons. (This is what it means to see oneself democratically.) But he does not think that this being is without substance, as it were transparent [in the same sense that Kateb does, for example]. It will necessarily have substance (that is, it will exist historically); and it will gain this substance from the interaction that it will perforce have with others.[7]

Strong suggests that by locating the subject in a particular history and community, we receive our substance from one another. Thus we are both transparent and filled at the same time.

Thus, it would seem that unlike Locke, Rousseau avoids the dilemmas of the doctrine of love because he does not see us as being "hollowed out" and waiting to be filled by an external source of judgment and truth. With Rousseau, we are our own sources, our own judges. The very ways in which Locke's self does not work provides the grounds for the general will to fill in the vacuum of self and script us into being.

But has Rousseau really succeeded in overcoming the doctrine of love? It is certainly true that Rousseau responds to the problems inherent in Locke's notion of self. Throughout his life and work, Rousseau exposes the contradictions of such a self, offering a subversive glimpse at its dysfunction. In his struggle with the liberal subject, Rousseau offers us one of the first modern extrapolations of the "perhaps," the democratic possibility within liberal subjectivity itself.

And yet there is a way in which Rousseau reproduces as much as he critiques this self and this idea of nature. Although he distinguishes himself from Locke in many important ways, Rousseau remains deeply rooted in Locke's epistemological foundations. Although he deeply secularizes Locke's already substantially secular-ized notion of nature, truth, and reason, I will argue that Rousseau nonetheless retains the essential structure of the doctrine of love, albeit in a wholly modern and secular guise. Although Rousseau localizes the truth in the general will, it remains, as far as the individuals who receive it are concerned, prior and more nat-ural, more original than they are themselves; their "original nothingness" becomes less a gap for them to fill but a zone that has already been structured. However secular, however local, the general will remains a kind of *agape*. Although he calls for our nothingness and our making of ourselves, Rousseau is at least as concerned as Locke is with questions of *real* substance, truth and hierarchy.

In saying this, I align myself with Jean Starobinski and also Derrida in their interpretations of Rousseau, particularly in terms of their doubts as to Rousseau's notion of transparency, a concept which Strong is more sanguine about.[8] They claim that Rousseau's desire for transparency is impossible and contains the seeds of its own destruction. In my own case, I argue this by locating Rousseau's work back in the doctrine of love itself. I see the notion of "transparency" as another version of the kind of self-hollowing that *agape* requires. I see "obstruction" as those factors which mitigate against this hollowing, the self-regarding that, for better or worse, comes along with a notion of *eros*.

Thus, while the fracturing of the self does indeed suggest the possibility of a democratic polity for Rousseau, it also presupposes its own limitations. In the end, Rousseau remains suspended between the "nature" that we give to ourselves, and the "nature" that is really true. He is suspended between the desire of the self to merge and lose himself in the general will, to "be the other," and the desire for the self to be and own only himself. He is suspended between his need for unconditional love and his sense of his own particularity. As much as he answers Locke's epistemological crisis, he reproduces it in a new guise, one that is not simply a philosophical suspension but in Rousseau's case offers a profound psychic crisis over the boundaries and substance of his own identity. It is in this darker sense that I agree with Strong's contention that Rousseau is modern, a self that is as much disabled as enabled by the constructs which produce it.

Rousseau's intellectual legacy in Locke

For all of his struggles against the politics that come out of Locke's philosophy, Rousseau's roots in Lockeanism are well established. In general, early-eighteenth-century French thought was deeply influenced by Locke. During Locke's exile in Holland, he came into contact with a great many French Protestant thinkers such as Pierre Bayle and Jean Le Clerc who were refugees from the repeal of the Edict of Nantes.[9] Through them, Locke become known to other French and particularly French Protestant thinkers. The most important figure in making Locke's works widely known in France was the legal theorist Jean Barbeyrac. Barbeyrac corresponded several times with Locke and wrote extensively about Locke's work, especially the *Essay concerning Human Understanding,* making it widely known and appreciated in French intellectual circles so that the text became a central influence on French empirical thought.[10]

Coming to the intellectual milieu of Paris, Rousseau, like many of his contemporaries, read and was deeply influenced by Locke. He was also influenced by Locke through his French counterparts, including empiricists such as Condillac and Buffon, as well through Locke's more diffuse influence on the *philosophe* movement in general.[11] Rousseau's complicated relationship to his own Calvinist background and subsequent conversion to Catholicism may help to explain his predisposition to both accept and react against Lockean thought.

Essentially the French readers of Locke sought to build on Locke's basis of the self as an empirical and historical phenomenon. These thinkers were attracted to what they saw as Locke's role in liberating the self from its prison in abstract metaphysics, via his grounding of the subject in the world of experience. In Locke's version of the doctrine of tabula rasa, they saw redemption from original sin and the grounds for a new conviction in the ethical goodness of humankind. In being so drawn, they sought to save Locke from his own tendency to reintroduce all-but-innate principles into his empiricism, principally, as we have already seen, in his treatment of the abstract mental faculties in general and in his treatment of reason in particular.

In the concept of "reflection" whereby the mind is aware of itself as a pure (and higher) entity, Locke was seen as insufficiently subscribing to his own empiricist philosophy.[12] French empiricism sought to reconcile Locke's notion of reason with a stricter empirical foundation, arguing that reason's special claims to know and discern truth must be limited to serving within the confines of available sensory data alone.

Despite his public and extensive feuds and breaks with the *philosophes,* there is a way in which Rousseau is not so much the anti-*philosophe* he claimed to be but rather the best, more ardent "rescuer" of Locke in the group. This is not to say that Rousseau either explicitly or even unconsciously sought to make Locke work in his own terms; on the contrary, Rousseau is often a virulent critic of Locke both implicitly and explicitly, as can be seen in the *Discourse on the Origins of Inequality.* But Rousseau, of all the French rethinkers of Locke, comes closest to making plausible a liberatory, secular, and progressive philosophy out of a Lockean epistemological foundation, in part by clarifying those complicated and ambivalent ideas about nature, the senses, and truth which he receives from Locke himself. It is Rousseau who takes most seriously the notion that what we see before us in society is not "natural," as many of the *philosophes* somewhat contradictorily believed, but rather a product of social engineering. Furthermore, Rousseau shows that our reason as well as our passions are themselves products of history and so are not "natural" and/or given either.[13] Here we see the basis for Rousseau's notion of what Strong calls "denaturing" the self in order to return it to a sort of second nature which is wholly one's own.

Yet, even if he is the greatest and best *philosophe,* Rousseau ultimately does not solve the basic epistemological problems that he inherits from Locke and the French empiricists. As Derrida tells us, for example:

> If he denies himself the theological facilities of Condillac when he looks for the natural origin of society, speech and writing, Rousseau makes the substitutive concepts of nature or origin play an analogous role. . . . The differences between Rousseau and Condillac will always be contained within the same closure.[14]

In other words, for all of his secularizing, his moving toward local and self-produced ideas of truth, Rousseau remains bound by his intellectual heritage, leading back to Locke himself. Rousseau's "improvement" on the earlier French empiricists reintroduces the same epistemological abstractions that they sought to do away with. In "denaturing" nature, Rousseau lets his own "substitutive" concept of nature stand in for the original, not replacing but rather reproducing it. The desire for nature itself remains, preserved by the attempt to mimic it.[15] Locke's natural law is not denied but simply stood in for.

And, in so doing, Rousseau is substituting for what, as we have already seen with Locke, is itself a substitution, and an inadequate one at that. For both Locke and Rousseau, the idea of nature constitutes a relationship between a lost origin which is "true" and an inferior copy. For Locke the origin is the age of revelation and the substitution is "common" reason. For Rousseau the origin is the original state of nature and the substitution is the general will. In both cases we are left with an inadequate means for retrieving and preserving the lost original. In *Of Grammatology,* Derrida writes of Rousseau that:

[Nature] suffices and is self-sufficient; but that also means that it is irreplaceable. . . . Nature's supplement does not proceed from Nature, it is not only inferior to but other than Nature.[16]

Given the inferiority of the substitute, one can see how Rousseau preserves the epistemological crisis of Lockean empiricism, even without his theological trappings. The original nature cannot be reproduced, and yet we are compelled to attempt to reproduce it nonetheless; rather than abandon nature, we must give ourselves another one.

Derrida tells us that "what one would substitute for [nature] would not equal it, would be only a mediocre makeshift."[17] Just as for Locke, reason, when left to its own devices, leads us into a "wild wood . . . an endless maze," so too for Rousseau do our own attempts to reproduce the lost, original nature lead us nowhere at all.

Or rather they lead, not nowhere, but, as with Locke, to the production of an entire political and philosophical system hopelessly in search of some lost authenticity; they lead, in other words, to the reproduction of the doctrine of love itself. Derrida calls the attempt to impose a substitute for the lost origin of nature a "scandal" because despite its impossible nature, "the sign . . . become[s] force . . . and make[s] 'the world move.' "[18] And he writes:

[The scandal] is also the moment when maternal nature, ceasing to be loved, as she ought to be for herself and in an immediate proximity . . . becomes the substitute for another love and for another attachment.[19]

Here we come full circle: The lost origin, the idea of nature itself becomes employed by the system which pretends to realize it, as just another sign presupposing itself. Thus "nature" becomes not only the basis for, but also the sign of truth, the epistemological dog chasing its own tail.

Gender, hierarchy, and autonomy

The fact that the tension between nature and self is expressed by Rousseau in specifically gendered terms (as the "maternal nature") is telling insofar as it reveals the degree to which the doctrine of love both explains and typifies Rousseau's political philosophy. As we have already seen in *The Discovery of the New World*, Rousseau's understanding of gender, and more particularly of women, offers clues to his deeper, underlying vision. For Rousseau, women represent a sweet sort of bond, the promise of moral and social freedom, and yet at the same time they also pose a real threat to the autonomy or even the existence of the (male) self. As we will see further, women for Rousseau can be either vast and universal, stand-in's for the original and lost maternal nature herself, or they can be particular and merely bodies, an empty sign, pointing to the original's ongoing absence. As a category women encompass and also inhabit, preserve, and subvert Rousseau's own ontological foundations.

In his understanding of gender we come closest to realizing both the promise and threat of a Rousseauvian politics. Strong's claim that Rousseau seeks transparency and denaturalization, while accurate, must be understood in light of his gendered idea of nature. If Rousseau seeks to become "nothing" on the one hand, he simultaneously fears nothingness, because it suggests his own absorption and destruction at the hands of an alien "other" who is always female. The vision that Strong promotes whereby selves can create a world together by voiding themselves of their own falsely produced "natures" and identities, must contend with the fact that these identities are produced and maintained by an extraordinary tension. "I" cannot become "the other" when she constitutes a threat to my very being.

As such, we must proceed cautiously in considering Rousseau's democratic potential. In a very important sense, neither of the options Rousseau initially presents us with—rapturous merger with the other (as "citizens"), or radical isolation (as "men")—are particularly democratic principles; both contain and preserve the struggle with otherness, the struggle to be a self. In a sense, these do not represent two "options" at all, but delineate the terrain of the doctrine of love. The society that is produced between these "opposites" is one marked by the same threat, hierarchy, and need that we have already seen with Locke. The "scandal" is that Rousseau tends, as we will see further, to produce a notion of self out of this contested terrain which preserves the privilege and autonomy of the isolated self even as it is absorbed into the social. The resultant "transparent" society disguises and presupposes that power, preserving these gendered identities in the guise of overcoming them. This is the realization of Derrida's circle; the maternal other—nature herself—becomes not an origin to return to, but rather the grounds upon which Rousseau imposes his sign.

Patriarchy, the scandalous imposition of substance where it is clearly absent, is Rousseau's attempt to resolve Locke's epistemological crisis. Although inadequate and "makeshift," the promise of patriarchy is that Rousseau can have it all, autonomy as well as union, the self-regarding of *eros* as well as a merger with the maternal *agape*. But in this union, the self will not be lost or abolished. It remains to structure and occupy the maternal as its own terrain. Rousseau holds out the wild hope that by so dominating and imitating nature, the patriarch can finally, safely have her once again. The makeshift substitute becomes true nature herself, only now she is mediated and tamed. This is the dream that animates Rousseau, but as we will see, it leads not to fulfillment, but to despair. As much as he is the architect of the substitute, Rousseau is also its fiercest critic, exposing the masquerade he perpetuates.

2. The History of Love and Freedom

In order to better establish these arguments, we must turn to a closer reading of Rousseau's understanding of human history. For Rousseau, history is the search for love and for freedom, two concepts which are symbiotic, even as they exist in dynamic tension. In *The Social Contract*, Rousseau presents us with a terrible paradox in the quest for freedom:

> Among the Greeks, all that which the people had to do, they did themselves: they were ceaselessly assembled in the market place. They lived in a mild climate...slaves did all of their work; their one great interest was their liberty. Not having these same advantages, how can one have these same rights? [You moderns] your climates are harsher, making you needier: six months of the year, the public places are uninhabitable...you care more for gain than for liberty and you fear slavery far less than misery.
>
> What? Is liberty to be maintained only through the use of slavery? Perhaps. The two extremes meet. Everything in nature has its inconveniences, and civil society more than the rest.[20]

The contentious relationship between slavery and freedom points to the fact that for Rousseau, as for Locke, freedom is produced through a properly balanced relationship with desire and need. Rousseau too sees unmediated desire as a danger to freedom "because the impulse of mere appetite is slavery."[21] And he too requires other people to mediate our desires for us, hence the requirement for others to stand in for the enslavement of the self. Yet, unlike Locke, Rousseau directly acknowledges (as Hegel will in turn) that the master is not freed by his slave's mediation, because he then becomes dependent, cut off from the source of his power. For Rousseau, the Greek masters are no more free than their slaves, as he tells us at the very beginning of *The Social Contract*, since "those who think themselves the master of others, are yet greater slaves than they."[22]

Thus we can't be free without other people and we can't be free with them either. For Rousseau, history becomes the process whereby humanity seeks a way out of this dilemma. In so much of his writing, Rousseau bemoans the loss of our original freedom, that unmediated connection to desire, to the maternal nature which is so threatening and yet so compelling. In *Émile*, he writes:

> Oh man! live your own life and you will no longer be wretched. Keep to your appointed place in the order of nature and nothing can tear you from it.... Your freedom and your power extend as far and no further than your natural strength; anything more is but slavery, deceit and treachery.[23]

And yet even in terms of his supposed yearning for the original, lost nature, Rousseau reveals a typical ambiguity.[24] He extols the freedom and the wholeness of such a period, and yet he refuses to countenance a return to such a state:

Must societies be abolished?... [M]ust we return to the forest to live among bears?... You...who think man destined only to live this little life and die in peace...your corrupt hearts and endless desires, resume...your ancient and primitive innocence. Retire to the woods.... For men like me, whose passions have destroyed their original simplicity, who can no longer subsist on plants or acorns, or live without laws and magistrates...they will respect the sacred bonds of their respective communities, they will love their fellow creatures.[25]

Rousseau attributes his inability to return to the state of nature to his "passions." It is love for his fellow creatures, however little they may deserve it, that has made him sociable.

Rousseau imagines that part of what was so blissful about the early state of nature was that it had no love, at least not in the romantic sense of the word:

Among [the appetites of mankind] was one which caused [*l'invita*] him to propagate his species; and this blind propensity, without any sentiment of the heart, only produced a purely animal act. The need satisfied, the two sexes knew each other no more; and even the child meant nothing to the mother, as soon as he could go off on his own.[26]

And yet, despite the appearance of isolation, unlike Hobbes, Rousseau doesn't really grant even these first people a life without any sense of family at all:

Those who seemed to resemble him [i.e., other human beings] were not yet to him what they are for us, and he had no greater commerce with them than with other animals. Yet they were not ignored by his observations either. The similarities which he came to discover between himself and them, *his* female [*sa femelle*] and himself led him to...see that they conducted themselves just as he would have under similar circumstances. (emphasis added)[27]

Here, Rousseau speaks of a man and *his* female although according to his own narrative the creation of the family was still to come. The presence of this female, and the relationship that is implied, however obliquely, already casts doubt on the original (male) subject's solitude.[28]

Another example of this reluctance to imagine true isolation comes when Rousseau discusses the all-important question of maternal love. Ironically, it is unclear whether Rousseau thought that the bond between mother and child was natural at all.[29] He writes that "As soon as they could forage for themselves, the children did not hesitate to leave the mother behind."[30] Rousseau felt that initially mothers took care of their children for their own benefit:

The mother nursed her child at first for her own need; then habit having made them dear to her, she nourished them afterward for theirs.[31]

This does not really explain how it could benefit a mother personally to take care of her child. If anything, it seems like the presence of children would hamper a mother's efforts to survive.

Even if we grant the argument that there are selfish reasons for a natural mother to nurture her children, Rousseau ends up postulating maternal love in the state of nature despite his own claims to the contrary. After a while, merely through the act of nurturing her child, the mother develops sentimental ties for her children.

In other words, even during the most savage, most "natural" period of life, we find loving relationships. Even at the dawn of humankind for Rousseau, there were selves and there were others (i.e. women), already portending the changes that were to come. In seeking to imagine a world without love, Rousseau has contaminated the past with the present, the origin with the sign, but in doing so, he reveals a confusion, or perhaps even a subversion of signification. Here, the sign, the isolated Patriarch becomes prior to his own maternal love, even as he is "already" contaminated by her.

The Golden Age

For Rousseau, the real watershed to demarcate the purely natural from a more socially oriented transitional state occurred when people began to live together in artificial houses. The huts that were created allowed men and women continual exposure to one another, and inevitably this led to a higher birth rate. "Natural" women were more or less able to handle one baby on their own, but now, saddled with several babies, they were unable to take on all of the new responsibilities without help. The fathers of those children began to go forth and find food for their offspring, and hence the first families were born. This in turn created the first social (and sexual) division of labor.

For Rousseau, family life led to feelings of "conjugal and paternal love."[32] Familial love, like maternal love before it, is a product of habit: "The habit of living together gave rise to the sweetest sentiments that are known by men."[33]

Initially, these first families were autonomous societies, completely self-sufficient and therefore in some sense replicating the "radical" freedom of the natural man. The first families lived in a "Golden Age" and were untroubled by strife and selfishness. In this period, love remains unthreatening because it is general, communal, and, crucially, incestuous:

> There were marriages but there was no love at all. Each family was self-sufficient and perpetuated itself exclusively by inbreeding.... Instinct held the place of passion.... *They became husband and wife without ceasing to be sister and brother.*[34] (emphasis added)

The family of the Golden Age represented an extension of the individual's self-love (*amour de soi*) to a collectivity. Familial love, which bound parents and children, husbands and wives, and brothers and sisters (as we have seen, often overlapping categories), allowed collective interests to be concurrent with one's own self-interest because all "others" were beloved by and intimately connected to the "individual."[35] Here, we can truly say "the other is me."

The Golden Age "works" for Rousseau because the boundaries of the self are flexible enough to incorporate not just one person but an entire harmoniously ordered family. When self and collective interest are not in conflict, the expanded self as family can still offer the individual freedom without compromising their particular desire. But here already, we see that in this harmonious order there are already nodes of power, centers of privilege which once again tend to revolve around the role that Rousseau might imagine for himself. As a harmonious unity, Golden Age families were for Rousseau, as for Locke, absolute patriarchies.[36] True, the patriarch did not "own" everything in the modern sense of the word and he is not a tyrant despite his absolute power. The power of the father did not constitute inequality for Rousseau because ties of love made the rule of the father benign, "his only commandment being not to succumb to depravity."[37] As Judith Shklar writes:

> Rousseau is not a proponent of equality but rather against inequality. Inequality for him is not an absolute but a relative concept. If the father is loving, his power is justified, the family is formally not unequal.[38]

Shklar considers that even the presence of servants in the Golden Age family household does not constitute inequality because "A wise, patriarchal employer can do much to diminish injustice and impersonal cruelty," although, she concedes, "he cannot erase it." She concludes, "The family is the one and only society that is not subject to the evils of inequality. That is why it is the essence of the golden age."[39]

I do not agree with her judgment that patriarchy is just a (minor) unfortunate side effect of the Golden Age, which is otherwise essentially just. Rather, I see patriarchy as being essential, the very bedrock of Rousseau's vision of the Golden Age. To put it bluntly, there has to be something in this for Rousseau himself in order to risk his own autonomy in such a merging of selves. Rousseau is not looking for total immersion into the public to the point of losing himself entirely. Rather, he is attempting to maintain a privileged center in which he (or some stand-in for him) can remain intact, while all others become "one" with and transparent to him. He can even become transparent himself at this point; once the hierarchy is presupposed, the privileged self can "afford" to become one with everyone else because his uniqueness as patriarch is preserved in its very merging with the "other." Patriarchy offers Rousseau a way to become transparent without disappearing, to organize the "nature" of this community in such a way as to preserve his own particular interest in "the general will."

But how golden is this age? For Rousseau, even this most harmonious of periods is already fraught with peril. Deep social fissures are already present but disguised by the incestuous generality (a precursor to the "general will" itself) of the Golden Age. As usual, for Rousseau, the element that destroys the social harmony is love, particularly in its sexual and romantic guise. In this Golden Age, the practice of incest is critical because the love that a brother felt for his sister was not particular to her. She just happened to be available. Just as the subject must accept himself as the person who happens to inhabit his own body, the brother accepts the sister because they share a common sense of self. The brother can love his sister safely, then, without danger of rejection. He can exist as if he were alone and complete unto himself, while still benefiting from the delights of love and society. As we have seen, although the trappings of love are present, Rousseau does not consider this relationship to be marked by love at all.

But for all this familial "sameness," difference is preserved and even magnified in this incestuous age. Clearly the status of the patriarchal brother is above that of his sister. The entire question of sexual access is fairly one-sided. For Rousseau, it is not that the sister can sleep with her brother, it is that he gets to sleep with her. Her access is assumed and the perspective of power is male (and again, Rousseau's). But when mankind becomes more abundant, when other families and other huts appear down the road, the Golden Age sister/wife finally gets her revenge. The fiction of the Golden Age that "everyone" loves everyone else and everyone lives in harmony is revealed to be a sham. Beneath its surface, the Golden Age contains hierarchy and tension that fissure the family as soon as these allegiances are put to the test (as is inevitable).

For Rousseau, the sudden abundance of suitors made it possible, even inevitable for human beings to begin to pick their lovers not on the basis of convenience but based on their particular qualities.[40] Suddenly, given a choice, the Golden Age sister began to see other, perhaps better options. Worse yet, for Rousseau, the patriarchal brother is no longer content with his sister even if she remains faithful to him; he too becomes enraptured with some particular other woman, thereby becoming dependent on a stranger who owes him nothing, losing his autonomy and his power in the process. The results are catastrophic:

> Men began to accustom themselves to making distinctions among things; imperceptibly, they came to acquire ideas of merit and beauty which produced in them feelings of preference.... A tender and sweet sentiment insinuated itself into their soul, and given the least opposition led to an impetuous fury: jealousy rose up along with love; discord triumphed and the sweetest passions received sacrifices of human blood.[41]

Whereas Golden Age "love" is carefree, the new particular love carried with it the risk of loss and failure. Natural inequalities which once were essentially meaningless take on a deadly importance in this new age. Now a man needed to appear desirable in the eyes of his beloved, and he had rivals for her affection, leading to an endless interpersonal comparison.[42]

With the downfall of the Golden Age, *amour propre* is born, the love of the self which is defined against and in tension with other selves. *Amour propre* replaces and renders impossible *amour de soi,* the love of the self *qua* self, the love of the self (or enlarged self) which regards only itself. *Amour propre* is the name that Rousseau gives to love in its darkest incarnations.

The return of amour de soi

If we complete Rousseau's history, extending forward into time, we come to his redemptive project; the resuscitation of *amour de soi.* Of course, as we have already seen, Rousseau cannot and does not want to "return" to a primitive age of isolation, which as it turns out was never all that isolated. How can we find a "self-regarding" love in the context of society? How can we partake in love without being overwhelmed by it? How can we substitute for what was lost?

Rousseau's solution to this dilemma, his "substitute" if you will, is to call for the "general will." He writes:

> [W]e must clearly distinguish natural liberty, which has as its limits only the power of the individual, from civil liberty, which is limited by the general will.[43]

The general will, the will of the entire community, stands for Rousseau as a barrier between one's self and one's own passions. Natural liberty is revealed to be slavery because one individual cannot mediate their desires for themselves; instead, they become captive to them. Rousseau's contemporary society does not mediate desire either but is consumed by it. A society that follows its general will, on the other hand, can avoid this pitfall by offering for the lost, original love a new supplement, a new love whereby "each gives himself to everyone, thus giving himself to no one."[44] The myriad wills of society become reduced to a "common me [*moi commun*].... This public person, which is thus formed by the union of all the others."[45]

It is instructive that Rousseau calls this a common "me," rather than a common "us" or "self." This is one more hint that Rousseau, even in the guise of promoting this kind of transparency, retains a desire to have a self, a particular "me" that persists even after it has been absorbed into the generality.

We can see inklings of this too when Rousseau speaks of moral freedom:

> Besides the preceding, we can add to the acquisition of the civil state moral liberty, which alone makes man truly master of himself... obedience to a law one prescribes to oneself is liberty.[46]

Here Rousseau speaks of this common me as he would speak of his own self. The self gives himself to "nobody," as if this one individual were the only person actually present. This person is "truly master of himself" and the law he follows is "self-prescribed." In this language, Rousseau takes the state and uses it as the vehicle for the realization of the interests of a particular citizen (his own, perhaps). The preservation of the language of self in this most social of contexts further suggests that the perspective of self will not be annihilated but preserved precisely through the social.

We see that Rousseau's strategy to revive *amour de soi* is also meant to revive the Golden Age in a new, modern guise. In the Golden Age, patriarchy was the foundation that allowed *amour de soi* to continue to exist despite the social setting. The original "*soi*" in question (but really more of a *moi*), the patriarch himself, is not in opposition to his loved ones. In a very Aristotelian (or Lockean) way love smoothes over the hierarchies that hold it together. The general will, as I will argue further, becomes a similar vehicle to achieve a kind of transparency, a "common me," that preserves and depoliticizes the hierarchies and identities that it is intended to eradicate. This new *amour de soi* seems to offer just what Rousseau has always been looking for—union and autonomy, love and freedom.

Scandalously, Rousseau seeks to replace the lost maternal with a new kind of nature, a "nothingness" which is aware of itself as such. This new *amour de soi,* a political and secular love, unlike its earlier incarnations, will never die. Unlike the original *amour de soi,* Rousseau seems to feel that this one is impervious to further social developments. Preserved as the basis for the general will, it can never abandon its recipient (even if he abandons it). It loves unconditionally; it is available to all of its subjects, regardless of their differences.

And yet, even as he constructs this "scandal," this sign that becomes its own ground for truth, Rousseau gives us ample evidence that it is an impossibility. Just as the Golden Age itself succumbed and fractured along the lines of identity that were smuggled within its golden harmony, so too does the "common me" contain and preserve difference, creating a social time bomb waiting to go off. When we examine Rousseau's various iterations of the return to *amour de soi,* of his attempts to reestablish the Golden Age, we see time and time again how this is the case.

In each case, it is Rousseau himself who reveals how his project must be a failure, how the transparent patriarchy cannot succeed. It is in his guise as a thinker who subverts his own utopias, rather than as a planner of the utopias themselves, that I believe Rousseau reveals his true democratic colors. In demonstrating the futility of attempting to resolve the doctrine of love from within its own grounds, Rousseau inherently points us elsewhere, toward other understandings of love and of freedom.

Let us follow him through some of these iterations, some specific attempts to restore the Golden Age and save us from *amour propre,* beginning with his attempt to save that all-important subject—himself.

3. ROUSSEAU'S SEARCH FOR LOVE AND FREEDOM

A. Himself

In terms of the possibility of freeing himself, of finding a love that did not threaten, Rousseau was at times especially optimistic. He believed that as an exceptional person, he could avoid a fate that had condemned most of his fellow men. In *The Confessions,* he writes: "I will even venture to say that I am like no one in the whole world."[47] In *Rousseau, Judge of Jean-Jacques,* Rousseau portrays himself as having the power to transcend society and the terrible threat that it poses to individual integrity. In that book, after describing an ideal citizen who is completely autonomous, in harmony with nature and yet fully aware of and benefiting from society, his imaginary interlocutor says, "My dear M. Rousseau, You certainly look to me like one of the inhabitants of that world." And Rousseau answers, "I recognize one at least... in the Author of *Émile* and *Héloïse*."[48] If his characters were not successful in escaping society (as we shall see), at least their author will be.

But for all his confidence, Rousseau often despaired for himself, realizing that he had never been able to achieve his own freedom. Early on in *The Confessions,* he bemoans the fact that he needed to be loved:

> Of all the gifts which my parents possessed, they left me only a sensitive heart. It had been the making of their happiness, but for me it has been the cause of all of the misfortunes in my life.[49]

From the beginning of his life, Rousseau's relationships with women dominated his life. His mother died shortly after giving birth to him, and he spent the rest of his life trying to (re)create this missing idyllic childhood relationship, to fill this lack of the maternal *agape.* He attempts to reproduce this last relationship throughout his life, often in explicitly self-punishing ways.[50] One of his earliest sexual memories, for example, was the punishments that he received at the hands of his surrogate mother, Mademoiselle Lambercier:

> Since Mlle. Lambercier treated us with a mother's love, she also had a mother's authority, which she exercised sometimes by inflicting on us such childish chastisements as we had earned.... [When] I was beaten... the very strange thing was that this punishment increased my affection for the inflicter.... I had dis-

85

covered in the shame and pain of the punishment an admixture of sensuality which had left me rather eager than otherwise for a repetition by the same hand.[51]

Rousseau goes on to write:

Who could have supposed that this childish punishment, received at the age of eight at the hands of a woman of thirty, would determine my tastes and desires, my passions, my very self for the rest of my life.... At the moment when my senses were aroused my desires took a false turn and confining themselves to this early experience, never set about seeking a different one.[52]

As Rousseau sees it, his life was dominated by these so-called childish fancies. Too shy to admit his unusual tastes to women, he "spent [his] days in silent longing in the presence of those [he] most loved."[53] Rather than having actual love, he therefore spent much of his life imagining it. Living through fantasies, Rousseau replicated in his own mind his relationship with women and thus brought the "other" with him wherever he might go. He could escape individual women (and frequently he did), but he could not escape his own mind.[54]

Rousseau's relationship with Madame de Warens was a case in point. Throughout most of their relationship, they remained chaste. He called her "Mamma" and she called him "Little One" even though they weren't all that different in age. As with Mlle. Lambercier, Rousseau could not separate maternal and sensual love:

To me, she was the most tender of mothers, who never thought of her own pleasure but always of my good. And if there was a sensual side of my attachment to her, that did not alter its character, but only made it more enchanting.[55]

As with all women, Rousseau's best relationship with Madame de Warens was in his own head: "I only felt the full strength of my attachment to her when she was out of my sight. When I could see her, I was merely happy."[56] When Madame de Warens was absent, "My inability to live without her caused me outbreaks of tenderness which often concluded with tears."[57]

Rousseau's attachment to Madame de Warens quite often borders on the obsessive: "How often have I kissed my bed because she had slept in it...even the floor on which I threw myself, calling to mind how she had walked there."[58]

After all this, when he finally does sleep with Madame de Warens, it is worse than anticlimactic:

How could I see the moment approaching with more pain than pleasure? How was it that instead of the delight which should have intoxicated me, I felt almost repugnance and fear?[59]

Madame de Warens sleeps with Rousseau, he writes, to protect him from other women. She knew that he was becoming dangerously obsessed with sexuality and needed to furnish him with an outlet. "Without desiring to possess her, I was glad that she robbed me of any desire to possess other women."[60] Faced with reality, rather than the fantasy of love, Rousseau is repulsed:

> By calling her Mamma and treating her with the familiarity of a son, I had grown to look on myself as such; and I think that is the real cause of my lack of eagerness to possess her. I remember very well then my first feelings for her, though no stronger, were more voluptuous.... She was to me more than a sister, more than a mother, more than a friend, more even than a mistress; and that is why is was not a mistress to me. In short I loved her too much to desire her; that is the clearest idea I have on the subject.[61]

Here we see, in his discussion of his relationship to Madame de Warens, a reproduction of the fall of the Golden Age. The harmonious incestuous promise of Golden Age love, which is not threatening to the self ("she was to me, more than a sister, more than a mother..."), becomes supplanted by particular, romantic, and dangerous love. When he says, "I loved her too much to desire her," I believe that he means that his particular love for her was too strong to allow for a safer, merely animal desire (such as is characteristic of the Golden Age). By consummating their relationship, Rousseau is forced to acknowledge that the real-life Madame de Warens is not simply a figment of his imagination. The carnal moment that he experiences with her throws her true, exterior "otherness" into full view. Even as (and because) he sees her as foreign, he is reminded that within the boundaries of his "self" a separate self exists, not of his own creation, but rather a reflection of the actual self that is before him, unknown and hence uncontrollable. Her presence exposes his need for her to mediate his desire, his inability to be whole without her and her power over him ("those who think themselves the masters of others are greater slaves than they"). He can never be free with or from such a woman.

Even while pursuing these fantastic loves, Rousseau also developed a taste for a radical personal autonomy. Judith Shklar describes the delight that he drew from his personal experiences as a vagabond. This was, she writes, the "greatest happiness that he had ever experienced":

> Never had he thought so much, existed so much, lived so much, or been so much "himself" as when he wandered about aimlessly and alone.... Vagrancy thus became the model of natural freedom, the condition of natural man as he aimlessly wanders about the uncultivated earth.[62]

She also attributes his vision of freedom to his own laziness. She writes:

> [Rousseau's] laziness was his substitute for virtue.... Since he did nothing, he did no harm. This extreme love of liberty he, moreover, knew to be the fruit of pure laziness. Laziness, Rousseau assumed, was part of everyone's nature, just as labor was the characteristic pain of civilization.[63]

Enraptured and obsessed with women on the one hand, aimless and lazy on the other—we can see the twin demands on Rousseau, self and other, working themselves out in his personal life.

As he grew older, torn by these tendencies and unable to settle anywhere, Rousseau grew fearful that he would never find a true and safe companion.

> How could it be that, with a naturally expansive nature for which to live was to love, I had not hitherto found a friend entirely my own, a true friend—I who felt so truly formed to be a friend?... Devoured by a need to love that I had never been able to satisfy, I saw myself coming to the gates of old age, and dying without having lived.[64]

When he wrote this, Rousseau had already found a compromise of sorts in the figure of Thérèse Lavasseur. He writes that given the fact that he lived with her for twenty-five years and married her in his old age, "it may be supposed that a mad passion turned my head from the first day."[65] And yet:

> I have never felt the least glimmering of love for her.... I no more desired to possess her than I had desired Mme. de Warens, and...the sensual needs I satisfied with her were for me purely sexual and had nothing to do with her as an individual.[66]

Thérèse seems to be a perfect companion for Rousseau because, as he does not (romantically) love her, she apparently poses no threat to him. At the same time, Thérèse is fully devoted to Rousseau and "would have absorbed my whole existence within herself if I could have absorbed hers in me."[67]

Able to take Thérèse for granted, he barely notes her "actual" presence. As Starobinski writes in *Transparency and Obstruction:*

> [In Thérèse, Rousseau] found someone whom he could easily identify with his own flesh and who never had raised the problem of the *other.* Thérèse is not a partner in a dialogue but an auxiliary to Rousseau's physical presence. With other women he sought the miraculous moment when the presence of the flesh would cease to be an obstacle. But in Thérèse he found flesh that simply was not an obstacle.[68]

Thus Thérèse doesn't appear to constitute a threat to Rousseau's attempts at independence. Rather, she serves as a way to keep him relatively chaste (and thus plays for him the same role as a wife that Locke ascribed). With her, he can release sexual energy that would otherwise turn him away from the goal of autonomy. Thérèse herself "doesn't count" as an other; she is merely a vehicle to further Rousseau's ambitions of self-liberation and freedom from the need to love.[69] She is the Golden Age sister/wife, accessible because she is simply there. She does not threaten, but rather enables his *amour de soi*.

One could consider Thérèse to "free" Rousseau in a way that Madame de Warens cannot. Since he doesn't love her, he also doesn't "need" her. He doesn't have an idealized relationship in his mind of her. She doesn't exist as an other for him; she becomes in his mind a thing, a part of the background of his life. In so utterly dominating her, has he achieved his transparent patriarchy?

The parallels between Rousseau's "marriage" to Thérèse and the Golden Age itself become most explicit at a point in his life that he describes in his *Confessions*. There, Rousseau writes that late in his life he discovered the island of St. Pierre on Lake Bienne in Switzerland (a place he also describes in his *Reveries of a Solitary Walker).*[70] This island offered itself as a refuge from the persecution of society. He wrote:

> It seemed to me that on that island I should be further removed from men, safer from their insults, and more forgotten by them; freer, in a word, to surrender to the pleasures of idleness and the contemplative life. I should have liked to be so cut off on that island as to have no more traffic with mortal men; and I certainly took every possible precaution to excuse myself from the necessity of any intercourse with them.[71]

Rousseau compares himself to Robinson Crusoe on his island (as he will compare Emile).[72] This is apt in that neither is truly alone on their island. This island too is already inhabited, including by Thérèse. On this island, Rousseau creates a society of "one"—with external income, a wife, and so forth not constituting a part of his society, but rather serving as the basis for it, as part of his enlarged "*soi/moi* "—here he sets up a new patriarchy.

Although desiring to "have no more traffic with mortal men," Rousseau himself seems to suggest that he is far from autonomous on this island. Just as the Golden Patriarch *did* need his sister, so too does Rousseau need Thérèse. For all her supposed non-presence, Thérèse can never cease to be a threat. Even as the most dutiful subject of patriarchy, as someone who could literally be anybody else, Thérèse remains all too present. Perhaps Rousseau even recognizes this when he writes, "I have always regarded the day which united me to my Thérèse as the one that determined my mortal being."[73]

Before Rousseau met Thérèse, before he could not count on her silent and presupposed support, he was forever foiled in his attempts to achieve this sort of idleness, this "aloneness." At an earlier point in the narrative of his *Confessions,*

Rousseau procures a dwelling place where he could "live after my own fashion without requiring anyone to control me." This place, however,

> imposed on me…duties which…could not be ignored. My whole liberty was no more than precarious. I was in a state of greater subjection than if I had been under orders because I had to submit of my own free will. I had not a single day on which I could say as I got up: "this day I will spend as I please."[74]

Without a wife to do everything (and perhaps a sure income), Rousseau found that he was forced to do everything for himself. The freedom that he seeks is quickly shown to be "precarious" without the help of others.

On St. Pierre, on the other hand, Rousseau offers a paean to idleness. In contrast to the idleness of society, which is "obligatory,"

> the idleness of solitude is delightful because it is free and voluntary. In company it is a torture to do nothing, because there I am compelled to inaction…[the idleness of solitude] is the idleness of a child who is incessantly on the move without ever doing anything.[75]

Immediately after this he writes, almost as an afterthought, "I sent for Thérèse to bring my books and belongings."[76]

Clearly, the "transparent" and merged selves on St. Pierre do not exist in a democratic relationship. This "nothingness" invites self-scripting only for the patriarch himself. Nor does this arrangement offer Rousseau the final resolution that he seeks, either literally or metaphorically.[77] Relying on Thérèse as a body, he cannot erase her utterly. Although Thérèse never lifted a finger (so far as we know) against her husband, her mere presence suggests a permanent "other" that lives within the bounds of the "common me," a stubborn reminder of the original maternal that refuses to be written away. As Rousseau tells us, he is a greater slave than she.

And, by living with a woman whom he does not love, Rousseau denies himself the real delights of love which have consumed him for his entire life. His substitution, his scandal, stands in for and in fact preempts the search for the pure maternal itself. With Thérèse he has only a "makeshift," a compromise that cannot really replace what it substitutes for. As we have already seen, even with her by his side, Rousseau remains dissatisfied that he has never found "a friend entirely my own, a true friend." One can almost hear in this complaint the voice of Aristotle intoning, "O my friends, there is no friend."

B. The individual: Émile

If Rousseau does not find a perfect combination of love and freedom for himself, what of his more literary attempts? There, it would appear, he is far more in control of the narrative, better able to dispense the endings that he seeks in life but does not necessarily find. In *Émile*, he seeks to resolve these issues within the pages of a novel where he, in his guise as author (as well as his foil as the tutor) can offer Emile the love and the liberty that he sought for himself.

In *Émile*, Rousseau revisits human history as compressed into the life of a single, imaginary boy. *Émile* is written as a tract on education in part modeled on Locke's own work. Before writing *Émile* itself, Rousseau studied and wrote on Locke's *Some Thoughts Concerning Education*.[78] For Rousseau, as for Locke, education is far from a matter of teaching books and skills; instead, it consists in nothing less than teaching a young boy (and like Locke, most likely *not* a girl) how to be free, how to contend with desire and need, and love.

As with Locke, Rousseau held that education could either be redemptive or venal. Rousseau says that when we look at the final "wretched" and "perverse" product of societal education, we lament man's nature. But this is not nature at all; this is "the creation of our fantasy; the natural man is cast in another mold."[79] In fact, for Rousseau, in the context of society, even a bad education is better than no education at all, for, "Under existing conditions, a man left to himself from birth would be more of a monster than the rest."[80]

As might be expected, a good education for Rousseau follows the laws of nature to the highest degree possible. He begins *Émile* by writing that "God makes all things good; man meddles with them and they become evil."[81] Because of his "perfectibility," man is incapable of leaving good enough alone. "He will have nothing as nature has made it, not even man himself."[82]

The task of the tutor then is to fight the tendency to reject "true" nature as best as he can. Rousseau's educational credo is "[f]ix your eyes on nature, follow the path traced by her."[83] But how do we identify nature? What is natural and what is not? In *Émile*, perhaps Rousseau's most Lockean text, he reveals an ambiguous empiricism, quite similar to Locke's own. On the one hand he subscribes to the Lockean notion of tabula rasa:

> We are born capable of learning but knowing nothing, perceiving nothing. The mind, bound up within imperfection and half grown organs, is not even aware of its own existence. The movements and cries of a newborn child are purely reflex, without knowledge or will.[84]

Yet elsewhere he tells us that "Nature is what is innate, not learned by man."[85] So Nature is both innate and learned, both inside us and outside us. It seems to be everywhere and nowhere.

Judith Shklar calls Rousseau's educational philosophy "negative education."[86] A negative education is one that is chiefly concerned with keeping the pupil free from all foreign influences. The pupil must be allowed to develop "naturally" without interference from outside, societal sources. Rousseau, in idealizing Emile, writes that "[h]e is alone in the midst of human society, he depends on himself alone."[87]

In speaking of negative education, Shklar implicitly allows that there is "something" original and pure to preserve at the heart of the liberal self. And yet, as with Locke and for much the same reason, Rousseau complicates this view by denying the grounds for such an original or natural self to be known or even to exist. Even as he seeks to preserve a self, Rousseau, like Locke, also must create it sprung wholly from the very social fabric which he sees as anathema to its freedom.

The savage who must live in the town

We can see gain insight into Rousseau's notions of self and nature by noting the model that he offers for Emile. Rousseau announces that the only book he would have Emile study is *Robinson Crusoe*. This book provides Emile with an idealized vision of what true freedom might be like. According to Rousseau (in his guise as the tutor), "Robinson Crusoe on his island, deprived of the help of his fellow men, yet find[s] food, preserv[es] his life, and procur[es] a certain amount of comfort."[88] He concludes that:

> We shall...make a reality of that desert island which formerly served as an illustration. The condition, I confess is not that of a social being, nor is it in all probability, Emile's own condition, but he should use it as a standard of comparison for all other conditions. The surest way to raise him above prejudice and to base his judgments on the true relations of things, is to put him in the place of a solitary man, and to judge all things as they would be judged by such a man in relation to their own utility.[89]

In seeking to emulate Robinson Crusoe, Rousseau wants nothing less than to create a (metaphorical) desert island for Emile to live on even while he is surrounded by society. Emile "is a savage who has to live in the town."[90]

As such, Emile can engage with society, benefit from it, find his mediation through it, but always be safe behind the boundaries of his island. This is not a manifesto to melt Emile into the social, but rather a quest to maintain his integrity, and what will become his manhood in the context of society, without having to give up his identity and uniqueness.

Even in this ideal, however, Rousseau recognizes that there are risks. Obliquely anticipating the fact that Robinson is never alone, even on his "desert island," he recognizes that this metaphysical island, no less than Ile St. Pierre, cannot remain unsullied and impervious to invasion and threat:

> Make haste therefore to establish him on his island while this is all he needs to make him happy; for the day is at hand, when, if he must still live on his island, he will not be content to live alone, when even the companionship of Man Friday, who is almost disregarded now, will no longer suffice.[91]

As with other islands, other selves, there is no "natural" wholeness to encapsulate, no original self to preserve. The island itself is already inhabited with others, already full of need, desire, and danger.

Emile and the tutor

Realizing the dangers posed to the child, even on his island, Rousseau explicitly seeks to limit the child's dependence on others:

> Can we conceive a more senseless plan than to educate a child as if he would never leave his room, as if he would always have his servants about him? If the wretched creature takes a single step up or down he is lost.[92]

And yet he makes it clear that throughout Emile's upbringing the tutor will practically never leave him alone:

> We must never be separated except by mutual consent. This clause is essential and I would have tutor and scholar so inseparable that they should regard their fate as one.[93]

And further:

> While the child is still unconscious, there is time to prepare his surroundings so that nothing shall strike his eye but what is fit for his sight. . . . You will not be the master of the child if you cannot control every one around him.[94]

He justifies this domination by arguing, "[w]hen they consider that they must always live together, they must needs love one another, and in this way they really learn to love one another."[95] Being with Emile for his entire childhood then, Rousseau-as-tutor seeks to become as familiar to him as his own body, not something "other" but simply an aspect of his own self.

Here Rousseau once again uses the method of Golden Age love: freedom through union and liberation as a family. The family in question is none other than the tutor and Emile themselves. Arguing that "the charms of home are the best antidote to vice,"[96] Rousseau in his guise as the tutor seeks to constitute a family with Emile that seems to be without distinction, and without tyranny, whereby they can form a "common me." Best of all, there appears to be no gender, no otherness, to threaten this union.

And yet even this relationship carries aspects of tension, and difference, indeed of gender itself. The members of this family are not equal partners. The tutor acknowledges his power, his patriarchy over Emile, as when he writes:

> It is I who am really Emile's father. It is I who have made a man of him.[97]

Seeing himself as a man, as the familial patriarch, the tutor proclaims, "you must be a man yourself before you try to train a man; you yourself must set the pattern he shall copy."[98]

Yet, although he sees himself as Emile's father, there is also a way in which the tutor plays a far more feminine role as well. In many ways, the tutor is also Emile's mother (and sister and wife—the incestuous roles of the Golden Age overlap). The tutor lives vicariously through his pupil, dedicating his life to freeing Emile rather than himself. At one point he writes:

> Oh, Emile, my son! If I were to lose you, what would be left of myself? And yet, I must learn to lose you, for who knows when you may be taken from me?[99]

The tutor must mediate Emile's desire for him, living chastely and lovelessly; there are no women to perform this function in this patriarchy.[100] In a maternal fashion, the tutor is forced to operate behind the scenes, manipulating Emile's opinions and ideas indirectly. From the tutor's perspective, if Emile can be led to believe that he *is* free, then he is free, revealing what Rousseau considers to be a "female" way of thinking, as when he writes elsewhere, "'What will people think?' is the grave of a man's virtue and the throne of a woman's."[101] This is hardly the language of patriarchy, of scandalous self-imposition, that comes with the notion of fatherhood.

Rousseau suggests the tutor's substitution for and merger between parental roles when he writes: "Emile is an orphan. No matter whether he has father or mother, having undertaken their duties I am invested with their rights. He must honor his parents but he must obey me. That is my first and only condition."[102]

What does it mean that the tutor is in some sense both Emile's mother and his father? It suggests a conflation of origin and sign, of the lost nature and the substitute which seeks to replace it. Will the tutor bring Emile to his own nature through a scandalous act of imposition, as a father might? Or through gentle loving and quiet control, as a mother would? Is the tutor a presence that dissolves otherness into himself, like the Golden Age patriarch, or is he a mere body whose seeming non-presence masks a need that leads to other needs, like the Golden Age sister (or indeed Thérèse Lavasseur)? In either case, what is instructive is not the particularities of the relationship but the fact that the unity of the Golden Age is always revealed to be a sham. Even a "genderless" family like the tutor and Emile reproduces difference and hierarchy. Even this harmony preserves within it not one but at least two perspectives.

And, as we saw in his consideration of the Golden Age, as with Robinson Crusoe's island itself, such "unity" can, indeed must be, treacherous, unsustainable in the long run. In creating Emile's intense and loving bond with the tutor, Rousseau is condemning him to a lifetime of dependency:

> His first affections [for his tutor] are the reins by which you control his movements; he was free and now I behold him in your power. So long as he loved nothing, he was independent of everything but himself and his own necessities; as soon as he loves, he is dependent on his affections.[103]

Recognizing that his control over Emile is only getting stronger, even while he appears to be relinquishing power, the tutor says: "But see what fresh chains you have bound about his heart. Reason, friendship, affection, gratitude, a thousand bonds of affection, speak to him in a voice he cannot fail to hear."[104] The tutor has spun his webs of love, his community of reason. That it is invisible makes the power of love all the stronger.

Just as the Golden Age family members themselves moved from general love for family members to a particular love outside the walls of the family compound, so too with Emile, love learned within the family leads necessarily to the undoing of the Golden Age itself.

Even on its own terms, before the catastrophes which are to come ("[m]ake haste therefore to establish him on his island while this is all he needs to make him happy"), we get a sense that the "family" of the tutor and Emile has already failed to deliver what it set out to do: to give Emile his true nature, to deliver him his autonomy amid a social setting. Unlike Locke, Rousseau openly doubts the ways in which "manhood" and authenticity are imparted by this educational process. If the tutor's own manhood is questionable (is he father or mother?), if he lives vicariously off his pupil, how can he teach him to be a man?

Rousseau's answer is always to "let nature be your guide." But this advice, as with Locke, doesn't get us that far. In both cases "nature" is as much a product of engineering and manipulation as the social notion of being it is supposed to be distinct from. Once again, however, where Locke does this covertly, Rousseau leads our eye to his own conflation. Frequently the tutor speaks as if he were a force of nature itself (and by extension, Rousseau):

> Keep the child dependent on nature only. By this course of education you will have followed the order of nature. Let his unreasonable wishes meet with physical obstacles only, or the punishment which results from his own actions.... Give him, not what he wants but what he needs. Let there be no question of obedience for him or tyranny for you. Supply the strength he lacks just so far as it is required for freedom, not for power, so that he may receive your services with a sort of shame, and look forward to the time when he may dispense with them and may achieve the honor of self help.[105]

In reality, the child isn't dependent on nature, he is dependent on the tutor, and there is no "necessity," only that which the tutor deems necessary. This conflation becomes such that the tutor openly equates himself with a natural force:

> *As for my pupil, or rather nature's pupil,* he has been trained from the outset to be as self reliant as possible he has not formed the habit of constantly seeking help from others, still less of displaying his stores of learning.... Nature not man is his schoolmaster, and he learns all the quicker because he is not aware that he has any lessons to learn.[106]

While as usual with Rousseau there is a certain ironical detachment in this, the fact that the tutor conflates himself with nature shows that we are not dealing with the simple question of whether Emile or the tutor are "natural" or "unnatural" but whether there is any meaningful category known as "nature" at all.

The tutor seeks to improve on the absence of original nature by becoming nature himself. But what kind of nature? The original maternal or the new paternal? In the end, we get neither, but are instead suspended in-between. Inside of this masquerade of nature lives a separate subjectivity, the tutor himself. For all of his self-sacrifice, for all his transparency, the tutor can no more will his body to disappear than can any of the women in Rousseau's novels. His own presence defies the dreams of unity and autonomy which he offers Emile; it is as pernicious to Emile's liberty as Sophie's will be (or the Golden Age sister will be to her brother or Thérèse to Rousseau). And because his masquerade is so successful, because Emile does not even realize that he is being offered a substitute or that his "own" autonomy includes a separate identity, Emile does not even realize that he is being slowly enslaved.

Society and the "need" for women

Emile's childhood is clearly the happiest period of his life. As in the Golden Age, he spends his days content and carefree. Yet his tutor realizes that this state of affairs is doomed from its inception. As he approaches manhood, an inevitable crisis occurs: Emile must have a woman. Rousseau calls this the "yoke of manhood."[107]

In the same way that he speculated on the naturalness of maternal love in the state of nature, Rousseau equivocates on whether the "need" for a woman is natural or not. On the one hand, he writes that this desire is not a "physical need. It is not true that it is a need at all."[108] For Rousseau, the need for a woman is externally imposed by the woman herself.

> If no lascivious object had met our eye, if no unclean thought had entered our mind, this so-called need might never have made itself felt, and we should have remained chaste, without temptation, effort or merit.[109]

On the other hand, Rousseau speaks of passion between the sexes as "a bond of nature."[110] As such, "nature has endowed women with a power of stimulating man's passions in excess of a man's power of satisfying those passions, and has thus made him dependent on her goodwill."[111] Here, men cannot be free *without* women.[112] We see that the passion that men feel is not an external implant but something inevitable, part of their nature. Hence it is incumbent on men to cooperate with women in order to be able to get this desire under "control," in order to allow women to embody and mediate men's own desires.[113]

Through the love of women, Emile can become "all the more himself." Through this union, he can achieve the substitute for the lost maternal. Emile needs a woman to be a man. He needs an other to be a self, an embodiment of an original to substitute for.

In seeking to reconcile these two disparate views of women, as threat and as liberator, the tutor sees himself as instrumental in making this necessary but dangerous liaison as safe as can be for Emile:

> If you cannot attain to the mastery of your passions, dear Emile, I pity you. . . . I will not permit the purposes of nature to be evaded. If you must be a slave, I prefer to surrender you to a tyrant from whom I may deliver you; whatever happens, I can free you more easily from the slavery of women than from yourself.[114]

Accordingly, the tutor finds a "perfect" woman for Emile, Sophie.[115] Sophie is demure, modest, fully in control of her passions.[116] Yet, despite her being "perfect" and custom designed by Rousseau to offer Emile maximum autonomy, the tutor displays anxiety about her from the outset. When Emile first sees Sophie, Rousseau writes, "farewell, liberty,"[117] and:

> O Emile! what art thou now? . . . How art thou fallen? Where is that young man so sternly fashioned, who braved all weathers . . . swayed by reason only? . . . Living in softness and idleness he now lets himself be ruled by women . . . a young girl is the arbiter of his fate . . . the earnest Emile is the plaything of a child.[118]

However, Rousseau also sees that this is the ultimate test of his work. If Emile can maintain his freedom with Sophie, gaining what he must from her and refusing to sacrifice his autonomy, if he can maintain his manhood even as he depends upon her to mediate his desire, he will have succeeded in achieving Rousseau's dream of having both love and autonomy:

> So far, you [Emile, up until the time that he met Sophie] have only had the semblance of liberty, the precarious liberty of the slave who has not received his orders. Now is the time for real freedom: learn to be your own master; control your heart my Emile and you will be virtuous.[119]

In other words, rather than hide from the "yoke of manhood" with the tutor on his desert island, Emile must face the enemy squarely and dominate her. The immature family between Emile and the tutor must give way to a family worthy of a man, establishing Emile as a rightful patriarch.

Accordingly, the tutor urges the couple to seek "a patriarchal, rural life, the earliest life of man, the most peaceful, the most natural, and the most attractive to the uncorrupted heart."[120] If Emile can completely dominate Sophie then perhaps her glaring "otherness" might be overcome.[121] She might then finally become incorporated into his enlarged sense of self, into the "common me." But we know in advance that this attempt too is futile. Ever the master of bittersweet irony, Rousseau writes: "What is needed for [the Golden Age's] restoration? One thing only and that is an impossibility; we must love the golden age."[122]

If the sisters of the Golden Age do not offer a safe and permanent outlet for their brother's lusts, if the tutor's relationship with Emile is only setting him up for a loss of autonomy, then how can Sophie save him? Emile is already lost. Even Sophie's chastity only reinforces his dependence upon her because it reinscribes the very power system that holds him in check, and makes his self-control dependent upon hers. Recognizing this implicitly, Emile says to the tutor:

> But for my passions, I should be in my manhood independent as God himself, for I only desire what is, and I should never fight against fate. At least, there is only one chain, a chain which I shall ever wear. . . . Come then, give me Sophie and I am free.[123]

Émile and Sophie

Émile ends on a dubious note, with Emile telling his tutor, "I need you more than ever now that I am taking up the duties of manhood."[124] This foreshadows what will happen in the sequel to *Émile,* entitled *Émile and Sophie or the Solitary Ones* [*Émile et Sophie ou les solitaires*]. This fragment of a book, which Rousseau never finished, is as tragic as *Émile* is hopeful. It is an epistolary novel written by Emile to his tutor. We are never sure if the tutor actually receives these letters, or indeed, if Emile even sent them. Emile begins the book by bewailing his fate to his former tutor:

> I was free, I was happy, oh, my master, you gave me a heart ready for the taste of happiness and you gave me Sophie . . . everything was set up to provide me with an agreeable life. . . . Alas what happened to that happy time of joy and hope?[125]

Without the tutor's guidance, Emile's life is a miserable failure. Initially, the couple followed the tutor's advice and created a rural patriarchy, but then tragedy struck their family, almost as if the fates (but more accurately, Rousseau himself) intended that they should not remain content. Sophie's parents die, as does "her" daughter (who is also of course Emile's daughter, although he never refers to her as such), and the fragility of the family's autonomy is destroyed. Seeking to distract her from her sorrows, Emile takes Sophie to Paris, which proves to be a complete fiasco. The lovers grow distant, worldly. Finally Sophie has an affair and Emile is shattered.

In the utter and rapid collapse of this "new Golden Age," we can see how, if anything, the grounds for harmony and patriarchy are even weaker than the original. In contrast to the indiscriminate love of the first Golden Age, Sophie and Emile's explicitly particular love makes their unity far more problematic. They *have* chosen one another; they do love and need one another. The separateness and distinction maintained by their romantic passion for one another becomes a fault line which splits them apart the minute the couple is put under any pressure (exactly as in the Golden Age itself, only more swiftly and definitively).

After his family falls apart, Emile lashes out at the tutor for making him dependent upon him and then abandoning him:

> Fickle happiness!...Was it by you, cruel father, that this decline had to begin?...you were complacent in your work.... You loved us and you left us. If you hadn't left, I would still be happy.... I would still have my wife in my arms.... In having abandoned me, you have done me more harm than you ever did me good![126]

Here, Emile finally recognizes that it is the tutor himself who has condemned him to dependency, but now it is too late. In despair, he leaves Paris to wander the earth in misery. During his wanderings he takes to the sea and is captured and sold into slavery by pirates. While in chains in the galley of the pirate ship, he realizes that he is finally perfectly free because his literal chains are a force of necessity that he can completely surrender himself to.

> What have I lost of my primitive liberty? Wasn't I born a slave to necessity? What new yoke can man impose on me? Work? Didn't I work when I was free? Hunger? How many times have I known that voluntarily?... Constraint? Could it be any worse than my first chains? Submitted since birth to human passions, whether their yoke is imposed by me or by others, what does it matter so long as I have to bear them?[127]

For Emile, freedom can be found only by giving up the search for freedom altogether, by ceasing to struggle and accept and love the chains that are always around his heart:

> Besides, what would I do if I was free? In the state that I am in, would I even want it? Ah! so as to avoid annihilation, I need to be animated by the will of another instead of my own.[128]

Rousseau never finished *Émile and Sophie,* but through conversations with his contemporaries there is evidence of how he intended to end his work.[129] In the version that I have available, Emile is eventually stranded on a desert island, where by a freakish coincidence Sophie has also been shipwrecked.[130] After some initial drama, Emile forgives Sophie and the couple are reunited. But the reason

Emile can now be safe with Sophie is that he no longer loves her; indeed he seems no longer to be capable of feeling love at all.

If we accept this ending as definitive, we might argue that Emile has a "happy" ending after all. True freedom lies in gazing on human society, with all its passions, longings, and so forth, as something apart from oneself. Having made this realization, it is now safe for Emile to embrace Sophie because she can do him no further harm. He has escaped within himself—he no longer "needs" Sophie to be free and so can revert to his original and lost autonomy.

Here again is Derrida's full circle: The maternal presence is reduced to merely another sign, giving Emile, finally, his own autonomy, his own substance, and the patriarchy he has so long sought. In many ways, this ending resembles the resolution that Rousseau achieved in his own life with Thérèse. As with Rousseau's feelings for Thérèse, Emile is now "safe" with Sophie.

And yet, also like Thérèse, Sophie's reduction to a mere body "that simply was not an obstacle" does not finally create a pure and safe "common me." She remains another distinct body. It still matters that she is there. Emile may not love her anymore, but he still requires her presence, he still remains dependent on her. Whether Sophie is a visible threat that Emile can't escape from (like Madame de Warens) or an invisible presence that he can't even see (like Thérèse), she remains defiantly other. This "solution" still doesn't offer Emile his *own* identity. His sense of self, his autonomy, is still screened through and mediated by an other. It is received by contrast, by "no longer being in love with Sophie," by having conquered (and presupposed) that love. Emile remains dependent upon a prehistory with the absent mother, the original nature that seduced him out of his autonomy in the first place and never let him go back. What we get at the end of *Émile and Sophie* is not so much resolution but deflation; he may no longer be in love, but he still remains bound by love's tenets.

C. The Golden Age family revisited (La Nouvelle Héloïse)

Having sketched out the problems that Rousseau has in freeing himself and the individual, I turn now to a consideration of how this problem manifests itself in the collective context, in terms of Rousseau's hope both for the family and for society as a whole.

Julie, ou La Nouvelle Héloïse is the main work in which Rousseau attempts to re-create the Golden Age family amid modern society. In this novel, the heroine, Julie, is in love with a man named Saint Preux, but she cannot marry him because they are from different classes and her parents do not approve. With society as corrupting and unredeemable as it is, Julie can never find true happiness. Rousseau has Julie escape the sorrows of society by renouncing love altogether and retreating to the isolation of the country. She opts to wed Monsieur de Wolmar, a respectable man, whom she pointedly does not love. This is akin to Rousseau's own purposes in marrying Thérèse. But whereas Thérèse is portrayed as being almost animal-like, Wolmar is a mysterious, almost divine figure.[131] In both cases, the hope is that the mediator will not be another "person," not an other at all. Such a mediator can be below the self: an animal, a mere body; or above the self: a disembodied god. Neither category threatens the autonomy of the individual in question.

Wolmar has an estate called Clarens, and there Julie seems to thrive. Their life is indeed quite nice. Julie writes:

> Everything here is pleasant and cheerful. Everything breathes an air of plenty and propriety; nothing savors of pomp and luxury. There is not a single room in which one may not recognize that he is in the country and yet in which he may not find all the conveniences of the city.[132]

Note that in describing Clarens, Rousseau is not really re-creating the Golden Age itself but rather revisiting it from the perspective of modern society. The Golden Age was crude, whereas Clarens is sumptuous. But the essential form is the same. As with the Golden Age, Clarens is a patriarchy. Wolmar is an autocratic ruler, but he, like the Golden Age father, is just, and so the entire miniature society at Clarens, with all of its servants and retinue, appears to be harmonious and without conflict. Clarens represents a community of interest:

> There is never either sullenness or discontent in obedience because there is neither haughtiness nor capriciousness in the house.... The master and mistress sufficiently respect the dignity of a man, even though he is a servant....The servants know well that their most assured fortune is attached to that of the master and that tie will never want for anything as long as the house is seen to prosper. In serving it, therefore, they are taking care of their own patrimony...this is to their greatest self-interest.... *[At Clarens,] [a]ll is done through affection.*[133] (emphasis added)

Ultimately, however, despite the otherworldly perfection of Wolmar, this new Golden Age is not destined to last, and indeed turns out to be a sham, another masquerade. While Julie is dying, she writes Saint Preux a letter confessing that her love for him never ceased:

> I have for a long time deluded myself. This delusion was advantageous to me; it vanished when I no longer needed it. You had thought me cured of my love for you and I thought I was too.... Yes, I tried in vain to stifle the first sentiment which inspired me.[134]

Julie has no regrets, since her virtue is "unblemished," but she ends her final letter on a tragic note:

Without you, what happiness could I enjoy? No, I do not leave you; I go to wait for you. The virtue which separated us on earth will unite us in eternal dwelling. I am dying in this sweet hope, only too happy to purchase at the price of my life the right of loving you forever without crime and of telling you one more time.[135]

Aware that particular love undermines the community of the Golden Age, Rousseau sought to have his heroine refuse its urges. He depicts a modern individual attempting to revisit a bygone time by submitting herself to patriarchal rule, by forgoing particular for general love. The "actual" families of the Golden Age were not aware that romantic love would be their undoing and so they did nothing to prevent it. But Julie is all too aware of the dangers and allures of romantic love, inequality, and so forth. Yet even with her eyes open, she cannot overcome her love for Saint Preux; for her, it is already too late.

As with the Golden Age itself, particular love inexorably, inevitably (re)surfaces, not only for Julie, but for Rousseau as well. At best, *La Nouvelle Héloïse* represents a community temporarily play-acting at familial, rustic innocence, another "makeshift" substitution doomed to failure.

Besides the failure inherent in the plot of the book, there is another way in which Rousseau suggests the ultimate hopelessness of its project, and this lies in his choice to narrate this tale from the perspective of a woman. Julie is the self who is to be freed and the other in fact is a man (or two men: a patriarch set over her and the object of her love that she cannot have). This conflation points us to what will be the novel's conclusion—the impossibility of the very merger of self and other, of mother and father, which Julie's double identity suggests. For Rousseau to "be Julie" implies giving up his manhood, that mystical source of self which has no tangible source either in society or even in nature (since natural progression leads to its undoing). While he may give up his own manhood, he will not give up on manhood or patriarchy itself. Even a woman who is a foil for Rousseau himself must submit to a higher power in the form of Wolmar (who in some way is *also* Rousseau). If Rousseau/Julie will not be patriarch, someone else must be.

Perhaps even more importantly, by narrating this book as a woman, Rousseau offers us a subversive view of the Golden Age family itself. By inhabiting Julie's perspective, we know that Wolmar is not loved. We know that his power is not total, that Julie preserves within herself an alien, other perspective that Wolmar has no access to. We also know that this Golden Age family is a farce and has not created anything like a "common me," despite its external appearances. We know that it must and will crumble over time. In *La Nouvelle Héloïse*, Rousseau leaves us little doubt as to the futility of his plan, the futility of the substitution. In this book he seems to mock his own aspirations, and as such, once again point us in another direction.

D. The social (Sparta, Poland)

If the family poses for Rousseau a problematical point from which to free the individual (either as a separate entity or as part of a harmonious collective unit), one can surmise that society is even worse. For Rousseau, society is itself gendered; like a woman, it mediates the world to each of us, and in turn makes us dependent upon it.

But, as ever, Rousseau is unwilling to give up on society (or women), finding, in the very contradictions it produces, hope for a solution. In "The General Society of the Human Race," the original (and excised) introduction to *The Social Contract,* Rousseau writes:

> Although there is no natural and general society among men, although they become unhappy and wicked in becoming sociable...yet we should not think that there is neither virtue nor happiness for us and that heaven has abandoned us without remedy to depravity. We should rather try to extract from the evil itself the remedy which can cure it.[136]

The "evil" is society itself, which becomes its own remedy, a substitute for what is lost. Calling the state "the mother of us all," Rousseau seeks to re-create the Golden Age family on this ultimate level.[137] As we have already seen, just as the generalized love of the Golden Age families served to mediate each member's individual desire without enslaving them, so too can society as a whole (through the mediation of the state) overcome particularity and hence offer freedom through its chains. In this ideal, the state itself becomes the patriarch, ordering and preserving our distinctness and yet bringing us into a unified whole; the "mother of us all" becomes the father as well—the maternal origin and paternal substitution become one, once again bringing us full circle.

Sparta

For Rousseau, the society that came closest to ever realizing this dream was Sparta. He praised the Spartans for having so structured their society as to make it completely in accord with the laws of nature (no small feat, as we have seen). The Spartans made themselves hard and fierce like natural man, obeying "necessity" rather than opinion. Constantly on the move, the militaristic Spartans avoided the softness and idleness of modern men, re-creating through artificial means the wandering life of natural man.[138] In their child-rearing practices, for example, Rousseau notes approvingly that

> Nature treats [children] precisely as Sparta treated the children of her citizens; she makes strong and robust those who are well constituted, and she causes the rest to perish.[139]

In short, Sparta allows for the possibility of men, solid and natural men who can therefore safely become citizens without losing themselves and their "natural" particularity.

In Sparta, the state is modeled on the Golden Age family, but as such, individual families must be subsumed. In *Émile,* Rousseau tells the story of the Spartan mother whose five sons have all been killed in a war. When she asks a slave as to the outcome of the war and is told about her sons, she becomes angry, saying, "Vile slave, is that what I asked thee?" The slave replies, "We have won the victory," and the mother goes to a temple to give thanks. Rousseau approvingly notes, "[t]hat was a citizen."[140] In Sparta, even the mothers seem to be "men," so that here even the permanent threat of gender seems finally to have been overcome. The mothers have become the fathers.

The Spartan mother has put the interests of the state over her own concerns for her children—her love is not particular for her own children, but general for all her fellow Spartans. Particular maternal love becomes subsumed into patriarchal generality.[141] Thus when Rousseau says that the Spartans follow nature, part of what he means is that they have "naturalized" political power (i.e., rendered it invisible) in such a way that it no longer compromises one's autonomy to obey it. Society itself has become (or poses as) natural and so the chains of society are legitimized; as with the Greeks' use of slaves, "the extremes meet."

Yet once again Rousseau is incapable of sustaining a vision of such perfect union and autonomy, even in the example of Sparta. Despite his praise for the Spartans' subsumption of particular families in the name of the larger state-as-family, they have only subordinated rather than eliminated the family; it remains intact, a constant possible source of contention within the city.[142] Even as the mother becomes the father, she is retained in her feminine role, presupposed as the basis of patriarchal society.

Rousseau doesn't criticize the decision to retain families, and it's worth considering why. In commenting on Plato's more radical "community of women" and the complete abolition of the family in *The Republic,* Rousseau opposes

> that subversion of all the tenderest of our natural feelings, which [Plato] sacrificed to an artificial sentiment which can only exist by their aid. Will the bonds of convention hold firm without some foundation in nature? Can devotion to the state exist apart from the love of those near and dear to us? Can patriotism thrive except in the soil of that miniature fatherland, the home? Is it not the good son, the good husband, the good father, who makes the good citizen?[143]

The Spartan citizen, as paternalistic as she is, preserves the figure and the hope for the lost maternal after all. Despite his confidence that the mother can become the father, that the second nature can substitute for the first, Rousseau reveals that he is not willing to give up the link to the original maternal after all, despite the risks that she poses. He reveals the inadequacy of the substitute, its need to be rooted in the original itself. Even if she doesn't care about their personal fates, the Spartan mother still knows who her sons are, still preserves the maternal, which is crucial for its own overcoming.[144]

Rousseau reveals that his heart is not with the substitute; it cannot replace but must still search for the lost original. Its identity is derived from that which it conquers and defines itself against. Without mothers, we could not have fathers. To be a good citizen is to be a good husband, father, and brother. Thus we require wives, mothers, and sisters as well.

Patriarchy keeps these selves ordered in a proper hierarchy, and Rousseau's citizen mother, like Thérèse, wholly buys into her subversion. Yet the state depends on her ongoing devotion—it has not freed itself from the "yoke of manhood." In this vision of citizenship, it is the mother who makes the sacrifices, to her state, to the patriarch himself. It is her interests, her love, that must be given up. Once again, under the veil of selfless publicness, we see different roles, different duties within the transparency of selves.

At the same time, it is possible too that the Spartan mother may reflect (as with La Nouvelle Héloïse, but in a different fashion) the inevitable breakdown in the patriarchy—where the mother becomes more of a man than the father himself. Even in her subservience to patriarchy, the mother poses a threat. Rousseau raises the spectre openly when he speaks of "the ambition of the Spartan women to rule over men."[145] In the very delight that Rousseau takes in her acting against her own self-interest ("*that* is a citizen"), we see evidence of just how subjugated she is. We see evidence of her own agenda precisely in its occlusion. This forgotten and yet preserved agenda, this maternal difference, does not "go away." It is not banished by the substitution of public love. It remains, dangerous and resentful, eating away at the foundations of patriarchy even as it seeks "a place at the table," until one day, as it must, Sparta rots and falls away.

Ultimately, Rousseau sees that even Sparta is imperfect, unrealizable as a model for liberation, and doomed to failure. In *The Social Contract* he writes:

> If Sparta and Rome perished, what state can hope to last for ever? If we want to set up a long lasting government, let us not dream of making it eternal. To succeed, we must not attempt the impossible, nor flatter ourselves by giving our work a permanence which the human condition does not allow for.[146]

There can be no re-creation of the Golden Age, there can be no return to Sparta. In his most somber mood, Rousseau despairs of human freedom:

> A thousand nations have shone on the earth who could never have accepted good laws; and even those who could have, could have done so only for an insufficient time [given the enormity of the requirement].[147]

How to make a free state

Despite his gloom, there remained some places that Rousseau considered possible sites of freedom, places that had not yet become corrupted. In *The Social Contract* he considered Corsica to be such a place (although to his disgust, the island was annexed by France). In his *Government of Poland,* Rousseau sets out a blueprint for reestablishing the Spartan model in contemporary Poland. Though in his mind the Poles, like all modern people, did not necessarily display the virtues of the Spartans, there was still hope for them to rise to the occasion:

> Give a different bent to the passions of the Poles; in doing so...[y]ou will give [them] a spiritual vigor...and will cause them to do by inclination...the things that men motivated by duty or interest never do quite well enough.[148]

Thus, as with Emile, as with Sparta itself, the proper institutions, the correct manipulations, can create an artificial nature offering a diffuse Golden Age love in its new guise of nationalism. Rousseau felt that for Poland to be free, it must focus exclusively on its Polishness (i.e., "Polishness" as the natural aspect of the Poles). Displaying a similar logic in *The Social Contract,* he chides Peter the Great for trying to turn Russians into "Germans or Englishmen" instead of Russians, saying, "he prevented his subjects from ever becoming what they could have been by persuading them to be what they are not."[149]

As with the individual, Rousseau sees national autonomy as a process of shutting out the world, of "negative education." Yet ultimately he locates what will set the Poles free not in something "authentic" to themselves, but rather in something external to them. He looks to the figure of a great Legislator to set the Polish nation on a righteous path (not unlike Solon and Lycurgus of Greece). The Legislator is also seen in *The Social Contract,* a Godlike, physically removed figure. As Rousseau puts it, "It would take gods to give laws to men."[150]

It often appears that Rousseau fancies himself to be a candidate for the Legislator. His *Government of Poland* seems to attest to this ambition.[151] If this is the case, we see a way for Rousseau to preserve not only patriarchy but also his own individuality in the very foundations of a state. As Legislator, Rousseau can safely inhabit the public (if not literally, then as a ghostly presence which, having no body, can never be removed) because it is very much of his own devising; it creates a "public" that is created according to his own wishes, which preserves his autonomy and his privilege even while giving himself over to the common me. Truly, he can say, *"l'état, c'est moi."*

But as such, Rousseau sees that he has a hard task ahead of him. In *The Social Contract,* the Legislator's task is nothing less than "changing human nature."[152] But here we come to the same dilemma that the tutor faced with Emile. If the Legislator for Poland is meant to preserve Poland's Polishness as the source of the collective *amour de soi*, what does it mean that Rousseau himself is not Polish? How can he "give" the Poles to their own, Polish nature and simultaneously "change" their nature?

Indeed it would appear that Rousseau doesn't actually want a nation of Poles but of Spartans (or Genevans?) and so, as with Émile, an external standard of autonomy is being foisted onto a people under the guise of their own "nature" or authenticity.

Although he may well recognize this dilemma, Rousseau seems to hope that a veil of mystification will prevent the Polish people (just as with Émile) from realizing the foreign origins of their own national "authenticity." If the Polish people think they are receiving Polishness, then perhaps they really are (if Émile thinks he is free, then perhaps he really is). Perhaps, through this act of masquerade, the "real" nature of Polishness will be produced after all.

Here too, the Legislator is both mother and father, original "nature" and transparent patriarch. Rousseau openly suggests as much when he writes, "Your true republican is a man who imbibed love of the fatherland, which is to say love of the laws and liberty, with his mother's milk."[153] The Legislator must on the one hand mediate the desire of the people for them and show them their "true nature" (mother), but at the same time embody the distance and overcoming of desire which renders such mediation safe, to give them, as it were, a second birth as citizens (father).

But does this unity work any better than those we have seen before? Does the absent Legislator offer the harmony that Rousseau has found to be so elusive elsewhere? In *The Social Contract,* immediately following his comments about Peter the Great's attempt to make Russians into Germans, Rousseau writes: "in the same way, a French tutor made his student [i.e., Émile] shine for a moment of his youth, only to amount to nothing in the end."[154] As in *Émile* itself, Rousseau warns us that the creation of authenticity out of whole cloth can never succeed. As in so many cases, the "unity" which results from such a construction preserves a number of discordances, beginning with that between the Legislator's own particularity and the "general" will, the Polish nature that he invents for himself.

In some sense, the Legislator must be a disembodied, Godlike figure to the community he produces, a dispenser of *agape* itself, filling and creating his subjects and giving them to themselves.[155] And yet this figure, perhaps Rousseau himself, has a very human and particular origin (not unlike the tutor in his own masquerade as nature). Rousseau expresses fears that the Legislator's "private aims would mar the sanctity of his work."[156] Given the fact that, for all his disembodiedness, all his masquerading as nature, the Legislator retains a particularity which might persist even after his absence, what of the "common me" that he inspires? How much does it remain "his" as opposed to the people who inhabit this society?

For Rousseau, because of questions like these, the Legislator must, like Moses, remove himself from the community that he forms, lest his particularity threaten the general will that he has created. But what will the people have when the "me" at the heart of their commonality removes himself? Will they do any better than Emile did when the tutor abandoned him? Can a people be any more free of the need for an "other" than Rousseau (or Émile) himself? Has the Legislator truly given them to themselves, or has he, like the tutor, suspended his pupils between an idea of their nature, and his own manipulations?

Recognizing to some degree the problematic nature of the Legislator and the inculcation of freedom in a people, Rousseau sees this process as being at best a long, painful path. It must involve paradoxically ignoring and avoiding all external influences, even while submitting to a radical national reconstruction at the Legislator's hands. And ultimately for Rousseau, the ruse will fail:

> Entirely contrary to what we have supposed we shall find that the progress of society stifles humanity in men's hearts by arousing personal interest.... From this it is apparent that this so-called *social treaty, dictated by nature, is a pure fantasy,* since its conditions are always unknown or impracticable and men must either be unaware of them or infringe them.[157] (emphasis added)

Here Rousseau finally admits that this is a story that he himself has invented. Instead of giving us all, we are left, as we always are, with Rousseau dissatisfied. Promised unity, we get a "makeshift." Promised mother and father, we get neither: neither a sense of our true and original nature ("mother") nor a satisfactory and self-created identity ("father"). Rather than provide the grounds for a democratic polity in which we embrace our nothingness and give ourselves to ourselves and to one another, Rousseau, like Locke, suspends us, however regretfully, between nature and patriarchy, between maternal *agape* and patriarchal *eros*. From this vantage point, the "common me" that constitutes society reveals itself, like Clarens, to be inhabited not by men, nor women, nor citizens, but rather by masqueraders in search of an identity.

O my friends...

As we've seen, Rousseau subverts, even as he suffers from, his participation in the doctrine of love. He reveals his solutions to be "fantasies" which he exposes and foils with aplomb throughout his works. He has succeeded in making the liberal subject "incredible" (to use Judith Butler's term), and sometimes even absurd.[158] By theorizing from both the center and periphery of his system, from both male and female perspectives, he exposes not only the hierarchies themselves, but the ongoing threats to those hierarchies. He points to the absence of unity beneath the facade of transparency.

And, in the discordance of the self that he reveals, there exists also evidence of the Nietzschean "perhaps." This is particularly true in Rousseau's distinction between *amour propre* and *amour de soi*. With the concept of *amour propre,* Rousseau offers a clear critique of the very system which inscribes him. *Amour propre* reveals the smoldering resentment, the conflict which is preserved in the heart of love. *Amour de soi,* a concept that we see he has an immense difficulty conceptualizing, much less bringing into being, offers a model of what love "was" or could yet be.[159]

But, before we can think further about what could be, we must recognize that Rousseau's critique and subversive possibilities are contained by his ongoing inscription within the doctrine of love. With Rousseau, we are not yet ready for the kind of democracy that Strong sees, for a transparency in which "I am the other." Such a sentiment still contains a very dangerous ambivalence for Rousseau, a threat and a need.

Rousseau himself points out why he is not yet a democratic thinker. He makes us aware of the fantasy, of the masquerade and the scandal which he participates in. Yet he retains hope that his masquerade will succeed, that he can have it all, despite the incoherence and suffering of liberal identity. Despite his secularization of Lockeanism, Rousseau remains very much animated by, if not faith, then hope, hope that "true" nature can be found despite the fact that he knows better, hope that he can have love without being compromised, hope that mother can become father, that he can be filled again with the love that was lost, the love that he is inadequate without.

Perhaps because of this hope, Rousseau remains suspended in the same trap that holds Locke; he can't go forward, renouncing the lost origin, but he can't go back either. I think that Rousseau's greatest gift to us is his despair and his doubt. He doubts the truth of nature. He doubts the possibility of freedom. He doubts himself. He doubts if all the sacrifices and hierarchies that are called for are justified. Although Rousseau, like Locke, is not unwilling to carve out a privileged space for himself, he recognizes the price that must be paid for his privilege, not only for those who must sacrifice themselves for him, but even for himself. He spells out the dangers and lures of *eros* benefit of *agape,* of the hollowed out subject forced to fill himself. Even as he offers us a beautiful vision of the "perhaps," Rousseau shows us the path *not* to take. We should heed his words carefully.

When we move from Locke and Rousseau, European social contract theorists during the early age of liberalism, to Emerson and Thoreau, nineteenth-century American writers, we see that, for all of their differences, the essential doctrines and dilemmas of love remain. The American transcendentalist movement, which both of these authors represent, was a refounding of the liberal self in its new American context. Transcendentalism was dedicated to giving Europeans a second chance for freedom in the New World. Accordingly, there was an explicit break with many of the old ways—principally with the ambivalent legacy of empiricism and with secularism itself. And yet, I will argue in the next two chapters, the fundamental problems that begin with Locke remain; we remain suspended between earth and heaven, inadequate, hollowed out, waiting to be filled and dreaming of our own power.

In many ways, Emerson is like Locke, masterful and confident, a man of supreme faith. For all his hierarchical tendencies, he too bears the same democratic dreams as Locke (and, at times, Rousseau as well), seeing in transparency the possibility of redemption. In many ways too, Thoreau's treatment of and problem with the question of freedom is astonishingly similar to Rousseau's. Like Rousseau, Thoreau insists on seeing for himself the price of liberal subjectivity; he sees how in seeking his own sense of self, he is choosing himself over others. And he, like Rousseau, is driven to despair by this realization. He too is a thinker who offers us his doubt.

So now we will reinvent the wheel, so to speak, moving on to Ralph Waldo Emerson and the refounding of the Lockean dilemma on new shores and during new times. And along with the tensions and doubts comes, as always, the "immense rumor," the ancient promise of *philia politike* reborn out of the ongoing conflicts of European (and European-American) subjectivity.

4

EMERSON'S CELESTIAL
DEMOCRACY

1. THE EMERSONIAN EYE

One of Emerson's best-known and most revealing passages can be found in the first of his two essays entitled "Nature" (written in 1836), where he writes:

> Crossing a bare common, in snow puddles, at twilight, under a clouded sky...I have enjoyed a perfect exhilaration.[1]

He goes on to say:

> Standing on the bare ground—my head bathed by the blithe air and uplifted into infinite space—all mean egotism vanishes. I become a transparent eyeball; I am nothing; I see all; the currents of the Universal Being circulate through me; I am part or parcel of God.[2]

This statement epitomizes an Emersonian transcendental moment. In his guise as this "transparent eyeball," Emerson has described a mood where he seems to no longer be himself.[3] Here we see, as with Rousseau, a desire for "nothingness" or transparency, for the overcoming of our selfhood as the basis for a return to our "true" nature.

Emerson seems to be entirely selfless at this moment, but we see that even in this transcendent state his self is not really extinguished, for he continues to narrate this passage in the first person: "*I* am nothing, *I* see all" (a statement that seems to both defy and support Cartesian logic). After all, Emerson doesn't say "all egotism vanishes" but "all *mean* egotism vanishes." Like Rousseau, even after his abandonment of his own identity, Emerson maintains a presence that continues to linger, to insist on its own selfhood despite the appearance of becoming resolved into something larger. There still remains some desire for substance, for an autonomous sense of self which persists. Such a remnant of self remains to narrate the extraordinary transformation of the self from a partial, problematic social being into something else.

What that something else is, Emerson makes clear in the preface which immediately precedes this passage:

LOVE IS A SWEET CHAIN

> Philosophically speaking, the universe is composed of Nature and the Soul. Strictly speaking therefore, all that is separate from us, all which philosophy distinguishes as the NOT ME, that is both nature and art, all other men and my own body, must be ranked under this name NATURE.[4] (his emphasis)

Thus, in contrast to the "not me," the "me" for Emerson is the original and true self, the soul, which we can experience only in these ecstatic moments of self-transparency. Everything else about us, our desires, our relationships, our own bodies, are "not me" and extraneous, part of the "mean egotism" which falls away. And we see here too that our own body, the source of our desires, is directly linked to "other men" as well as nature, a vast complex of otherness that exists within the subject as well as without. The original self is a celestial being, pure and unattached. By reducing himself to the "me," Emerson is free from dangerous associations with others, with his own body, and even with nature. He doesn't need his desires to be mediated by anyone. He doesn't seem to need love anymore.

Indeed, as this essay develops, we see that the transcendental moment involves an explicit break with human interactions:

> The name of the nearest friend sounds then foreign and accidental: to be brothers, to be acquaintances, master or servant, is then a trifle and a disturbance. I am the lover of uncontained and immortal beauty. In the wilderness, I find something more dear and connate than in streets or villages.[5]

For Emerson, a close relationship, even brotherhood, is a "disturbance," having nothing to do with his own transcendence.

Crossing this bare common, the Emersonian subject appears to have overcome the European dilemma, where desire, partiality, and the sheer crowdedness of Europe have reduced humans to an interdependent, non-autonomous mass. Whereas Emerson recognized that the very same phenomenon was occurring in Boston and New York and even Concord, he felt that it was still possible to be free in America. In America one could leave the teeming masses and come upon a bare common. It was still possible to achieve a transcendental moment where one could discover what one "was" (i.e., the "me") without recourse to the confused interplay of boundaries that characterized the life of society. Crossing this common, Emerson is finally free because he is alone; all other selves, all other perspectives of what he calls "that great defying eye" of the other, are gone.[6] Has he then rescued us, finally, from the embrace of love? Has he found a way to make us free?

The many moods of Emerson

In "Thinking of Emerson" and "An Emerson Mood," two essays which he appends to *The Senses of Walden,* Stanley Cavell offers us a valuable rethinking of

Emerson's writing. He considers the way in which Emerson's "epistemology of moods" reflects upon and departs from the Kantian (and generally liberal) understanding of experience, suggesting that Emerson himself is more progressive, more democratic than he first appears. Kant, despite his concern for what he saw as nihilism in the empiricist tradition, nevertheless insists that all that we can know of the world must be grounded in our experience. As we have seen, for Kant even metaphysics must reflect its empirical and human-centric basis, since the metaphysical realm is only produced as a "something" through an act of exclusion from the "world of sense."[7]

In this way, Kant is able to reintroduce a moral imperative without violating the sanctity of a human perspective. He allows for a valid position for human experience while simultaneously locating that value in a sense of "higherness" and externality.

For Cavell, Emerson offers a response to the Kantian notion of experience by taking a different position on what constitutes an experience in the first place. It is not so much that Emerson rejects Kantian empiricism as that he expands the ways in which we "experience experience" by including visitations of mood along with our other sensory inputs. In this way, Cavell tells us, for Emerson the world around us is no longer simply something "of my making," or a projection of our own partial understandings.[8] For Emerson "inevitably... the universe wears our color," and we wear its.[9] Moods come to us in a succession. They "take us over." We are as much framed by them as we serve as their author.

For Cavell, Emerson's notion of mood enables us to simultaneously be "ourselves," solipsistic and partial, and yet also part of something much larger; this is not Kant's "larger," which is our own projection into the universe, our own searching for the perspective of God, but rather something which is simply bigger than us, something we can only dimly comprehend. Cavell writes that through moods:

> we are in a state of "romance" with the universe (to use a word from the last sentence of "Experience"); we do not possess it, but our life is to return to it, in ever-widening circles, onward and onward, but with as directed a goal as any quest can have.[10]

Ultimately, Cavell tells us, it is not the *having* of moods, but their coming and going which establishes our sense of our self and our world for Emerson:

> This very evanescence of the world proves its existence to me; it *is* what vanishes from me. I guess this is not realism exactly, but it is not solipsism either.[11]

In such an evanescent world, we must not cling to the phenomena of the "not me" but rather, as Cavell tells us, abandon the world.[12] In this way, the transcendental subject achieves transparency, abandoning one notion of self in order to find another in the swirl and chaos of life; by leaving the world, his own self, and "all other men," he becomes filled up, given his substance through his connection with nature.

For Cavell, Emerson's notion of whim encapsulates the kind of self-reliant thinking that is the hallmark of this abandonment:

> I shun father and mother and wife and brother when my genius calls me. I would write on the lintels of the door-post, *Whim*. I hope it is somewhat better than whim at last, but we cannot spend the day in explanation.[13]

Cavell writes that statements such as these are "hard" sayings, but argues that it is "no harder than the fact that he is the one he is and that each of us is the one each of us is."[14] Whim here stands in for the honoring of one's own thoughts, following them where they lead, a precursor to Nietzschean perspectivism whereby whim becomes the means to "become what one is."

For Cavell, this act of abandonment does not preclude the possibility of "father and mother and wife and brother" also coming to their own self-reliance and their own whims. Each of us by virtue of being a self has the capacity for self-reliance and greatness. He quotes Emerson as saying:

> To believe in your own thought, to believe that what is true for you in your private heart, is true for all men—that is genius.[15]

Cavell offers a vision of Emersonian democracy whereby our individual genius does not come at anyone's expense. In this mood, we see Emerson as a deeply democratic thinker. His denigration of the masses means only that nobody should have to live as a part of a mass. Cavell tells us that Emerson, far from being an elitist, "embrac[es] the common," and "sit[s] at the feet of the low" and the "vulgar."[16] For Emerson, the "low" is not something to be overcome, but something to learn from and to cherish. In this vision we see a validation of difference and even serendipity. Validating "whim" as he does, Cavell suggests that with Emerson (and of course Thoreau as well) we find a doctrine that does not judge and rank us at all, but simply locates us in terms of our "nextness" and our neighborliness to one another and to ourselves.[17] The transcendental subject, while far from his neighbors and friends, is still spatially related to them, still "next" to them even when he is (metaphysically speaking) a million miles away.

Cavell's appreciation for Emersonian transcendence must be taken very seriously. He articulates the democratic possibility in Emerson and sees him as offering a deeply nuanced understanding of self and relationship that goes well beyond the promise of Kant. Yet if it is true that Emerson is a philosopher of moods, not all of his moods are quite so hopeful, quite so democratic. While appreciating and taking seriously those democratic aspects of Emerson, in this chapter I will argue that Emersonian transcendentalism still reveals its origins in and ongoing connection to the doctrine of love. We have seen the idea of abandonment before, in the insistence that our "true" self is not the one we occupy but the one that receives the universe and is open to God's love as *agape*. Understood in these terms, transcendence achieves its "self"-reliance through an act of surrender and abandonment, hollowing out the self.[18] Such abandonment is not yet what Cavell is looking for.

The question Cavell raises for both Emerson and Thoreau is whether the inadequacy of language, of meaning (of the "filledness" of words), is a cause for despair or for hope. With Emerson we are in a "romance" with the universe, because we want once again to feel and connect to that which we are in love with, that which gives us to ourselves. Kant, in his own attempt to colonize the transcendent from the perspective of human beings (his "scandal" or substitute, if you will), does not offer us this connection; it remains bound by the inherent problems of inadequacy. It seeks to reproduce the original through an act of substitution and thereby cannot succeed. Emerson on the other hand wants us to open ourselves up, to receive what is always "out there." And yet, for Cavell, Emerson too sees a limitation; our outermost circles grow distant and faint. Cavell writes: "That [the universe] has no more than I can give it is a fact that Emerson calls my poverty (other philosophers may speak of the emptiness of the self)."[19] Thus Emerson too offers a vision of inadequacy, of being suspended between two realms.

In this chapter, I will be both agreeing with and arguing against Cavell, and in a very different way, George Kateb and Judith Shklar as well, in order to show how Emerson's democratic moods cannot be divorced from other, darker moods, moods of inadequacy and unfilledness. I will attempt to show that these moods do not simply coexist but rather the democratic moods presuppose and build upon those less- or even undemocratic tendencies in Emerson's thought. As with Locke and Rousseau, we must not be too hasty in proclaiming the democratic potential in Emerson.

Accordingly, I will argue that Emerson's appreciation for the low and vulgar, while genuine and important, is not always all that different from Locke's—an appreciation for something which, when in its proper place, serves to advance the self to a higher, better position. The very use of terms like "low," "common," and "vulgar" suggests a complex and perhaps less than flattering relationship to what is to be appreciated. As I will argue throughout this chapter, Emerson's "appreciation" of the world at times serves to reinforce the basic hierarchies that Kant (and Locke) subscribes to, in which the common, vulgar, and low are not only below but also *worse* than the higher and better. And while Emerson does indeed often promote an idea of whim, he tells us himself that he hopes that it is more than that; whim itself is not Emerson's final goal. Indeed, there is another mood in Emerson which is almost hostile to whim, which insists upon a real sense of progress and hence reintroduces precisely those judgments and rankings which the idea of whim seeks to dissolve.

In terms of the political questions that arise from Emerson's work we see a similar disjuncture. While Emerson writes, often quite beautifully, of perfect friendship between two great friends, and hence promotes the possibility of equality that goes beyond reciprocity, we will also see that this friendship, like Aristotle's own notion, does not exist in a vacuum but presupposes an entire (and by now familiar) network of hierarchies, a lower to serve the higher, in order to produce and sustain it.

Ultimately, we will see that for all its promise, Emerson's notion of transcendentalism reproduces as much as it resolves the dilemma of love. His transparency reveals itself, like Rousseau's own version, to have smuggled in a perspective of privilege; his transparent eyeball, like Locke, achieves a state of "indifference," beyond all need and desire because of a prior network of hierarchy and dependency that vanishes along with the rest of the "not me," not to be annihilated but simply presupposed.

I read Emerson as a thinker and poet who seeks to return us to the romance of *eros* and *agape,* to the *caritas* synthesis itself; he is desecularizing love and delivering us from a profound and ongoing crisis. Yet Emerson's return to love cannot be complete; the self he inherits is already the liberal subject, self-regarding, unable and unwilling to give himself over absolutely. As such, the promise of Emerson comes with concomitant and familiar baggage; we see a profound struggle between democratic and hierarchical notions, a struggle we shall see even more starkly with Thoreau. Emerson's democracy works at the celestial level, at the level of the "me," where we are indeed all equal and all autonomous, but in terms of politics, the presupposed world of connections and relationships, Emersonian democracy must remain at the level of the "perhaps."

2. NATURE AND THE SELF

To establish these claims, we must begin by examining Emerson's understanding of nature. As we have seen, when he uses the term "Nature" he sometimes means different things. "Philosophically speaking," as we have seen, nature means the "not me"—that is, "both nature and art, all other men, and my own body." "Commonly speaking," on the other hand, nature means the physical things that exist outside of human art and society—trees, birds, mountains. However, these two terms are always interrelated; the nature "out there" in the woods and the nature in society and even within the self are all intimately connected, collectively serving as the grounds upon which the "me" distinguishes itself—it being the one category which is defined as not belonging to nature at all.

In considering the proper relationship of human beings and nature in its "common" form, Emerson is markedly different from Thoreau. Whereas Thoreau reveals a considerable interest in nature as a phenomenon separate from human agendas, with its own validity, for Emerson nature mainly serves to teach us what we are not.

Thoreau's interest in nature *qua* nature extended to the point where he, unlike Emerson, insisted on physically experiencing the wilderness, living in the woods at Walden Pond and going on long expeditions into the forests of Maine and Minnesota. In thinking about a life in the wilds such as Thoreau himself practiced, Emerson wrote:

> We think we shall be grand as [natural objects] if we camp out and eat roots, but let us be men instead of woodchucks, and the oak and the elm shall gladly serve us though we sit in chairs of ivory on carpets of silk.[20]

Because for Emerson nature is primarily a basis for transcendence, he is less appreciative of its untamed qualities as such.

Transforming the landscape

Even when he reveres nature, Emerson does not see it as the highest manifestation of God incarnate on earth. That honor goes to human beings, and nature is our servant:

> Nature is thoroughly mediate. It is made to serve. It receives the domination of man as meekly as the ass on which the Saviour rode. It offers all its kingdoms to man as the raw material which he may mould into what is useful. Man is never weary of working it up.... One after the other his victorious thought comes up with and reduces all things *until the world becomes at last only a realized will—the double of the man.*[21] (emphasis added)

This passage is critical to Emerson's understanding of the material world because it establishes an agenda: the realization of man's will in nature, not necessarily in terms of a literal transformation of the landscape, but insofar as each person is concerned. The world exists to show him who he is.[22]

The transparent eyeball that surveys all does not only look outward, but inward as well. Thus "[t]he lover of nature is he whose inward and outward senses are truly adjusted to each other."[23] For Emerson, we never lose the possibility of such "insight" and nature holds out a standard for us to surpass. In his second essay entitled "Nature," he states:

Man is fallen, nature is erect and serves as a differential thermometer, detecting the presence or absence of the divine sentiment in man. By fault of our dullness and selfishness, we are looking up to nature, but when we are convalescent, nature will look up to us. We see the foaming brook with compunction: if our own life flowed with the right energy, we should shame the brook.[24]

The animal and the rational eye

How can this redemption come about? How can we purify ourselves, distinguish ourselves from the "not me"? Emerson answers these questions once again using the motif of the human eye. He sees us as having two eyes occupying the same organ, one animal and one rational. The relationship between these two eyes forms the basis of our ability to see the truth and to know ourselves. For Emerson, the animal eye is the sensory eye, the eye of the "not me." It is the flesh organ itself which discerns material reality, partial and desirous. Suspicious as he is of empiricism, Emerson does not trust this eye, at least not when it is left to its own devices. The animal eye must be subsumed to the higher, rational eye (the eye of the "me"), which sees connections between the apparent randomness of phenomena in the world and can therefore discern to some degree the vastness of eternity through its myriad particular manifestations.

The rational eye, and in particular the eye of the poet, sees the unity of "the all." But for Emerson the rational eye is not possible without the animal eye as a base; he needs to be able to see here on earth in order to "see" what is in heaven. The animal eye contributes its share in the rational eye's ability to know and perceive:

Until this higher agency [the rational eye] intervened, the animal eye sees, with wonderful accuracy, sharp outlines and colored surfaces. When the eye of Reason opens, to outline and surface are at once added grace and expression. These proceed from imagination and affection and abate somewhat of the angular distinctness of objects. If the Reason be stimulated to more earnest vision, outlines and surfaces become transparent, and are no longer seen, cause and spirit are seen through them.[25]

The two eyes are symbiotic: Without the animal eye, the rational eye could not even exist; without the rational eye, the animal eye does not know what it is seeing.

Various natural phenomena (including "man-made" ones) induce the rational eye to develop from the animal:

Nature is made to conspire with spirit to emancipate us.... We are strangely affected by seeing the shore from a moving ship, from a balloon, or through the tints of an usual sky. The least change in our point of view gives the whole world a pictorial air.... What new thoughts are suggested by seeing a face of country quite familiar, in the rapid movement of a railroad car![26]

This new and different perspective Emerson calls a "low degree of the sublime."[27] It is part of the process of training the eye to transcend its animal origins going up the "ladder of being." Emerson's use of the term "low" in this case is telling. He sees this drawing out of the self as a necessary but insufficient basis for transcendence: "Beauty in nature is not ultimate. It is the herald of inward and external beauty."[28]

The change in vision leads to a change in our identity as well. Corresponding to the animal eye is "the aboriginal Self, on which a universal reliance may be grounded."[29] Frequently Emerson likens the aboriginal self to a state of childhood—as with Rousseau, it is an innocent and uncorrupted but unfulfilled state that inevitably must be overcome. As Emerson writes of children, "their eye is as yet unconquered."[30]

With each new child, Emerson holds out a hope, however slight, that they might avoid the same fate as his elders. As human beings, we inevitably develop a will of our own (a "divided and rebel mind").[31] The will, the source of our self-reliance, is also what corrupts us in the first place. Most of us will be led astray by our animal desires and remain aboriginal selves, unrealized "me"s. The lower desires, the animal eye, the aboriginal self, are like Locke's worker—something to be learned from, depended upon, but yet kept separate from the true owner of the self. To rely on them too heavily is to become mired in sensuality, in the "not me."[32]

The poet

For Emerson, although most of us remain part of "a mass" there are those who are attuned to nature and to the all. He writes that in "the thick darkness" of confusion there are "gleams of better light."[33]

Ultimately, he places his faith for our future redemption in a figure he calls "the poet":

> The poet, the orator bred in the woods, whose senses have been nourished by their fair and appeasing changes, year after year, without design and without heed—shall not lose their lesson altogether in the roar of cities or the broil of politics.... At the call of a noble sentiment, again the woods wave, the pines murmur, the river rolls and shines.... And with these forms, the spells of persuasion, the keys of power are put in his hands.[34]

What does the poet (Emerson himself?) have that no one else has? His is the most reasonable eye, the one least tainted by need and desire. He surveys the landscape without partiality. He can reconcile nature and art.[35] In a passage immediately following the one quoted above about the effects of technology on our vision, Emerson writes:

> In a higher manner the poet communicates the same pleasure. By a few strokes he delineates on the air, the sun . . . the city, the hero, the maiden, not different from what we know them, but only lifted from the ground and before the eye.[36]

The poet learns from and improves upon the ways that technology and beauty lift the vision of the eye. Unlike the rest of us, the poet can see beauty for what it is: a signpost pointing to the all, a harbinger of the infinite. He can love beauty and the "not me" without falling for its lures, without being defined by it. Rooted from his "infancy" as a woods dweller, the poet abstracts from nature. He sees "the world in God." An idealist, he:

> beholds the whole circles of persons and things, of actions and events, of country and religion not painfully accumulated, atom after atom, act after act, in an aged creeping past, but as one vast picture which God paints on the instant eternal for the contemplation of the soul.[37]

The poet sees Being itself, the "all-at-onceness" of the world, of time, and of space. In nature, he sees an "instant eternity," the relationship between the particular and "the all." The poet is our vehicle for our return to *agape*. He is Emerson's modern-day prophet. His power is entirely metaphysical in nature, but suggests too a great political possibility; to speak freely, to know the meaning of words, to locate a fact in its relation to eternity, to have access to truths and virtues which society is desperately in need of. Thus are the "keys to power" put into his hands.

Desire and the poet

As we have seen, what the poet negotiates better than the rest of us is his relationship with desire. As with Locke and Rousseau, Emerson is not ready to write off desire, however dangerous it might be. In "The Poet," for example, he writes:

> All the faces of the animal economy, sex, nutriment, gestation, birth, growth are symbols of the passage of the world into the soul of men, to suffer there a change and reap a new and higher fact.[38]

The poet, the transcendent figure himself, is not what he initially appears to be. He is not completely cut off from or indifferent to desire after all; he must engage with it in order to achieve transcendence itself. And because the poet's engagement with desire is not a one-time event but rather an ongoing process, he can't afford to rest on his laurels; he is, like Locke's subject, perpetually threatened by temptation, by backsliding.

Emerson writes in "The Poet" about the poet's use of "wine, mead, narcotics"[39] in order to escape his body and "that jail-yard of individual relations in which he is enclosed." He goes on to say:

> Hence a great number of such as were professionally expressers of Beauty, as painters, poets...have been more than others wont to lead a life of pleasure and indulgence; all but the few who received the true nectar; and it was a spurious mode of attaining freedom, as it was an emancipation not into the heavens but not the freedom of baser places, they were punished for that advantage they won by a dissipation and deterioration.[40]

Emerson admonishes us that "the sublime vision comes to the pure and simple soul in a clean and chaste body."[41] The poet is not constitutionally immune from the lures of beauty.

The transcendent mood

We can begin to see more clearly how Emerson's different moods might coexist with one another. The poet, who achieves a liberation from desire, and from the "not me," has done so by presupposing and subsuming those desires, not by actually ridding himself of them. He still sees with the animal eye—without it he could have no vision at all. He still occupies an aboriginal self—without it he could have no self at all. Despite portraying himself as a disembodied transparent eyeball, the "not me" in all of its forms is still there, still needed. And as such, the hierarchy between lower and higher remains. The whim and freedom of the self-reliant person is built on a series of prior and presupposed relationships.

This leads to questions that we have already seen with Locke and Rousseau, questions of autonomy and authenticity. If the "me" exists only in relationship to the "not me," what exactly is the substance of the "me"? In what ways does achieving the "me" make it "my own"? How can it be called "self"-reliant?[42]

Perhaps the poet can resolve these questions for us by showing that we are "both" animal and rational, united as part of "the all" (i.e., the *caritas* synthesis), that, as Cavell tells us, we are connected to the universe only by our experience of it. But for the poet himself, such a resolution seems elusive. He contains within him the tension between the "me" and the "not me." He is both human and tempted, in love with the beauty of nature even as he is also superhuman, chaste, and above the fray. As we will see, his is not an easy balance. Emerson tells us that "man is a golden impossibility. The line he must walk is a hair's breadth."[43] And he says further:

We may climb into the thin and cold realm of pure geometry and lifeless science or sink into that sensation. Between these extremes is the equator of life, of thought, of spirit of poetry, a narrow belt.[44]

This is once again the "Scylla and Charybdis" that Locke spoke of.

And even if the poet was never tempted, always in control, and even if the "Me" could be known against the "not me" (very big ifs indeed), it is not always clear that Emerson is willing to pay the price for such hierarchies or even for transcendence itself. In some sense, for Emerson as much as for Locke, part of what makes us free, part of what makes us important and "self"-reliant is precisely this animality, this "aboriginal" self that has the right to determine its own fate as it sees fit and without reference to higher truth. This tension becomes even more prominent in Thoreau, but Emerson does not ignore it entirely; we see in his calls for whim and even for democracy itself something that tugs him toward what he is overcoming, even as his belief in the higher requires him to move relentlessly on.

Far from being dispassionate about the elements he is treating fairly instrumentally in his search for the higher, Emerson is a man who struggles with himself ("I would write on the lintels of the door-posts, *Whim.* I hope it is somewhat better than whim at last"). He shows rare but important moments when he reveals his genuine love for nature *qua* nature, for the very sort of spontaneous, serendipitous way of life that he frequently preaches in his texts. In "Nature" (first series), he writes:

> I have no hostility to nature, but a child's love to it. I expand and live in the warm day like corn and melons. Let us speak her fair. I do not want to fling stones at my beautiful mother, nor soil my gentle nest.[45]

Throughout his texts, throughout his life, we see Emerson struggling with himself as he fights over this balance, claiming that "a self-denial no less austere than the saints is demanded of the scholar."[46] Mostly, he is a stern advocate for the dispassionate, lonely road. And yet he often regrets having to make the choices that he does. In "Experience," one of his most personal and reflective of essays, he writes:

> The life of truth is cold and so far mournful, but it is not the slave of tears contritions and perturbations. It does not attempt another's work, nor adopt another's facts. It is a main lesson of wisdom to know your own from another's.[47]

Emerson loves nature as something pure and true, and yet reviles it as a force of corruption, a tempting away from a higher path. Similarly he loves our will, our ability to be independent, and yet reviles it for what we have chosen to do with our unique gift. His ambivalence about the desirability of human agency and the question of freedom haunts his attempt to reconcile human beings with the world around them (and with each other). He remains bound by even as he struggles against the doctrine of love.

And this is where the political salience of Emerson's vision becomes important. If Emerson himself had his own doubts about himself, what of those "other men," those teeming masses who are "low" and "coarse" and "vulgar"? The transformation of the external world is one thing. When it comes to transforming the nature of human beings ("other men"), things get more complicated. Once relationships with other people are involved, the question of "high" and "low," the problem of the diversity of the human will, the question of whim itself, becomes not simply a philosophical matter but a question of democracy. But before we can discuss democracy, we must first discuss what for Emerson are its forerunners: romantic love and friendship, the bonds which both hold us together and threaten us.

3. ROMANTIC LOVE AND FRIENDSHIP: EMERSON AND HUMAN RELATIONSHIPS

Given the fact that the "not me" includes "other men," as well as nature and our own bodies, Emerson includes social relationships as a crucial part of the desires that the poet must interact with in order to achieve transcendence. In his book, *Society and Solitude,* he writes:

> The capital defect of cold, arid natures is the want of animal spirits.... Animal spirits constitute the power of the present and their feats are like the structure of a pyramid. Their result is a lord, a general, or a boon companion.... But this *genial heat* is latent in all constitutions and is disengaged only by the friction of society.[48] (emphasis added)

The poet cannot afford to remove himself from society lest he become, like Locke's automaton, a "cold, arid nature." But what of the danger that society poses to him? *Society and Solitude,* written in 1870 and toward the very end of Emerson's life, attempts to reconcile the need for society with the need for transcendence, abandonment, and isolation. Emerson writes:

> Nature delights to put us between extreme antagonisms, and our safety is in the skill with which we keep the diagonal line. Solitude is impracticable and society fatal. We must keep our head in the one and our hands in the other. The conditions are met, if we keep our independence, yet do not lose our sympathy. These wonderful horses need to be driven by fine hands.[49]

In his own life, Emerson found it difficult to achieve a proper balance between society and solitude. For all of his attempts to live on a most spiritual and intellectual plane, we must credit him with having been dedicated to his family and friends. And yet these relationships caused him much grief, especially because of the many deaths that he suffered.[50]

The two losses which pained him the most were undoubtedly that of his first wife, Ellen, and of his son, Waldo. Emerson's biographer Robert D. Richardson Jr. writes that with the loss of Ellen, Emerson began his lifelong devotion to the spiritual realm. According to Richardson:

> Her loss and the simultaneous spiritual crisis Emerson was undergoing constitute his second birth. Before this time Emerson was a rationalist who was fascinated but not wholly convinced by the truth of idealism. After this time Emerson believed completely, implicitly and viscerally in the reality and primacy of the spirit, though he was always aware that the spirit can manifest itself only in the corporeal world.[51]

If it is true that Emerson began to retreat from the sensual world, we see even in this description evidence of his recognition that this retreat could be only partial. As painful as the world was for him, it nonetheless provided the grounds for the spiritual world that he sought out.[52]

In "Experience," Emerson wrote about the loss of his son, Waldo Jr.:

> In the death of my son, now more than two years ago, I seem to have lost a beautiful estate, no more. I cannot get it nearer to me . . . [this calamity] does not touch me: some thing which I fancied was a part of me, which could not be torn away without tearing me, nor enlarged without enriching me, falls off from me, and leaves no scar.[53]

Tragically, he is both threatened by loss and unable to feel it. He feels both the pain of separation and the pain of self-denial. For all his urging of balance between society and solitude, Emerson seems at times to have received the worst of both worlds. On the one hand he complains that the life of an ascetic was "cold and so far mournful."[54] Yet in his essay "Love" he writes:

> It is strange how painful is the actual world—the painful kingdom of time and place. There dwells care and canker and fear.[55]

Romantic love

For Emerson, as for Locke and Rousseau, relationships go beyond a simple harnessing of heat, need, and desire. As with nature itself (narrowly conceived), "other men" (and women too) serve a yet higher purpose, to embody a grounds of contrast, to constitute a "not me," against which the "me" can know itself.

This can be clearly seen in Emerson's depiction of personal relationships, beginning with the most intimate of all, romantic love. In "Love," Emerson writes:

> We feel that what we love is not your will but above it. It is the radiance of *you and not you*. It is that which you know not in yourself and can never know.[56] (emphasis added)

By having a relationship with another person, the subject can begin to know about himself. Love for another teaches the subject about the "you and not you," which in turn teaches him about the "me" and the "not me."

In "Love," Emerson expands on how romantic love teaches us to become more than ourselves. He writes that the man in love "is twice a man"[57] and that love:

> makes the clown gentle and gives the coward heart. Into the most pitiful and abject it will infuse a heart and courage to defy the world. . . . In giving him to another, *it still more gives him to himself.* He is a new man with new perceptions, new and keener purposes, and a religious solemnity of character and aims. *He* does not longer appertain to his family and society. He is somewhat. *He* is a person. *He* is a soul.[58]

As with the relationship between the animal and the rational eye, love works its transformation by lifting the subject from his self-obsession, his utter partiality. For Emerson, romantic love is divisive. It separates us from ourselves by taking us out from our own animal preoccupations. Furthermore it separates us from our families and society by "giving us to ourselves." Rather than receive our sense of self from those around us, we simply respond to their being not us. We become open to "becoming who we are." This is the first step (and for most of us, the only step) toward *self*-reliance.

In discussing the love of a "maiden," Emerson writes, "Her existence makes the world rich . . . the maiden stands to him for a representative of all select things and virtues."[59] Such love isn't really about "the maiden" at all; she represents something larger and impersonal to him. Emerson notes that while the subject's friends see his object of love as looking like his mother or sister, for the subject himself she has no resemblance "except to summer evenings and diamond mornings, to rainbows and the song of birds."[60] His love for her draws him toward the all.

But, for all of its utility, the beauty of the beloved is not to be dwelt on overlong. As with the love of nature's beauty, to become too enamored of the maiden herself is to fail to realize the true purpose of desire:

> If however, from too much conversing with material objects, the soul was gross, and misplaced its satisfaction in the body, it reaped nothing but sorrow; body being unable to fulfill the promise which beauty holds out. . . . But if . . . the lovers contemplate one another in their discourses and their actions, then they

pass to the true palace of beauty.... The lover comes to a warmer love of these nobilities...he passes from loving them in one to loving them in all, and so is the one beautiful soul only the door through which he enters to the society of all true and pure souls.[61]

Romantic love takes us through a double movement from our animal self, to the other and then to the all, bringing us back to our "true" self. The other is merely a stepping stone on a higher path, one that we remain too close to at our peril.

For Emerson, romantic love is something that affects us all the same way; it is open to all of us and it doesn't matter if we are worthy of love; great or not great, requited or not requited, we all receive its grace. He insists that in this most intimate of experiences, we are all worthy of another chance to become more truly "ourselves," whether or not we succeed. By the time we come to a higher form of intimacy—friendship—Emerson has already begun to make stricter distinctions.

Friendship

Ultimately, for Emerson, romantic love itself has little to do with the higher truth:

Never can love make consciousness and ascription equal in force. There will be the same gulf between every me and thee, as between the original and the picture. The universe is the pride of the soul, all private sympathy is partial.[62]

For Emerson, romantic love gives us only a glimmering of ourselves but not a more solid picture; it exaggerates our virtues and underplays our faults. Friendship, on the other hand, because it is (at least relatively) above the carnal, because it is about the essence of a person and not their body is, if not divine itself, then at least more divine, higher than romantic love. But friendship too has a carnal origin, representing "love in the sexes," as he writes:

Of such friendships love in the sexes is the first symbol, as all other things are symbols of love. Those relationships to the best men, which at one time we reckoned the romances of youth, become, in the progress of the character the most solid enjoyment.[63]

As we see, Emerson locates friendship between two men as having its origin in "the romances of youth." This ties in with his own personal experiences, where, as a young man, he had at least one important same-sex crush, on a fellow student named (appropriately enough) Martin Gay. Richardson notes that Emerson experienced the glances that he exchanged with Gay as powerful invasions of his autonomy:

The glance thus exchanged was so significant, so striking that he remarked on it at the time. He spoke of eyetraps, and even constructed a sort of theory of 'the glance.' 'There are some occult facts in human nature that are natural magic,' he wrote. 'The chief of these is the glance (oeillade).'[64]

In thinking about these glances Emerson came to realize the power, the "differentness," of another person, the power and autonomy of their eye, of their gaze. Yet for all the power of this relationship, Emerson censored himself. When he wrote about Gay in his journals, he concealed his infatuation for him, crossing out or writing about his feelings in Latin.[65] In the tradition of a Derridean *sousrature*, Emerson preserves his same-sex desire even while he is in the process of denying it.

This might help explain Emerson's valuation of same-sex friendships thereafter. Unlike heterosexual love, for Emerson romance between the sexes (more accurately, between men) is checked by the homosexual taboo. From "the romances of youth" this friendship necessarily becomes "the most solid enjoyment." The carnality is repressed, harnessed early and totally, hence it becomes "solid." For Emerson, the friend can mediate our desires in a way that is safer, less likely to fail, than the lover.

And yet, although checked, the carnal desires in friendship remain at the heart of this solidity. In this sense friendship too poses a threat to the subject; it remains tainted by, even as it seeks to transcend, desire. Yet it is paradoxically the very mixture of attraction and repulsion, desire and control (or to use Emerson's terms "truth" and "tenderness"), which allows us to come the closest we ever will to seeing ourselves in our friend, precisely because of the mixture of difference and sameness which the relationship contains:

> A friend therefore is a sort of paradox in nature. I who alone am, I who see nothing in nature whose existence I can affirm with equal evidence to my own, behold now the semblance of my being, in all its height variety and curiosity, reiterated in a foreign form; so that a friend may well be reckoned the masterpiece of nature.[66]

Our friends must be what Emerson calls "a beautiful enemy, untamable, devoutly revered."[67]

Greatness and friendship

Emerson's model of friendship, like Aristotle's, suggests a model for democracy itself—a respect for distance and otherness, as opposed to the smothering sameness of love itself. George Kateb remarks in his analysis of friendship in Emerson that "friends are equal," evoking once again the possibility of Aristotle's *philia politike*.[68] But this friendship is a strange sort of equality. It is not a model of equality with any widespread political ramifications (certainly not for women!), for those worthy of being called friends are culled only from the highest (in the spiritual sense) circles. As with Aristotle, such friendship does not exist in a vacuum. It presupposes a great chain of other sorts of (unequal) relationships, "not me"s against which the "me" can define itself. As the animal eye stands to the rational eye, so too do the masses, the "not me" with their "genial heat," stand to the friends.

Ultimately for Emerson, true friendship is only possible between the great. A real spirit of equality is only possible between self-reliant men. As with Aristotle, these friendships are few in number. They are "[t]hose rare pilgrims whereof only one or two wander in nature at once."[69] This friendship *is* equal, but only because most relationships between people are not really friendships in Emerson's eyes. Between the great and the rest of us, there remains difference. The "not me"-ness of the masses is as necessary for the friends to know themselves as each is to the other.

And yet ultimately even this sort of friendship is not an end in itself. Emerson writes that "[t]he soul environs itself with friends so that it may enter into a grander self-acquaintance or solitude,"[70] and "[i]n the last analysis love is only the reflection of a man's own worthiness from other men."[71]

For Emerson, the friend is ultimately an instrument for one's own self-reliance; an instrument which can become an obstacle to further progress:

> Let us even bid our dearest friends farewell and defy them, saying "who are you? Unhand me; I will be dependent no more." Ah! seest thou not, O brother, that thus we part only to meet again on a higher platform, and only be more each other's because we are more our own?[72]

Thus Emerson sees even the friendship between the most self-reliant and great individuals as being a potential source of dependency. Even as he is another "me," the friend is also "not me," as far as the self is concerned.

Yet we see too that Emerson is not really willing to give up on the possibility of companionship.[73] He insists that by physically leaving the friend (perhaps forever), one can really come to them in a "truer" way—even though all of his language suggests the necessity of sending them away forever. He implies that the carnal roots of friendship can be overcome altogether, and friendship becomes a safe relationship within the "all." Can it be that two disembodied selves will haunt the "all" without conflict, sharing a single subjectivity? Can there be "one soul" with (or better yet without) "two bodies"? We see here, as we saw with Rousseau, a yearning for the lost origin to be replaced in the transcendent, transparent heights.

Even if such a resolution were possible, Emerson remains bittersweet about the costs of such an approach to friendship. Is such an abstracted friendship truly an adequate substitute for the flesh-and-blood relationship that is left behind? In one of his more candid moments in all of his works, he writes:

> It would indeed give me a certain household joy to quit this lofty seeking, this spiritual astronomy or search of stars, and come down to warm sympathies with you; but then I know well I shall mourn always the vanishing of my mighty gods. It is true, next week I shall have languid times, when I can well afford to occupy myself with foreign objects; then I shall regret the lost literature of your mind, and wish you were by my side again.[74]

Despite such sentiments, Emerson remains grimly resolute. Haunted by loss, by dead but not forgotten bodies, by cancelled desires and dangerous loves, he sees that our fate is to be alone. As if answering the question posed by Aristotle of whether two bodies can share a soul, he writes:

> The soul is not twin-born but the only begotten, and though revealing itself as a child in time, child in appearance, is of a fatal and universal power, admitting no co-life.[75]

If Emerson's vision of friendship begins with an invocation of *philia politike,* ultimately the doctrine of love demands that he not linger over it. If love asks us to look higher, to fill ourselves and our relationships with something beyond us, then even the most exalted friendships cannot be valued on their own terms; there can never be a moment when we say "this is good enough," never a valuation of human politics and community on their own terms. Ultimately, as we have seen, even the love of the neighbor must become seen as a reflection only of a much higher and much greater love: "O my friends, there is no friend."

Friendship and social hierarchy

When we look at relationships that are not friendships for Emerson—unequal relationships, between men and women, between greater and lesser men—we see the political ramifications of love even more clearly than with friendship itself. If the democratic potential in friendship is compromised by love, what of other relationships? Can "other men" (including women) provide their "genial heat" to the poet as self-reliant and transcendent beings in their own right (where, as Cavell suggests, we are all partaking of "genius" to some extent)? Can we all be great, all be poets, if not today then someday?

As ever, the answer must remain at best as a "perhaps." The greatest obstacle, as in the case of friendship itself, is the question of substance, of our inadequacy and lacking as a foundational principle of the doctrine of love. As we have seen, the friends are distinguished and equal to one another by their greatness. But even between them, Emerson demands distinction, resistence, and distance. In "Friendship," Emerson writes:

> The only joy I have in his being mine, is that the *not mine* is *mine*. It turns the stomach, it blots the daylight where I look for a manly furtherance or at least a manly resistance, to find a mush of concession. Better to be a nettle in the side of your friend than his echo.... There must be very two before there can be very one.[76]

Manhood for Emerson is predicated on the search for substance. He writes in "Character" that "a man should give us a sense of mass."[77] A man knows himself by what he isn't, a "solidity" instead of a "mush," even as, in some sense, the solidity is predicated on its own repression of "mushiness." It is worth considering the degree to which Emerson links "manliness" to the repression of homoeroticism. If homoeroticism is the desire (or tenderness) that is held in check as the basis of friendship between men, then male effeminacy is the failure to adequately negotiate between truth and tenderness. The effeminate man loves the body of the other (man) instead of loving those virtues that he represents. Instead of serving as the basis of a "most solid enjoyment," effeminacy results when mushy schoolboy crushes are never overcome (a fate that is clearly more dangerous for Thoreau than for Emerson). Given that a man is not only situated above, but in some sense defined against, the populace, Emerson expects that such a man will constantly be under attack. He writes in "Self-Reliance" that "society everywhere is in a conspiracy against the manhood of every one of its members,"[78] and that

> For non-conformity the world whips you with its displeasure.... It is easy enough for a *firm man* who knows the world to brook the rage of the cultivated classes. Their rage is decorous and prudent, for they are timid, as being very vulnerable themselves. But when to their feminine rage the indignation of the people is added, when the ignorant and the poor are aroused, when the unintelligent brute force that lies at the bottom of society is made to growl and mow, it needs the habit of magnanimity and religion to treat it godlike as a trifle of no concernment.[79] (emphasis added)

This is a dark but revealing mood for Emerson. I see in this passage a social analysis that is remarkably similar to Locke. The urban masses (a category which must be kept distinct from the yeomen farmers who I will discuss shortly), like Locke's workers, have little to no opportunity to discern the truth. Their rational eye is largely undeveloped and they are themselves almost like animals—hence their "growling" and "mowing." As for the rest of society, they divide into the effete, cultivated class of men who appear to have settled for sensuality at the price of their potential manhood with their "feminine rage"(much like what Locke called the depraved), and the "firm men" themselves (the rational subjects) who somehow manage to successfully negotiate the golden impossibility of manhood.

The hermaphroditic subject

For Emerson, the contentious relation between unequal subjects has its mirror in an internal struggle between our own unequal aspects, making the question of substance and identity even more complicated. In "Character," he writes:

> Everything in nature...has a positive and a negative pole. There is a male and a female, a spirit and a fact, a north and a south. Spirit is the positive, the event is the negative.... The feeble souls are drawn to the south or negative pole.... They do not wish to be lovely but to be loved.[80]

George Kateb calls this Emerson's doctrine of hermaphroditism. This is a vision of two opposite forces (or sexes) living within each person in a sort of permanent contest. We see that for all persons there are two possibilities. One can exist dominated by the feminine, negative pole and thus be effeminate if one is male (or a "lady," I suppose, if one is female). Or one can be dominated by the positive masculine pole—a "firm man" if one is a male or perhaps even if one is biologically a woman (a statement which is only a slight exaggeration of some of Emerson's journal entries from which Kateb quotes regarding this idea, including backhanded compliments like "Thus Mrs. B. is a man").[81] In either case, it is those dominated by the masculine pole that are "great" and have substance, while the rest of us are "feeble souls."

Kateb argues that this vision contains within it the possibility of an emancipatory idea of women's nature (and I suppose of men's as well) in that Emerson goes beyond a simple biological determinism, although he concedes that he "loosens but does not abandon" such categories.[82] To back this claim up, Kateb cites Emerson's claim that "in both men and women [there is] a deeper and more important *sex of mind*, namely the inventive or creative class of both men and women, and the uninventive or accepting class."[83] This is to say that since both men and women are hermaphrodites, either sex has the opportunity to have the "masculine" pole dominate; thus we can all be self-reliant. Kateb further argues that the negative or female pole is not "evil" for Emerson but valid in its own right.

For Kateb then, Emerson is radical because "the independent mind has no categorical fixity."[84] That is, one's sex in and of itself does not determine the chance for greatness. But if women can only be valued insofar as they "think like men," and if men are feeble and effeminate if they "think like women" or have "feminine rages," then the original subjugation of female to male, the essential core of the gender subjugation system, remains intact and preserved at the heart of this "new" idea of gender. Self-reliance and even whim must be contained within the behaviors prescribed by this internal hermaphroditic hierarchy.

Kateb writes that it is "unfortunate" that Emerson seems to "place the masculine above the feminine" and that he "assume[s] that the good hermaphroditic opportunity is for men, not women."[85] But the important point to grasp is that it is not just "unfortunate" that the feminine is subordinate, but absolutely essential to Emerson's system. The masculine pole must be based on top of the feminine for Emerson's entire system to function. It can only exist, only know itself as the masculine, exactly because it has this "other" pole, this lower and *worse* feminine below it from which to distinguish itself. Even before men come to know themselves against their effeminate counterparts and even before the great know themselves against the masses, within each of us our better parts know themselves only against our worse parts. As we have already seen, manhood (and womanhood too) is not so much a state of substance as it is a mirror reflection of what it is defined against.

These internal and external differences keep the self going on his path upward. The animal growling and feminine rage of the feeble and the urban masses are very much part of what keeps the man on the narrow path that he must exercise. And "Men" also need "Women" to define themselves against; gender itself is conceived of in this system as a state of engaging with and overcoming desires. Women (of both sexes) embody the lower position of this hierarchy.[86]

What are the political consequences of such a view of self and society? What can the relationship be between the great and the rest, between men and women? In this mood, it seems unlikely that Emerson can offer us even a vision of tutelary democracy where the great show everyone else how to realize their potential. The struggle and threat between the great and the many, between the masculine and feminine poles, is not a temporary state but an ongoing element in the subject's move toward transcendence.

One essay in which a vision of permanent and Aristotelian hierarchy is particularly clear is entitled "Manners." In this essay, Emerson quite explicitly considers how the great and the non-great can relate to one another. Here he breaks with his usual assault on opinion and fashion to put forth the notion that manners are in fact a means by which the greatness of the great can be communicated to the masses of society:

> Fashion, though in a strange way, *represents all manly virtue.* It is virtue gone to seed: it is a kind of posthumous honor. It does not often caress the great, but the children of the great.... Great men are not commonly in its halls...they are working not triumphing. Fashion is made up of their children, of those, who, through the value and virtue of somebody which secures to them...if not the highest power to work, yet high power to enjoy.[87] (emphasis added)

Emerson goes on to say that fashion, and indeed aristocracy, are "inevitable." Sounding very much like Plato in his myth of the metals, Emerson says:

> Each returns to his degree in the scale of good society, porcelain remains porcelain, and earthen. The objects of fashion may be frivolous, or fashion may be objectless but the nature of this union and selection can be neither frivolous nor accidental. Each man's rank in that perfect graduation depends on some symmetry in his structure, or some agreement in his structure to the symmetry of society.[88]

Ultimately, fashion becomes a vehicle whereby the learning of the self-reliant becomes the dogma of the many, for "there is almost no kind of self-reliance, so it be sane and proportioned, which fashion does not occasionally adopt."[89]

Emerson's elitist tone needs to be qualified: He takes care to note that "The persons who constitute the natural aristocracy, are not found in the actual aristocracy, only on its edge."[90] His hierarchy is based on merit, not birth, and it is not a question of material success, of property or ownership, but of self-reliance itself. And yet if the "me" requires the "not me" to know itself, is it not the case that one understanding of hierarchy has been replaced with another?

Can such a "trickling down" of manners lead the many to be self-reliant? As we have already seen with Locke and Rousseau, for Emerson the essence of self-reliance is to be able to figure things out for oneself. The masses receive these gifts wholesale and are not taught to reason on their own. Instead, this is another version of an Aristotelian society whereby greatness is conferred vicariously from top to bottom.

Such fashion constitutes a loving relationship, uniting the community even while it presupposes hierarchy:

> All individual natures stand in a scale according to the purity of this element in them. The will of the pure runs down from them into other natures as water runs down from a higher into a lower vessel.[91]

Human potential is fully realized for Emerson by the few great men in society. They do a better job, it would seem, of realizing the human spirit than any of the rest of us ever could:

> The poet is representative. He stands among partial men for the complete man and appraises us not of his wealth but of commonwealth. The young man reveres men of genius because to speak truly, *they are more himself than he is.*[92] (emphasis added)

Since most of us are "partial men," it falls to the great (and complete) man to represent the lost potential in the many. They stand as the purest of "me"s, emblematic of the many other "me"s that are not realized, that remain determined by their own "not me." Their "pure" will stands for and fills in the fallen wills of the masses themselves.

"Manners" suggests at the very least one end of a spectrum that determines Emerson's thoughts on democracy. As we have already seen, he is a harsh critic of following opinion, as it limits the self's ability to think autonomously. In fact, he ends this section of musing on fashion by baldly stating:

> But any deference to some eminent man or woman of the world forfeits all privilege of nobility. He is an underling; I have nothing to do with him: I will speak with his master.[93]

When we look at his notions of manhood and substance, at the relationship between the great, the poets, and the masses, we come to the core of Emerson's undemocratic mood.[94] But what then of Cavell's vision? What of *philia politike*? Emerson is widely considered to be and called himself a democrat. What sort of democratic polity, if any, can he offer us? How do his democratic moods sit with sentiments such as these? Can Emerson's vision ever be more than a "perhaps"?

4. SELF-RELIANCE AND DEMOCRACY

In addition to Cavell himself, who I will refrain from contending with for now, there are two important thinkers who have helped set the stage for how we come to terms with Emerson's democratic tendencies, namely George Kateb and Judith Shklar. Both of them write from a liberal perspective. Kateb in particular is optimistic about the ways that Emerson can help us understand how the self can be preserved and unthreatened in the context of society, while Shklar is somewhat more critical.

In *Emerson and Self-Reliance,* Kateb argues that proper understanding of Emerson's concept of self-reliance takes us a long way in the search for democratic individualism. He states that for Emerson, self-reliance is more of a method than any particular sort of ideology. Similar to Cavell's analysis of Emerson as a writer of moods, Kateb's arguement is that Emerson's famously contradictory writing style is the result of the fact that at different times he tries on different versions of the truth (i.e., whims). For Kateb, Emersonian self-reliance involves sitting with an idea, and judging for oneself whether it is ultimately truthful or not, much as one might try on several pairs of shoes to find the one that fits best. The key point is to avoid the influence of commonly held opinion or the beliefs of other people who might interfere with your own thinking. Even if you end up agreeing with them, you must come to this conclusion on your own.

And, like Cavell, Kateb also appreciates a kind of abandonment that takes place in Emerson's work. He has invented a term, deindividualization, to describe Emerson's vision of the individual finding the truth via connecting to "the all." As with Rousseau, deindividualization involves abandoning one's own particularity in order to rediscover the true self that lies beneath it. In thinking about this process, Kateb sees Emerson's relationship between the "me" and the "not me" in a far less problematic light than I have. Rather than seeing this relationship as an inevitable and permanent source of conflict, Kateb imagines it as precisely that which can reach across the "innavigable sea" between each of us and connect us without violating the safety of our boundaries. For Kateb, Emerson's understanding of the connection between the "me" and "not me" is the essence of what is attractive about his vision of politics. According to him, for Emerson, the only way to connect with the entirety of the "not me" is by leaving the specific confines of our bodies, our relationships and entanglements with the world. As Kateb puts it:

> Only [by deindividualizing ourselves]...can the observer individualize the world: change it in thought from masses to individuals. One mitigates one's own identity to make room for the identity of other particular persons, creatures, and things. Impersonality is a kind of selflessness, which allows what is outside oneself to fill one's inner space, and which prepares the way for piercing and expressing the identity of the otherwise indistinct or unappreciated.[95]

Thus we see here that the process of transcendentalism, the leaving of the body to become "all eyeball," is in fact the centerpiece of what Kateb sees as vital to Emerson's vision of democracy. The "filling in" of the self, rather than being a problem, delivers us to common life, making us able to coexist. Issues that might lead to selfishness, struggle, and anger when understood from our own limited perspective can be resolved at the transcendental level because, just as with Rousseau, this is a space where we are "all part of the all."

Before going on to critique this interpretation of Emerson as a visionary who resolves the individual's conflict with society, I'd like to take issue with part of Kateb's analysis of Emerson at the most fundamental level: his understanding of Emerson's methodology. As we have seen, Emerson's appreciation for "whim" is heavily qualified. Particularly in his less democratic moods, I don't see him as trying on different ideas to see how they work for him. Rather, as I've already suggested with Cavell, I find Emerson often to have a strong sense of moral direction; there is a real "up" and a real "down" for him; without these, the world deteriorates into void and chaos. The self-reliant mind is not expected to discover, for example, that "drinking wine is better than poetry" or that "effeminacy is better than manhood." Emerson's "contradictoriness" for me is much more about how hopeful he is regarding the outcome of his strongly held goals than a serendipitous trying on of different views. The self-reliant mind must be nimble, and must not stay for too long on any perch. This may look like serendipity (or whim) to Kateb, but in my opinion it is more likely a way to keep the mind sharp for its constant movement upward.

Does Emerson love the vulgar?

Even the most enthusiastic promoter of Emerson's democratic possibility must contend with his language, which, as we have already seen, is often (although by no means always) quite elitist in tone. Kateb discusses one instance in the essay "Self-Reliance," where Emerson writes:

> As soon as the man is at one with God, he will not beg. He will then see prayer in all action. The prayer of the farmer kneeling in his field to weed it, the prayer of the rower kneeling with the stroke of his oar, are true prayers heard throughout nature, though for *cheap ends.*[96] (emphasis added)

Kateb is disturbed by the contention that self-reliance, when expressed as physical labor instead of as thought, appears to Emerson to have "cheap ends." Kateb writes of this:

> Just as steady as Emerson's praise of vocation is his dismay at most occupations. We thus come up against a major obstacle in our efforts to see the essence of self-reliance as a principle of action.... He can go only so far in investing daily work, even when undertaken as prayer, with...dignity.... The abrupt phrase "though for cheap ends"...is indicative of Emerson's attitude.... Emerson sees the coarseness, not only the sincerity.... He labors to love labor and succeeds partly.[97]

Kateb tries to resolve this by showing that physical or "active" self-reliance is modeled on mental self-reliance. Mental self-reliance is more "pure" because, remaining at the level of internal thought, it does not bring in all of the conflicts that come with social interaction. Although Kateb contends that self-reliance works better at a mental level, he will not give up on active self-reliance; this, after all, is the realm of politics itself.[98] Although it bothers him (and to his credit, he points out its occurrence), Kateb has no choice but to discount the gravity of Emerson's denigration of necessity and his use of words like "cheap" or "coarse" or "low."

We must ask whether those who practice self-reliance for "cheap ends" are or could be equal to those who practice a higher mental self-reliance. How does this yardstick of higher and lower translate into political terms?

Kateb contends with this issue often and in various ways. He seeks to deal with the problem of hierarchy in Emerson by claiming, as Emerson often does himself, that difference can and must be the basis of any democratic society. Kateb includes a quote from Emerson to stake this claim:

But there remains the indefeasible persistency of the individual to be himself.... Every mind is different; and the more it is unfolded, the more pronounced that difference.... And what is originality? It is being, being one's self, and reporting accurately what we see and are.[99]

It is indeed desirable that democracy be based on difference, but the question is whether the differences between members exist in a hierarchical order to one another. If they do, then the value of each member will be found in accordance with their rank in the hierarchy in both a political as well as "personal" manner. I don't see these words of Emerson as necessarily serving as a manifesto of democracy, or of the possibility or desirability of difference as the cornerstone of democracy. One's reading of this passage may depend on Emerson's mood. The very difference that Emerson praises could itself be a model for an inherently hierarchical system. "Being one's self" might mean something like, "I'm great and you aren't great. Therefore I am better than you/therefore I know the truth in a way that you cannot (if not an absolute than in a relative sense)."

The critical question to ask here is, "Given the things that are different about us, what are the things that link and unite us, that make us a viable and equitable political community whereby each of us has something to offer that is not ranked but simply accepted?" How can we make our "originality" the basis of a democratic polity? Simply thinking that the low (or as we saw earlier, the "female pole") is not evil, and has a valid position in society, does not in itself constitute a democratic viewpoint.

Kateb seeks to make a place for each of us through Emerson's concept of vocation, which is reminiscent of Luther's notion of the calling. For Kateb, the concept of vocation (the physical manifestation of "being one's self") is central to his notion of active self-reliance. The vocation that each person chooses links them into a collective (and hence political) web of meaning. Through private property, through self-ownership, each person, each self-reliant individual:

cannot be dependent on the contributions or services of others to such an extent as to be unable to reciprocate. The needy cannot seem to render service, direct or indirect. There must be moral equality otherwise there would not be democratic individuality.[100]

Kateb cites many passages of Emerson to show that there is a sort of grace in self-reliance as a vocation, a connection to "the all" even in the most basic and coarse ways of life. To the degree that anyone is self-reliant in any way, those following their vocation partake in that grace and thereby partake in some worthy vision of political community.[101]

But if action is somehow "dirtied" by a connection to the earth, can this really be a source of meaningful democratic principles? Emerson suggests a tension between poets and laborers, for example, when he writes

> Is not the landscape every glimpse of which hath a grandeur, a face of [God]? Yet this may show us what discord is between man and nature, for you cannot freely admire a noble landscape if laborers are digging in the field hard by. The poet finds something ridiculous in his delight until he is out of the sight of men.[102]

If desire is dangerous as well as necessary, if dwelling on beauty, and working with the land, are embodiments of precisely that which must be overcome, how could such duties also be taken as valid endeavors in and of themselves? Must we read so hard against the text? Emerson tells us that labor is "sublime" but also "low." Clearly it *is* valid, but only in terms of its position in the social division of labor, in the hierarchy it perpetuates.[103] Thus although even the farmer with cheap ends achieves a "low degree of the sublime," he also achieves lowness in general in his life.

Emerson, as Kateb admits, "labors to love labor," and although he "succeeds partly," he does not succeed to the point that there is a meaningfully political vision of non-hierarchicalism operative in his political vision. And here I've made this argument in looking at a group he favors (however much with a backhanded compliment): farmers. When we think about Emerson's view of the masses with their "animal growls" and "feminine rages," the issue only seems to become more problematic.

The inhibition of democracy

We have been dwelling on Emerson's darker moods, but as we have seen he has other, more progressive moods as well. For all his problematic understanding of the masses, for all of his promotion of greatness, Emerson nonetheless remains committed to a democratic polity. How do his love of greatness and his democratic tendencies coexist? Here we turn to the ideas of Judith Shklar, who deals directly with Emersonian ideas of greatness and its relationship to the masses, particularly in her article entitled "Emerson and the Inhibitions of Democracy."

For Shklar, there is a clear tension in Emerson between his acceptance of democratic ideals on the one hand, and his suspicion of the effects of a democratic polity on the other. For all of this tension, Shklar accepts that his commitment to democracy is genuine. She reminds us of his great respect for the yeomen farmers of Vermont and New Hampshire, his frequent and genuine praise for the "greatness" of simplicity, even of poverty. But why then, if greatness can be found among the poorest of the poor, does greatness (or even humanity) seem to recede among the masses in general, and in the "animal" urban lower-class masses in particular? Shklar writes that for Emerson "most people are simply too timid and too dependent to try [for greatness], especially in the big cities."[104]

Even if Emerson's writings tend to suggest that the low are a permanent underclass, Shklar writes that "what Emerson could not get himself to say was the great are absolutely different and better within their sphere. That was the inhibition of democracy."[105] She concludes that Emerson's commitment was such that he was willing to tolerate the unfortunate aspects of democracy—its leveling nature, its cheapness—as the price to be paid for a democratic polity.

Seeing Emerson as having at best a grudging respect for democracy already takes us past Kateb's view of Emerson's democratic potential. But Shklar's contention that there could be some kind of functional balance between Emerson's "moods" must be carefully considered. Can a theory of greatness and a desire for democracy be reconciled at all? An argument could be made (one that Kateb and Shklar both imply at points) that whereas Emerson has given up on "the masses" of Boston and New York, he retains hope for the unity of greatness and democratic spirit among the yeomen farmers of Vermont and New Hampshire. As Shklar writes, these farmers were for Emerson "no less than for Jefferson before him the embodiment of democratic ideals."[106] Couldn't one argue then that the yeomen farmers are proof that for Emerson, democracy and greatness are compatible, that the many can each be great in their own terms if only we had a country exclusively composed of such people?

Let us move past the obvious criticism that we don't and never really did have such a country and take this claim seriously.[107] It is certainly true that Emerson praised the yeomen farmers for their self-reliant qualities. His great love for their simplicity and purity is one of the things that redeems him from seeming a true elitist. Yet his admiration for the yeomen farmers is not unlike his admiration for all simple states, such as childhood, a nostalgia, a desire to hold on to a way of life that by definition cannot be maintained. In this sense it is not unlike Rousseau's own nostalgia for the "Golden Age." Consider for example this quote from Emerson's chapter entitled "Farming" from his book *Society and Solitude.* He writes:

> The great elements with which [the farmer] deals cannot leave him unaffected... their influence somewhat resembles that which the same Nature has on the child—of subduing and silencing him.... [The farmer] changes the face of the landscape.... [H]e stands well on the world—as Adam did, as an Indian does.... He is a person whom a poet of any clime...would appreciate as being really a piece of the old nature...because he is, as all natural persons are, representative of Nature.... That uncorrupted behavior which we admire in animals and in young children belongs to him.[108]

Most of this chapter on farming shows how the farmer improves on nature, learns from it, and is in turn the inspiration for science. There is a progressive development in this chapter, beginning with the "first planter, the savage," who is a "a poor creature; he scratches with a sharp stick.... He falls and is lame,"[109] whereupon "The Indian...is overpowered by the gaze of the white and his eye sinks."[110] After the elimination of the Indian comes the yeoman farmer. Even he is "a piece of old nature"—that is, of the "not me," and, by implication, a further development to higher levels yet. Here again we see how for Emerson the natural serves as a building block upon which the higher can be established.

Emerson praises the farmer for his simplicity, but also describes him as "primitive" and argues that he "represents the necessities."[111] For all of his nostalgia, one does not get the feeling that Emerson would be content to return America to its "past" as a nation of yeomen farmers. We have already seen his denigration of going "back to the woods" like Thoreau. Emerson accepts the railroad and the factory as reconcilable with nature through the intervention of the poet. The progress of the human race toward a higher end demands that we move away from this simple, albeit pure point of origin.

As we have already seen, when Emerson praises the yeoman farmer, it is with a certain reserve, as when he writes in "Self-Reliance" that the farmer kneeling in his field is involved in a kind of prayer, "though for cheap ends." This line troubled Kateb, for good reason. Why would Emerson's model of a democratic subject have "cheap ends"? The essence of the yeoman farmers can serve as a model for greatness, but are they themselves are too compromised by their relationship to necessity, to the earth itself.

An alternative argument could also be made in reconciling Emerson's love of greatness and his democratic tendencies: He is seeking not just individual greatness but the greatness of an entire people, the greatness of America. To the degree that each person in America participates in that greatness by virtue of their participation in its society, one could say that "greatness is democratized." Emerson can and often has been accused of strong nationalistic fervors, praising the "Anglo-Saxon" race at the expense of others. The great, as "representatives" of our nationhood, make our nation a great place that all of us then can, in our own way, help to fulfill and express. Meanwhile, the masses do their part in national greatness by supporting the great.

Emerson may indeed have occasionally thought along these lines. Yet if his idea of self-reliance is to mean anything at all, the notion of collective greatness is one that he must be ultimately dissatisfied with. It is clear that for him, if anything is true, it is that the benefits he looks for are for the sake of individuals, not for society itself (the very use of his derogatory concept of "the masses" suggests as much).[112] As he writes: "Progress is not for society. Progress belongs to the Individual."[113] There is thus no necessary connection between the greatness of America and the greatness of its individual citizens.

We see then that it is rather difficult to reconcile greatness and democracy after all. In suggesting that there is an opposition between them, I am not trying to make an argument for some kind of human leveling. I am not arguing that a society that views a musician like Mozart or an author like Shakespeare as "great" cannot therefore practice democracy. Rather, I am taking issue with the idea of what greatness means, what its political salience is. With Emerson we get the sense that greatness is not something we confer on one another, but rather is received in accordance with our "higherness." Shklar herself concedes that "[Emerson] *did* believe in something more, in an Eternal Cause, a supersensible Nature, an intimation of another World."[114] In the same way that Emerson's support for whim is predicated upon having our whims serve in the purpose of our higherness, the idea of greatness too presupposes an orientation toward an external yardstick of judgment.

If the idea of greatness was not politically salient for Emerson, it might not matter so much how he thought about it; it is certainly possible to be culturally elitist and still be committed to democratic principles. Indeed, this is the portrait of Emerson that Shklar promotes. But for Emerson the question of greatness, of genius, *is* explicitly political. At the end of "Experience," furnishing the notion of romance that Cavell draws upon in his own explication of Emerson's work, Emerson writes:

> [T]he true romance which the world exists to realize will be the transformation of genius into practical power.[115]

Emerson's appreciation for greatness therefore is not merely cultural or philosophical; any tension between his appreciation for genius and his democratic spirit is not merely an issue of taste or belief, but points to serious questions when it comes to thinking about the implementation of an Emersonian political vision.

God and genius

If it is so difficult to reconcile democracy and greatness, why would Emerson choose democracy in any form at all, given his apparent contempt for the masses? Why not openly advocate for a meritocratic hierarchy?

In my mind, the answer lies in Emerson's religious nature. Certainly he was an ardent foe of most organized religion. This represented for him just one more way that opinion is dictated to us, one more way that the masses are rendered without a will of their own. But there is no doubt that Emerson was a deeply religious man. The entirety of his transcendentalism, his vision of redemption, his entire notion of progress, all are deeply informed by a notion of divinity, and, with it, his acceptance of the doctrine of love. It is his through his own homegrown religion that he comes to accept and advance the cause of democracy.

Why would such a believer in "natural aristocracy," in "higher" and "lower" truths, hold democratic principles unless he was motivated by a belief in the soul (in the "me"?) which exists even in the most wretched of vehicles? Remember that for Emerson the truth, the highest order, is not to be found in the visible but in the invisible world. Ultimately our various differences, questions of whether we are made of porcelain or earth, are unimportant. Rather, what matters about each of us is that we have a soul. Thus when Shklar writes that for Emerson the "the qualities that truly distinguish us are not those that are available to only exceptional individuals [i.e., the great] but those which we can all potentially achieve,"[116] I agree, but see that what is "best" about us for Emerson is that most abstract, least political of concepts, the soul itself. In "The Over-Soul," he writes:

> All goes to show that the soul in man is not an organ, but animates and exercises all the organs; is not a function, like the power of memory...but uses these as hands and feet; is not a faculty but a light; is not the intellect or the will, but the master of the intellect and the will;— is the vast background of our being, in which they lie,—an immensity not possessed and that cannot be possessed.[117]

Emerson writes that "in their habitual and mean service to the world...[souls] resemble those Arabian sheiks who dwell in mean houses and affect an external poverty."[118] Similarly, from the perspective of the soul, genius is nothing special, rather it is a reflection of the truth and beauty of the all, of God. Emerson seeks democracy because he loves us as he loves God:

> The same Omniscience flows into the intellect and makes what we call genius. Much of the wisdom of the world is not wisdom.... Among the multitude of scholars and authors...we are sensible of a knack and skill rather than inspiration; they have a light and know not whence it comes and call it their own.... But *genius is religious. it is a larger imbibing of the common heart.* It is not anomalous but more like and not less like other men.[119] (emphasis added)

Here then we find a strong statement of non-hierarchicalism and of genius. But note that this sort of language comes only when considering humanity at its most abstract, sublime level. The passage goes on to discuss the merits of Homer and Shakespeare, but to offer that even "the lowly and simple" can and do participate in the "energy" of the divine.

This celestial, divine community manifests itself in the world, particularly through its earthly corollary, love:

> Here is the use of Society: it is so easy with the great to be great; so easy to come up to an existing standard—as easy as it is to the lover to swim to his maiden through waves so grim before. The benefits of affection are immense; and the one event which never loses its romance is the encounter with the superior person on terms allowing the happiest intercourse.[120]

Here, in one of his most democratic-sounding moments, we see that the "benefits of affection" can solve so many issues for Emerson. With love, "it is so easy with the great to be great." With love, born of an appreciation for the "all," for the soul that each of us has, the dangers of the lower classes and effeminate men vanish and we are left with a vision, not only of harmony but of the betterment of each of us—the love for the great allows the lower to be "great" themselves, at least in the confines of this relationship.

At this celestial level, Emerson is clearly a kind of democrat; at this sublime level all of the contradictions and struggles of the world are indeed "trivial" and meaningless. Harmony is already present; we engage in a "happy intercourse." This is a vision of *agape,* of seeking to fill us with the divine truth, regardless of whether we are sinner or saved.

Ironically, Kateb, in his own assessment of Emerson's vision of democracy, seeks to distance himself from this religious vision. He frets that religiousness itself will impede the possibility of a meaningful democratic self-reliance:

> It is obvious that I find the religiousness of Emerson an impediment to my reception. I certainly do not deny that because the theory of democratic individuality commits one to the hope that a secular...form of the philosophical conception of self-reliance can gain acceptance among ordinary persons, the fact of pervasive religiousness remains a tremendous problem.[121]

Kateb seeks to read Emerson—despite his own admission of Emerson's deep spirituality—as a secular thinker (or "near enough to secularism"). He makes various arguments in this regard, including asserting that despite Emerson's stated belief in the "the all," most of his "exposures" of God's complexity are not particularly insightful not really heartfelt (and certainly the idea of the "all" does not necessarily need to be read as religious). Kateb calls Emerson's religiosity an "impediment," a "flaw," and an "obstacle."[122] Basically, Kateb is saying that Emerson's faith is interfering with his reason, and that, under all his religious fervor, Emerson knows better. He implies that Emerson desperately seeks morality but is unable to accept that morality can (or must) be determined in a secular order.

Why go to such lengths to separate Emerson from his own words when it makes much more sense to go the other way and accept Emerson's religiosity? In casting off Emerson's faith, Kateb not only avoids the real source of terrestrial hierarchies for Emerson, but also and paradoxically avoids what is truly democratic about Emerson himself. As we have seen, it is Emerson's love for the soul in each of us, no matter how miserable the external frame it lies in, that causes him to cast in his lot with the many. It is, I think, both what is most problematic but also most attractive about Emerson, not something to discard but to reconsider.

From the perspective of secular liberals like Kateb, and to a lesser extent Shklar, we see the limits of what Emerson can offer them. From within the confines of a system defined by love, Emerson's democratic possibility must always be compromised by its source in the relationship between *eros* and *agape.* The democratic spirit, received from on high, is on its own terms, always inadequate, never the point. It is the "makeshift" substitute. We must stand outside of this tradition in order to be able to discern and perhaps partake in something of the *philia politike* that Emerson seems to offer us but which remains so elusive to realize something other than a celestial democracy.

Democratizing genius

With this in mind, let us finally return to Cavell and his own vision of what Emerson does and does not offer to us. In this chapter I have spent a great deal more time critiquing Kateb's reading of Emerson than Cavell's, in part because I am much closer to Cavell's position. Kateb sees in Emerson an idea of self that is much more substantial, much more unproblematical than Cavell's. For Kateb, it seems as if the "me," even if complex and hermaphroditic, is also authentic and autonomous, the basic building block of a democratic polity. "Deindividualization" works for Kateb because such selves are not at risk; they have nothing to lose, and can only gain by achieving the transcendental perspective. In the transcendent heights, we can safely join together, overcome our own limited perspective, because back on earth we fully inhabit our bodies.

But as we have seen, such authentic selves are exactly what liberalism does not deliver. Instead it gives us interdependent and overlapping selves, selves which are hollow and need to be filled, selves which must be defined against one another and remain contentious and in opposition. Resolving our differences in the transcendental realm does not recognize but rather presupposes our differences in the world. Politics takes place in the realm of the "not me," which serves as the platform upon which the "me" is built.

Cavell, on the other hand, does not presume such selves. He offers a vision of how we can forge a democratic polity out of the disintegration of selves, into persons that are "next to" themselves and to one another. He offers a new idea of "neighborliness," a new and interesting reading of the tenet "love thy neighbor." Yet we need to be careful in conceding Cavell's idea of nextness as the basis of Emerson's democratic promise. If nextness presupposes, as I have argued, hierarchy itself, if I am not only next to you but also necessarily above you, then an idea of nextness alone cannot deliver on the democratic promise, at least not yet. With Emerson we are still left with the quandary of how one can love one's neighbor and love oneself as one loves God (and is loved in return). How far can we go with Cavell then in appreciating a democratic vision of friendship in Emerson?

In *Conditions Handsome and Unhandsome,* Cavell considers what he calls Emerson's "moral perfectionism"—that is, the question of the development of the soul (of the "me"). Cavell argues against thinkers such as Rawls who claim that this is an inherently elitist doctrine. He claims that to have an idea of "the great" is not in itself elitist, nor is an idea of having "representative men." Cavell tells us that "anyone is entitled and no one is, to stand for this election."[123] In other words, greatness is not conferred by the self but conferred upon it by the esteem and respect of others. Cavell goes on to argue, as we have already seen, that as Emerson's categories have no material basis, there is no "zero-sum" problem in his idea of greatness. For me to be great, to be self-reliant, costs you nothing and certainly does not come at your expense.[124] Greatness can be merely an "illustration" for the other to take or not take as they please.

In this argument, Cavell is not all that different from Kateb and shares with him an interest in a reinvigorated notion of democracy, one that does not ask for conformity as its goal but rather autonomy, the giving of the law and truth to oneself. In this sense, one can speak of what Kateb calls "democratizing genius" as part of the democratic project.[125] This an idea that Cavell also alludes to, as we have already seen, when he quotes Emerson as writing:

> To believe in your own thought, to believe that what is true for you in your private heart, is true for all men—that is genius.[126]

In this view, genius does not mean having access to something arcane and difficult (as it might be argued it does for Locke), rather it simply constitutes sitting with our self. But here my argument with Cavell is the same argument I make with Kateb: if the self *qua* self were in fact the ultimate goal, then an idea of self-reliance might indeed be a basis for democratic thought, and maybe we therefore could all be geniuses together. And indeed, to the degree that this is a possibility within Emerson's work, we should be encouraged to think further about this question. As we have seen, there are moments when Emerson himself laments his choices, offers a vision of a very different kind of life, other kinds of friendships. But despite all of his lamentation, Emerson still participates in the doctrine of love; the self is not given over to itself, it is meant to be filled up with something higher; the self as such does not offer substance, does not have its own validity. If the self chooses certain whims which are not conducive to higherness, then it is not a self at all. As with Locke, although we "own" ourselves, that ownership is subject to our conformity to a prior, deeper ownership, by God himself.

Cavell frequently compares Emerson to Nietzsche, and rightly so, but there is this one great difference: Nietzsche might believe in truths, but he does not believe in The Truth to the degree that Emerson does. Whereas what Nietzsche calls "homespun, severe, ugly, obnoxious, un-Christian, unmoral" truths are products of our own understanding, products of human history, Emersonian truth lies beyond us.[127] Both thinkers are moody; Nietzsche certainly has anti-democratic and elitist moments of his own, ones which make Emerson's seem quite mild in comparison. Yet unlike Emerson, Nietzsche has unambiguously and radically democratized the truth and the self which is to receive it.[128] Thus we are not only invited but indeed forced to take his claims with a grain of salt. Although Nietzsche is far from being a total relativist, he is also more of a true perspectivist than Emerson. Emersonian "perspectivism" remains contained by an external rubric, by the need to transcend and move higher.

Nietzsche's own embracing of "whim" therefore does not have the same built-in conflict that Emerson's does, because it is not being held against some absolute standard of judgment. In the end, it matters less for Nietzsche than for Emerson what he says or thinks about a particular issue. Nietzsche offers us only our own devices; his reader's must judge for themselves.

Yet, for all of this, it is true that Nietzsche, and Cavell himself, both recognize something in Emerson. In the very struggle that we can see in Emerson, in his moods, lies this "perhaps" that should not be discounted, however compromised. Perhaps as much *because* as *despite* his ensconcement in the doctrine of love, Emerson does tell us something about friendship, about *philia politike*. As Cavell tells us:

> Here, in this constraint by recognition and negation, is the place of the high role assigned in moral perfection to friendship. Aristotle speaks of a friend as "another myself." To see Emerson's philosophical authorship as taking up the ancient position of the friend, we have to include the inflection (more brazen in Nietzsche but no less explicit in Emerson) of my friend as my enemy (contesting my present attainments). If the position of that loved one were not also feared and hated, why would the thoughts from that place remain rejected?[129]

In a sense, it might be precisely Emerson's struggle between love and threat discernible in his notion of friendship that helps him to understand what friendship is or could be: not a utopian harmony, but an endless struggle, a relationship that is always (and should always be) in some kind of tension. As I will argue further in the final chapter, this vision of the friend as an enemy is as much produced from as it is an alternative to the doctrine of love. From his vision of friendship ensconced in love, Emerson can see, or Nietzsche (or Cavell) can see in him, something else, something that goes beyond his doubts and struggles.

But we will not find this vision entirely within Emerson himself. Emerson's friends are not democratic friends—not yet, anyway. Emerson himself helps us to recognize this. Arguing that there is something necessarily exclusive about "perfect" friendship, he writes:

> In good company there is never such discourse between two, across the tale, as takes place when you leave them alone. In good company the individuals at once merge their egotism into a social soul exactly coextensive with the several consciousnesses there present.... Only he may then speak who can sail

on the common thought of the party, and not poorly limited to his own. Now this convention, which good sense demands, destroys the high freedom of great conversation, which requires an absolute running of two souls into one.[130]

Emerson concedes that "you shall have very useful and cheering discourse at several times with two several men," allowing for multiple friendships over a period of time, suggesting future possibilities.[131] But for now, as a model for politics, Emerson's notion of friendship remains tied up with greatness; it is not only hostile to number and to plurality, but also, in a sense, set against it.[132]

And even on its own terms, Emerson's model of friendship is not yet democratic. Because their friendship is not itself the point, because their friendship exists on the basis of an entire network of difference, of higherness and lowerness, because even their enmity presupposes this hierarchy, we remain at the level of the perhaps with Emerson.

Emerson may have been responding to the kind of epistemological crises that we have seen from Locke onward, but in a sense he does so returning us not to ourselves but to a fuller embrace of *agape.* Yet even as he seeks to fill us with the all, Emerson retains much of the human-centered, autonomy-seeking notions that animate post-Lockean European and American philosophy—something we will see even more clearly with his own disciple, Thoreau. For Emerson, as for Locke, the desire for *agape,* the yearnings of *eros,* do not coexist easily; *caritas* has unraveled. A productive tension exists to be sure, one that Nietzsche recognized and made much use of. But these tensions are also the source of something disabling and even disheartening about Emerson.

In my mind, what *is* heartening about Emerson is that in many ways he did not practice what he preached. He allowed his different moods to coexist in his life and to some degree in his work as well. Although he may have been committed to a rather Platonic notion of truth, he both suffered from and enjoyed the "canker" of life. He is not the completely austere, chaste, and isolated figure that the poet needs to be. It is with Thoreau perhaps that the real test of Emerson's theories comes to light. Thoreau was (or at least tried to be) everything in life that Emerson called for in word. To a far greater degree than Emerson, Thoreau seeks out nature; he is chaste and strives for (at least more than Emerson) isolation. He makes a lifetime career out of following his whims. Where Emerson seems to banish contradiction to the transcendent heights, Thoreau experiences these contradictions directly. What is a source of creative and disturbing tension for Emerson becomes for Thoreau a way of life. In his elations, in his struggles, and in his despair, Thoreau reveals the literal workings of love. His is perhaps the most acutely political, the most worldly understanding of its costs and its benefits.

HENRY DAVID THOREAU:
DEEPER INTO THE WOODS

1. THE WALKER

Early on in his essay entitled "Walking" Thoreau writes:

> If you are ready to leave father and mother, brother and sister, and wife and child and friends, and never see them again—if you have paid your debts and made your will, and settled all your affairs and are a free man, then you are ready for a walk.[1]

For Thoreau, freedom is clearly conceived of as a state of removal and isolation from society. His "Walking" is reminiscent of Rousseau's *Reveries of a Solitary Walker*. Only in this instance Thoreau intends to literally leave society behind. Rather than reaching a transcendent distance in the middle of a common, the walker leaves his house and never comes back.

Thoreau's aversion to society is well known; he is one of America's most vociferous critics of urban life and most social institutions. In "Walking," as in many of his works, Thoreau contrasts the unhealthy, crowded, and artificial world of (white society) with a life spent in nature: "Give me the ocean, the desert, or the wilderness! In the desert, pure air and solitude compensate for want of moisture and fertility."[2] Quoting an imaginary walker who traveled "the steppes of Tartary," he writes:

> on reentering cultivated lands, the agitation, perplexity and turmoil of civilization oppressed and suffocated us. The air seemed to fill us, and we felt every moment as if about to die of asphyxia.[3]

And yet this complicated thinker does not exactly advocate, nor did he practice in his own life, a complete and permanent removal from society. Whenever Thoreau waxes poetic about the beauties of the wild, he usually qualifies this imagery with a nod to the necessities and benefits of civilized life. In "Walking," he sees the walker as someone who travels a boundary between nature and civilization:

For my part, I feel that with regard to Nature I live a sort of border life, on the confines of a world into which I make occasional and transient forays only, and my patriotism and allegiance to the state into whose territories I seem to retreat are those of a moss-trooper. Unto a life which I call natural I would gladly follow even a will-o-the wisp through bogs and sloughs unimaginable, but no moon nor firefly has shown me the causeway to it.[4]

It is a telling irony that Thoreau, a staunch advocate of setting one's own path, of striking out into the world alone and defying convention, sees himself as waiting for an invitation to go into nature. For him nature is an ideal, one that he can approach but never quite reach. He can travel in the woods but the original nature eludes him. Thus he endlessly "walks" back and forth between society and the woods, at home in neither terrain.

In his wanderings, Thoreau compares himself to a Native American, a subject which in his mind personified the reconciliation of nature and society.[5] For Thoreau, Native Americans inhabit the same boundary zone that the walker moves through. He felt that as a white man and a privileged person, he could never have the entree into nature that was available to darker-skinned people:

A tanned skin is something more respectable, and perhaps olive skin is a fitter color than white for a man—a denizen of the woods. "The pale white man!" I do not wonder that the African pitied him. Darwin the naturalist says, "A white man bathing by the side of a Tahitian was like a plant bleached by the gardener's art, compared with a fine, dark green one, growing vigorously in the open fields."[6]

And yet, while lauding Native American superiority, and greater "naturalness," Thoreau ultimately, albeit reluctantly, throws his lot in with white society. As the essay progresses, the true walker, the one who leaves home and never comes back, is revealed to be a pioneer, a white settler who leaves Europe and moves to America in search of new lands to conquer. Thoreau lauds the settlers and pioneers who follow the sun westward, including Columbus, who "felt the westward tendency more strongly than any before. He obeyed it and found a New World for Castile and Leon."[7]

Thoreau is not asking his (white) readers to settle in the wild as "savages" themselves. Rather in "Walking" he advocates leaving an established, settled society and re-creating that society in a new, wilder setting. At one point, he even justifies the European's usurpation of the Native American's land, writing: "I think the farmer displaces the Indian even because he redeems the meadow, and so makes himself stronger and in some respects *more natural*."[8] Sounding very much like Locke, Thoreau writes that the white settler has the right to till the land because "the Indian" is incapable of acquiring the skills to maximize efficient use of it:

The very winds blew the Indian's cornfield into the meadow, and pointed out the way which he had not the skill to follow. He had no better implement with which to entrench himself in the land than a clamshell. But the farmer is armed with plow and spade.[9]

As pioneers, living at the boundary between society and nature, the settlers are able to appreciate and benefit from nature even as they improve the earth. The pioneers use wildness as a way to revitalize the Europeans who follow in their wake. A successful human society is one that literally grows out of the decaying matter of old conquered forests:

> A town is saved not by the righteous men in it than by the woods and swamps that surround it. A township where one primitive forest waves above while another primitive forest rots below—such a town is fitted to raise not only corn and potatoes, but poets and philosophers for the coming ages.[10]

For Thoreau, the trouble with Europe is that its forests are cut down, its land all cultivated. He says, "Alas for human culture! little is to be expected of a nation, when the vegetable mould is exhausted, and it is compelled to make manure of the bones of its fathers."[11] America is for Thoreau as for Emerson, the promised land, wild and new, full of potential and invigorating life. He quotes an English traveler as saying: "the heavens of America appear infinitely higher, the sky is bluer, the air is fresher."[12]

Yet for all the newness of America, the walker is very much rooted in European notions of self. As with Locke and Rousseau (and Emerson too, of course), Thoreau's understanding of nature has as much to say about the internal self as it does an external phenomenon. "Nature" is revealed once again to be the elusive source of authenticity, that which gives us to ourselves. And once again the essential question of nature is a question of desire: "The wildness of the savage is but a faint symbol of the awful ferity with which good men and lovers meet."[13]

Thoreau sees that the American wilderness corresponds to our "inner nature." Whether in its guise as forest or internal nature, wildness is to be subordinated to, although not exterminated by, the needs of white society:

> I would not have every man nor every part of a man cultivated, any more than I would have every acre of earth cultivated; part will be tillage, but the greater part will be meadowed and forest, not only serving an immediate use, but preparing a mould against a distant future, by the annual decay of the vegetation which it supports.[14]

Internally and externally, we should create a parkland, with areas of cultivation admixed with areas of wildness.[15] We should strive to incorporate the boundary region, the parkland, into ourselves. To do so gives us "the best of both worlds," the energy and dynamism, the raw desire of the woods, and the order, power, and destiny of society.

To achieve this state, Thoreau turns, as Emerson did before him, to the poet, a figure who can see and understand the boundaries in ways that no one else can. He asks:

> Where is the literature which gives expression to Nature? He would be a poet who could impress the winds and streams into his service...who nailed words to their primitive senses...who...transplanted [his words] to his page with earth adhering to their roots; whose words were so true and fresh and natural that they would appear to expand like the buds at the approach of spring.[16]

It is thus the (white) poet, even more than the Native Americans, who can reconcile nature and society. The Native Americans themselves, although epitomizing a border life, are in a sense too compromised by the wildness they inhabit. Nature, "this vast savage howling mother of ours," is so complex and vast and unknowable that merely living amid her is not enough:[17]

> The pines have developed their delicate blossoms on the highest twigs of the wood every summer for ages, as well over the heads of Nature's red children as of her white ones. Yet scarcely a farmer or hunter in the land has ever seen them.[18]

Thus, despite his initial conviction that as a white man he cannot have the same relationship to nature as "the Indian," Thoreau sees that as a poet, he can once again have the "best of both worlds." The poet, removed from nature by his status as a white man, has just the right combination of distance and proximity to negotiate the balance with nature. We see here once again an echo of Emerson's conviction that only the poet can really harness desire without losing his self. To become too ensconced in nature suggests sharing the fate of the Native Americans, becoming compromised by her wildness and then swept away by the tide of white progress.

Thoreau ends "Walking" with a scene in which he describes the redemptive power of nature:

> The west side of every wood and rising ground gleamed like the boundary of Elysium and the sun on our backs seemed like a gentle herdsman driving us home at evening.[19]

Here, Thoreau is in a fully transcendentalist, we might even say Emersonian mood. Despite an earlier assurance that the walker was to leave his home forever, he returns after all, reconciled with society but changed and invigorated through an interaction with nature that can only be described through poetic imagery.

Clearly this is an essay filled with contradiction, the overriding paradox being the contrast between the apparent resolution at the end and the motif of endless walking itself. In a sense, this essay perfectly captures the ways in which Thoreau is, even more than Emerson, a man at struggle with himself. For all his tone of resolution and return, we see several elements in "Walking" that suggest a less sanguine resolution and, in its very difficulty, points us to other possibilities, other accomodations.

As if countering his own notion of turning America and ourselves into parklands, Thoreau reminds us that on his own walks he fears that this accomodation is being overrun, being turned into simply more urbanity:

> At present, in this vicinity, the best part of the land is not private property; the landscape is not owned, and the walker enjoys comparative freedom. But possibly the day will come when it will be partitioned off... when fences shall be multiplied, and man-traps and other engines invented to confine man to the *public* road, and walking over the surface of God's earth shall be construed to mean trespassing on some gentleman's grounds.... Let us improve our opportunities, then before the evil days come.[20]

The careful balance between nature and civilization may not be tenable in the long run. Although the poet seeks the eternal, he exists in and draws upon a world bounded and ruled by time and space. There is only so much land to be used up. For all his lauding of the pioneer, we also get a sense of the walker as one who brings destruction with him, who ruins and uses up precisely that which is most precious. The wildness that is preserved in the parkland is not held purely for its own sake. It also serves a purpose, to stand as a "mould" to be used up in the future; eventually the parkland must give way to feed the ongoing needs of a dynamic and outward-expanding white society. Thoreau seems to suggest the impossibility of this balance when he writes:

> At the same time that we are earnest to explore and learn all things, we require that all things be mysterious and unexplorable, that land and sea be infinitely wild, unsurveyed and unfathomed by us because unfathomable. We can never have enough of Nature.[21]

Can he, should we, have it both ways? And what is Thoreau implying by making the conflict seem so stark?

Thoreau raises these kinds of questions throughout his work, but perhaps "Walking" expresses his dilemma most succinctly. Can nature be known and controlled even as it remains pure? Can it be worshiped and appreciated on its own terms even as it is a "mould" to be used up by an onward civilization? Can we live and appreciate the particular and local on its own terms even as we relate to the eternal?

Thoreau's ambivalence about the uses of nature also extends to his attitude to his own "wildness," his own inner "nature," desires, and needs. Should he be like "the Indian," wild and natural (or as natural as a transplant can be)? But as we see, the fate of the Native Americans is to disappear along with nature itself. Is this the price of authenticity, of wildness itself? In the seemingly inevitable conquest of America, Thoreau seeks to have it both ways, but as he shows us, time is not on his side.

We see here, in another guise, familiar questions stemming from the doctrine of love. Thoreau, through the figure of the poet, introduces the same desire for reconciliation, the same "coming home" to ourselves that we find with Emerson through poetry, art, and transcendence itself. The poet, through his connection to *agape*, is best able to describe what is really true about each of us. The physical manifestations of nature are not really what is central. It is the metaphorical essence of nature that matters, and this is something that only the poet has access to.

By this way of thinking, the reality of nature is, if anything, dangerous and corrupting, because, as we have already seen with Emerson, desire if unmediated can be overwhelming, can disrupt us from our true purpose. But unlike Emerson, Thoreau must see for himself what is given up in this act of submission. He wants to experience raw desire, the heart of the woods, even as he struggles against it. He wants to know what is being lost through the act of transcendence itself.

And yet for all of his seeking of rawness, Thoreau too remains mediated, removed from nature's mysteries, exactly because he participates in the movement to overcome and harness it. So long as he is engaged in transcendental philosophy, in poetry itself, "no moon nor firefly has shown [him] the causeway to [nature]." "Nature" remains for him, as for Emerson, a cipher; if the farmer can be more natural than "the Indian," and the poet more natural still, then the meaning of nature is once again a substitute, a sign searching for its own origin. Thoreau remains, like Rousseau himself, hoping that the substitute can discover or reproduce the original which it replaces.

Uninvited, walking at the outskirts of nature, the walker cannot be certain that in "transcending" nature he has captured its true essence. Thoreau himself tells us that the walker, the poet, the pioneer are unnatural transplants. Can they really tell us what nature is? If anything, "the Indian" may yet be better acquainted with whatever nature really is (if it is anything at all). Hence the walker is compelled to walk deeper into the woods, still searching for what his own presence destroys.

In the end, "Walking" leaves us with more questions than answers. What of Thoreau's original idea of freedom? What is our nature? Where is our home? Although he participates in liberal theory, in the ongoing development of the doctrine of love I find Thoreau to have the most subversive contribution of all of the thinkers that I have considered thus far. He struggles with his legacy from

Emerson and earlier European thinkers, with his own privilege, with the nature outside and within his own body. All of these struggles serve to expose the liberal project as impossible, even as he subscribes to it, however reluctantly. In the project of seeking out *philia politike,* Thoreau tells us, "Give me for my friends and neighbors wild men, not tame ones."[22]

2. A POLITICS OF WILDNESS

As we have seen, Thoreau's notion of transcendentalism is not so much vertical as it is horizontal; he keeps the form of his mentor's philosophy but radically subverts its content. Where Emerson looks up to the heavens, Thoreau looks down, as he tells us in *Walden* where he writes, "my head is an organ for burrowing." He tells us also that, looking down, he sees "fish in the sky, whose bottom is pebbly with stars."[23] For Thoreau, to retain a terrestrial perspective means that even in his most transcendent raptures, whatever is being transcended—be it nature, desire, one's own body, or other people—remains present, hiding in plain sight. For Thoreau, even more than Emerson, despite a similar yearning for transparency, bodies and particular things have a way of lingering even after they have been presupposed, dissolved into the "all." In this view, the heavens are revealed to contain, not abstractions, but the very matter, the fish and pebbles of the world he lives in.

In general, it seems safe to say that Thoreau has more of a democratic disposition than Emerson. He does not have to "labor to love labor"; he not only appreciates but emulates "the low." But does this get him any closer than Emerson in the end to a vision of a democratic polity, to a *philia politike?*

In *The Senses of Walden Pond,* Cavell details the ways in which Thoreau's project, being so different from Emerson's, results in a very different kind of subject and politics. He quotes Thoreau from his chapter entitled "Solitude" in *Walden:*

> With thinking we may be beside ourselves in a sane sense.... I only know myself as a human entity; the scene, so to speak, of thoughts and affections; and am sensible of a certain doubleness by which I can stand as remote from myself as from another.[24]

Cavell goes on to say:

> This is not Emerson's idea of an Over-Soul, most importantly because Emerson locates that, among other places, *within* the self, as a unity, or *the* Unity; and he leaves me the habitual spectator of my world. That is where Emerson is always stuck, with his sense, not his achievement, of outsideness, the yearning for the thing to happen to him.[25]

In other words, with Thoreau we get a greater acceptance of the ways that the self is *not* coherent, not unified. For Thoreau the self is wilder, more democratic and decentered.

Cavell himself maintains Thoreau's doubleness by calling him "the writer of *Walden,*" allowing him to maintain a perspective outside of himself:

> The name we find for the writer's description of the double does not at the moment matter; what is essential is that he gives his own view of what is apparently an ancient and recurring intimation of the wholeness of the self ("holiness groping for expression") out of a present sense of incoherence or division or incompleteness.[26]

As we have seen, Cavell accepts our disunity, not so much as a source of despair but of opportunity. It allows for this doubleness, this nextness which itself serves as the basis for a democratic notion of self and citizenship.

In Thoreau's "double self," his detached and alienated self is not "him" but rather "next to" him. The "real" self is a kind of accommodation between these various separate subjects. Cavell writes:

> We are to reinterpret our sense of doubleness as a relation between ourselves in the aspect of indweller, unconsciously building, and in the aspect of spectator, impartially observing. Unity between these aspects is viewed not as a mutual absorption, but as a perpetual nextness, an act of neighboring or befriending.[27]

Cavell further writes that "*Walden's* underlying notion, in its account of doubleness—as opposed say to Plato's notion of the harmony of the soul, is one of integrity conceived as an activity."[28] In other words, our coherence is not a given, we have to make it ourselves.

Cavell suggests that this concept of a democratized self also leads to the possibility of democratic subjects. Here, as he did with Emerson, Cavell appreciates a notion of abandonment as an essential part of how we can be together without smothering or overruling one another. Paraphrasing Thoreau, he writes that "I do not know whether I have finally been able to leave you sufficiently alone, to make you go far enough to find us both."[29] Here too we see a vision of *philia politike,* a notion of distance, even enmity as part of the relationship that we have with one another, even with ourselves. The selves Cavell envisions are not merged threateningly into one another but keep their distance ("a perpetual nextness").

Through "nextness," we are permitted to create and acknowledge fixed spatial location as an anchor of identity and see it as that which both separates us (hence rendering us *not* a threat to one another) and also binds us, allowing for a non-harmonious, but still coherent unity. Cavell writes:

Walden is among other things, a tract of political education, education for membership in the polis. It locates authority in the citizens and it identifies citizens—those with whom one is in membership as "neighbors." What it shows is that education for citizenship is education for isolation. (In this sense, *Walden* is Emile grown up. The absence of Sophie only purifies the point).[30]

Once again, I am drawn by Cavell's interpretation of an author, but hold myself out as more cautious, more concerned with the baggage that comes with this generally positive vision. The very notion that Emile ever could "grow" up or be "free" from Sophie suggests a resolution to a struggle which, as we saw in the case of Rousseau himself, is impossible insofar as Rousseau himself was concerned. Perhaps more accurately, it recognizes the implicit "perhaps" in Rousseau's work but seems to suggest that this perhaps is already or imminently at hand.

Cavell offers us a vision of the "perhaps" but also hints of the complexity of the project. As he tells us, Thoreau's radical deconstruction of the subject is accompanied by a hope, a faith in the possibility of solidity, as when he writes:

Let us settle ourselves and work and wedge our feet downward through the mud and slush of opinion and prejudice and tradition and delusion and appearance, that alluvion which covers the globe... through church and state, through poetry and philosophy and religion, till we come to a hard bottom and rocks in place, which we can call reality and say, This is it, and no mistake.... Be it life or death we crave only reality.[31]

In all of his acknowledgment of the makeshift nature of the subject, Thoreau remains animated by a hope for substance and filledness. But where do we find this "hard bottom"? Is it like the bottom of Walden Pond itself ontologically present, ready to recieve those who seek it out? Or is it rather elusive, eternally hoped for but never discovered?

As attractive as the idea of nextness is, I want to suggest, as I did in the previous chapter as well, that we must engage with it through an awareness of the fact that in many ways Thoreau is a bad neighbor or at least not yet a good one, both to himself and to others.

For all of his love of nature, his need for unmediated desire, his celebration of Native Americans and the unmolested woods, we have already seen how Thoreau is also a pioneer, a bringer of transcendence, a harnesser of desire. He carries with him a swath of destruction even as he seeks reconciliation. He is "next" to himself, but also engaged in a fierce struggle with himself. He does not want desire to die but he needs to harness and use it up. He adores "the Indian" as having a closer connection to nature and yet he also needs for "the Indian" to disappear (or at least can't preclude that outcome) in order to make way for his own society. Enmity and distance are one thing, but in a sense Thoreau is engaged, however reluctantly, in something far worse—conquest, the destruction of nature, the harnessing and using up of desire, even genocide. He is seeking to reconcile things that by his own accounting are irreconcilable. If coexistence is his desire, he seeks to make compromises in a battle which he himself often recognizes as being one to the death.

Of the liberal thinkers that I treat in this book, Thoreau is the most earthbound, the one who is least satisfied with transcendence, reason, and the gifts of *agape*. As such, he is also the thinker most rooted in the dimensions of earth, namely space and time. In terms of space, we have already seen how he seeks to literally cover the earth, to endlessly journey and see for himself the process of transcendence, and, as we will see, to witness the sacrifice of nature, the murder of Native American society, firsthand.

But Thoreau is also a thinker ensconced in human time. In *Walden,* Thoreau tells us that

> time is but the stream I go a-fishing in. I drink at it but while I drink I see the sandy bottom and detect how shallow it is. Its thin current slides by, but eternity remains. I would drink deeper."[32]

Even as he recognizes the limitations and rules of time, Thoreau seeks to drink deeper, to get to the bottom, to drink up eternity moment by moment, yet even as he is so engaged, he realizes how little ('how shallow") time is. This fishing is a brave (Cavell would say heroic) act. Thoreau might have chosen to ignore the ravages of time, both in terms of the past and the future, and thereby be far more content with the progress of white society. In New England, much of the genocide and overcoming of nature had already taken place, not directly before Thoreau's eyes. The sanitization of nature, which makes the world safe for the white settler and the woods safe for the poet has already occurred. But Thoreau insists, as we shall see clearly, on visiting the "scene of the crime," on going "a-fishing," going into the deepest heart of the woods to witness its overcoming. Even at "home," Thoreau is constantly reminded of the vanished ghosts of the wild beasts and Native Americans who had to make way for white progress.

Furthermore, Thoreau is not content to ignore the future either—the balance of nature and society that he calls for, the parkland within and without, is untenable, as he himself will tell us. America may be vast and may have years left before the last vestiges of wildness are overcome, but eventually everything will be used up and there will be nowhere left for the human subject to go. Thoreau is a man aware of the passing of time, aware of the unstableness of the contradictions that he is seeking to contend with and the inevitable results that must one day come. Even as he seeks a relationship with eternity, Thoreau lives in the world, in space and in time, and as such reveals the price of liberal polity, the price of love itself. He shows the immense difficulty in the reconciliation between human and celestial dimensions, offering further evidence that what frustrates Arendt about Saint Augustine cannot easily be overcome.

Given this irreconcilability, must Thoreau always be a bad neighbor? What vision of friendship, of community and love itself, does he offer in all of this struggle? What is produced out of this tension? What democratic vision can we derive from this most democratic of writers?

I began this chapter with a consideration of "Walking" because it offers us a model for Thoreau's dilemma. In his endless journeys, Thoreau was only able to connect in fleeting glimpses with what he was looking for. For so much of his life he was discontented and frustrated. We need to better understand why. I thus propose to follow Thoreau through his actual and literary wanderings from society (by examining a section drawn from *A Week on the Concord and Merrimack Rivers*), to the borderlands (with an analysis of *Walden*), and then on into the deep woods themselves (by examining the three essays of *The Maine Woods*). In looking at these different literary and philosophical settings, I will ask why Thoreau found happiness so elusive no matter where he was. Why could he never settle on just one place? And most importantly, for the purposes of this book, what implication does Thoreau's endless searching have for questions of liberal identity, friendship, and democracy?

3. FRIENDSHIP: LIFE IN SOCIETY

I begin with a consideration of the social because, despite a widespread perception that Thoreau's chief concern is nature itself, I will be consistently arguing that most of his life and works are centrally concerned with human (and perhaps more accurately, white) society and relationships. Above all, Thoreau is searching for a perfect love, a true friend. That he sought to escape society and go deeper into the woods to find such a love may seem paradoxical. Yet when we consider that for Thoreau the heart of the wilderness is also in a sense the heart of his own desire, we can see why he makes the connection. The deep woods promises him a raw and direct experience of love ("give me for my friends and neighbors wild men, not tame ones").

Before we consider Thoreau's search for love in the woods, let us first try to understand why he found love in society so difficult to find. A key text to help us understand his frustrated search for love can be found in the excerpt entitled "Friendship" from *A Week on the Concord and Merrimack Rivers*.[33] This book is a description of a two-week hiking and boating trip that Thoreau undertook with his brother John in New Hampshire during the summer of 1839. Initially a commercial flop, the book does not have a straightforward narrative. Rather, it is divided into seven "days" in which the events of the trip serve as a unifying device to pull together a vast assortment of thoughts, meandering up and branching as the rivers he is paddling along. "Friendship" comes from the chapter entitled "Wednesday."

A Week on the Concord and Merrimack Rivers is written as a memorial to Thoreau's brother John, who died just three years after this trip to New Hampshire.[34] Until fairly recently, the conventional reading of this trip was that the Thoreau brothers were making their peace with one another, having just fought over the love of the same woman. Henry Seidel Canby makes the claim in his biography *Thoreau* that both Henry and John were smitten by a woman named Ellen Sewall.[35] According to Canby, John initially asked her to marry him; she accepted at first and then refused. Then Henry had his chance but, being shy and reticent, he bungled it. After this, the brothers good-naturedly set aside their differences and went "a-fishing."

This account of the brother's fight, however, is quite suspect, because although Canby declares that Thoreau loved Ellen Sewall, a reading even of Canby's own text suggests otherwise. Apparently before he met Ellen, Thoreau had met her brother, Edmund. Canby acknowledges that Thoreau was taken with the beauty of this youth: "There was to Thoreau's seeing a spiritual beauty in the face of this boy."[36] Canby quotes a poem entitled "Sympathy" that Thoreau wrote about Edmund (which is to be found at the very beginning of "Friendship"). Jonathan Ned Katz also quotes this poem in *Gay American History* as part of his argument that Thoreau was actually gay. The poem includes lines like "I might have loved him, had I loved him less," and "Each moment, as we nearer draw to each, a stern respect withheld us further yet," suggesting a struggle within Thoreau to deal with his feelings for the boy. Canby seems clueless about this possibility:

> This is clearly Transcendental love-making in search of someone so virtuous that the emotions of love lose their personal character. A dangerous kind of love-making for a young man of twenty-two, yet safe enough with a pure uncompromising spirit, settled not positively anywhere, for the love was only ideal. But suppose such sympathy should flow out to a lovely and high-spirited girl![37]

For Canby, such tender expressions of love are only practice for the "real thing" with Ellen. He goes on to suggest that works of poetry that would seem to be addressed by Thoreau to Edmund Sewall really refer to his sister and that he used "a camouflage of masculine pronouns[!]"[38]

Shortly after the situation with Ellen was "resolved," Thoreau wrote in his journal:

To sigh under the cold, cold moon for a love unrequited is but a slight on nature; the natural remedy would be to fall in love with the moon and the night and find our love requited.[39]

Whether he pines for Ellen or Edmund is worth pondering further. If Thoreau is repressing his same-sex yearnings (which seems clear to me), it goes a long way in explaining his ambivalent attitude toward relationships and society. It helps us to understand better Thoreau's concept of transcendence and "pure love"; perhaps these terms mask an internal struggle with sexuality—one that Thoreau does not seem to be able to handle as readily as Emerson did in his own struggle for "that great defying eye" of Martin Gay. We can see here more evidence for the different temperament between these authors. Thoreau suffers from a conflict that Emerson turns to his advantage—what for Emerson becomes the basis of "the most solid enjoyment" is for Thoreau a torment, an unrequited, unstoppable yearning.[40] Where Emerson is able to transcend his forbidden romances, making the forbidding itself the basis by which desire is safely mediated, Thoreau gets stuck, caught on the object of transcendence itself.

Regardless of who he desired, Thoreau experienced great frustration in his life due to his inability to find or enjoy love.[41] In another journal entry during this period, he wrote:

How alone must our life be lived.... Men are my merry companions...who beguile the way but leave me at the first turn in the road—for none are traveling one road so far as myself.[42]

Interdependence means taking risks; love can be unrequited. The fact that a person needs someone does not ensure that they will actually get to be with them. In a sense, Thoreau's same-sex desires only complicate this issue. As Michael Warner tells us in "Thoreau's Bottom," whereas heterosexual love presupposes gender differences as a mediating agent to provide some safe distance between the lovers, Thoreau's same-sex yearnings are even more challenging, more threatening to his precarious sense of self. How "other" is the same-sex lover?[43]

The peacefulness demonstrated in Thoreau's relationship with his brother during the narrative of *A Week on the Concord and Merrimack Rivers* may not so much indicate reconciliation as the fact that both brothers are seeking comfort in each other's company. They share a love that, because it is chaste, seems sure to be requited. Like Rousseau's Golden Age love, the love between Henry and John Thoreau is held within the safe confines of family.

Yet, as we know, even the relationship with John is not all that safe, for John actually died (from lockjaw and in Henry's arms) just a few years after this trip and before the book itself was written. From the standpoint of this loss, even the characterization of this safe, chaste, and requited love is haunted by doubt and risk. As a commemoration of love lost, "Friendship" is both an act of mourning and a continuing search for a perfect love which gives comfort and companionship but brings no risk.

Thoreau expresses such an ideal, writing:

> This is what I would like,—to be as intimate with you as our spirits are intimate,—respecting you as I respect my ideal. Never to profane one another by word or action, even by a thought. Between us, if necessary, let there be no acquaintance.
> I have discovered you; how can you be concealed from me?[44]

Whatever their relation as living brothers, in death, Henry Thoreau has transformed John into such an absent, perfect lover. Thoreau writes:

> Even the death of Friends will inspire us as much as their lives. They will leave consolation to the mourners, as the rich leave money to defray the expenses of their funerals, and their memories will be incrusted over with sublime and pleasing thoughts, as their monuments are overgrown with moss.
> This to our cis-Alpine and cis-Atlantic Friends.[45]

Thoreau has a gone a-fishing in the streams of time. Can he pluck from its waters a moment now lost to him? Can he journey to the past via this act of memory, or does the love he seeks remain determined by its temporal location, gone and lost to him forever?

Some fair floating isle of palms

The tendency to abstract from and transcend loss is repeated throughout "Friendship," beginning with the loss of Edmund Sewall. "Friendship" begins with the poem "Sympathy" (quoted by Canby), which deals with the transformation of his desire:

> Lately, alas I knew a gentle boy
> Whose features all were cast in Virtue's mould,
> As one she had designed for Beauty's toy,
> But after manned him for her own stronghold.[46]

The poem turns tragic when he writes:

> Eternity may not the chance repeat,
> But I must tread my single way alone,
> In sad remembrance that we once did meet,
> And know that bliss irrevocably gone.[47]

As Emerson's student, Thoreau turns this tragic love affair into an opportunity for transcendence:

If I but love that virtue which he is,
Though it be scented in the morning air,
Still shall we be truest acquaintances,
Nor mortals know a sympathy more rare.[48]

Here we see that Thoreau must love not the boy himself but the boy's virtue, and in so doing he can have true acquaintance with him—an intimacy few mortals can know. The sort of transcendent, abstract love that he calls for here is typical of most of this short excerpt, and sounds very much like Emerson's own conceptions of friendship.

In an inversion that is typical of Thoreau, physical proximity is seen as an obstacle to intimacy. If we see Thoreau as repressing his sexuality, this particular inversion makes sense. Too much physical proximity is a cruel reminder of all that Thoreau wants and cannot have. Able to love only from afar, it would appear as though intimacy and love can only be achieved by Thoreau through abstraction and sublimation.[49] By abandoning the actual lover, he can have him all the more in the abstract realm. Thoreau follows the poem with these lines:

The Friend is some fair floating isle of palms eluding the mariner in Pacific seas. Many are the dangers to be encountered.... But who would not sail through mutiny and storm, even over Atlantic waves, to reach the fabulous retreating shores of some continent man?[50]

For Thoreau, as for Emerson (as for Aristotle), true friendship does not ask anything of the other.[51] It only asks that you "[c]onsent only to be what you are."[52] It runs no risk of being unrequited because it is by nature so abstract:

I never asked thy leave to let me love thee, I have a right. I love thee not as something private and personal, which is *your own*, but as something universal and worthy of love, *which I have found.*[53]

Thus the risk, the very *otherness* of conventional love, is not present in true friendship. The love of another is not an object which can be given or withheld; it is rather an objective fact that stands on its own.

Difference and brotherhood

But is this abstract perfect friendship enough? Is the substitute more than a "mediocre makeshift"? What does it mean for Thoreau to "have" the absent John or to have Edmund's virtue but not his body? What is lost in this transcendence? We have seen Emerson's agonized response to the loss of his son, bewailing his inability to connect to his own grief. Thoreau himself will not sit with this failure; he is compelled to revisit the loss itself.

He does this perhaps most tangibly in one of the only sections of "Friendship" that directly describes an actual flesh-and-blood relationship (and the only relationship where the friends are actually given names). The friendship he describes is between a Native American named Wawatam and a fur trader named Henry. Thoreau writes:

> The Friendship which Wawatam testified for Henry the fur-trader, as described in the latter's Adventures, so almost bare and leafless yet not blossomless nor fruitless, is remembered with satisfaction and security. The stern imperturbable warrior, after fasting, solitude and mortification of body, comes to the white man's lodge and affirms that he is the white brother who he saw in his dream and adopts him henceforth.[54]

Wawatam, realizing his deep bond with Henry, saves him from his fellow Native Americans by removing him into the deep woods. Although this tale seems to be loosely based on some actual account, it is fairly clear that Henry Thoreau depicts himself as "Henry the fur-trader," where his brother John is "Wawatam."[55]

This story portrays an ideal, bucolic friendship. Yet like the real-life relationship that it describes, it ends in tragedy and separation. Eventually, "after a long winter of undisturbed and happy intercourse" in the wilderness, Wawatam must leave.[56] Henry bids Wawatam farewell, supposing that they were to be separated for a short time only. Yet he concludes, "we never hear of him again."[57]

Thoreau laments that love can bring such sorrow. He writes: "The only danger in Friendship is that it will end. It is a delicate plant, though a native."[58] What does racial difference ("a native plant") offer Thoreau in his attempt to reproduce his love for John? It seems as if Wawatam offers Henry access to unmediated, "native" desire but at the same time it provides a safe distance. The racial distance also preserves John's absence; however blissful it may be, the friendship between Henry and Wawatam must end.

In the end, after Wawatam's disappearance, Thoreau returns to an abstract vision of friendship. In the abstract, Thoreau sees that all differences, all separations between self and other, can be overcome, leading to a divine intimacy that he can only dream of on earth:

> My Friend is not of some other race or family of men, but flesh of my flesh, bone of my bone. *He is my real brother.* I see his nature groping yonder so like mine. We do not live far apart.[59] (emphasis added)

And yet, in comparing the abstract story of friendship in general and this specific tale of Henry and Wawatam, we see that the transcendental story is much less problematic, but also much less fulfilling; it is only an inadequate substitute for what was lost.

The abstract relationship between friends is "a relationship of perfect equality. It cannot well spare any outward sign of equal obligation and advantage."[60] It is a relationship between two autonomous beings who owe each other nothing. The concrete relationship depicted between Henry and Wawatam, on the other hand, is unequal and dependent but also much more vivid, more sensual; these friends have names; we know who they are.

Whereas the abstract friendship is marked by a transcendence of necessity...

> Few things are more difficult than to help a Friend in matters which do not require the aid of Friendship, but only a cheap and trivial service, if your Friendship wants the basis of a thorough practical acquaintance. I stand in the friendliest relation, on social and spiritual grounds, to one who does not perceive what practical skill I have.[61]

... the concrete relationship is marked by necessity itself. Thoreau introduces the story of Wawatam and Henry by noting that

> The Friend is a *necesarius,* and meets his Friend on homely ground; not on carpets and cushions, but on the ground and on rocks they will sit, obeying the natural and primitive laws.[62]

Here we have a contrast between a white, abstract, equal, and necessity-free transcendent love and the "Indian," concrete, unequal, and necessity-bound actual love. It is the very necessity, difference, and inequality of this "real" friendship that allows Thoreau to know the real beauty and experience of love, even while seeing that real love is painful and marked by conflict and inevitability of loss. Whereas for Thoreau the higher friendship is eternal, real friendship exists in space and time. Its very tangibility marks it as unsafe, as mortal, but also gives it its value.

Despite the greater power and allure of the real love, in concluding the story of Henry and Wawatam, Thoreau seems to be (indeed must be) in favor of the transcendent. He writes:

> Friendship is not so kind as is imagined; it has not much human blood in it; but consists with a certain disregard for men and their erections.... We may call [friendship] an essentially heathenish intercourse, free and irresponsible in its nature.[63]

Once again, Thoreau seems to throw his lot in with transcendence rather than the flesh, with society and art rather than nature. But even at this transcendent level, we are reminded of the "heathenish" Wawatam.

Thoreau goes on to argue that the overcoming of this "heathenism" in a sense destroys the very object of love itself:

> When the Friend comes out of his heathenism and superstition, and breaks his idols, being converted by the precepts of a newer testament; when he forgets his mythology, and treats his Friend like a Christian, or as he can afford; then Friendship ceased to be Friendship and becomes charity.[64]

Here we can see that Thoreau, if not explicitly condemning the notion of *caritas* which binds him, at least resents its most explicit manifestations, as well as the Christian doctrine which sustains it. When the friend is converted, when he is transcended and abstracted, he ceases to be a Friend at all. In the movement toward the higher, Thoreau loses the very thing that he came to find, the actual having of love, the presence of the other. If Thoreau expects to be filled with *agape* itself, with the divine love that lies at the heart of all mortal relationships, he is disappointed—he finds not God's love but an emptiness, a mediocre makeshift.

In his transcendentalist moods, Thoreau sees that it is necessary that Wawatam disappear in order that Henry can experience a safe and abstracted friendship, lest he love Wawatam too much (and possibly therefore share his fate). Is it therefore also necessary for John to have died so that Thoreau can safely love him? By rendering John into a Native American himself, does Thoreau ask him to share a similar fate to "the Indian," loved from afar, useful only at a distance, despite the promise of real affection and intimacy that such a treatment betrays?

John's death may have afforded Thoreau an opportunity to write an elegiac transcendent account of perfect love, but the transcendence of John is marred by the loss that it contains. Simply put: Thoreau misses John too much to enjoy a perfect, safe, and eternally requited relationship in the abstract. In the end, Thoreau has all the autonomy he wants; in fact, he has far too much. He is experiencing a form of love free from all sorts of entanglements, but it is not what he is looking for. At the heart of this abstraction of love remains the body that was transcended, the dead body of John, the discarded body of Wawatam, the desired body of Edmund.

"Friendship" ultimately paints a portrait of the impossibility of what its title asks for. Far from being what it is for Emerson, a stepladder upward, friendship for Thoreau takes him nowhere at all. Neither the flesh nor the abstraction satisfy; the one is too dangerous, the other too empty. Thoreau remains suspended between *eros* and *agape,* between earthly and terrestrial love. Where Emerson insists on finding authenticity and coherence in the transcendent realm itself, Thoreau sees with his own eyes how the search for love is full of pain and loss, and so we must look elsewhere for the possibility of love. In society, Thoreau has not found the love that he seeks.

4. WALDEN POND: LIFE ON THE BOUNDARY

Experiencing the loss of John very painfully, and having failed to find a perfect, abstract friendship in society, Thoreau moves to the fringes of society in the hope that this will afford him the hybrid of security and freedom which he seeks. Here at last is the "parkland" he speaks of in "Walking," a boundary area which promises a transcendent life and yet does not lose a connection with the object of transcendence, the desires and necessities inherent in the woods themselves. As such, Walden Pond, which is semi-natural and semi-isolated, appears a good place to find peace and freedom and perhaps even love itself.

In the very first paragraph of *Walden,* Thoreau writes that "[a]t present, I am a sojourner in civilized life again."[65] Even at the outset of this book, we are reminded that the perspective of this work is written from within society, and that Thoreau's partial retreat into the woods has led to a "sojourn" back into civilization; the walker keeps on walking.

Given his critique of life in cities and the dangers of social influences, it is no wonder that so many think of Thoreau as a renegade who, in moving to Walden Pond, sought to cut off all ties with his fellow members of society. But of course this is hardly true. Thoreau's cabin, which he built himself, was located about a mile from his nearest neighbor. Granted, this was quite a distance in an era before automobiles, but it hardly qualified as inaccessible wilderness. Thoreau's house was on a well-traveled path and across the pond from an active railway line. The land that he lived on belonged to none other than Emerson himself.[66] And he spent much time in the company of his own family as well as the Emersons.

Henry Seidel Canby takes issue with those who make light of Thoreau's continued dependence on and frequent visits to his family:

> The oft-told story that Henry, posing as a hermit, used to help himself stealthily to doughnuts from his mother's kitchen, has no point. Of course he did; but not stealthily. He was not trying to live *out* of the world; he was trying to live without being inconveniently dependent upon the world.[67]

In fact, as Canby, other biographers, and Thoreau himself frequently point out, the two years that Thoreau spent at Walden Pond were very busy not only socially but also economically and artistically. Thoreau made an expedition to Maine in the summer of the second year (which went into writing part of *The Maine Woods*).

Canby writes that at Walden Thoreau wanted "a room of his own," where he sought to prove that he could live on his own and give himself time to write and think and commune with nature. It is true that at the Emerson home he had all the time, resources, and encouragement to write that he needed. Yet it was around this time that Thoreau had come to realize just how dependent he was (both economically and intellectually) on his mentor, and he needed a bit of distance from him.[68] In 1845, a year after Emerson's remarks against living in the woods like "woodchucks" was published in his second series of essays, Thoreau moved to Walden Pond.

In his own journal writings of the period, Thoreau clearly states his frustration and need for a break from the Emerson household, and in particular Emerson himself:

> My life will wait for nobody, but is being matured still irresistibly while I go about the streets and chaffer with this man [Emerson] and that to secure it a living.... This staying to buy me a farm is as if the Mississippi should stop to chaffer with a clamshell.[69]

Clearly Walden offered only a partial distance from Emerson, perhaps not enough of one. Even there, Thoreau retains a strong connection, both physical and philosophical, to Emerson, even while struggling against him.

The parkland

In coming to Walden, Thoreau writes:

> It would be some advantage to live a primitive and frontier life though in the midst of an outward civilization if only to learn what are the gross necessaries of life.[70]

In the yearning for the parkland we see the possibility of living, as Rousseau put it, as "the savage who must live in the town." What relationship to nature and to love itself does life in this parkland afford? Walden is not the deep wilderness; it is a site of conquest, rich with the mould of that which has been overcome. Can Thoreau live here, learn from nature, even while remaining to some extent separate from it, associated with that which has harnessed and conquered it?

Nowhere do we see the struggle between Thoreau's own desires and his Emersonian transcendentalism more clearly than in the chapter of Walden entitled "Higher Laws." At one point in this chapter, Thoreau calls on us to repress what is animal about us:

> We are conscious of an animal in us, which awakens in proportion as our *higher nature* slumbers. It is reptile and sensual, and perhaps cannot be wholly expelled.... Possibly we may withdraw from it, but never change its nature.[71]

This "animal" is in fact our inner nature, the savage, primitive aspect of and basis for civilized people. For Thoreau this "animal" is manifested most directly and troublingly as our sexuality. All that is noble in us is based on its taming and harnessing:

> The generative energy, which when we are loose, dissipates and makes us unclean, when we are continent invigorates and inspires us. Chastity is the

flowering of man; and what are called Genius, Heroism, Holiness and the like are but various fruits which succeed it.[72]

Thoreau held that "he is blessed who is assured that the animal is dying out in him day by day and the divine being established."[73] He even gives us a line which appears shocking for anyone slightly acquainted with Thoreau: "Nature is hard to overcome, but she must be overcome."[74]

As a student of Emerson, Thoreau knows that freedom can only lie in subjecting base nature to higher nature, to struggling against the animals within and the animals without. But even in his most Emersonian mood, in "Higher Laws," he writes:

> I found in myself…an instinct toward a higher, or, as it is named spiritual life, as do most men, and another toward a primitive rank and savage one, and I reverence them both. *I love the wild not less the good.*[75]

Thoreau, who one page later will call for destroying the "animal" within us, here states, "I like sometimes to take rank hold on life and spend my day more as the animals do,"[76] and "I could sometimes eat a fried rat with good relish."[77] Whereas for Emerson words like "low" and "coarse" often have a disapproving tone, for Thoreau such words can be full of deep longing and even hope.

The Native Americans of Walden Pond

As in "Walking," and "Friendship" too, at Walden Pond Thoreau turns to Native Americans to help him in his dilemma. From this borderline perspective, he found himself identifying more and more with this community in terms of deciding how he lives, what he eats, and what his value systems are. In *Thoreau and the American Indians*, Robert F. Sayre claims that the entire structure of the book is deliberately organized as an "Indian vision quest."[78] As an academic subject, Native Americans fascinated, even obsessed Thoreau.[79] He had long determined to write "an Indian book," which he thought would become the definitive sourcebook on Native American folklore and knowledge about nature. While he never actually wrote this book, he did compile thousands of pages of notes on Native Americans, and in addition he undertook several journeys into their territory. If there was a way to avoid choosing, to avoid having to be either social or natural (or neither), perhaps the Native Americans could point out that way.

Here again, racial difference affords Thoreau a way to consider dangerous issues such as the nature of desire, the lure of love, all through an intermediary that he relates himself to but remains differentiated from by race. Thoreau can imagine himself as a Native American, to connect with nature as he sees them doing, but his "whiteness" prevents that association from becoming overly contaminating.

At Walden Pond, a connection to Native Americans offers not only the mediation of race, but also of time; here all of the Native Americans are long dead. In his chapter entitled "Former Inhabitants," Thoreau describes the escaped slaves, Irish workers, and deceased Native Americans who still haunt his cabin and the local woods. His occupation of a cabin in this location is laden with symbolic importance.[80] In this chapter, Thoreau is telling us about his neighborhood.

If the Native Americans themselves are dead, Thoreau does come into contact with several white men who appear to have "gone native," returning to the same kind of pure relationship to nature that the Native Americans represent for Thoreau. He tells the tale of a French Canadian whom he encountered in the woods. Something struck Thoreau about this man, and he finally realized that this isolated woodsman was thinking for himself, "a phenomenon so rare that I would any day walk ten miles to observe it."[81]

Yet this self-motivated thinker did not have much to offer the world: "his thinking was so primitive and immersed in his animal life that, though more promising than a merely learned man's, it rarely ripened into anything which can be reported."[82] This man is not unlike Emerson's yeoman farmer, self-reliant and pure but not able to transcend the lowness that he engages with. Yet, more than Emerson, Thoreau admires precisely the very primitiveness that spawned this French Canadian's thoughts. His primitiveness makes him what he is, and yet it also prevents him from serving as a model that Thoreau could himself follow.

There are other, darker models in this book of Europeans being overcome by the lowness of their environs, particularly in terms of the Irish immigrants that Thoreau encounters. The Irishmen in the vicinity of Walden Pond seem to stand for the idea of the European who has given up his birthright and become degenerate in a way that the Native Americans themselves never were. Thoreau writes, for example, of his Irish neighbor "John Field," whose name is itself instructive given Thoreau's tendency (like Locke's) to see our internal state as a kind of landscape related to the world without; this John is indeed a "field," but one that is not as well utilized as other neighbors, including Thoreau himself. The two go out fishing on one occasion, and while Thoreau "was catching a fair string," John Field, using the wrong bait, was catching nothing at all.[83] Thoreau writes:

> Poor John Field!—I trust he does not read this, unless he will improve by it,—thinking to live by some derivative old country mode in this primitive new country.... With his horizon all his own, yet he a poor man, born to be poor, with his inherited Irish poverty or poor life, his Adam's grandmother and boggy ways, not to rise in this world, he nor his posterity, till their wading webbed bog-trotting feet get *talaria* to their heels.[84]

Thoreau shows how he has learned, better than John Field, how best to flourish in America. Unlike Field, Thoreau does not attempt to live as his European ancestors did, a non-native plant. In this new world, it becomes "derivative" to follow one's own traditions and "original" to follow Native American fashions. Unlike Field, Thoreau has substituted one origin for another, mediating his relationship to nature through "the Indian" example.

Hunting

For Thoreau, this story of fishing with John Field is illustrative because fishing and especially hunting are the single most important things that the Native Americans have to teach him. For all of his willingness to see Native Americans in ways that aren't entirely stereotypical, "the Indian" as hunter remains the prime metaphor for his understanding of that society. The hunter, a man alone in nature, is an emblem of the sort of independence and freedom that seems to drive all of Thoreau's work. Yet the hunter is doomed as are all Native Americans by the advance of white society. Here we come to the same quandary as we found in "Walking": How can Thoreau learn from the hunter, emulate his freedom, autonomy, and power, gain his access to nature and desire and yet not share his fate?

For Thoreau, hunting is not purely a Native American activity. He fondly remembers the hunting that he did as a boy, and which nearly every boy in New England learned to do. It was "one of the best parts of my education."[85] For Thoreau, the hunter is one stage in an evolutionary process that is not only historical but also personal:

> Thus even in civilized communities, the embryo man passes through the hunter stage of development.[86]

We begin our lives as hunters of literal wild animals, but as we develop, Thoreau would have us sublimate this hunt into a metaphoric, transcendent level so that we may become "hunters as well as fishers of men."[87]

Thoreau writes that hunting "is oftenest the young man's introduction to the forest, and the most original part of himself," and that "We cannot but pity the boy who has never fired a gun; he is no more humane, while his education has been sadly neglected."[88] Ultimately, however, to retain an interest in literal hunting is to remain trapped in boyhood forever:

> No human creature past the thoughtless age of boyhood, will wantonly murder any creature, which holds its life by the same tenure that he does.[89]

And then:

> He goes thither at first as a hunter and fisher, until at last, if he has the seeds of a better life, he distinguishes his proper objects as a poet or naturalist it may be, and leaves the gun and fish-pole behind. The mass of men are still and always young in this respect.[90]

As hunters of literal beasts, Native Americans serve as models but not ones that are to be followed too closely. For all their manliness (Thoreau writes that the Algonquins called the hunters "the best men"), they remain for Thoreau at the level of children.[91] As culture "develops" (that is, as we turn from Native American to white society), the actual hunters must give way, becoming abstracted into metaphorical hunters of "the reptile" within.

Thus, in precisely the same way that with Locke the laborer provides a service and a lesson for the master, for Thoreau the hunter is a basis for transcendence itself. On the one hand, the hunter is necessary for the task of actually clearing the woods themselves of wild beasts. Like the logger and the pioneer, the hunter is part of a series of actions taken that precede the poet, making the woods safe for his entry. As Thoreau tells us in "Chesuncook":

> The poet's commonly is not a logger's path, but a woodman's. The logger and pioneer have preceded him like John the Baptist; eaten the wild honey, it may be, but the locusts also; banished decaying wood and the spongy mosses which feed on it, and built hearth and humanized nature for him.[92]

Only a wood conquered and "humanized" serves as the site of transcendence. Free as it is of dangerous beasts, the poet can now "commune with nature." Furthermore, as we have seen, the hunter provides a model for how the poet can contend with the "inner" animals. Just as the hunter helped to humanize the woods, so does his model help the poet to "humanize" himself, applying the lessons of boyhood hunting to the stalking of his own inner beasts.

In this case, even more than with Locke, there is a need to distance oneself from the lesson giver. To remain a hunter is to be too bonded to nature to ever be able to fully master the animal, or to escape its fate. On the other hand, an effete, modern person who has no experience of hunting would not be able to defeat the animal either, having lived too long a soft and interdependent life.

Ultimately, the most developed hunter is the poet himself:

> A farmer, a hunter, a soldier, a reporter, even a philosopher may be daunted, but nothing can deter a poet, for he is actuated by pure love.[93]

It is the poet who can do what the hunter cannot, not just kill but harness the desire inherent in the deepest part of the woods. His is a more subtle kind of power, characteristic of love itself (albeit a power based on a prior act of killing).

But, as always with Thoreau, there is an ambivalence expressed about this kind of metaphorical hunting, about what is lost in the process of this transformation. In the space of one paragraph we can see Thoreau equivocating both on his firm disavowal of hunting and on the desirability of social creature comforts:

> With every year, I am less a fisherman, though without more humanity or even wisdom; at present I am no fisherman at all. But I see that if I were to live in a

wilderness I should again be tempted to become a fisher and hunter in earnest. Beside, there is something essentially unclean about this diet and all flesh and I began to see where housework commences and whence the endeavor, which costs so much to keep a tidy and respectable appearance each day, to keep the house sweet and free from all ill odors and sights.... A little bread or a few potatoes would have done as well, with less trouble and filth.[94]

Here again, we see Thoreau torn between two worlds. He still yearns to be a hunter, but at the same time he is disgusted by the carnage and dirtiness that he imagines such a life would bring. Would he eat meat or bread and potatoes, or can he have them both?

At Walden Pond, the Native American hunters are all long gone. But their work and their ghosts live on. If boyhood hunting is the prerequisite to manhood, then so too are the Native American hunters the prerequisite to poetry. Thoreau's relationship to the desire inherent in the woods is mediated, as we have seen, by racial difference and also by time itself. For a different kind of thinker, this might offer a perfect solution to the constituent threat posed by those who must sacrifice themselves for others in liberal society. The Native Americans are dead and gone; they can't threaten anyone now. But Thoreau is not this kind of thinker. He insists on seeing for himself what went on in the past, insists on considering that the life that has been overcome might be a better life than that which replaces it.

And, perhaps too, Thoreau suspects that the extinction of the Native American hunter points to the impossibility of the balance that he seeks, of having both society and nature coexisting. The hunter, who epitomizes such a balance, ends up dead and gone. Thoreau comes to Walden Pond to test the possibility of balance, but such an outcome is undermined by its own preconditions. Thoreau knows in a sense that he cannot ignore the past because it tells him something about the future.

Time is as much Thoreau's enemy as it is his ally. True, it protects him, gives him distance, allows him to avoid seeing the slaughter of animals and genocide of people that preceded him, but it also means that eventually, inevitably, Walden itself will become not a parkland but part of the city. Thoreau knows that the border between nature and society is not static but always moving west. In "Higher Laws," he notes that even boyhood hunting itself is endangered:

[A]lready a change is taking place, owing not to increased humanity, but to an increased scarcity of game, for perhaps the hunter is the greatest friend of the animals hunted.[95]

Time is running out for Thoreau, and for society as well. The animals and the hunters follow each other in death, leaving white settlers with less and less to teach them, less of a mould with every passing year.

And this is equally true for Thoreau himself in his own internal struggle. His internal "mould," the nature and the reptile willing, will also be used up, the desires harnessed and tamed. Like the Native American hunter who follows his prey in death, Thoreau might die, at least in terms of all that matters for him. As he colonizes himself in this way, he too will be "humanized," which is to say left emptier than ever, conquered and hollowed out, waiting to be filled.

The borderlands do not have answers for Thoreau. We must go one step deeper, away from society, into the heart of the wilderness itself, following the walker into the heart of what he most desires. We see that Thoreau is not certain what he will find there, or what he will do when he gets there. Will he finally learn to kill the beast within once and for all and achieve some safe and chaste and distant form of love? Or will he embrace it, abandoning the hunt? Can he find a balance at last? Can he find the love that he has been seeking all along?

5. THE MAINE WOODS: LIFE AND DEATH IN THE WILD

In terms of the conquest of the American wilderness, in Concord, and even at Walden Pond, Thoreau lives in the future, when the necessary hard work has all been accomplished. But as we've seen, he is not content to simply feast on the mould of what was accomplished before; he wants a direct link to the manifestation of desire that has long ago been tamed and humanized. By going to Maine, Thoreau is seeking contact with the past, the necessity-bound world that he draws inspiration from. Seeing for himself the prehistory of what went into creating the "balance" of wildness and cultivation in the parkland at Walden Pond, he does learn something in the woods, but perhaps not what he expected to.

Unlike at Walden Pond, where he is only a short walk from the town of Concord, in the woods of Maine Thoreau is truly on his own. In the woods he is dependent upon his traveling companions to some degree, but especially on his Native American guides. It is ironic that for all his feelings that "social" necessity is enslaving, and a relationship to base necessity liberating, in Maine, if anything, the exact opposite is true. While marveling at the grandeur and the beauty of nature, Thoreau finds himself very much a displaced white man, out of his element—his distance from nature becomes more rather than less apparent. Most importantly, Thoreau sees to his horror the exact costs of "progress." In Maine he has face-to-face contact with "the Indian," he sees also the brutality of slaughter, of hunting and death in the woods. At the same time, I find the writings in *The Maine Woods* to be among his most beautiful and most engaged, precisely because, having the courage to look beneath the facade of his privilege and his subjectivity, he is truly on the trail of the "truth" that he has long been searching for.

The Maine Woods is actually three separate essays, "Ktaadn," "Chesuncook," and "The Allegash and East Branch," each of which chronicles a separate journey to the wilds of Maine (in 1846, 1853, and 1857, respectively). At each trip, Thoreau was in a very different stage of his life. The first trip, which he describes in "Ktaadn," was written during his sojourn at Walden Pond. By the time he wrote "The Allegash and East Branch," he was ailing from tuberculosis and nearing the end of his life.

At the time of Thoreau's visits to Maine, this area was the last real frontier area left on the upper East Coast. Whereas most New England Native Americans had been decimated or expelled, those of Maine (he deals mainly with the Penobscot Nation) had managed to survive the onslaught of disease and white imperialism, at least enough to offer a sizable community adapting to their colonized status. Maine, then, represented for Thoreau a relatively accessible opportunity to visit the wild and those human beings who made their life in it.

In terms of his attitude toward actual Native American persons (as opposed to long-vanished ghosts), Robert Sayre contends that Thoreau moves beyond the stereotypes of "savagism" popular during his day. He writes that Thoreau's understanding of Native American culture and society was ameliorated through repeated contact with and study of actual people. According to Sayre, as we move from one volume of *The Maine Woods* to the next, Thoreau comes to a somewhat more enlightened position. While he might offer an improvement upon savagist depictions, Thoreau retains a tendency to speak of the flesh-and-blood Native Americans which he encounters as "the Indian," enlisting them as metaphors in the service of his own philosophical purposes.[96]

And yet there is a way that Thoreau allows Native American people whom he encounters to offer their own personalities and foibles, even when they run counter to his own uses for "the Indian." He is often confounded by the Native Americans that he meets, by their *non*-exoticism, by their similarity to himself. Thus the "obvious" distance of race is diminished in the deep woods, making his connection to them all too vivid, all too immediate, even as he also sees how dangerous, how difficult, how terrifying a life encountering raw nature really is.

The doomed Native American?

"Ktaadn," Thoreau's description of his first Maine expedition, begins by musing on the decline of Native American culture. For Thoreau, Native Americans are indeed "savages," a word that he derives from "salvage," which he in turn derives from the Latin *sylva* or "woods."[97] The Native Americans then are woodspeople and Thoreau's project is to salvage from their experience what he can—indeed, *The Maine Woods* is often animated by a sense of urgency, a desire to derive what can be had from a dying people while some of them yet remain.

Yet Thoreau's personal experience of Native American people defies his expectations. He describes going along the Penobscot River, telling us that an island in the middle of the river belongs to the Penobscots. From his boat he sees on the island "a short shabby, washer woman-looking Indian."[98] The image of this woman impressed him with the sorry state of the Native Americans of Maine. He wrote: "This picture will do to put before the Indian's history, that is, the history of his extinction."[99] Yet, confounding his own convictions, Thoreau notes:

> The island seemed deserted today, yet I observed some new houses among the weather stained ones, as if the tribe had still a design on life.[100]

In general, one can see that Thoreau is surprised by what he sees among Maine's Native American people. His guides lived in well-made cabins ("as good as an average one on a New England village street"), were practicing Christians, and often knew little about their own histories and backgrounds.[101] Nor were they always as curious about their own past or their "naturalness" as he expected them to be.

The tenaciousness with which "the Indian" clings to life is just one of the many ambiguities Thoreau has to face in his study of Native American people. The living example of Native Americans adapting to survive in the face of white society suggests an exception to Thoreau's certainty that a life in nature is untenable and that the power of white society is inevitable. It disturbs his conviction that his choices are "necessary" and inevitable. It also upsets his notion of "the Indian" as a model which offers some safe, mediating distance.

Three guides

In *The Maine Woods,* as we progress from his first guide to his last (Louis Neptune, Joe Aitteon, and Joe Polis, respectively), we can see both an unraveling of stereotypes about Native Americans and a decrease in self-confidence on Thoreau's part.[102] From Thoreau's own perspective, the increasingly intimate connection between himself and his Native American guides leads him deeper into the mysteries of their society and thereby into nature itself. But at the same time, his sense of alienation from what he is searching for grows apace. The more he knows and experiences, the less he can grasp.

The first guide that Thoreau engages, in "Ktaadn," is Louis Neptune. In his description of Neptune, Thoreau evinces a viewpoint that was perhaps typical of his period:

> Met face to face, these Indians in their native woods looked like the sinister and slouching fellows whom you meet picking up strings and paper in the streets of a city. There is, in fact, a remarkable and unexpected resemblance between the

degraded savage and the lowest classes in a great city. The one is no more a child of nature than the other. In the progress of degradation the distinction of race is soon lost.[103]

The connection to the white underclass suggests that for Thoreau the Native American strategy of survival compromises all that is great about them, condemns them to a kind of "lowness" not unlike that of John Field, one that is not appropriate to or worthy of Thoreau's own image of "the Indian."

As a guide, Neptune is a disaster; he never shows up for an appointed meeting and Thoreau and his fellow white travelers are forced to do all the work and follow the trails themselves. Finally, he appears just as they are coming back from their trip. Thoreau writes that Neptune and his cohorts "had been delayed so long by a drunken frolic"[104] and sees him off in disgust. Once Neptune is out of sight, however, Thoreau lapses into a transcendentalist mode, musing at the vanishing back of his erstwhile first guide:

> He is but dim and misty to me, obscured by the aeons that lie between the bark-canoe and the batteau. He builds no house of logs, but a wigwam of skins. He eats no hot bread and sweet cake but musquash and moose-meat and the fat of bears. He glides up the Millinocket and is lost to my sight.... So he goes about his destiny, the red face of man.[105]

Freed from the reality of Joe Neptune, whom he seems to find fairly distasteful and about as exotic as a pauper on the streets of New York City, Thoreau reverts to a stereotype of "the Indian" that has nothing to do with Neptune's personal qualities. Neptune does in fact live in a European-style house, and it seems as if he would prefer freshly baked bread to bear fat if given the choice.

To be sure, Thoreau was able to achieve his goal without his Native American guide. The objective—to climb Mount Ktaadn in central Maine—was undertaken without fuss. But of his three voyages, "Ktaadn" is in some ways the most impoverished—it seems as if he is still missing something here. Certainly he is compelled to return two more times.

In "Chesuncook," Thoreau admits that "we had employed an Indian mainly that I might have the opportunity to study his ways."[106] Thoreau needs Native American guides not literally to find his way in the woods, but rather to direct him to the mysteries of the woods of which he, as a white man, has no experience and no invitation.[107]

The second guide, Joe Aitteon, is, from the outset, an improvement on Neptune. Early on, Thoreau notes that Aitteon disappears "Indian like"[108] but soon returns, and he says, "we had no reason to complain of him afterwards." Aitteon is a contemporary Native American, brought up under the auspices of white society. As such, he evinces attitudes that Thoreau finds to be somewhat disappointing. For example, Aitteon admits to Thoreau that although his ancestors subsisted on berries and game from the woods, he had not been brought up to do so himself. Thoreau quotes him as saying, "By George! I shan't go into the woods without provisions."[109]

But in other ways Aitteon impressed Thoreau very much. In marveling at Aitteon's skill as a navigator and guide, Thoreau writes that the ways in which he excels are completely unlike those skills that white woodsmen possess:

> He and other Indians generally...are not able to describe dimensions or distances in our measures with any accuracy. He could tell, perhaps what time we should arrive, but not how far it was.[110]

Electing to spend the night camping with Aitteon and his Native American friend, because the white campground "had an ill smell," Thoreau observes the Native Americans speaking their own language:[111]

> It took me by surprise, though I had found so many arrow-heads and convinced me that the Indian was not the invention of historians and poets. It was a purely wild and primitive American sound, as much as the barking of a *chickaree.*"[112]

Transfixed by this "wild and primitive American sound," Thoreau felt "that I stood...as near to the primitive man of America, that night, as any of its discoverers ever did."[113] Here he is reverting to his tendency to metamorphosize a flesh-and-blood Native American person in his presence into an icon of wildness and purity. Because the Native Americans are speaking their own language, Thoreau is once again thrown onto his own devices; he readily lapses into transcendental reverie. And yet the thrill that he feels is an indication that there is more to find, that he has something to learn from these men.

Joe Polis, the third of Thoreau's guides, was such a success and revealed so much about Native American culture and woodlore to Thoreau that the latter came to see him as something of an obstacle. Thoreau wrote to a would-be editor:

> The more fatal objection to printing my last Maine-wood experience, is that my Indian guide, whose words and deeds I report very faithfully,—and they are the most interesting part of the story,—knows how to read and takes a newspaper so that I could not face him again.[114]

Thoreau's experience in "The Allegash and East Branch" is certainly his most vivid and captivating account of his travels in Maine. And, as we see, Thoreau himself recognized that he owed most of this to Polis himself. During this trip, which went into some of the wildest parts of Maine, Thoreau was constantly reminded of how little he knew the woods compared to Polis.

In fact, Polis was no ordinary guide; he was one of the few in the area who knew much about ancient customs. He had acquired his knowledge from his

Penobscot elders and "lamented that the present generation of Indians 'had lost a great deal.' "[115] By the time Thoreau meets Polis, the Penobscot community has suffered a plague of smallpox—thus Thoreau's dire predictions about Native American extinction seem to finally be coming true. Ironically, just as the Native Americans appear to be disappearing, so too is Thoreau himself. He is very ill at this point with tuberculosis—the disease that will kill him while still quite young.

At the outset of this trip, Thoreau is warned not to expect to find a worthy guide under the circumstances, but as luck will have it, Polis, a member of the "Indian aristocracy," wants the job. Against this background of loss, Polis's vitality and adaptability seem to defy the role that Thoreau has cut out for him as the last voice of a dying culture. In his ongoing relationship to Polis, Thoreau comes both to respect and resent the ways in which Polis does not readily lend himself to being typecast.

As with the other guides, Thoreau often sees Polis as a metaphor. In commenting, for example, on his accent, Thoreau writes, "it was a wild and refreshing sound, like that of the wind among the pines, or the booming of the surf on the shore."[116] Or, when Polis sings a song in his own language, it carries Thoreau "back to the period of the discovery of America, to San Salvadore and the Inca."[117] At one point Polis calls to a wild animal by emitting a "curious squeaking wiry sound with his lips." Thoreau thought "I had at last got into the wilderness, and that he was a wild man indeed to be talking to a musquash."[118] Polis seems to give Thoreau an entree, a glimpse into the deep woods, the wilderness that he had been seeking all along. If Thoreau seeks wild men as friends, he seems to have found one in Joe Polis, a flesh-and-blood incarnation of "Wawatam."

At other times, Thoreau records unique attributes of Polis that run counter to any stereotyped representation of "the Indian" that he might hold. For example, Polis is a devout Christian and insists that he won't work on Sundays. Thoreau, who came to the woods in part to escape white institutions, writes that as a non-believer among Christians, he "found himself in the minority."[119] He also records Polis's interest in leaving the woods to move to a major metropolitan area. At the same time, he shows how Polis himself felt this was probably not feasible, saying, "I suppose I live in New York, I be poorest hunter, I expect," and Thoreau comments that "he understood very well both his superiority and inferiority to the whites."[120]

As with Aitteon, Thoreau sees Polis as having a unique sense of woodcraft which as a white man he is incapable of. Ultimately, he views Polis's wisdom as stemming, as with the French Canadian he encounters in *Walden,* from an ability to think for himself:

Often when an Indian says "I don't know" in regard to the route he is to take, he does not mean what a white man would by those words, for his Indian instinct may tell him still as much as the most confident white man knows. He does not carry things in his head...but *relies on himself* for the moment.[121] (emphasis added)

Here again we see that Thoreau sees "natural" self-reliance all around him, but he cannot himself directly experience it. Like Rousseau, Thoreau is jealous of and wistful for those who mediate his desire, who touch wildness itself.

At one point during the voyage, Thoreau ruefully records that he and his white companions have lost Polis's track, noting that "The Indian was greatly surprised that...we had not followed his tracks,—said it was 'strange' and evidently thought little of our woodcraft."[122] When he traveled without his white followers, Polis dispensed with the need for trails altogether, traveling cross country "over the unaltered face of nature."[123]

Thoreau's disadvantages as a woodsman vis-à-vis Polis are brought into the open when his companion, Edward Hoar, gets lost. Straining to keep up with Polis, Thoreau loses track of Hoar and comes to realize that the latter is lost. Polis and Thoreau search for him everywhere, and at one point Thoreau loses sight of Polis too and panics somewhat, "halooing and searching for him." Polis turns up, but in his concern for Hoar's whereabouts, Thoreau is made painfully aware of his own limitations. "I thought what I should do the next day, if I did not find him, what I *could* do in such a wilderness."[124] Hoar is found the next day, but the entire experience serves as a reminder of Thoreau's incapacity, vulnerability, and dependence in the wilderness.[125] He never considers that Polis was the one who was lost—it is always he or his white companion who cannot find their way. He assumes that Polis knows exactly where he is at all times.

As Thoreau sees it, for Polis (unlike Thoreau himself), the wilderness is his home. When they finish their trip and return to Polis's lodging, Thoreau asks him if he is glad to be back home. Thoreau records that

there was no relenting to his wildness, and he said, "It makes no difference to me where I am." Such is the Indian's pretense always.[126]

Thoreau's relationship with Polis is complicated; he praises Polis at one moment and makes fun of him the next. He invariably points out how Polis says "lock" instead of rock or how excessively Polis complains when he gets sick, yet at the same time he evinces a deep respect and envy for his skills. If in some way Thoreau sees Polis as the true author of "The Allegash and East Branch," then what of Thoreau's own autonomous vision? Has he learned anything about self-reliance on this trip? If he insists on thinking for himself, how does he reconcile himself as a purveyor of Polis's knowledge? How can the desire and nature he encounters be really "his own" when it is so clearly mediated? Polis's vitality, his refusal to submit to stereotypes of "the Indian," and his complex personality in general are a challenge to Thoreau's need to use him as an icon that must be transcended. And, to his credit, Thoreau portrays Polis in a way that is honest, which allows these challenges to emerge. Polis resists becoming a shadowy metaphor. His is a body that comes so vividly to life that he is not only a mediator of Thoreau's desire but also an obstacle. He is a separate body, with a separate agenda defying a unifying harmony (a Golden Age oneness) both in the writing and the experience of "The Allegash and East Branch." Polis is "different" from Thoreau but not so different. He is not dead (in fact he is much more robust and healthy than Thoreau) and can speak for himself—he resists reification by his every word and deed, and Thoreau cannot decide if he is thrilled or in despair. Does Thoreau want to *be* Polis? Could he be his friend?

As we move from Neptune to Aitteon to Polis, we travel deeper into the woods both literally and metaphorically. With Neptune's protracted absence, Thoreau has an experience of the woods essentially without a guide. He comments on the flora and so forth, but his experience is clearly shy of the transcendental redemption that he is looking for. It is with the very present, very much alive Joe Polis that he comes closest to what he is looking for, yet what Thoreau experiences isn't freedom, autonomy, and full communion with nature but rather his own distance from and dependence upon what he is seeking.

Hunting (and poetry) revisited

Just as the physical presence of his guides mars Thoreau's quest for transcendence, so do the habits and lifestyle of the wilderness. Here in the deep woods, we see that Thoreau's understanding of hunting has changed as he has outgrown and transcended it. At Walden Pond, hunting is a metaphor, a sport for boys to be cast off during adulthood. Here in the woods, however, hunting is a way of life. In revisiting the experience of hunting as a grown man and as a poet, Thoreau sees clearly the murderous impulse, the bad neighboring, that is presupposed by transcendence.

In "Chesuncook," Thoreau gives us a protracted description of a moose hunt in which he participates very peripherally. This account mixes admiration for Aitteon's skills ("he stepped lightly and gracefully, stealing through the bushes with the least possible noise in a way in which no white man does") with revulsion at the blood and carnage involved.[127] Thoreau reflects:

> I had had enough of moose-hunting. I had not come to the woods for this purpose...though I had been willing to learn how the Indian manoeuvered.... This afternoon's tragedy, and my share in it, as it affected the innocence, destroyed the pleasure of my adventure. It is true, I came as near as possible to being a hunter and miss it, myself; as it is, I think that I could spend a year in

the woods, fishing and hunting, just enough to sustain myself, with satisfaction. This would be next to living like a philosopher on the fruits of the earth which you had raised.[128]

Even at this moment, Thoreau's denunciation of hunting is not total. His main complaint here is that the hunting was purely for sport and without purpose, "not even for the sake of [the moose's] hide."[129] He writes that in the woods, hunters, both Native American and white, have become little more than mercenaries "whose object is to slay as many moose and other wild animals as possible."[130]

> What a coarse and imperfect use Indians and hunters make of Nature! No wonder that their race is so soon exterminated. I already, and for weeks afterward felt my nature the coarser for this part of my woodland experience, and was reminded that our life should be lived as tenderly and daintily as one would pluck a flower.[131]

But of course, the purpose of hunting *must* be mercenary in this time and in this place. As a disappearing community, there can be no question of "ways of life" for the Native American hunters. In Maine, hunting has a serious and even urgent purpose, to clear the woods, conquering and humanizing them as part of the ongoing path of settlement. There is not only no need for sustaining the wild, but such sentiments run counter to the purposes of progress.

There is a sense in which Thoreau seems to realize that he ought not to have witnessed this degree of brutality and slaughter, however necessary it has been. Having participated in the moose hunt, he begins to feel afraid:

> I remembered how far on every hand that wilderness stretched, before you came to cleared or cultivated fields, and wondered if any bear or moose was watching the light of my fire; for Nature looked sternly upon me on account of the murder of the moose.[132]

Suddenly, the woods, where Thoreau seeks redemption and love, become transformed into a hostile environment. Ironically it is "the Indian," to whom Thoreau turned to initiate himself into the mysteries of the wild, who is the cause of this sense of separation from nature; the mediator is once again transformed into barrier, his very difference enabling but also defying Thoreau's purpose.

In "The Allegash and East Branch," with the unpleasant memory of the moose hunt in "Chesuncook" a long way behind him, Thoreau redescribes the hunter's role to himself in a way that more closely suits his purposes. After denouncing urban living as being "like vermin clubs together in alleys and drinking saloons," he writes:

> [the Hunter] is comparatively an independent and successful man, getting his living in a way that he likes, without disturbing his human neighbors. How

much more respectable also is the life of a solitary pioneer or settler in these, or any woods,—having real difficulties, not of his own creation, drawing his subsistence directly from nature,—than the helpless multitudes in the towns who depend on gratifying the extremely artificial wants of society.[133]

This is vintage Thoreau as he lives in the popular consciousness, advocating a life in the woods as wholesome and pure, the antidote to civilization and characterized by blissful isolation, autonomy, and freedom. But where is this hunter during the description of actual moose hunting in "Chesuncook"? Commenting on hunting as a pastime in that essay, with the dead body of a slaughtered moose at his feet, Thoreau writes that whereas white settlers and Native Americans only take from the woods, the poet takes nothing at all:

> Strange that so few ever come to the woods to see how the pine lives and grows and spires, lifting its evergreen arms to the light.... There is a higher law affecting our relation to pines as well as to men.... Every creature is better alive than dead, men and moose, and pine-trees.... Is it the lumberman, then, who is the friend and lover of the pine? No! no! it is the poet; he is who makes the truest use of the pine.... No, it is the poet who loves them, as his own shadow in the air, and lets them stand.[134]

In the woods of Maine, Thoreau has indeed learned something. Whereas at Walden Pond he could exist without violating nature, hoeing beans, and so forth, to sustain human life here in the wilderness, especially during this transitional period, requires a certain violence against nature that Thoreau is not willing to commit and does not even care to witness.

And yet witnessed it he has. And he knows that he is dependent upon this slaughter. As we have seen, in order to be have poetry, Thoreau, like Emerson before him, requires that in the distant past there had been hunting and logging. The poet can only exist in a wood that has already been "humanized," sanitized by conquest. He tells us that "it is the poet who loves them all." But what kind of love is this which is born out of murder? The walker, as pioneer in effect, comes to a land that has already been subjugated for him by those who came before him. Thoreau perhaps shows us more clearly than anyone else how it is that the higher is built on the subjugation of the lower, how this "loving unity" presupposes not just hierarchy, but slaughter and colonization as well.

And the same argument holds true for the parallel development of Thoreau's struggle with the animal within; he wants to kill the beast within, but cannot bear to see it die or to live without it. Perhaps he sees that the hunting of the beast within is no less awful than the hunt of the moose in "Chesuncook." There too, the purpose of the hunt is not to honor the beast but to use it, even to kill it off once and for all.

After his experience of the woods as they "really are," he seeks to return to the safe and comfortable world of white society. Once out of the woods, Thoreau feels tremendous relief:

> It was a relief to get back to our smooth but still varied landscape. For a permanent residence, it seemed to me that there could be no comparison between this and the wilderness, necessary as the latter is for a resource and a background, the raw material of all our civilization. The wilderness is simple, almost to barrenness. The partially cultivated country it is which chiefly has inspired and will inspire the strains of poets.... The civilized man must at length pine there, like a cultivated plant.[135]

Thoreau realizes that the wilderness is no place for a transplant, a non-native plant. His intent was always to learn from the forest and bring that lesson home to society; he is a "cultivated plant" who always meant to return home.

Thoreau went into the woods to discover how to (or if one could) love and be free at the same time. He came to find his authentic self, to make peace with the past, with the original nature that he can never find. Yet as he probes deeper into the Maine wilderness, with each trip he learns to an increasing degree that he is not capable of the task that is before him. He can neither connect with the wild nor overcome it, but he is rather haunted by it, even as he is haunted by the absence of love itself. He finds not himself, not the other, but simply a tantalizing vision of those things which he desperately needs. He learns too that the mediation of desire does not preserve what he looks for but destroys it. Unlike Emerson, Thoreau cannot be content with abstraction because he knows as Emerson does not (or at least not to the same extent) that abstraction does not substitute for the original, it murders it (or at least its vestiges).

In a sense, Thoreau can never find the idyllic past he is looking for. Going to Maine, he finds not the eternal peace of the wild, but a zone of conquest, a land in transition, a near past. Thoreau's own presence in a sense denies his access to the perfect vista he seeks. His presence already implies the coming of white society, of death and slaughter. Once again we see the "scandal" of the sign seeking to both find and replace the lost original.

And without true wilderness, Thoreau can't find true love either. In his search for perfect companionship and perfect freedom, Thoreau finds, as others have before him, that bodies have a way of lingering, serving as testaments to that which has been lost, that which cannot be replaced. John (whether as himself or as Wawatam) is gone but is dearly missed; the desire for Edmund is not overcome by its transposition to his virtue; "the Indian" continues to haunt the groves of Walden Pond; Joe Polis serves as much as obstacle as bridge to the heart of the woods. These bodies linger not just because of the role they play, but also because Thoreau himself is a party in maintaining their continued, lingering presence. In the search for self-reliance, autonomy, and freedom, Thoreau discovers at the heart of this search that his self is empty because it is built upon the loss of those whom he needs and loves the most, the loss and destruction of nature and the wild and even friendship itself.

6. WILD, DEMOCRATIC FRIENDS

What do we make of Thoreau's despair, of the failure of his search for love and friendship? Cavell himself admits that there is a despair in Thoreau that he worries will undermine the conviction of his arguments:

> [T]here is a recurrent form of doubt about Thoreau's writing which may threaten the balance of my deliberations with his book and thereby take the heart out of the reader's effort to try it further. The form of doubt is caused partly by the depth of the book's depressions and the height of its elevations, and more nearly by the absence of reconciliation between them.[136]

I think Cavell has perfectly captured something about Thoreau, if we understand these elevations and depressions as a model for the ways in which Thoreau seeks to reconcile his Emersonian transcendentalism with his own much more democratic soul.

Cavell takes seriously Thoreau's claim that "I do not propose to write an ode to dejection." Yet Cavell writes that "every line of his account is cause for despair, because each is an expression he has waited for, and yet with each he is not transformed."[137] And again:

> This is the characteristic threat of prophecy, and of the knowledge of the gospel.... If Thoreau's words merely show us promises we can never accept, then his beauty mocks us; he has realized the fear in his epigraph and written an ode to dejection.[138]

And yet there is always hope, because

> That was always the knack of faith. Crowing, if it is not followed by the last day, will at any rate express acceptance of that promise; if there is not dawn in him, the crower is at any rate studying "an infinite expectation of dawn."[139]

Thus we are once again face-to-face with the Nietzschan "perhaps," the possibility of a democratic vision amid Thoreau's despair.

But where is it? As we have seen, Cavell uses the concept of "nextness" as a way to redeem the liberal self from all of his complexities. Cavell himself considers the kinds of neighbors that Thoreau finds in the woods:

> [The writer of *Walden*] keeps alive the fact and the imagination of injustice, and inhabiting "the more free and honorable ground" on which to be found by "the

fugitive slave, and the Mexican prisoner on parole, and the Indian come to plead the wrongs of his race"...all of whom make their appearance to him at Walden. He went there to "repeople the woods"...first by being there, second, by imaging those who were before, third by anticipating those for whom he is preparing the ground, those who have come to the woods and must be renewed.[140]

Of course this is all true, but at the same time Thoreau is not only a chronicler in the destruction of these people, but also in some sense a benefactor. He lives in a wood humanized by conquest; he has learned how to hunt without sharing the doom of those who have taught him. Thoreau tries to be a good neighbor, but he is a bad one as well. Whereas "nextness" allows for hostility and difference, it also presumes the possibility of coexistence. Thoreau's tragic vision does not permit this, at least not yet.

But Thoreau's despair does offer us something. It tells us the dangers of trying to pursue nextness and democracy from within the confines of love. Perhaps the ultimate irony for Thoreau is that within the rubric of the doctrine of love, terrestrial love itself remains eternally elusive. Indeed, Thoreau himself offers that under existing circumstances, neighborliness, like most relationships, merely reinforces our alienation from ourselves:

> For the most part, we are contented so to deal and to be dealt with, and we do not think that for the mass of men there is any truer and nobler relation possible. A man may have good neighbors, so called, and acquaintances, and even companions, wife, parents, brothers, sisters, children, who meet himself and one another on this ground only. The state does not demand justice of its members...what is commonly called Friendship is only a little more than honor among rogues.[141]

But can there ever be friends? Thoreau's concept of friendship presupposes other relationships, just as with Emerson and Aristotle before him. As with Emerson (and Aristotle), episodes of true friendship are rare indeed. For Thoreau, most so-called friendships are not worthy of their name, for "they are not often transfigured and translated by love in each other's presence."[142] Without love, there can be no friendship, but it seems just as true to say that there can't be any friendship with love either. "O my friends, there is no friend."

In "Friendship," Thoreau explicitly links the search for a friend to the same imagery of the pioneer, and to Columbus himself, that we saw in "Walking," This Columbus is the searcher for lovers who have:

> sailed westward of these isles...but neither he nor his successors have found them [friends].... The earnest seeker and hopeful discoverer of this New World always haunts the outskirts of his time and walks through the densest crowd uninterrupted, and, as it were, in a straight line.[143]

As Rousseau told us in *The Discovery of the New World,* Columbus did indeed find love and friendship across the ocean. And even as he created a new unity, he also instigated an attack on nature and a genocide that was still being carried out in Thoreau's own lifetime. Whether as the pioneer or Columbus, the searcher for friendship is destroying the very thing he seeks in the searching.

Perhaps Thoreau recognizes this when he writes, "Men do not, after all, love their Friends greatly."[144] But maybe this is also a recognition on his part that love itself is complex and treacherous. By rendering friendship and love literally impossible, is it not possible (therefore) that Thoreau is suggesting an entirely other notion of friendship, one that does not yet exist but which still might? He writes:

> How often we find ourselves turning on our back on our actual Friends, that we may go and meet their ideal cousins. I would that I were worthy to be any man's Friend.[145]

Perhaps, suffering from the loss of John, unable to find love, unable to connect to nature, unwilling to simply accept his privilege, Thoreau realizes that friendship may not lie where he has been told to look that he is not yet a good friend. Perhaps the ideal of Friendship stands in for what is and what could yet be. Perhaps one day Thoreau would be worthy, could be worthy to be anyone's Friend.

In the meantime, he ends "Friendship" with this thought, anticipating Nietzsche by some fifty years:

> Ah my dear Strangers and Enemies, I would not forget you. I can well afford to welcome you.... We have nothing to fear from our foes; God keeps a standing army for that service; but we have no ally against our Friends, those ruthless Vandals.[146]

THOMAS HOBBES:
THE ROAD NOT TAKEN[1]

1. A Love More Loving than Love

With Thoreau we have come to the darkest heart of the doctrine of love. Thoreau reveals, even more clearly than Rousseau, not just the inadequacy of the makeshift, but its terrible, even murderous consequences. As a religious doctrine, love serves as a metaphor for the mysterious relationship that mortal beings have with God. The attempt to love one's neighbor as oneself becomes a question of relating the finite with the infinite, the fallen with the divine. The fact that such love seems impossible is irrelevant; through God's grace, we can know and receive such a love.

But in the attempt to render a politics out of such a love, such impossible questions become much more problematic, particularly as love becomes more secularized. Politics is necessarily conceived of and implemented in the human realm, bound by space and time. Absent revelation itself, the eternal can be nothing more than a notion from this perspective. To build a politics of love necessarily means to order ourselves as we imagine God requires us to; it means loving and relating and existing in our most intimate lives in accordance with something that we cannot see or know. In so doing, we are not at liberty to invent a God to suit our purposes; our freedom as mortal, fallible people is only the freedom to discover what is eternally true. But as we grow more secular, as we further politicize love, that truth becomes ever more elusive.

As Derrida tells us, in our frustrated quest for the eternal, we are seeking to substitute for a lost original. In this case, the lost original, the true nature that we seek, is revealed to be God himself, whom we identify through the concept of *agape*. The substitute is our own attempts to reconstruct *agape* from the position of *eros*, to fill ourselves while we wait for God to fill us. But by definition, *eros* is not up to the task. Eros constitutes *our* desires, not God's will. By definition, the substitute is makeshift and will fail.

Liberalism, in its attempts to find our true nature, to educate us and make us reasonable and free, is premised on the makeshift, on this "scandal." Politically speaking, the unmet expectation of fulfillment with *agape,* creates a vacuum, an emptiness which we fill with our own substitutes. Passively receptive to God, we are also passive towards the notions of state, law, sovereignty, and self which come to stand in for God's love and truth. So long as we remain bound by the doctrine of love, we have no means by which to challenge the makeshift; it colonized us, takes us over; it becomes our nature, our "hard bottom."

Liberalism has made its task to create a politics out of love; it is devoted to the possibility of the substitute, even as it exacerbates the divide between *eros* and *agape*. If liberalism does not and cannot know what our real nature is, it must reinvent nature, give it back to us, however artificial this concept may be. The faith of liberalism is premised on the expectation of grace; if we believe that we are free, then we will be. If we believe that we are whole selves, then it will be so; God helps those who help themselves.

And yet, as I have tried to show, it is the liberal theorists themselves (especially after Locke) who, even while they are involved in this project, reveal to us why this masquerade will never work. Liberalism cannot believe in its own fabrications because it remains in a state of expectation, waiting in messianic time for the arrival of true *agape,* rendering its own efforts and judgments mere substitutes, empty and without their own validity. Implicitly, they show us how the substitute obscures and writes over any possibility of "real" messianism, how the "original" God—itself a projection of our desires—precludes any knowing or glimpsing of God, even as it precludes any terrestrial, democratic politics. In the gap between the promise and the substitute, we see a murderous rage, a desire to destroy, grown out of our failure and disappointment, As Derrida tells us, the scandal makes "the world move." And move it does, through violence and blood. In the end of course, we have not been colonized by heaven at all, but only by our own fantasies of power and substance.

We seem to face a stark choice: To avoid the suspension between earth and heaven that typifies liberal theory, we must choose one or the other; either total passivity or total relativism, either complete submission or absolute atheism. Clearly, the former choice does not appear to be politically viable. To believe that there is a truth but that we have to wait to receive it (and, in the meantime, we can't make up any truths of our own), seems like a very poor, even paralyzing, doctrine upon which to base a political system.

And yet the alternative does not seem particularly attractive either. Absolute atheism seems to suggest total relativism, in which any of us can do anything we please. Is there any possibility of *philia politike* in such a society? Don't we lose, along with the tensions of love, the notion of human worth, of community itself? Must it really be all or nothing?

Derrida suggests other possibilities when considering the "immense rumor" that persists throughout the history of Western philosophy. Toward the end of *Politics of Friendship,* he tells us that he stands not so much in opposition to the course of Western philosophy as in contention with it. Derrida ends this book, which is dedicated to rethinking the fraternal and hence "natural" origins of friendship, by musing on that which he has contested:

> It is rather late in the day now to issue a warning. Despite the appearances that this book has multiplied, nothing in it says anything *against* the brother or against fraternity.... This history will not be thought, it will not be recalled, by taking up *this* side. In my own special way, like everyone else, I no doubt love, yes, in my own way, my brother, my only brother.[2]

If Western philosophy in general (and for my own interests, liberalism in particular) has given us the dream of friendship, must we pursue this dream by completely rejecting the system that produced it? Can we not love the brother and still seek the friend? Must we not begin where we already are, with brotherhood, with ideas about nature and democratic dreams?

Nietzsche tells us that Western philosophy has produced "a magnificent tension of soul."[3] Rather than deny this tension, Nietzsche uses the analogy of the tension of a bowstring, allowing us to engage with the tension as a means to move beyond existing categories. As Nietzsche tells us in *The Genealogy of Morals,* the very life-denying fabrications of Western philosophy have preserved and complicated us, making new truths and new states of being possible. He writes:

> In all fairness it should be added however, that only on this soil...has man been able to develop into an interesting creature; that only here has the human mind grown both profound and evil; and it is in these two respects after all, that man has proved his superiority over the rest of creation.[4]

In all of its searching for some otherworldly perfection, Western thought has yet maintained a perspective for human agency and power, preserving and developing those very desires it seeks to overcome.[5] Nietzsche tells us that for all its ascetic self-denial Western philosophy has been "pregnant" (memories of Diotima here) with the possibilities of the future.[6] He writes, "Far from denying 'existence,'... [asceticism] affirms [the Western subject's] existence."[7] Thus this most life-denying of systems preserves and even expands the possibility of life. And, by the same token, this most love-hating of all systems preserves and even expands the possibilities of love itself.[8]

And yet Nietzsche cautions us not to confuse being pregnant with possibility with the reality of our lives, not to confuse the "perhaps" with what we have before us. In our current position, we have only loss itself:

> This is Europe's true predicament: together with the fear of man we have also lost the love of man, reverence for man, confidence in man, indeed the *will to man*. Now the sight of man makes us despond. What is nihilism today if not that?[9]

In response to Aristotle, Nietzsche, the living fool, tells us, "Foes, there is no foe." This "apostrophe," this stand-in for the occluded friendship itself, tells us something. It tells us that enmity is a bridge to friendship. The living fool, for whom friendship still remains only a perhaps, must be an enemy before he can be a friend:

> The noble person will respect his enemy, and respect is already a bridge to love.[10]

In *The Gay Science,* Nietzsche tells us what love consists of in our own day. "Our love of our neighbors—is it not a lust for new possessions?"[11] Here we see a clear articulation of *amour propre,* love that is born out of *ressentiment,* out of always comparing ourselves to others. Such love becomes a "property right," an "avarice" to own the property in another's person (as well as a fear of being owned). As Nietzsche explains, such a love is always in tension, never satisfied. "Gradually we become tired of the old, of what we safely possess, and we stretch out our hands again."[12]

Nietzsche further recognizes that "[t]o become tired of some possession means tiring of ourselves."[13] Without a source of substance, an idea of selfhood that is wholly our own, we are always seeking to colonize the other as a way to delineate and define (and protect) the self. The absence of selfhood at the core of this doctrine of love means a profound dissatisfaction, an inadequacy inherent in the search for love, and always, the need for fresh conquests.

In his analysis of sexual love, Nietzsche perfectly articulates the goal that we have seen Rousseau set for himself, the desire for total union (two bodies, one soul) and yet also the desire for total power (patriarchy):

> [The lover] desires equally unconditional power over the soul and over the body of the beloved; he alone wants to be loved and desires to live and rule in the other as supreme and supremely desirable.[14]

This lover is hardly the model for a democratic subject; he "aims at the impoverishment and deprivations of all competitors."[15]

In *Politics of Friendship,* Derrida reflects upon these passages from *The Gay Science.* For Derrida, Nietzsche identifies the murderous desires that lie behind the gentle facade of *caritas* itself:

> [E]ven the very Christian "love of one's neighbor"—charity, perhaps—would reveal only a new lust in this fundamental drive: "Our love of our neighbor—is it not a lust for new *possessions*?"[16]

Derrida picks up Nietzsche's call here for a "new justice," one that is not calibrated on *amour propre.* A new justice would abrogate the endless reckoning of status, equivalency and reciprocity, reward and debt, which determines, orders (and defeats) existing notions of *philia*.[17] This new justice, Derrida tells us, would "quite simply, no longer calculate at all." It would "carry itself beyond proportion, beyond appropriation, thereby exceeding all reappropriation of the proper."[18] Derrida calls this a "rupture in reciprocity" and writes:

> This "disappropriation" [*dépropriation*] would undoubtedly beckon this other "love" whose true name, says Nietzsche...whose "just name" is *friendship (Ihr rechter Name ist Freundschaft)*. This friendship is a species of love, but of a love more loving than love.[19]

2. THE LOVE OF THOMAS HOBBES

Where can we look for such love that is "more loving than love"? How can we think more about the perhaps? Derrida offers us many thinkers to illuminate his claims—Nietzsche himself, obviously, Carl Schmitt, and even Aristotle. To this group, I propose to add Thomas Hobbes, a thinker who writes not entirely outside of but alongside the liberal tradition, a thinker who therefore preserves the tension, enlists the same vocabulary.

As I will argue further, Hobbes embraces neither religious submission nor atheism. He doesn't reject but rather revisits the tension between heaven and earth, preserving and maintaining a zone for human agency, substance, and action without depriving us of some notion of an outside, some idea of the "wholly other."

In this way, Hobbes is reminiscent of Aristophanes, who also had a place for humans and a place for gods. For both thinkers, this possibility of coexistence was ultimately superseded by a conquest from "heaven."[20]

As I argued earlier, Hobbes offers us something very precious, a fully articulated foundation of self and community, an entire epistemology. With Hobbes, we are in a position to rethink a genealogy of liberalism as if it had had very different directions, and very different results. Hobbes, in my mind, represents "a road not taken," a rupture in reciprocity that was not pursued. With Hobbes, we can think not only of the "perhaps" but also of the "could have been" (and "perhaps" could yet be).

Historically we have received Hobbes very much as proto-liberal, a thinker who, but for his times and his obsession with absolutism, might have been the thinker that Locke himself was.[21] In recent years, however, there has been a renewed appreciation for Hobbes on his own terms.[22] Thinkers ranging from Michael Oakeshott to Richard Flathman have undertaken a revision of Hobbes that links him neither simply to Locke, nor even to the conventional paths of liberalism itself.[23] In my own view, I see Hobbes less as someone who might be able to "save" or reform liberalism than as someone who helps us rethink the liberal project, imagining it in entirely other guises.

Hobbes and religion

Among the early moderns, Hobbes is perhaps the most forceful in his rejection of classical theories. Among his many attacks on Aristotle, Hobbes called him "the worst teacher that ever was, the worst politician and ethick."[24] But if he is rejecting Aristotle, is he also rejecting Christian Aristotelianism, or even Christianity itself? Is Hobbes the atheist he was so often accused of being?

Some contemporary scholars have argued that Hobbes was an atheist and used religious language only as a screen to allow his books to be published.[25] As it was, the publication of *Leviathan* in England led to a storm of controversy; copies of the book were burned in public. After the Restoration, Hobbes may have tried to regain the trust of royalists and Anglican ministers by republishing *Leviathan* with some of the offending passages altered or taken out—including his perceived defense of independency, the Puritan doctrine of individual church autonomy.[26]

Others, however, argue that Hobbes's religiosity must be accepted as given.[27] *Leviathan* (at least the original version of it) is hardly a book written to appease certain political and religious views. It marks something of a departure from some of his earlier works such as *Elements of Law* and even *De Cive,* which were accepted as royalist and, at least nominally, pro-Anglican texts.[28] And if religion is a subterfuge for Hobbes, he devotes an enormous amount of time to this disguise.

There is also some debate about what kind of Christianity, if any, Hobbes actually supported. Nominally, he was a lifelong Anglican; he was always associated with Anglican royalists, particularly the Cavendish family, who were his employers for much of his life. He is certainly a bitter foe of both Catholicism and Presbyterianism. But some scholars have suggested that Hobbes is sympathetic to some of the doctrines of radical Puritanism. Richard Tuck argues that Hobbes strongly supported independency, as demonstrated by passages in *Leviathan* such as "we are reduced to the Independency of the Primitive Christians to follow Paul, or Cephas, or Apollos, every man as he liketh best: which . . . is perhaps the best."[29] But A. P. Martinich challenges this interpretation, arguing that Hobbes hedges a great deal ("reduced," "perhaps") and that in his own stated preference for a state church he evinces little tolerance for heterodoxy.[30]

Ultimately, I think the important question to ask with Hobbes is not whether he is religious or not (I think that he is) or whether he is an Anglican, a closeted Puritan, or something else (a more nuanced question), but rather what the political and empirical salience of religion is for him.

It is here that he offers us a glimpse of another possible relationship between heaven and earth. He does not deny God's existence; as we will see, the existence of God is central to his entire system. And yet, unlike Locke, his understanding of God is premised on and even enabled by the deity's silence. Perhaps not unlike orthodox Jews who, not knowing where the holy of holies lies, refuse to tread upon any part of the mount of the temple of Solomon, even while continuing to devoutly worship God along the temple's lower wall, Hobbes, in reconciling himself with the uncertainty of truth in the modern age, avoids making assumptions about how God wants us to order ourselves when it comes to matters of secular life. For Hobbes, we have no choice but to make our own meanings, give ourselves our own substance, even as we are contained and made sacred by the silent presence of God.

In his religious views, Hobbes, for all of his conservatism, often does seem to be aligned with many of the more radical Puritan clergymen, Ranters, Quakers, Levellers, and Diggers of his day.[31] Like Richard Overton, Hobbes rejects the separation of the body and the soul as a basis for subjectivity.[32] Like William Walwyn, he rejects a literal vision of hell and everlasting punishment.[33] Like Gerrard Winstanley, he rejects Scripture as a basis for political guidance.[34] At times, the words of Winstanley could easily be the words of Hobbes, such as when the former writes:

> While men are gazing up to heaven, imagining after a happiness or fearing a hell after they are dead, their eyes are put out, that they see not what is their birthrights, and what is to be done by them here on earth while they are living.[35]

Yet for all of this similarity, it is Hobbes who takes these eschatological principles and turns them into a fully developed political philosophy. While Winstanley derives a critique of property ownership and other secular matters from his theology, Hobbes takes on the mandate of rethinking human agency itself. As Richard Flathman argues, it is Hobbes who makes us "[m]akers of [our]selves."[36]

Accordingly, Hobbes practices a radical empiricism which as its grounding premise accepts the loss of absolute truths in the world. He writes:

> No Discourse whatsoever, can End in absolute knowledge of Fact, past, or to come. For, as for the knowledge of Fact, it is originally, Sense; and ever after, Memory. [37]

Since we never know things absolutely, we are forced to rely entirely on our own judgments to make decisions. Hobbes's empiricism goes far beyond what Locke and later empiricists will profess (with some interesting exceptions such as Hume). Whereas, as we have seen, Locke equivocates on questions of abstraction and "higher faculties," Hobbes truly gives meaning to the term "tabula rasa."

Without the possibility of absolute truth, the church can no longer lay claim to having access to vision that is denied to the laypeople. In *Leviathan* he writes:

> [T]here is on Earth, no such universall Church as all Christians are bound to obey; because there is no power on Earth, to which all other Common-wealths are subject.... And therefore a Church...is the same thing with a Civil Common-wealth, consisting of Christian men; and is called a Civill State, for that of the subjects of it are Men; and a Church, for that the subjects thereof are Christians.... It is true, that the bodies of the faithfull, after the Resurrection shall be not only Spirituall but Eternall: but *in this life they are grosse, and corruptible.*[38] (emphasis added)

As far as the truth claims of a church are concerned, they are no truer (or less true) than a state. Neither church nor state has absolute knowledge. We live in the world of the "grosse, and corruptible," and religious and secular questions are necessarily determined from such a fallible position.

It is true that Hobbes calls for a state church in England, and an Anglican one at that. But for him, the purpose of such control is less because of his conviction of the rightness of the Anglican Church than because he is concerned that without some ecclesiastical unity the nation will continue to rip itself to pieces. Hobbes writes that with Scripture being available to infinite interpretations, there will be an infinite number of people all claiming that they have the correct answer, producing "a diversity of opinion, and consequently...disputation, breach of charity, disobedience, and at last rebellion."[39] For him, the English civil war can be directly blamed on such myriad competing interpretations. We must have unity "or else there must need follow Faction, and Civil war."[40]

But Hobbes's allegiance to the tenets of Anglicanism itself is negligible at best. As we have already seen, he takes the side of many of the Anglican Church's staunchest critics. This ambivalence toward Anglicanism was noted and resented by many of his contemporaries as well. Richard Tuck interprets Hobbes's "A Review and Conclusion" at the end of *Leviathan* as a kind of apology for his appearance to be "backing" Cromwell's commonwealth and the Independent church. It seems as if Hobbes is arguing that whoever runs the state should run the church as well.[41]

Upon closer examination, it can be seen that for Hobbes, religious peace has more value than simply preserving the social order—particularly since he does not seem to be overwhelmingly troubled by which particular social order might triumph, whether Anglican or something else.[42] He makes the case that within the framework of the calm provided by a state church, each person is able to come to their own beliefs.

Given our notions of Hobbes's absolutist tendencies, the degree to which Hobbes carves out a space for individual belief is fairly astonishing. In *Leviathan*, he asks what relationship we should have to the "Positive Laws of God."[43] His answer is a healthy skepticism. Even during periods of miracles and revelations, when it might seem that God's law is apparent to one and all, Hobbes questions whether God himself is doing the revealing. The presence of miracles are no real proof in themselves, since "that which is marvellous to one, may not be so to another." And anyway, "sanctity may be feigned."[44] He goes on to say that "no man can infallibly know by naturall reason, that another has had a supernaturall revelation of Gods will; but only a beliefe."[45] In other words, reason cannot compel us (as it seems to with Locke) to recognize and know higher truths as they manifest themselves in our world; rather, it is always up to each and every one of us to decide whether or not to believe. Belief itself is a political process for Hobbes. In this way, then, he preserves a crucial dimension of human decision making. It will be recalled that Locke, in his own consideration of miracles, acknowledged that "it is unavoidable that that should be a miracle to one, which is not so to another."[46] But Locke concludes that reason is designed to recognize a higher truth when presented with one. A reasonable person therefore will believe in miracles without question. Hobbes, on the other hand, carves out a crucial distinction between obeying and believing. Recognizing that God's law will have many claimants, he writes that men are

> not bound to believe [any particular divine manifestations]: for men's beliefe and interiour cogitations, are not subject to the commands, but only to the operation of God, ordinary or extraordinary.[47]

That Hobbes seems to be allowing for exactly the sort of heterodoxy in the minds of parishioners which he condemns so vigorously in public may seem surprising at first, but it should point us toward a fact which Hobbes's (and our own) attention to sovereign power tends to obscure; the inner life for Hobbes is not an irrelevancy but a zone of possibility. Despite the obvious threat that it poses to his much-vaunted security and peace, Hobbes insists on preserving the subject's inner autonomy.[48] Much of his opposition to the Catholic Church stems from that church's claims to sovereignty. He strongly disliked the church's claim of infallibility and, at the time, its political power based on such a claim.[49] He doesn't like the Presbyterian church of his time much better, for similar reasons. This alone should give pause to those who consider Hobbes to be a claimant for absolute sovereignty—as we see, for him, there is nothing absolute on this earth. In this case, the sovereignty of a state church is less a zone of absolute power than a mechanism that can preserve the ability of each of us to believe or not believe what we will.

As I will argue in more detail, I see Hobbes as a thinker with a developmental agenda. One must not assume that his vision of a unitary church in public and heterodoxy in private serves as a vision of a permanent political arrangement when it comes to matters of faith. Rather, I believe, as I will argue with his political vision of sovereignty as well, that for Hobbes the peace provided by a state church serves to create an embryonic space within which a genuine public discourse can evolve, beginning (but only beginning) with the untrammeled private thoughts of individual members, one that neither replaces nor substitutes for God's truth, but rather coexists with it.

Hobbes and nature

If Hobbes denies the political salience of religious orthodoxy, what then of his notions about natural law? Norberto Bobbio argues that Hobbes is one of the originators of the theory of natural law in its modern incarnation.[50] If this is the case, doesn't Hobbes, like Locke himself, replace a clear idea of God with a less clear (but no less sovereign) notion of natural law?

We must be careful to distinguish Hobbes from those natural-law theorists who come after him (as well as the reputation which he suffers from at their hands). It might seem as if Hobbes thinks that we are "naturally wicked" since we are so craven in his so-called state of nature. But he resists this notion, writing:

> For though from nature, that is from their first birth, as they are merely sensible creatures, they have this disposition, that immediately as much as in them lies they desire and do whatsoever is best pleasing to them...yet are they not for this reason to be accounted wicked.[51]

For Hobbes, the state of nature is not a kind of snapshot of us as we "really are." By "nature" he simply means how we comport ourselves "from...first birth." This is a descriptive rather than a prescriptive term for Hobbes (and therefore quite different from Locke's notion). Rather than making some absolute claim about what we truly are, the state of nature, like any period in history for Hobbes, tells us what we might be (or have been), given certain contexts, certain standards of behavior. As with all else for Hobbes, no absolute or essential fact of human "nature" can be derived from this or any other period in time. Elsewhere he writes:

> The Desire, and other Passions of man, are in themselves no Sin. No more are the Actions, that proceed from those Passions, till they know a law that forbids them: which till Laws be made they cannot know.[52]

Determinations of wickedness and goodness are therefore not "given" by nature. Until we make laws, until we engage in politics to determine what our "natures" will be, we remain relatively blank canvases. Those things which animate us, our desires and passions, rather than being lowly and shameful, are simply a part of our ever-changing and developing "natures."

Whereas Locke revives Aristotle's use of nature as a way to depoliticize social hierarchies, Hobbes's state of nature, if anything, has the opposite effect—it exposes all that we considered natural in our own society to be in fact a naked relationship of power (and therefore not "given" but subject to debate and alteration). Accordingly, for Hobbes (unlike Locke) neither class nor family relationships are in any way "natural." Even marriage is an artifact of power; even love is not "natural."

Hobbes's body

And yet, as with his thinking about God himself, Hobbes's attitude toward nature is not simply a matter of reinventing it for the purpose of human politics, not simply to substitute for it, but also to enlist it in the service of allowing us to become "makers of ourselves." Although no more "knowable" as a concept than God himself, for Hobbes we can yet derive one "truth" from nature which is removed from the realm of human contrivances: the human body, the terrain of the "grosse, and corruptible" itself.

For Hobbes, the corruptibility and mortality of the human body serves to establish rather than undermine its central importance. What for Locke serves as a source of inadequacy and limit, for Hobbes becomes the basis for our worth. We are valid and worthy, not despite but because we occupy mortal bodies. Remarking on the peculiar frailty of the body, he writes:

> For if we look on men full grown, and consider how brittle the frame of our human body is, which perishing, all its strength, vigour and wisdom itself perisheth with it; and how easy matter it is, even for the weakest man to kill the strongest: there is no reason why any man, trusting to his own strength, should conceive himself made by nature above others.... All men therefore among themselves are by nature equal; the inequality we now discern, hath its spring from the civil law.[53]

Thus we are equal because we will all die. The only thing that we do "know" from nature is how fragile and precious and irreplaceable we are. The body delimits the realm of human experience; it is the one thing that we "have" which we cannot undo or remake. Without knowing exactly what it is, we do know that it serves as the basis of our selfhood, and of the communities that we will forge.

Hobbes's valuation of the body *qua* body can be seen by looking at his version of the fall of Adam and Eve in *Leviathan*. As we might recall, Locke focuses on the temptation itself as the source of their sin, seeing them as "disobedient."[54] For Hobbes, Adam and Eve couldn't have been disobedient per se; they ate of the apple of knowledge but "acquired no new ability to distinguish between [good and evil] aright."[55] Thus Adam and Eve were like children who weren't capable of knowing what they were doing. Instead, Hobbes focuses on their real crime—having been ashamed at their nakedness:

> And whereas it is said, that having eaten, they saw they were naked; no man hath so interpreted that place, as if they had been formerly blind, and saw not their own skins: the meaning is plain, that it was then that they first judged their nakedness (wherein it was God's will to create them) to be uncomely; and by being ashamed did tacitly censure God.[56]

Thus the one real "sin" we can be said to have performed before we entered into society (wherein we learn to "distinguish" good from evil by adapting these terms to our own interests) was to have questioned that which God clearly gave us: our own bodies. For Hobbes, his doubting of the inherent worth of the body is a censure of God, in that it questions the only thing that we *know* that he has given us. For Hobbes, to truly love and trust God must mean to love and trust ourselves as his creation.

In this tale, we see a radically different understanding of *eros* and *agape*. *Eros* is not inadequate and waiting for *agape*; it is given its validity via its absence. In God's expelling Adam and Eve from the garden, he is reminding them that their validity is linked to his, even when he becomes silent. Without some original idea of "nature" or God, human life might indeed be empty and random. Without the idea that the human body is created by God, it would not be valid or worthy, it would not be necessary to treat it with reverence; the body would become, like all other things, merely and only an object of power.[57] We must think of ourselves as God-created. But that is all that we know about God; the rest is up to us. Founded as a gift of *agape*, *eros* is left to its own devices; it becomes democratized. The only way we can love God is to love ourselves.

Here it might seem as if Hobbes is arguing that we should essentialize the body even as everything else must be seen as a social contrivance. Yet his own methodology demands that we think otherwise. For Hobbes, as we have seen, no "facts" are absolute or essentially true. It seems to me that Hobbes is not essentializing the body so much as insisting that the body and the body alone be removed from epistemological contention—it is not so much that the body is "truer" than anything else, but that we cannot afford to put the body into the fray lest we remove the grounds of our being itself.[58]

A body politic

The idea of the body as inherently valid underscores a political vision that Hobbes produces via the interaction of different bodies in a common arena. As I will argue further, this foundation serves as a much more coherent and more desirable basis than Locke's much more problematic and complicated sense of self, something more in keeping with the possibility of *philia politike* itself.

As we have already seen, Hobbes argues that our common mortality makes us fundamentally equal. This equality is not merely rooted in the fact that Hobbes assumes we should fear death. Stephen Holmes points out that for Hobbes there are times when people will value other things over their life—the fear of death is but one of the many passions that make up the human psyche.[59] For Hobbes, it is mortality itself rather than simply the fear of death which makes us equal—it is the ongoing "fact" of the body, not the perceptions which we have of it, that anchors our individual worth. Here again, we see how Hobbes prevents endless relativism and nihilism by understanding the body; in this way. Our death is a solid "fact" that we all share in exactly the same way; none of us can be immortal, regardless of what we think.

Hobbes's focus on the body seems to challenge the traditional Christian doctrine that the body is merely the vehicle of the soul. But again he is challenging the political salience of such a doctrine more than the doctrine itself. True to his empirical stance, for Hobbes, from our "grosse, and corruptible" position, death is necessarily a mystery. While a more traditionally Christian doctrine might not see either the fear of death or death itself as making us equal (since in the afterlife, believers and non-believers have very different and *un*-equal fates), for Hobbes, so long as we live, this "vehicle" of the body is the one and only operative basis of political and personal identity, the only thing that we can be sure of.[60]

In this way, we are not so much self-"owning," as we are with Locke, as much as we *are* our own bodies. Without denying the possibility of our having souls, Hobbes insists on locating our equality in something far more tangible: the recognition of our own limitations and absence, our own death. There are therefore no complicating questions of overlapping subjectivity, of God owning us, of us owning others. Nor is there any question of some of us owning and managing ourselves better than others. For Hobbes, as with Derrida, death gives each of us to ourselves in a way that defies all talk of merit and ownership. We are always and only our own person. We can only cede such an identity by actually dying.

Accordingly, Hobbes's notion of freedom is far less complicated, and less compromising, than Locke's. Locke's notion, it will be recalled, involves obeying our "true" owner, God himself. We are not free to do what he does not please. Life becomes a matter of trying to live up to God's wishes in all things, however opaque they might be. An entire political edifice is built, as we have seen, on this idea of "freedom" which paradoxically involves a great deal of what might be considered to be slavery. For Hobbes, God is not our owner but rather, as Arendt would agree, our *creator*. As such, freedom is far less constrained although it necessarily means much less than it does for Locke. Hobbes writes:

> [A] FREE-MAN is he, that in those things, which by his strength and wit he is able to do, is not hindered to doe what he has a will to do. But when the words Free, and Liberty, are applyed to any thing but Bodies, they are abused.[61]

For Hobbes, freedom must always be rooted in the physicality of the body. Such freedom can never be vicarious—for a body to be called "free," it and only it must literally be free. There can be no freedom by proxy as we so often get with Locke (or Aristotle). As with his idea of equality, Hobbes's notion of freedom presupposes, not overlapping selves, but separate selves whose coexistence does not demand the kinds of hierarchy and sacrifice that we see Locke requires.

Even when his concept of freedom appears to violate the power of the sovereign himself, Hobbes does not relent. He offers us a series of seemingly bizarre "rights" when it comes to our behavior vis-à-vis the sovereign. We have the right to fight the sovereign when he condemns us to death (in practice this may only amount to the right to kick and scream on the way to the gallows). Hobbes also gives us the right to betray our original sovereign when another sovereign conquers us in war, and also the right to pay others to fight for us when we are too cowardly. And even if we are captured by an "infidel" sovereign, Hobbes, because he has always kept an interior space within which we can think what we want, allows that it is our right to follow that sovereign too.[62]

These rights may seem arbitrary, but they reflect Hobbes's commitment to never violate the one sacred thing in political life: the human body itself. As we have already seen, Hobbes's commitment to maintaining human life goes far beyond a craven fear of death and clinging to life at all costs. Hobbes has plans for us; he wants us to live so as to fulfill ourselves and thereby fulfill our worth as God's creations. The body serves as the basis not only of who we are but of who we might become—it is the holder of the "perhaps." Hobbes never compromises, never asks us to give this up.[63]

Will and the sovereign

We come closer to the question of who we might become when we consider Hobbes's notion of the human will and political sovereignty. Hobbes is probably most notorious for his understanding of sovereignty, earning him the nickname "the beast of Malmesbury."[64] If he were concerned only with preserving human life at all costs, if he were indifferent to how power was used and abused so long as some modicum of physical safety were preserved, he would indeed deserve this nickname and more.

Certainly he suffers in the opinion of a great many political philosophers, including Hannah Arendt.[65] Since I want to reconcile her thinking with that of Hobbes, let me contend with her criticisms in particular. She attacks Hobbes for his ideas about truth, as well as his notion of will and sovereignty. Her opinion of him is not unlike Kirstie McClure's, portraying him as the inventor of an unethical calculus, a harbinger of all that is horrible about modernity.

But whereas McClure, as we have seen, attacks Hobbes in order to promote a Lockean agenda, I believe that Arendt's own values are actually much closer to those of Hobbes himself. In her attacks on him, I believe that Arendt is subscribing at least partially to guilt by association. Her understanding of him (and I think his reputation in general) is marred, not only by his own gloomy and harsh tone (whereby his reputation is largely self-inflicted), but, as I've already noted, by those who follow after him and "develop" his ideas to the point that we cannot read the words "will" or "sovereignty" without connotations which have little to do with him.

In terms of the notion of will, Arendt's critique of Hobbes (among other modern political theorists, including Rousseau) is that his notion of action involves a completely internal dialogue. A subject's desire is projected into the world without any consideration of the social realm that it enters into.[66] Arendt calls this the "philosophical equation of freedom and free will," arguing that this serves as a solipsistic and tyrannical basis for action and politics.[67]

Yet Hobbes's idea of will is itself inherently interactive. Whereas both Locke and Rousseau require that we "submit" our will either to natural law (in Locke's case) or the general will (in Rousseau's), Hobbes's notion of the formation of the will insists on a far more democratic, genuinely social process.

It is true that in *Leviathan,* Hobbes describes the will as "the last Appetite in Deliberating" and therefore the product of an internal dialogue.[68] He tells us that the term "deliberating" is apt, for it consists of "putting an end to the Liberty [i.e., 'de-liberating'] we had of doing or omitting, according to our own Appetite or Aversion."[69] Although different desires may make equal demands upon our attention, we can only choose one at a time.

But for Hobbes the will as an internal process is not the last word in the process of making judgments and acting in the world. He goes on to say:

> And because in Deliberation, the Appetites, and Aversions are raised by foresight of the good and evil consequences, and sequels of the action whereof we Deliberate; the good or evil effect thereof we Deliberate; the good or evil effect thereof dependeth on the foresight of a long chain of consequences, *of which very seldome any man is able to see to the end.*[70] (emphasis added).

In other words, the will, as a process of internal dialogue, is in itself not only fallible (as all things are) but often does not lead to results that we are satisfied with. The will therefore is not supreme, not "right" on its own terms. Rather it should be seen as the result of a necessarily limited personal dialogue. "Very seldome" do we manage to produce a worthwhile decision from this solipsistic method of judgment.

For Hobbes, it is far better when the will is immersed in a social context.[71] Our internal ideas becomes worthwhile only when spoken before other persons. He writes:

> [A] man may play with the sounds and equivocall signfications of words; and that many times with encounters of extraordinary Fancy: but in a Sermon, or in public, or before persons unknown... there is no Gingling of words that will not be accounted folly....Judgment therefore without Fancy is Wit, but Fancy without Judgment not.[72]

The social context allows us to bounce ideas off of one another and submit ourselves to the judgments of others. Our internal process is completed by the need to actually convince other persons; we must take their judgments in as the culmination of our own. Hobbes distinguishes between belief—those judgments that are produced in the social context—and opinion, which is a "contemplation of his own" (akin to Plato's concept of thought as a dialogue with oneself).[73] Belief, which is a far more important category for Hobbes, arises based on our perception of the speaker's honesty rather than on the content of what he or she has to say.[74] As we have already seen, he always insists that any belief must be voluntary—we cannot force each other to believe, we must persuade. Interpersonal relationships thus undergird the entire system of what comes to be believed in by persons in a community. But Hobbes does not expect us to submit to one great "common me" as Rousseau does; he tells us repeatedly that the body politic that is produced by the covenant is an artifice. What really matters is the unstructured spaces within the covenant. There, we will talk and engage, one or more persons at a time. Through these relationships, "truths" are produced. Through speech and dialogue, we forge relationships, come to trust one another and ourselves. To speak, to hear, and have reactions, makes judgment possible, makes our ideas "real."

In my mind, this notion of speech and communication in Hobbes is precisely the same notion of collectively forging stories together, of building reality that Arendt calls for in her own work. She writes, "Man's reason, being fallible, can function only if he can make 'public use' of it."[75] Will (when defined as an isolated judgment) for Hobbes is not the end but the beginning of a story of how politics is forged.

In *Leviathan*, Hobbes offers us an image of how this collectivity will develop over time:

> For all men are by nature provided of notable multiplying glasses (that is their Passions and Self-Love,) through which, every little payment appeareth a great grievance but are destitute of those prospective glasses, (namely Morall and Civill Science,) to see a farre off the miseries that hang over them.[76]

It becomes ever clearer that with Hobbes, the true purpose of getting us into society is not to repress the appetite-crazed animals that we "truly are" (since Hobbes already told us that we are not "naturally wicked"). Rather, just as with his understanding of a state religion, the purpose of society is to allow us peaceful and prolonged access to one another and thereby to begin to produce collective judgments and make a world together.

Locke, in his own considerations on will and judgment, has a very different point to make. Like Hobbes, he argues that the mind, which is the determinant of will, can lead us into a "a variety of mistakes, errors, and faults which we run into in…our endeavors after happiness."[77] But for Locke the solution to this is not to externalize our judgments but rather to turn to an internal mental faculty. As we have already seen, this is the power of "indifference":

> To prevent this, we have a power to suspend the prosecution of this or that desire.… This seems to me the source of all liberty.… For, during this suspension…we have opportunity to examine, view and judge of the good and evil of what we are going to do.[78]

Unlike Hobbes, for Locke we do not need other people to improve our judgments; the truth lies "within," so long as we have the power to suspend desire.[79] Yet for Locke there *is* a social dimension to this process because, as I've argued, our power to suspend judgment is not actually "ours" at all but rather is produced by the social division of labor.

Based on their respective ideas of will, Hobbes and Locke offer us two very different attitudes toward other members of society. Locke's subject requires hierarchy to produce his own "internal" judgments. He does not engage in dialogue with others; they have nothing to offer him but their bodies, their labor, and their mediation. Hobbes, on the other hand, requires only our physical presence and individual perspectives in order to make valid judgments. As selves who are only our bodies, we all have something to offer one another, something that comes at no expense to ourselves or to anyone else. Regardless of our virtues, our powers or status, Hobbes's notion of collectivity provides a valid position for each of us. Each of us retains the control of our own belief.[80] We must be convinced (or not convinced), we must be engaged with one person at a time.

Hobbes's ideas about the will carry over into his notions of sovereignty as well. This idea of the sovereign, as Arendt points out, is the result of a solipsistic and anti-political process. The sovereign offers a single will which subsumes the entire populace, regardless of individual differences, even as it insists that by subscribing to the sovereign, each of us is "ruling ourselves."[81] In this way, the idea of sovereignty reproduces the doctrine of love itself, hollowing us out and filling us at the same time with something that determines "who we are" (i.e., citizens of the state). We love ourselves and one another, not with our own love, but with the love of the state.

I think that the usual reading of Hobbes's sovereign (including Arendt's) excludes an important fact: Hobbes's sovereign is not himself bound by the social contract; he is different, he is *outside*.[82] For Hobbes, the sovereign is not necessarily expected to act rationally, morally, or according to the dictates of civil science. While Hobbes *hopes* that the sovereign will comport himself well (and occasionally argues for why he should), he concedes that his system might be "obnoxious to the lusts, and other irregular passions of him, or them that have so unlimited a Power in their hands."[83]

As we have already seen with the question of the state church, Hobbes is quite willing to allow for a unitary power even while disdaining its particular qualities. This is because sovereignty itself is not Hobbes's main focus—it is a means rather than an end. Hobbes is interested not so much in the sovereign per se, but rather in the effect that the presence of the sovereign has on his subjects. When the people "author" the sovereign, they are also authoring (or "making") themselves, both individually and collectively.

Excluded as he is from the social realm, the sovereign himself will not take part in the developmental process; he will remain selfish and isolated, unenlightened by the process of collective judgment. Even if Hobbes hopes that the sovereign acts decently, his own system dictates that he probably won't.[84]

I think that Hobbes has "invented" sovereignty in the same way that he has "invented" nature as something which he defines in order to locate it outside of our selves. The sovereign represents the outer limit of the people's ongoing act of self-creation. It is Locke who brings nature and sovereignty back where Hobbes didn't want them—into the self and into the community. In declaring the people sovereign, Locke has colonized them in their entirety. In reinscribing them into the law of nature Locke denies them the space of self-creation that Hobbes so carefully carved out for them. Hobbes's sovereign is *not* the people, as it is for Locke, precisely because the people themselves are meant to develop as they will in the space that is excluded from sovereignty, that is to say the public space that is not solipsistic, not already scripted.

Hobbes tells us that "[i]n cases where the Sovereign has proscribed no rule, there the Subject hath the liberty to do, or forbearance, according to his own discretion."[85] We could read this as offering the people very little indeed, but we must remember that Hobbes is a theorist with a developmental agenda—he looks to a future of "morall and civill science." As we become self-governing, this space will necessarily grow larger, while the sovereign remains static. I would go so far as to argue that for Hobbes, eventually the sovereign will become entirely superfluous; having performed his function—to give the people their own space of self-creation—the sovereign can and will fade away.[86] At the very least, sovereignty itself is not the crucible of political life as it is for Locke.

Richard Flathman, in his discussions of Hobbes's sovereign, makes a somewhat different argument than I am making here, one that seeks to inscribe Hobbes more closely into the existing rubric of liberalism (even as he sees Hobbes as somehow redeeming the liberal project). For Flathman, we must accept the Leviathan as a necessary part of the price of politics. Its presence, although troubling, is crucial as an ongoing feature of society.

Flathman tells us that Hobbes's sovereign serves as the necessary basis for liberal freedoms. This state must be absolute not in the totalitarian sense, but rather in terms of not being subject to challenge from outside the processes of state power itself.[87] Without such sovereignty, Flathman argues, we would have not freedom but chaos.[88]

Flathman tells us that Hobbes's notions of sovereignty and absolutism actually presuppose the space of self scripting itself. To do away with sovereignty then would be to do away with freedom as well. For Flathman, the analogy that Hobbes makes between God and Leviathan tells us how Hobbesian sovereignty actually works. Flathman tells us that "although absolute, God's rule (and by extension the sovereign's rule) is far from total." And he further writes of Hobbes that "God's rule over the people not only permits but *obliges* them to rule themselves in some parts of their thought and action."[89] In other words, God's absolute power serves as both the limit to and the guarantor of our personal freedom. Under the umbrella of God's power over us, our freedom is preserved and becomes our very own. And it works the same way with the state.

Although I find Flathman's reading of Hobbes very compelling, I do not share his opinions about Hobbes's absolutism, particularly in terms of the ongoing need for the sovereign. Flathman himself argues that for Hobbes, God's absolute power and the sovereign's power are not "parallel" and not meant to be taken literally.[90] As we have seen, nothing on this earth is absolute for Hobbes, certainly not the sovereign himself. Hobbes certainly does not see the sovereign as ordered and logical but rather as a repository of random power—an insight that Carl Schmitt takes from him. And we have already seen the limits that Hobbes imposes on sovereign power. For Hobbes, sovereignty comes to mean "the last word" rather than "the diviner of truth," a significant difference. It is therefore like the will itself, the end product of a necessarily limited and solipsistic process which then becomes the grounds for the transformation of the social, something which it is then swallowed up into and forgotten.

Characteristically, for Hobbes, we do not depend so much on the presence, but rather on the absence of the sovereign, on the spaces where he is not, in order to produce truths. Thus the sovereign's power is not so much a foundation for our freedoms as Flathman argues, but rather a launching pad for them, something that can and should be left behind.

Furthermore, I think that the choice Flathman presents to us, between chaos (or anarchy) and absolutism, is overdrawn. To suggest as much is to deny Flathman's own valuable insight that voluntarism is not nihilism. The public sphere in which we are "makers of ourselves" is not anarchistic or nihilist for Hobbes. The sovereign, as a solipsistic and unresponsive entity, is the true force of chaos, not bound by any conventions or considerations of difference or social dynamics. The idea that state sovereignty is all that stands between us and chaos presupposes a particular (and liberal) vision of order, perhaps a consequence of Flathman's trying to read Hobbes into the contemporary liberal lexicon.

While Flathman deeply appreciates the democratic possibility inherent in the social act of self making, he sees it as inherently fragile, always requiring the strength of the sovereign to protect and bolster it, to keep it from tearing itself apart. Clearly this is Hobbes's opinion as well, in the initial stages of his political vision, but as the world becomes "real," as moral and civil science develops, it becomes stronger, sustained by the ties of belief. Such a society would no longer require a sovereign to define itself against; quite likely it would also no longer be willing to tolerate the inherently undemocratic nature of the sovereign.

Here, Hobbes offers us his own vision of the "perhaps," the possibility of a democratic result born from a most undemocratic of contexts. Perhaps we can have friendship. Perhaps we can have *philia politike.* Perhaps we can approach one another, not as entities filled from a common, sovereign source, but rather as separate, autonomous subjects, who are related voluntarily. Perhaps our worth is given, not from the state itself, not from the "outside," but rather as the selves and the social connections that we have created. I see a Hobbesian community as emerging according to the logic of Nietzsche's metaphor of pregnancy. From the chrysalis of sovereignty, the smothering envelope of love, perhaps we can emerge as something other than what we have been.

If Hobbes gives us a glimpse of the perhaps, it still remains unrealized. It is not a certainty for Hobbes, but a hope, and clearly, the direction of Western philosophy since Hobbes has, if anything, bound us together all the tighter. As we have seen, liberalism has secularized the doctrine of love, and in so doing, has transformed the central role of God himself to the state—a process we see in Locke and Rousseau quite clearly. As Hobbes tells us, sovereignty is the random repository of authorship, the empty and chaotic center of a system seeking to give substance and order to its population, seeking to substitute for the loss of *agape.* So long as we remain devoted to the expectation of being filled by its substance, we remain inadequate as ourselves, colonized and controlled.[91]

Hobbes dwells on sovereignty, not because he approves of it but in order to show us how to emerge from it. For Hobbes, we need sovereignty, as we need love initially, to create a context that makes the dream of friendship possible, but just as crucially, we need to abandon this empty father, this patriarchal transparency, and turn to the *philia politike* that is born out of it. The sovereign is the first enemy that Hobbes provides us with; he is our bridge to love.

3. IN SEARCH OF PHILIA POLITIKE

Hobbes was a road not taken by liberal theory. He remains part of the "immense rumor," the "perhaps." He stood at a moment of rupture, but rupture is part and parcel of the dynamic and unstable process of Western (and especially liberal) subjectivity. We have had, and we will have, other ruptures, other roads not taken. Hobbes does not invent the "perhaps," nor does he single-handedly redeem us. But he participates in a conversation, ranging from Aristophanes to Arendt to Derrida. As such, he has as much to learn from as to offer to this ongoing rumor. As is appropriate to his own philosophy, any engagement between Hobbes and other thinkers must be deeply interactive.

As I've suggested, Hobbes's own greatest contribution to this conversation is to offer a fully articulated foundation for subjectivity and community, one that stems from the heart of Western philosophy and yet does not simply replicate the doctrine of love itself. I believe that Hobbes, a consummate political theorist, can add to more contemporary philosophical inquiries by offering an alternative foundation for democratic dreams. I would like to focus on three particular components of the "perhaps" that I consider Hobbes to be particularly useful for: the idea of respect, the idea of responsibility, and the question of how to conceptualize an idea of the "outside" (or to use Levinas's term, the "wholly other"). In each case, as we will see, an engagement between Hobbes and contemporary thinkers works to enrich all parties, adds to the ongoing conversation, the "immense rumor" of democracy.

Respect

The notion of respect, which as a Latin cognate means "looking back," presupposes a distance between subjects (to look "back" one must be in a different space than the other) and thereby offers in its very linguistic meaning an alternative concept of love. It will be recalled that Arendt, in her own consideration of love, considered it apolitical, creating among us a terrible sameness, an overmerging of selves. As we have seen, she compares love with respect, writing:

> Respect not unlike the Aristotelian *philia politike*, is a kind of "friendship" without intimacy and without closeness.[92]

In evoking Aristotle, Arendt is also implicitly evoking the possibility of democratic friendship itself. Arendt believes that persons are supposed to relate ethically to one another through an operation called "representational thinking." For Arendt, I can make a moral decision as regards political arrangements first by placing myself in their context, or, as she puts it, by "being and thinking in my own identity where actually I am not."[93] To engage in representational thinking for Arendt means to keep our identity intact, to keep a respectful distance from others and yet still be able to think beyond one's own actual situation.

In contemporary society, marked by existing ideas of sovereignty, we do not engage in representational thinking. Instead we ask, "What would I do if I were them?" To ask such a question is to presume that we could know not only what it is like to be in their situation but to actually be them (we see such an impulse for example clearly in Rawls's original position). In such a viewpoint, I have nothing to learn from another actual person. I can learn all that I need to know through an internal journey, through an isolated act of will. The merging of selves which love allows for suggests that if the truth is "obvious" to me, then it is necessarily also "obvious" to you. Thus in our thought processes we internalize and reproduce the sovereign imperative and thereby make the other unreal to us, too close to ourselves.[94]

In arguing for respect, Arendt is inherently invoking Kant's notion. For Kant too, respect is an alternative to love. He tells us that "even the best of friends should not make themselves too familiar with each other."[95] Friends should be subjected to the same "looking back," the same respect that we owe ourselves as well.

As we have seen with Derrida (and Coles), Kant's notion of respect is too unstable for Arendt. The idea of distance he offers us is based on the principle of repulsion, which suggests and preserves a contentious spatial tension between selves. Kant's notion of respect offers, not a stable and permanent distance, but as we have already seen, an "oscillation," a dynamic constantly threatened by rupture and collapse.

Arendt might achieve a more stable notion of respect by grounding her subject in a Hobbesian epistemology. Hobbes offers Arendt the idea of the self as an inherently situated entity. For Hobbes, spatial relationships between members of a community are bounded and preserved by the fact that he makes no separation between "the me" and the body it occupies. Hobbes's self-as-body can only be in one place at a time by definition, and his idea of will mandates that we do indeed "look back" at one another. We are not complete without one another; the distance between us is required to make our community real.

Locke's subject, on the other hand, cannot *re*-present the other in his mind—they are always there, mixed together with the self. For Locke, we have very little to learn from one another. Love allows us to presuppose one another, to always be together, sovereign and whole.

Unlike Locke, Hobbes does not ask us to love each other, at least not in the way that Locke intends. He writes:

> [T]hey who shall more narrowly look into the causes for which men come together, and delight in each other's company, shall easily find that this happens not because naturally it could happen no otherwise, but by accident. For if by nature one man should love another... there could be (no) reason... why every man should not equally love every man, as being equally man.[96]

For Hobbes, such love makes no distinctions; it is like a flood that annihilates our particularity. It is not natural but an "accident"; Therefore we are not condemned to live by love.

As if anticipating Nietzsche's living fool, Hobbes tells us:

> We must therefore resolve that the original of all great and lasting societies consisted not in the mutual good will men had towards each other, but in the mutual fear they had of each other.[97]

"Foes, there is no foe."

Before we can be friends, we must be enemies. We must respect one another. In a footnote to this passage, Hobbes offers us a vision of how we can pass from enmity, through respect, to society itself:

> It is through fear that men secure themselves... whence it happens, that daring to come forth they know each other's spirits. But then if they fight, civil society ariseth from the victory; if they agree, from their agreement.[98]

Exactly as with Nietzsche, it is the "love of one's enemy" that serves as a bridge to another kind of love itself, to *philia politike* perhaps. Through our engagement as separate and dangerous beings, we come to "know each other's spirits," we form networks of belief, and this can lead to "agreement," to peace and community on a new, more solid foundation. The outcome of this engagement is not given, the process of coming together is the very point. Love must not be a mandate that we submit to but something that we make, something that we earn, or don't earn.[99]

Responsibility

From our distances, how do we respond to one another? How or why should we care about each other at all? What keeps respect from becoming an infinite distance, a separation of humanity into its component parts? In coming up with a reason to have a community at all, we come into treacherous waters because this is where love itself has always had an answer in Western philosophy, at least since Plato: Without love, it is argued, we have nothing at all.

The word "respond" comes from Latin and means "to promise in return," or perhaps we could say more broadly "to give back." It too implies the distance of respect but includes also a notion of exchange and communication, connection. As we have already seen, in *Politics of Friendship* Derrida seeks a "rupture of reciprocity," an idea of giving that is not tied up with an automatic and required response which stems from our sameness, from our lack of spatial distance from one another. Such an understanding does not preclude promising, or giving back, but only asks that we do so in a very different way. Here, we promise, we give without expecting to receive anything in return.[100]

In seeking a basis for responsibility, Derrida, like Hobbes himself, sees death as that which simultaneously confers our singularity and difference, even as it is common to each of us, offering us both distance and connection. As he tells us in *The Gift of Death:*

> Death is very much that which nobody else can undergo or confront in my place. My irreplaceability is therefore conferred, delivered, "given" one can say by death. It is the same gift, the same source, one could say the same goodness and the same law. It is from the site of death as the place of my irreplaceability, that is, of my singularity that I feel called to responsibility. In this sense, only a mortal can be responsible.[101]

Our "response" to one another, our responsibility, is given by death. In considering death in this way, Derrida describes a disagreement between Heidegger and Levinas. For Heidegger, the importance of death is that no one can die for you. They can die in your place at some particular instant, temporarily saving your life, but eventually you must die yourself. This singular fact reinforces the fact that "Dying is something that every *Dasein* itself must take upon itself at the time."[102] Death reinforces our finitude and thus gives us to ourselves.

Levinas complains that such a notion of death excludes the way that death does indeed ethically link us to one another. For Levinas, responsibility comes not from our being thrown onto our own limitations and hence toward Being itself, but rather toward one another. For Levinas, we are responsible for one another only by including ourselves in the other's death—in recognizing, across the infinite separation of death, a commonality.

In "On Death in Bloch's Thought," Levinas argues:

> [I]n Heidegger's celebrated analyses of time, the "ecstasy" of the future is privileged over those of the present and the past. This "Being-for-death," as a potential-to-be most proper to man because absolutely untransferable (each one dies for himself without a possible replacement), as the anguish wherein

the imminence of nothingness occurs is the original future. It is the most authentic modality of the humanity of man. This schema of pure future stands opposed to that which emerges from Bloch's thought.[103]

Levinas proposes instead the possibility of an "authentic future... the hope of realizing what is not yet," which is to say, the hope of living in human time, where what we will do, what we will become, is not already marked in terms of an unending relationship with the eternal sameness.[104] In making this claim, Levinas is not unlike Hannah Arendt herself, who, as we saw in the first chapter, looks to Saint Augustine for a way to understand the infinite that does not as he sees it simply reproduce the inadequacy of human life and human time, but rather serves as its foundation. In *Love and Saint Augustine,* Arendt is responding to Heidegger's notion of time, as when she writes:

> Since our expectations and desires are prompted by what we remember and guided by a previous knowledge, it is memory and not expectation (for instance, the expectation of death as in Heidegger's approach) that gives unity and wholeness to human existence.[105]

Arendt's treatment of Heidegger is gentler than Levinas's. She does not seek to replace Heidegger's notion of the future so much as bolster it. To Heidegger's expectation of death, which, even as it renders each of us unique (no one can die for us), also makes us all the same (we will *all* die), Arendt adds a new emphasis on the fact of our birth. This gives us to ourselves in a different way; each of us is given our lives to do as we will. The as yet unknown story of our life distinguishes us, makes us truly unique.

Perhaps even more than Levinas, Arendt seeks not only a human future but a present, a notion of human time and the possibility of action. For Arendt, a truly authentic future is one that escapes the demands of a solipsistic notion of sovereignty. Such an understanding of time allows for a future which can surprise us, which remains unscripted, located in the actions and reactions, that is to say the *responses* of the present, of the human beings who live among one another.

For Arendt, our ability to respond, to make promises, is the marker of a life lived in human time. In *The Human Condition* she writes:

> The function of the faculty of promising is to master this two fold darkness of human affairs [i.e., the human inability to rely either on one another or on oneself] and is, as such, the only alternative to a mastery which relies on domination of one's self and rule over others.... The moment promises lose their character as isolated islands of certainty in an ocean of uncertainty, that is, when this faculty is misused to cover the whole ground of the future and to map out a path secured in all directions, they lose their binding power and the whole enterprise becomes self-defeating.[106]

Promising becomes, like memory, a way to establish ourselves, to make ourselves into persons who can be trusted, to come to know one another. A promise, a response, does not presume its own certainty, or the certainty of other persons. It is a "let us see," an experiment whose outcome remains unknown. When we make promises, we are also making ourselves into the kind of responsible persons that we promise to become.

To achieve this, we require an epistemological foundation, a concept of time which allows for such promising. For Arendt, the idea of death alone will not serve as the grounds for respect and responsibility unless it can deliver us to our own time, unless it can provide an epistemological basis for action. Adding birth to death helps to achieve this foundation.[107] As she writes:

> The miracle that saves the world, the realm of human affairs, from its normal "natural" ruin is ultimately the fact of natality, in which the faculty of action is ontologically rooted. It is, in other words, the birth of new men and the new beginning, the action they are capable of by virtue of being born.[108]

Birth and death create a boundary around human times; as we have seen, we become "bounded by eternity" on two ends.[109] Between this lies the realm of human life and by extension, human responsibility.

As we have seen, Arendt, in turning to Augustine, remains ambivalent about what she is getting. In turning to Augustine's notion of creation, she is also accepting his notion of love, of *agape* itself. As we have seen too, by the time she writes *The Human Condition,* she sees that love undermines the very relationships, the very responses, that she would ask of us. Love has already mapped out our lives, provided us with its own future, leading us to an eternal sameness from which death itself is no release.

Once again, I believe that Hobbes (and Derrida as well) offers her an epistemological foundation for a notion of responsibility that includes both birth and death, our particularity and our commonality. With Hobbes, we reject a presupposed nature that orders our actions and determines our lives. As we have seen, nature is defined by Hobbes as stemming "from [our] first birth." It is simply the record, the memory of our lives, of how we create ourselves and one another. Such an idea of birth does not preclude and indeed requires an end; Hobbes accepts and celebrates, as Arendt does, our birth as mortal beings.[110] And he too accepts and celebrates, in a sense, our death. Death, as much as birth, confers onto us both a present as well as an "authentic future," that is to say a life that is wholly and only our own, but also one that is limited and finite; our finitude both binds us and separates us. It gives us respect and responsibility.

We begin to see even more clearly now why Hobbes puts such an enormous premium on life itself—life is not only the grounds for but also the essence of what develops through "morall and civill science." Life is filled with the endless possibility of human time and space; it becomes democratic. With Hobbes, responsibility becomes not so much an obligation, as it is with Levinas, but a privilege—it is not that we *must* respond to the other, it is rather that our presence with one another offers us this precious opportunity, one that we dismiss to our greatest possible detriment. "Perhaps," in our unpredictable, unscripted, and limited time here on earth, we just might choose to be friends.

The wholly other

There is one final but crucial element to what Hobbes offers to the "immense rumor," and that is the idea of a God who, while present, is silent and leaves us to our own devices. Although dangerous and colonizing the political, the idea of the eternal, of the "outside," is nonetheless crucial to the notion of *philia politike* because it offers a counterweight to the hubris, the excessive self-regarding, that might otherwise come with an entirely terrestrial politics. Thus not only do we need distance from one another, not only can we respond to one another, but the quality of that response, the nature of that distance, must also be considered.

Levinas argues that without the notion of God as wholly other, we would be incapable of any responsibility (he calls it "ethics," but Derrida avoids the word, ceding it to those thinkers who have enshrouded it in nature and fraternity). For Levinas, God's otherness lies precisely in his invisibility. Levinas speaks of "The God who hides His face."[111] He writes:

> The link between God and man is not an emotional communion that takes place within the love of a God incarnate.... It is precisely a word, not incarnate, from God that ensures a living God among us.[112]

Exactly as with Hobbes, for Levinas God's absence serves as the ground for humanity's own value and community. He writes that God "hide[s his] face so as to demand the superhuman of man."[113] Elsewhere he writes, "It is here that God has transcended creation itself. It is here that God 'has emptied himself.' He has created someone to talk to."[114] God's ultimate gift to us, for Levinas, is not to have emptied us in readiness for his presence, but rather to have emptied himself, withdrawn from the world to create a separate possibility, a separate worthiness, a different idea of love.

For Levinas, God becomes an analogy, a face that we cannot see which we then project onto other persons that we encounter—they become, like God himself, present but unknowable, hence affording the same "rupture of reciprocity" that Derrida speaks of.

Yet Derrida, in his own considerations of the infinite, argues for a somewhat different understanding of responsibility:

On what condition is responsibility possible? On a condition that the Good no longer be a transcendental objective, a relation between objective things, but the relation to the other, a response to the other.... On what condition does goodness exist beyond all calculation? *On the condition that goodness forget itself,* that the movement be a movement of the gift that renounces itself, hence a movement of infinite love. Only infinite love can renounce itself and, in order to become *finite* become incarnated in order to love the other, to love the other as a finite other. This gift of infinite love comes from someone and is addressed to someone; responsibility demands irreplaceable singularity.[115] (emphasis added)

In this analogy, God does not so much recede from the world as incarnate into it, take on a mortal form. In *The Gift of Death,* Derrida derives such an idea from a frankly Christian source, the Czech theologian Jan Patočka. But he argues that there is not anything "essentially Christian" about this notion. He tells us that there is something deeply heretical about Patočka; the idea of God that emerges almost obliterates itself in its transformation into finite form. In a sense, in becoming finite, God ceases to be infinite. As such, Derrida offers us less of a Christian philosophy than a philosophy born out of an engagement with Christian and Greek doctrines.[116]

And Jewish ones too. In "Violence and Metaphysics," Derrida considers how Levinas's philosophy, by its own logic, might itself lead to a not unsimilar viewpoint:

The positive Infinity (God)—if these words are meaningful—cannot be infinitely Other. If one thinks, as Levinas does, that positive infinity tolerates, or even requires, infinite alterity, then one must renounce all language, and first of all the words *infinite* and *other.* Infinity cannot be understood as Other except in the form of the in-finite.[117]

In a sense, then, Levinas's God must too become incarnated, must exist within the bounds of time and space to serve as the basis of human responsibility.

In considering the production of the in-finite from the infinite, Derrida shows us how, from a foundation in love, in Platonic and Christian (and perhaps Jewish) iconography, we can discern something else. Something very new (or, he tells us, also very old). In forgetting itself, Goodness becomes simply goodness, the infinite becomes finite, a terrain for human politics becomes born out of the very otherness of a forgotten God.[118]

What does it mean to "forget" God or to forget the Good? Does this entail the abandonment of these concepts altogether? Giorgio Agamben helps us think further about how such a transformation might come about. In *The Coming Community,* he offers us the image of limbo as a way to understand a terrestrial politics that is contained by even as it has forgotten God himself. According to Agamben, in traditional Catholic doctrine, when babies die too soon to be baptized, they cannot go to heaven but are too pure and innocent to go to hell either. In limbo they do not suffer but they are deprived of God's presence. Yet God gives them one great gift—they are allowed to forget God's very existence. As Agamben puts it:

> The greatest punishment—the lack of the vision of God—thus turns into a natural joy: Irremediably lost, they persist without pain in divine abandon. God has not forgotten them but rather they have...forgotten God....Neither blessed like the elected nor hopeless like the damned, they are infused with a joy with no outlet.[119]

For Agamben, life on earth itself could be rethought as a kind of limbo. Rather than wait in expectation of the divine to fill us up (and rather than be filled with rage and murderous intent when he doesn't), we forget God and turn to ourselves. Yet, to paraphrase (and reverse) Arendt, in so forgetting God, we do not deny him. The act of forgetting itself still retains a relationship with, dare we say, a memory of God. He is still "next to" us. We still preserve a relationship to the divine, only now the substance of it, the filledness of it, becomes by default our own.

For Agamben, such an act of forgetting can also be the basis of a new kind of love. He tells us that love is not (or should not be) a kind of grasping for power, or a will to already know all about myself and hence the universe. Love should not be sovereign, a randomness that imagines itself to be universal, that seeks to replace or substitute for God. Instead, love is (or should be) an embracing of our mortality, or as he puts it, the accepting of our "power not to be."

To remain bound by sovereign notions, by existing conventions of love, means that as mortals we cannot accept our limitations. Accordingly, Agamben tells us we are filled with rage at our impotence, at our inability to know all things, at our inadequacy. To try to be like God ourselves then is to feel God's absence, to feel our own futility. He argues that to accept our limitations on the other hand is not a submission to passivity and failure but rather a positive glorying in our own limitations, in "becoming who we are":

> Fleeing from our own impotence, or rather trying to adopt it as a weapon, we construct the malevolent power that oppresses those who show us their weakness, and failing our innermost possibility of not-being, we fall away from the only thing that makes love possible. Creation—or existence—is not the victorious struggle of a power to be against a power to not-be; it is rather the impotence of God with respect to his own impotence, his allowing—being able to *not* not be—a contingency to be. Or rather: It is the birth in God of love.[120]

217

Love here becomes reconceptualized as an "already filled-ness." Our birth, our creation, becomes the moment of "not-not" being, a conceptualization of life that holds both birth and death as its two boundaries. Such a love receives its adequacy from "the wholly other" even as it also erases all traces of such an event. The filledness that we expect from *agape* is no longer a "yet to be" but now is an "already was." What we do with ourselves becomes our own concern, a matter of politics, of *philia politike.*

In this sense, Arendt herself might benefit from this notion of forgetting. In her own search for *philia politike,* as we have seen, she turns not to forgetting but to its opposite: memory. And yet these need not be two contradictory gestures. As Agamben, and Hobbes as well, show us, the act of forgetting can itself contain, indeed can be the basis for the memory of our origin and creation. In this way, the concept of forgetting might aid Arendt in her frustration at being suspended between Greek freedom and Christian time. Arendt's own rootedness in Augustinian love can be not annihilated, but forgotten; out of the doctrine of love, something new can be born.[121]

Here again, Hobbes offers us an epistemological mechanism by which these democratic dreams of Arendt might begin to find their realization. For Hobbes, we can love one another not according to a lack (as with Locke) but rather according to a presence, to what God has vouchsafed to give us: our bodies and our communities or perhaps, rather, the lack has been reconceptualized into a having. Whereas it might appear that Locke's God has forgotten us, for Hobbes, we have "forgotten" him.[122]

It is true that both Hobbes and Locke view the subject as suspended between the absolute and the contingent; Hobbes mirrors Agamben's idea of a limbo between heaven and earth, and Locke attempts to reconcile God's law and earthly politics. Yet the crucial difference is that in Hobbes's case this suspension or in-betweenness serves to carve out a zone of freedom and unscripted possibilities—a true limbo that is divorced from any ongoing dependency upon its origins or creation, whereas Locke's suspendedness tends to collapse upon itself as divergent forces (God's truth and our truth, divine law and empiricism) attempt to occupy the same position.

What Hobbes offers above all is therefore human time and human space; he gives us his empiricism. This is not the pseudo-empiricism of Locke, but a real commitment to the earth and to our position upon it. Yet Hobbes's empiricism does not, as we have seen, preclude a relationship to God; it does not make us relativists or nihilists. Rather it allows for our experience of life to be "filled" with our own substance even as that substance is received from God. With God forgotten, truly we have only the world around us. But this world is one that has become sacred through that act of forgetting (and hence preserving), and we have become sacred as well. Hobbes has given us a notion of the wholly other which is incarnate in the world; it is the infinite become in-finite. When we look for the wholly other, we see not God himself, but one another and ourselves; our bodies become the carriers for a once divine but now entirely terrestrial alterity.

In this sense, Hobbes's empiricism is redolent of Levinas (at least as he appears in the hands of Jacques Derrida). In Derrida's treatment of him, Levinas emerges as a great empiricist in his own right. Near the end of "Violence and Metaphysics," Derrida writes that empiricism is the dream of the "wholly other":

> [T]he profundity of the empiricist tradition must be recognized beneath the naiveté of certain of its historical expressions. It is the *dream* of a purely *hetero-logical* thought at its source. A *pure* thought of *pure* difference.[123]

As with Cavell's notion of mood, Derrida sees in Levinas's empiricism "the experience of the infinitely [in-finitely] other," serving as the basis for our self and our responsibility, promising new horizons, new dreams.[124] Yet Derrida recognizes that as a dream "it must vanish *at daybreak,* as soon as language awakens.";[125] Language, that Greek gift of *logos,* resists and obliterates the dream of alterity; it offers that same smothering sameness of love itself.

But Derrida does not abandon the dream. He sees in Levinas a revived empiricism which "inverses [itself] by revealing it to itself as metaphysics."[126] In other words, like Aristophanes' globular humans, Levinas dares to challenge the Greek gods in their abode.

These "gods" are in fact those philosophers who have upheld Platonic thought, love itself, since Plato's time. Derrida writes that Levinasian empiricism is deemed a "nonphilosophy," an outsider to the great tradition of Platonic thought. An outsider, a Jew, Levinas makes his case for the wholly other amid a chorus of eternity-loving Greeks.[127]

Characteristically, however, Derrida does not call for the abandonment of the Greeks themselves (in part because he recognizes that Greek thought is a "miracle" which "forever has protected itself against every absolutely *surprising* convocation").[128] Like Arendt, he seeks reconciliation; after all, the dream of *philia politike* was born in Greece rather than Israel.

Derrida asks, "Are we Jews? Are we Greeks?" His answer: "We live in the difference between the Jew and the Greek."[129] The doctrine of love is to be found in this difference. This difference is our home, possibly the only home we will ever find. We must find *philia politike* here, if anywhere. At the end of "Violence and Metaphysics," in a phrase redolent of Rousseau's musings on Greek slavery, Derrida quotes James Joyce's *Ulysses:* "Jewgreek is greekjew. Extremes meet."[130]

To Derrida's and Arendt's attempts to reconcile Greek, Jewish, and Christian thought, let us consider adding Hobbes to the conversation. Is he a Jew? Is he a Greek?[131] Perhaps he offers us something of the "Jewish" vision of the wholly other, the creator, as well as the "Greek" vision of politics, of freedom and *philia politike.* Hobbes attempts a truce, coexistence between heaven and earth. Does he succeed in reconciling "the extremes"? Does he help us to realize these democratic dreams?

Perhaps...but not yet

The preceding can only hint at the kinds of conversations that might be envisioned between Hobbes, Derrida, Arendt, Agamben, Levinas, and others, the ongoing development of the "immense rumor." What can we take from Hobbes in the meantime? Hobbes offers us some advice on how to rethink love. He shows us a way that we can be enemies and yet build a community together. He shows us a way to have a relationship with God, if we so choose, and still have our own validity, our own sense of time and space. Hobbes tells us a story about the human body which, if not true, still serves as a suitable foundation for a polity, one that gives us each the space and the respect that we need without masking our differences. He offers a way to make our interactions not peripheral to but the basis of the society that we build together. This thinker, who argues that we can and must fear one another, yet shows us how we can trust one another, how we can come to believe in something that is of our own making and still treat it with reverence.

And Hobbes shows another important thing too, something that Derrida also reminds us of: that the "perhaps" lies not only in the future but in our past as well. Derrida shows us further that the "perhaps" can be found even in those thinkers who stand at the heart of the doctrine of love and friendship. We have seen this throughout this book, in the struggle within Locke, Rousseau, Emerson, and even Thoreau between democratic principles and the love of truth, between God and humanity, between *eros* and *agape.* This tension goes back to the founders of the doctrine of love themselves, to Aristotle, and even to Plato. Plato need not have included the critique of Aristophanes in his retelling of *The Symposium.* His choice to include this bit of subversion, and even the multiple and competing tales of the nature of love, he offers in general might itself suggest that perhaps Plato too was concerned that friendship was a hard thing to come across, that love was not a certain or easy prospect.

What does it take to begin to realize the "perhaps," the democratic dreams? Perhaps not very much at all. In *The Coming Community,* Agamben considers this Jewish parable:

> A rabbi, a real cabalist, once said that in order to establish the reign of peace it is not necessary to destroy everything nor to begin a completely new world. It is sufficient to displace this cup or this bus or this stone just a little, and thus everything. But this small displacement is so difficult to achieve and its measure

is so difficult to find that, with regard to the world, humans are incapable of it and it is necessary that the Messiah come.[132]

This story itself emerges as part of the immense rumor; Agamben tells us that Walter Benjamin told this story to Ernst Bloch, and he in turn heard it from Gershom Scholem. Now Agamben is telling this to us. We see how all of the building blocks of love and friendship are already present. The world does not need to be remade—to do so would be to lose the very basis for that which we seek. This world is our home. Yet for all this, this parable expresses a messianic sentiment. Does it offer us more than an "ode to dejection," waiting for a redemption that might never come?

Derrida himself reminds us these goals will always be elusive, always just around the corner. He writes at the end of *Politics of Friendship:*

> [D]emocracy remains to come; this is its essence in so far as it remains: not only will it remain indefinitely perfectible, hence always insufficient and future, but, belonging to the time of the promise, it will always remain, in each of its future times, to come: even when there is democracy, it never exists, it is never present. . . .
>
> When will we be ready for an experience of freedom and equality that is capable of respectfully experiencing that friendship, which would at last be just, just beyond the law, and measured up against its measurelessness?
>
> O my democratic friends.[133]

Even Derrida reveals his impatience, his desire for friendship itself, not just for the "perhaps." Maybe love itself has taught us to be impatient. But we want more than just to dream. We want to build and to live out a *philia politike.* Can a thinker like Hobbes help us in this endeavor?

E. M. Forster was a man who, in his own struggle with his longings, knew firsthand the traumas of love, the failed dreams of friendship. He also knew how to wait. At the end of *A Passage to India,* Aziz, a character full of anger at the injustice of British colonialism, tells Fielding (whose name is redolent of precisely the colonializing tendency—Locke's view of the self and the world as a field of conquest) that after the British are thrown out of India, after the enmity comes to the surface and distance is finally achieved,

> ". . . then," [Aziz] concluded, half kissing [Fielding], "you and I shall be friends."
>
> "Why can't we be friends now?" said the other, holding him affectionately. "It's what I want. It's what you want.'"
>
> But the horses didn't want it—they swerved apart. The earth didn't want it, sending up rocks through which the riders must pass single file; the temple, the tank, the jail, the birds, the carrion, the Guest House . . . they didn't want it.

They said in their hundred voices "No, not yet," and the sky said, "No, not there."[134]

Forster offers us a vision in which the very human dimensions of space and time realize that they remain colonized, fields of control. They have been and remain conquered and subdued by notions of sovereignty, by nature, by love itself. They know that as such, they cannot offer a place for friendship; all they can offer is a "perhaps." Perhaps one day we can be friends, but not yet, not here.

Notes

1. Jean-Jacques Rousseau, *La Découverte du nouveau monde*, in *Oeuvres Complètes de Jean-Jacques Rousseau*, vol. 3 (Paris: Furne et. Cie. Libraires—Editeurs, 1846), p. 260. Titles of French-language works will appear in the main texts in their English translation except for *Émile* and *La Nouvelle Héloïse*, which normally are cited in French. In the case of *The Discovery of the New World* and *Émile and Sophie, or the Solitary Ones,* there is no English translation available so, in my first citation, I give the title in both languages. In cases of French editions, I supply my own translations.
2. Ibid., p. 257.
3. By democracy I do not mean to refer to formalist structures of electoralism. Rather, I am addressing the substantive opportunities for more meaningful political participation. Throughout this book, I will be considering "democratic" in both a political and philosophical sense. Politically, the idea of democracy suggests a political system that does not mandate hierarchy or sacrifice as part of its foundational order. Democracy, which I relate closely to the unrealized Aristotelian dream of *philia politike*, involves a political structure which shifts and adjusts according to the discourse of its members, a discourse marked by surprise, struggle, agreement, and disagreement. Philosophically, democracy suggests an Archimedean point that remains on earth, a kind of "horizontal" epistemology contained within the boundaries of human time and space. Such a vision does not project power, value, or decision making into heaven, "the state," or "sovereignty" but contains it, once again, in the political realm itself.
4. Plato, *The Dialogues of Plato Volume II: The Symposium* (New Haven: Yale University Press, 1991), p. 153.
5. Ibid., p. 130.
6. It is worth pointing out that Aristophanes does not negate the notion of the Gods, he only asks that they remain out of the realm of politics and human desires. As I will be arguing later in this book, an idea of heaven or a "wholly other" serves as an important check on the relativism and hubris that could otherwise visit an entirely human-centered philosophy.
7. Jacques Derrida, *Politics of Friendship* (New York: Verso Press, 1997), p. 27.
8. In this case, the external standard of judgment is not "the truth," but nature, a somewhat more local category. Although nature is a more terrestrial form of judgment, Aristotle invests it with the same sort of external judgments, the same tendency to organize and order human societies according to its dictates as Plato's concept of the forms. In one important way, however, Aristotle does differ from Plato, namely in his idea of the possibility of human self-sufficiency as a polis. In this way he avoids the Platonic contention that regardless of their arrangements, human beings are never adequate, never worthy of the external standards that they are being measured by. Thus, although he reproduces the terrestrial organizations of *eros*, Aristotle's notion of *philia* does contain an element that sets it at odds against the Platonic system, offering an alternative vision to the doctrine of

love. In this way, we can consider Aristotle's contribution to the "immense rumor" to be more than simply a wistfulness for the possibility of friendship.

9. Aristotle, *Ethics* (New York: Penguin Books, 1976), p. 263.

10. Ibid., p. 301.

11. Ibid., p., 302.

12. Ibid., p. 264.

13. Ibid., p. 270.

14. Ibid., p. 278.

15. Saint Augustine, *The City of God* (New York: Doubleday, Image Books, 1958), p. 321.

16. Ibid., p. 460.

17. In *The Nature of Love,* Irving Singer argues that in so subsuming *eros* to *agape,* Saint Augustine has actually voided the concept of *eros* altogether, which if true certainly calls into question the criticisms that Nygren and de Rougemont make of him. Irving Singer, *The Nature of Love,* vol. I (New York: Random House, 1966).

18. Anders Nygren, *Agape and Eros,* vol. II (London: Society for Promoting Christian Knowledge, 1939), p. 492.

19. Ibid., p. 407.

20. As Singer puts it, "[Luther] not only denies that man has a free will (except in minor, material matters—'to milk kine, to build houses, etc.') but also he claims that men who expect to attain anything spiritual by means of free will thereby deny Christ." Singer, p. 334.

21. Ibid., p. 337.

22. Ibid., p. 344.

23. Ibid., p. 370.

24. Ibid., p. 365. Singer writes that there is something of a countertradition to this doctrine of love, a more "realist" or "terrestrial" notion of love that is wholly of the world. He specifically cites Ovid and Lucretius as epitomizing such an approach. But Singer suggests that although they have very opposite ideas about sexuality and love, both thinkers fail to promote a love that is more than selfish and self-reflexive. As he says of the Ovidian lovers, for example, "they *all* use the beloved as a way of loving themselves, and they all wish to be loved instead of loving someone else." Singer, p. 149. If the Christian doctrine of love fails because it makes love impossible by hollowing us out, failing to give us a love of our own, this "realist" tradition similarly seems to offer no mechanism by which to get us outside of ourselves and care about one another. Love, which demands a kind of crossing over of personal boundaries, has no place to take root in this "terrestrial" soil. In its rejection of love as a transcendent, Platonic concept, love has not been so much redeemed as undone.

25. Julia Kristeva, *Tales of Love* (New York: Columbia University, 1987), pp. 143–44.

26. Ibid., p. 144.

27. Such a love is "dominated by the idea that brotherly love is not a love for fallen strangers in the world but for beings that belong always already to the Name of the Father." Ibid., p. 148.

28. Ibid.

29. Ibid.

30. Nygren's earlier critics include Reinhold Niebuhr, who writes, "[Nygren's concept of] *agape* is really a complete impossibility and irrelevance to man. It describes the character of God but has no real relation, as source and end towards *philia* and *eros,* towards either mutual love or expressions of love, tainted by self-interest, which are the actual stuff of

human existence." Reinhold Niebuhr, *Faith and History* (New York: Charles Scribner's Sons, 1999), p. 178. If what Nygren asks of us is too much, then the various doctrines of love ranging from Augustine's to Calvin's and presumably even Luther's must not be as different as they seem, despite some important contentions.

31. Hannah Arendt, *Love and Saint Augustine* (Chicago: University of Chicago Press, 1996), pp. 25, 30.
32. Ibid., pp. 36, 38
33. Ibid., p. 39.
34. Ibid., p. 43, and footnote, p. 44.
35. Ibid., p. 49.
36. Ibid.
37. Ibid., p. 53.
38. Ibid., p. 58
39. Ibid., p. 69.
40. Ibid., p. 72.
41. Ibid., p. 75. This turn to metaphysics on Arendt's part is constituted to some degree by her complicated relationship to Martin Heidegger and his philosophy.
42. Ibid., p. 96.
43. Ibid., p. 108.
44. Ibid., p. 112
45. Hannah Arendt, *The Human Condition* (Chicago: University of Chicago Press, 1958), p. 242.
46. *Love and Saint Augustine,* pp. 38–39.
47. *The Human Condition,* p. 242 (footnote).
48. Ibid., p. 242.
49. Ibid., p. 243.
50. Arendt doesn't totally discount love, however, because she writes that it reveals *who* we are—as opposed to *what* we are. The difference seems to be between our essence, the person that we make ourselves be (who), and our "qualities and shortcomings...achievements, failings and transgressions" (what). Ibid., p. 242.
51. Ibid., p. 243.
52. Ibid., p. 246.
53. Ibid., p. 247.
54. Ibid.
55. *Politics of Friendship,* p. 1.
56. Aristotle himself seems to make no such distinction between love's public and private face. *Ethics,* pp. 276–77.
57. At several points in *Politics of Friendship,* Derrida acknowledges that he treats the subject as male, yet offers that this only deepens rather than answers the question of subjectivity.
58. *Politics of Friendship,* p. 11.
59. Ibid., p. 62.
60. Ibid., p. 50.
61. Ibid., p. 63.
62. Ibid., p. x.
63. John Locke, *Two Treatises of Government* (Cambridge: Cambridge University Press, 1965), 2:5 (p. 270), for one example. The term "judicious" is interesting insofar as it recalls the period of rule by judges in the Hebrew tradition. Locke, like many of his contemporaries,

saw the time of the Hebrew judges as an ideal political community when the word of God could be directly imparted to a community via a divinely inspired leader. Hooker holds on to the ongoing possibility of such judgment as the basis for a political order. As such, he might well be considered "judicious."

64. Richard Hooker, *Ecclesiastical Works (The Works of That Learned and Judicious Divine Mr. Richard Hooker)* (New York: D. Appleton & Company, 1851), p. 152. Note his use of word "contentions," which Locke might echo in his own talk about the "quarrelsom and contentious."

65. *Ethics,* p. 301.

66. Hooker, p. 129.

67. Ibid., pp. 129–30. Hooker goes on to write:

> But ye will say that if the guides of the people must be blind, the common sort of men must not close up their own eyes and be led by the conduct of such.... Which thing though in itself most true, is in your defence notwithstanding weak: because the matter wherein ye think that ye see, and imagine that your ways are sincere, is of far deeper consideration that any one amongst five hundred of you conceiveth. Let the vulgar sort amongst you know, that there is not the least branch of the cause wherein they are so resolute, but that to the trail of it a great deal more appertaineth than their conceit doth reach unto. Ibid., p. 130.

Here Hooker almost sounds like Robert Filmer, but of course, instead of Filmer's devotion to tradition *qua* tradition, Hooker stresses, as Locke will, devotion to truth itself, which may in fact be at odds with tradition (just as Christ himself was).

68. Ibid., p. 133.

69. Aristotle, *The Politics* (New York: Penguin Books, 1962), pp. 96–97.

70. *Two Treatises,* 2:5 (p. 270). It is clear in the text that Locke is quoting Hooker in order to establish his own basis for moral virtues.

71. Ibid., 2:6 (p. 271).

72. Locke's term for this is the "withdrawing of miracles." John Locke, *The Reasonableness of Christianity* (Stanford, Calif.: Stanford University Press, 1958), p. 97.

73. Immanuel Kant, *Groundwork of the Metaphysic of Morals* (New York: Harper Torchbooks, 1964), pp. 91–92, for one example.

74. Ibid., p. 130.

75. Immanuel Kant, *Perpetual Peace* (Indianapolis: Hackett Publishing Co., 1983), p. 41.

76. Romand Coles, *Rethinking Generosity* (Ithaca, N.Y.: Cornell University Press, 1997), p. 25.

77. *Politics of Friendship,* p. 254.

78. Ibid.

79. Ibid.

80. Ibid., p. 255.

81. John Stuart Mill, *On Liberty* (Indianapolis: Hackett Publishing, 1978), p. 42. Mill holds out the hope that some "mechanism" might arise to solve this problem, but in terms of what this deus ex machina might be or look like, he tells us nothing.

82. Ibid., p. 62.

83. I will be making a similar argument here about Emerson's theories of geniuses and the "masses."

84. Ibid., p. 64.

85. Leo Bersani, "Loving Men," in Maurice Berger, Brian Wallis, and Simon Watson, eds., *Constructing Masculinity* (New York: Routledge, 1995), p. 121.

86. Wendy Brown, "Liberalism's Family Values," in *States of Injury: Power and Freedom in Late Mondernity* (Princeton: Princeton University Press, 1995), p. 164.
87. Ibid., p. 156.
88. The term is Coles's.
89. Derrida, despite his formal areligiosity, by linking himself to religious thinkers like Patočka, Levinas, and Kierkegaard, also engages with what he calls "religion without religion." Jacques Derrida, *The Gift of Death* (Chicago: University of Chicago Press, 1995), p. 49. See also John D. Caputo, *The Prayer and Tears of Jacques Derrida* (Indianapolis: Indiana University Press, 1997).
90. Christopher Hill, *The World Turned Upside Down* (New York: Viking Press, 1972).

CHAPTER 2

1. This is certainly the argument of someone like C. B. MacPherson. Peter Laslett makes this argument in his introduction to the *Two Treatises of Government*, p. 67.
2. Kirstie M. McClure, *Judging Rights: Lockean Politics and the Limits of Consent* (Ithaca, N.Y.: Cornell University Press, 1996), p. 57. I would also challenge her categorizing Rousseau along with Hobbes and Hume (in my mind his epistemology is quite a bit like Locke's and is even directly influenced by Locke via Rousseau's connections to French Lockeans such as Condillac and Buffon).

    Elsewhere in the same volume, McClure also writes:

    > Locke's construction of human equality invests individual agency not only with the Hobbesian right and power to provide for one's own bodily needs and determine one's own individual actions, but with the reciprocal jurisdiction to judge and punish the actions of others for their deviations from the moral law. Ibid., p. 79.

3. Richard Ashcraft, *Revolutionary Politics and Locke's Two Treatises of Government* (Princeton: Princeton University Press, 1986), p. 258.
4. For more discussion of the concept of Locke's notion of "workmanship" see James Tully, *A Discourse of Property: John Locke and His Adversaries* (Cambridge, U.K.: Cambridge University Press, 1980), p. 9.
5. Ibid., p. 247. For an insightful account of the relationship between Locke's politics and those of the Levellers as articulated at the Army debates at Putney in 1647, see Jacqueline Stevens's article "The Reasonableness of John Locke's Majority," *Political Theory* 24: 3 (August 1996), pp. 423–63.
6. *Revolutionary Politics*, p. 249.
7. This position can be seen in Leveller discourse demonstrated for example by Colonel Rainborough, who at the Putney debates denies the suggestion that he is a communist or an anarchist. Ibid., p. 161. See also Christopher Hill, *The Century of Revolution* (Edinburgh, U.K.: Thomas Nelson and Sons, 1961), p. 132.
8. See Stevens, p. 445, for example. Also see Lois Schwoerer, "Locke and the Glorious Revolution," *Journal of the History of Ideas* 51 (October/December, 1990).
9. *Revolutionary Politics*, p. 165. For related arguments and documentation see Andrew Sharp, ed., *The English Levellers* (Cambridge, U.K.: Cambridge University Press, 1998); Kevin Sharp, ed., *Faction and Parliament* (Oxford: Clarendon Press, 1978); Kirstie M. McClure (already cited); and James Tully (already cited).
10. *Revolutionary Politics*, p. 157.

11. David Wootton argues that their position was in response to Cromwell's obstinacy at Putney. David Wootton, ed., *Divine Right and Democracy* (New York: Penguin Books, 1986), p. 51.

12. The first point is made by Wootton, Ibid. The latter, by Ashcraft, *Revolutionary Politics,* p. 160.

13. *The Century of Revolution,* p. 132.

14. Ibid., p. 131.

15. Ashcraft points out that Locke has made a vast improvement over the work of his contemporary James Tyrell, who sticks with the doctrine of property rights as given by occupancy. *Revolutionary Politics,* p. 282.

16. Ibid., p. 266.

17. Ibid.

18. Ibid., p. 270.

19. Ibid.

20. Ibid., p. 269. This is an argument that I will be returning to later.

21. John Locke, *Of the Conduct of the Understanding,* in *The Philosophical Works of John Locke* (London: George Bell & Sons, 1908), p. 32. [Henceforth *Conduct*]

22. In a way, I am not sure that it even really matters if Locke supports universal manhood suffrage or not (I doubt that he does, however), because for him the relationships of reason are such that the hierarchies that produce them are prepolitical. That is to say that the servant, worker, and even wife, by the time they might get to vote, have already (hopefully) submitted themselves to their masters' superior reason. Of course, given that the workers might *not* be so dutiful (as we will see, a perennial problem in Locke's system), it might just not be worth giving them (or at least their lower echelons) the vote after all; I tend to think that while Locke's principles may have been relatively redistributional (at least in terms of political, as opposed to economic rights), there is probably a limit to it lest the crucial economic order itself becomes threatened. Besides which, the series of arguments that Ashcraft provides us with whereby "Locke is probably like the Levellers who are themselves most likely proponents of universal manhood suffrage and therefore it is quite possible that Locke himself is so inclined" is rather tenuous in the first place.

23. John Dunn, *Locke* (Oxford, U.K.: Oxford University Press, 1984), p. 2.

24. John Dunn, *The Political Thought of John Locke* (Cambridge, U.K.: Cambridge University Press, 1969), pp. 256–57.

25. Ibid., p. 258.

26. Ibid., p. 225.

27. There is also a more secular Aristotelian influence on Locke from James Harrington.

28. *Revolutionary Politics,* p. 68.

29. Introduction to Book I of *Of the Laws of Ecclesiastical Polity.* R. W. Church, ed. (Oxford, U.K.: Clarendon Press, 1882), p. xvi.

30. Ibid., pp. x, xvi.

31. *Ecclesiastical Polity,* p. 133.

32. Michael Walzer, *The Revolution of the Saints* (Cambridge, Mass.: Harvard University Press, 1965), p. 36.

33. Calvin himself cites Augustine approvingly at times, suggesting a less than adversarial relationship between them. Luther is more critical, however. See *Luther and Calvin: On*

Secular Authority (Cambridge, U.K.: Cambridge University Press, 1991), pp. 63, 73, and footnotes.

34. Locke actually quotes this passage twice; see marginalia, *Two Treatises* 2:94 (p. 329) and 2:111 (p. 343). Elsewhere Locke cites Hooker as writing: "The lawful power of making Laws to Command whole Politick Societies of men belonging so properly unto the same entire Societies, that for any Prince or Potentate of what kind soever upon Earth, to exercise the same of himself, and not by express Commission immediately and personally received by God, or else by Authority derived a the first from their consent . . . is not better than meer Tyranny." Footnote, 2:134 (p. 356).

35. Ibid., footnote, 2:135 (p. 357).

36. In *Ecclesiastical Community*, Hooker writes: "True it is, that the kingdom of God must be the first thing in our purposes and desires. But inasmuch as religious life presupposeth life; inasmuch as to live virtuously it is impossible except we live; therefore, the first impediment . . . is penury and want of things without which we cannot live." p. 274.

37. Ibid., pp. 176, 178.

38. Ibid., p. 180.

39. He writes: "Capable we are of God both by understanding and will: by understanding, as he is that sovereign truth which comprehendeth the rich treasures of all wisdom; by will, as he is that sea of goodness whereof whoseo tasteth shall thirst no more. As the will doth now work upon that object by desire, which is as it were a motion towards the end as yet unobtained; so likewise upon the same hereafter received it shall work also by love." Ibid., p. 181.

40. *Two Treatises,* 2:5 (p. 270).

41. Ibid.

42. Ibid., 2:15 (pp. 277–78).

43. *The Reasonableness of Christianity,* p. 97.

44. Ibid., *A Discourse on Miracles,* p. 80.

45. He repeats this sort of idea, to give just one example, in the beginning of his chapter "Of Property" when he writes: "Whether we consider natural *Reason* . . . Or Revelation . . . 'tis very clear that God . . . *has given the Earth to the Children of Men.*" In other words, the same conclusions can be reached by either system, either together or independently. *Two Treatises,* 2:25 (p. 285).

46. Ibid., 1:46 (p. 173).

47. As I will argue in the next chapter, Derrida would call such an endeavor a "mediocre makeshift." Jacques Derrida, *Of Grammatology* (Baltimore: Johns Hopkins University Press, 1974), p. 145.

48. *The Reasonableness of Christianity,* p. 66.

49. Ibid., p. 64.

50. Ultimately, his best answer to this question is "the people," but as I shall show, the idea of "the people" itself presupposes many of the problems that lead to this epistemological crisis in the first place.

51. In many ways, the arguments over innate truths versus empiricism reproduce many of the questions we have already seen over whether God's love enables or preempts our own. If innate truths are truths that exist "in the mind of God," empiricism is the doctrine that insists that we are capable of knowing and understanding truths on our own.

52. The particular charge in this case was by John Edwards. John Dunn, for one, concedes that the charge made that Locke himself was a Socinianist was "extremely plausible." *Locke,* p. 15.

53. As I will argue further, Hobbes quite boldly promotes the concept of reason through a full and unapologetic empiricism. In this sense, he is quite like the Diggers themselves in making human reason, sense, and judgment the sole criteria by which we can come to know truths. But Hobbes's (and Winstanley's) version of empiricism was not to predominate.

54. *Revolutionary Politics,* p. 52. As Ashcraft tells us, Parker himself was, strangely enough, considered to be a Hobbesian, an idea that Parker contested strongly. Regardless of the merits of this argument, as I will argue later, the "Hobbesian" reading that Parker is said to echo is not an accurate portrayal of Hobbes himself. Ibid., p. 50.

55. *John Locke, An Essay concerning Human Understanding,* vol. I (New York: Dover Publications, 1959), p. 53. [Henceforth *Essay*]

56. Ibid., p. 37. Hooker makes a very similar argument and distinction himself.

57. Tully, p. 44. Tully writes that Locke rearticulates this claim of positive law himself in 2:57.

58. Thomas Hobbes, *Leviathan* (New York: Penguin Books, 1968), p. 88.

59. Michael Ayers, *Locke Volume I: Epistemology* (New York: Routledge, 1991), p. 245.

60. Ibid., p. 252–253.

61. Ernst Cassirer, *The Philosophy of the Enlightenment* (Princeton: Princeton University Press, 1968), p. 101.

62. Hooker, p. 164. Locke cites this in the *Essay,* p. 48.

63. Ibid.

64. Ibid., p. 57.

65. Hooker, p. 165.

66. *Essay,* p. 41.

67. Ibid., pp. 60, 61, and 58 respectively. It is deeply ironic to note that Locke argues against the notion of "tacit consent" when it comes to arguments against innate reason, but later will use exactly this argument to justify property relations. In the *Essay* he argues, "I have always thought the actions of men the best interpreters of their thoughts. But, since it is certain that most men's practices, and some men's open professions have either questioned or denied these principles it is impossible to establish an universal consent. Ibid., pp. 66–67. By this logic, the very grounds of property that Locke establishes in the *Second Treatise* seem to be called into question.

68. *Conduct,* p. 31.

69. *Essay,* p. 43.

70. *Conduct,* pp. 34–35.

71. *Essay,* p. 321.

72. Ibid., p. 43.

73. Ibid.

74. Ibid., p. 46.

75. Uday Singh Mehta, *The Anxiety of Freedom: Imagination and Individuality in Locke's Political Thought* (Ithaca, N.Y.: Cornell University Press, 1992).

76. *Two Treatises,* 2:173 (p. 383).

77. Peter Schouls, *Reasoned Freedom: John Locke and the Enlightenment* (Ithaca, N.Y. Cornell University Press, 1992), p. 50.

78. I think the harshness of Locke's language in such passages may in part be hyperbole born of his need to justify civil insurrection (the civil war and Glorious Revolution) but also born of his conviction that reason is an extremely fragile and yet vital thing and that no one should take it lightly.

79. *Essay,* p. 334. Locke writes, "but that which immediately determines the will . . . is the uneasiness of desire, fixed on some absent good."

80. Ibid., p. 345. Locke considers the term "free will" improper because he believes that the will is not the subject of human agency. It is merely a faculty, an executive aspect of the mind to act out the desires of the agent, which is none other than the subject himself. It makes sense that Locke would resist granting the will more power than he did, as it is the internal psyche's equivalent of a king. Since Locke was struggling against the undue power of the monarchy, he made an attempt to rein in the will as well. Ibid., p. 328.

81. The idea of indifferency brings with it shades of *agape.* As Peter Schouls points out, Locke uses "indifference" in two senses. One meaning is indifference as in a state of sufficient objectivity from a situation to be able to make a rational judgment. The other form of indifference is a moral one to good or evil. This latter sort of indifference Locke sees as detrimental, and in the treatment here I am only referring to the former sort of indifference. The very idea of indifference also relates to what Charles Taylor calls "the punctual self" who can step back from the world, analyze it critically, and respond accordingly. See Charles Taylor, *Sources of the Self* (Cambridge, Mass.: Harvard University Press, 1989), ch. 9, "Locke's Punctual Self."

82. *Conduct,* p. 51.

83. *Essay,* p. 344.

84. John Locke, *Some Thoughts concerning Education,* in *John Locke on Politics and Education* (Roslyn, N.Y.: Walter J. Black, Inc., 1947), p. 231. [Henceforth *Education*]

85. Ibid., pp. 233–34.

86. *Essay,* p. 68.

87. Ibid., p. 335.

88. Ibid.

89. *Conduct,* p. 32. In a section of the *Essay* entitled "Preference of Vice to Virtue as a Manifest Wrong Judgment," Locke writes:

> Whatever false notions, or shameful neglect of what is in their power, may put men out of their way to happiness and distract them, as we see, into so different courses of life . . . and he that will not be so far a rational creature as to reflect seriously upon infinite happiness and misery, must needs condemn himself as not making that use of his understanding he should. *Essay,* p. 364.

90. Quoted in *The Political Thought of John Locke,* p. 185.

91. *Essay,* p. 343.

92. Ibid.

93. *Education,* p. 210.

94. For boys, that is. Locke hardly mentions the education of girls and, as we will see, has a very different fate in mind for them.

95. Ibid. Schouls suggests that this is an exaggeration on Locke's part, not necessarily meant to be taken literally.

96. Nathan Tarcov, *Locke's Education for Liberty* (Chicago: University of Chicago Press, 1984), p. 81.

97. *Education,* p. 237.

98. Ibid.
99. Ibid., pp. 237–38.
100. Ibid., p. 238.
101. Ibid. In this sense, Locke is once again evocative of Aristotle, in this case in terms of the classical thinker's finding virtue in the doctrine of the means. As Aristotle writes in his *Ethics*:

    [E]very knowledgeable person avoids excess and deficiency, but looks for the mean and chooses it—not the mean of the thing but the mean relative to us. *Ethics*, p. 100.

    Locke's admonition here is akin to Aristotle's claim that one should avoid either licentiousness (*akolasia*) on the one hand or insensibility (*anaisthesia*) on the other and aim instead at what he calls temperance (*sophrosune*). Ibid., p. 104.
102. *Education*, p. 228.
103. Here we see elements of the kind of "Calvinist" self-restraint that Dunn to admires in Locke.
104. Ibid., p. 234.
105. Ibid., p. 229.
106. *Two Treatises*, 2:27 (pp. 287–88). This vision of us owning ourselves stands in direct contrast to Hobbes. For Hobbes, we can't own our bodies—we *are* our bodies.
107. Ibid., 2:34 (p. 291).
108. Ibid., 2:28 (p. 289).
109. This passage has elicited an enormous amount of scholastic comment. James Tully writes that there are at least three contemporary interpretations of it. One is that Locke is saying that labor and property are incompatible (i.e., one who actually labors cannot own the product of their efforts)—although to argue this is to strongly read against the text itself. Another interpretation is that Locke is being inconsistent, simultaneously advancing a socialist view of labor and ownership with a capitalist one. The third interpretation seeks to reconcile the contradiction, or to simply point to it. C. B. MacPherson is associated with the latter two theories, arguing that Locke "take[s] the wage relationship entirely for granted." Tully, pp. 135–36.

    J. P. Day suggests that C. B. MacPherson confuses the word "labor" meaning "laborer" with "labor" meaning "physical labor." Having bought the labor on the open market, it is not necessarily so strange that Locke claims that the labor is "mine," i.e., the owner's. J. P. Day, "Locke on Property," in *Life, Liberty, and Property*, p. 113. I don't find this explanation entirely convincing, however, since the possession of labor (understood as physical labor) is, in Locke's own understanding, a principal marker of identity and therefore too tied to a person's sense of self to be so readily alienable. Furthermore, this explanation does not lessen the fact that for Locke such an understanding renders the master economically non-autonomous in contrast to his characterization of the first economic man as laboring alone, "without asking leave or depending upon the Will of any other Man" (2:4, p. 269).
110. In Jean Starobinski's terms, the servant is both transparent and an obstacle to the master in terms of his relationships to his own desire. Jean Starobinski, *Jean-Jacques Rousseau: Transparency and Obstruction* (Chicago: University of Chicago Press, 1971).
111. From "The Commonplace Book," quoted in *Political Writings of John Locke*, David Wootton, ed. (New York: Mentor Books, 1993), p. 441.
112. Ibid., p. 441–42.

113. Ibid., p. 442.

114. *Revolutionary Politics,* p. 270.

115. Ibid., p. 269.

116. "Draft of a Representation Containing a Scheme of Methods for the Employment of the Poor," quoted in *Political Writings of John Locke,* p. 447.

117. C. B. MacPherson, *The Political Theory of Possessive Individualism* (New York: Oxford University Press, 1962), p. 223.

118. *Two Treatises,* 2:85 (p. 322).

119. *Education,* pp. 221–22. He also writes: "The great difficulty here is, I imagine, from the folly and perverseness of servants, who are hardly to be hindered from crossing herein the designs of the father and mother. Children, discountenanced by their parents for any fault, find usually a refuge and relief in the caresses of those foolish flatterers, who thereby undo whatever the parents endeavor to establish." Ibid., p. 243.

120. Ibid., p. 252.

121. Ibid. Locke, perhaps charitably, but certainly revealing a strong sense of class privilege, states that children should not be allowed to treat servants rudely. If they could exercise

> a gentle, courteous, affable carriage towards the lower ranks of men...No part of their superiority will be hereby lost, but the distinction increased, and their authority strengthened, when love in inferiors is joined to outward respect, and an esteem of the person has a share in their submission: and domestics will pay a more ready and cheerful service, when they find themselves not spurned, because fortune has laid them below the level of others, at their master's feet. Ibid., p. 307.

To allow a child to mistreat servants, Locke holds, is problematic, not so much because it makes the servants miserable (which is not really Locke's concern) but rather because it would tend to make the child "oppressive and cruel."

122. *Two Treatises,* 1:47 (p. 174). The idea that men and women have "different understandings" can also be found in the *Second Treatise,* 2:82 (p. 321).

123. Although I think this is as true for working-class gender roles as it is for privileged ones, as far as Locke is concerned the category of "women" tends to mean rich mothers, wives, and daughters. So whereas the distinction between "the working class" and "women" is artificial (since there are obviously working-class women as well as men), I am basically maintaining the distinction in order to continue to follow Locke's own logic. Most of the things that Locke says about rich women are also most likely true about poor ones as far as he is concerned, it is only that poor women as a category are largely invisible for him.

124. He does not describe Eve's origins himself but rather allows Sir Robert Filmer to do so for him (perhaps because Filmer is more suited to portray a person in this "old-fashioned" or prepolitical manner). He quotes Filmer as saying: "God Created only Adam, and of a piece of him made the Woman, and...by Generation from them two, as parts of them, all Mankind be propagated." Ibid., 1:14 (p. 150).

125. Ibid., 1:44 (p. 172).

126. This is somewhat illogical since even if Eve herself became depraved, the punishment for her should not have been visited upon all future women each of whom should have their own potential. We see how the category of "women's nature" and Eve's own merit overlap.

127. Ibid., 1:47 (p. 174).

128. Ibid., 2:64 (p. 310).
129. Ibid., 2:69 (p. 313). Peter Laslett, the editor, notes that Locke neglects to retain his use of the term "parental" here. Ibid.
130. Ibid., 2:72 (pp. 314–15). The term "ordinarily" in this quote may indicate that there are times when women can transmit property to their children. It could also mean foster parents, governors, guardians, or any number of possibilities. While I don't think that Locke ruled out the possibility of women property owners (indeed, he probably knew quite a few), I will argue shortly that, as a rule, Locke had another purpose in mind for women.
131. Ibid., 2:58 (p. 306).
132. Ibid., 2:65 (p. 310).
133. Ibid., 1:55 (p. 180).
134. Ibid., 2:65 (p. 310). There are tantalizing clues that Locke considers the subjection of Eve to Adam to partially derive from the fact that he "begot" her. At one point in the *First Treatise,* he plays devil's advocate to Filmer's claim that fatherhood itself bestows power. Rhetorically, he questions whether Adam's heir should have sovereign power over his mother, Eve. Locke concludes that the heir most likely would not have dominion over his mother

> or if it did, it being nothing but the Fatherhood of Adam descended by inheritance, the Heir must have the right to govern Eve, because Adam begot her; for fatherhood is nothing else. Ibid., 1:99 (p. 213).

While this passage is complicated, one must note the casual reference to Adam having begotten Eve. Not to mention the fact that even if Adam did beget Eve, she should then by all rights be his eldest. Another complicated passage has Locke writing:

> [I]f Adam had any such Regal Power over Eve . . . it must be by some other title than that of begetting. 1:73 (p. 195–96).

Here, Locke is not saying that Adam didn't "beget" Eve, only that begetting itself does not grant a right of "Regal Power."
135. *Education,* p. 234.
136. Ibid., p. 211.
137. Ibid., p. 17. Here again he sounds exactly like Rousseau.
138. Ibid., p. 214.
139. Ibid., p. 298.
140. Ibid., 2:65 (p. 311). In so quoting from Genesis, Locke does not complete the phrase, which goes on to say, "and they shall be one flesh," itself an evocation of the same spirit as "two friends, one soul." Genesis 2:24.
141. *Two Treatises,* 1:59 (p. 183).
142. As well as the "female" education she may have received from her own father.
143. *Education,* p. 257. It is interesting to speculate that homosexuality, with its suggestion of a violation of personal boundaries between autonomous peers, is particularly distressing for Locke, suggesting not only a sexual but a personal and propertied intermingling as well.

> Even without a sexual connotation, Locke fretted about the influence of his peers on a young boy seeing "a spreading contagion if you will venture (the young man) abroad in the herd." Ibid., p. 256.

144. *Two Treatises,* 2:65 (p. 311).

145. *Education,* p. 235.
146. Ibid., p. 236.
147. Ibid., p. 284.
148. *Two Treatises,* 2:66 (p. 311).
149. *Education,* pp. 284–85.
150. Ibid., p. 385. This is precisely the anxiety voiced by Rousseau in *Émile,* which in many ways matches the concerns and issues that Locke poses here.
151. Ibid., p. 285.
152. *Two Treatises,* 2:119 (p. 347).
153. Ibid., 2:73 (p. 315).
154. Ibid., 2:60 (pp. 307–8).
155. *Education,* p. 236.
156. This is more clearly true with questions of class than gender, where Locke complicates things with his talk of "natural" differences.
157. In this approach, Locke is quite like Rousseau. For Rousseau, in his own ideas about education, the son's "authentic" being is what must be honored and sheltered from others. For Rousseau, education becomes what Judith Shklar describes as "negative education," keeping out external influences, nurturing the "true" self that the subject possesses. Judith Shklar, *Men and Citizens* (Cambridge: Cambridge University Press, 1969), pp. 148–49.

    Both Locke and Rousseau subscribe to the idea that freedom can be found only in conforming to "nature," as opposed to conforming to the will of other people. But as we have seen with Locke (and as a reading of *Émile* demonstrates to be the case with Rousseau as well), there is nothing "authentic" (or natural) about the educational process; it is a very complex series of carefully considered and often hidden manipulations seeking to instill in the student exactly the appropriate amount of passion and exactly the appropriate amount of control to make him "autonomous." For both authors, actually leaving the boy to his own devices would be ruinous.
158. Quoted from Charles Taylor, *Sources of the Self,* pp. 167–68.
159. This question of how the son's reason is or is not different from the father's has been taken up by many scholars of Locke, and there are several possible answers. One solution, which is advocated by Peter Schouls, is that there is no contradiction between the reason that a child gains at his father's knee and the reason that the child comes into on his own, because reason is after all the practice of following "the good," which is a universal construct. Schouls makes the argument that the freedom that children acquire is precisely the freedom that any one has: the "freedom" to follow natural law and reason. So the discrepancy between "forced submission" to a parent's reason and "free submission" to their own reason is unimportant. Schouls, p. 214. Schouls's answer, while very clever and compelling, does not entirely answer the question. It does not explain, for example, how the child switches over from external to internal reasoning. Rather, Schouls collapses the two types of reasoning without telling us how (or if) this transition occurs. Yet Locke finds it natural that the son and father, even if both are perfectly reasonable, will not agree on everything. Thus, for example, Locke writes: "Imperiousness and severity is but an ill way of treating men, who have reason to guide them unless you have a mind to make your children, when grown up, weary of you and secretly to say within themselves 'when will you die, father?'" *Education,* p. 235. In a way, Schouls's view of reason is anthropomorphized, as if reason was itself an entity rather than a

process. But reason is, after all, in Locke's mind, a faculty which needs to be exercised—a faculty which can be unlearned just as it can be learned.

Another answer, which arrives at similar answers to Schouls but from a very different point of view, is that promoted by Nathan Tarcov. Tarcov holds that Locke's notion of reason is simply a code-word for "community standards." Tarcov argues that for all his railing against custom and opinion, Locke's recommendation for children's upbringing is to make them followers of reputation after all. Tarcov, p. 101. He argues that "one can say that [Locke] teaches that all good things come from virtue by way of esteem." Ibid., p. 103. In other words, one knows the good by that which is said to be good. Tarcov considers a quote from *Some Thoughts concerning Education* which states: "If you can once get into children love of credit, and an apprehension of shame and disgrace, you have put into them the true principle, which will constantly work, and incline them to the right." *Education,* pp. 241–42. Here he argues that this can be extended to adulthood as well. Locke's attacks on depravity then would be akin to arguing that it is wrong to be depraved because the community has traditionally frowned upon such behavior (the community in question presumably being Locke's community, that of the landed gentry). Tarcov's argument is that (1) one is always motivated even as an adult by rewards and punishments, including divine favor or reprobation; and (2) the question of whether the reason that children receive in their family is in fact "reason" itself can also be posed for an adult in their standing in the community.

Clearly, I do not share Tarcov's read on Locke as a largely secular thinker. Putting this aside, I would also argue that Tarcov downplays something that is very important for Locke: the major transition from childhood to adulthood on the one hand and the autonomy of the subject from society (and their own family) on the other. By arguing (elsewhere) that the child's relationship to reason (i.e., reputation) is a model for the adult, Tarcov is denying Locke's insistence that one must think for oneself—that the ways children and adults think are radically different. At the same time, because Locke clearly sees the opinions of society as being not a norm to be adopted but a *threat* to be avoided, community standards cannot be the basis of autonomous thought.

160. Ibid., p. 249.
161. Ibid., p. 236.
162. Once again, Locke has a more difficult task than Aristotle did. In his *Ethics,* Aristotle poses a question quite similar to the one I have just been treating with Locke:

> A difficulty however may be raised as to how we can say that people must perform just actions if they are to become just, and temperate ones if they are to become temperate; because if they do what is just and temperate they are just and temperate already. *Ethics,* p. 97.

In other words, Aristotle is asking how we can learn to be good. It is one thing simply to say a person who is good by nature will do good things but how can virtue be understood and instilled in others who might not otherwise be good? Aristotle's answer to this is that it is the actions themselves that make a person just and temperate, saying, "like activities produce like dispositions." Ibid., p. 92. In other words, it is by doing right that one becomes right, so that in this instance there is no contradiction between right habit and right reason. As Aristotle puts it further:

> The moral virtues, then, are engendered in us neither by nor contrary to nature; we are constituted by nature to receive them, but their full development in us is due to habit. Ibid., p. 91.

But Aristotle is able to do this rather unproblematically because he is not interested in independent and autonomous souls, only in (publicly) virtuous ones. His notion of what nature tells us is not in tension with human agency; this *telos* can be known and expressed. And furthermore, Aristotle is not troubled by interdependence. He sees the "reliance" of a master upon his slave as perfectly natural and in no way reducing the master's capacity or power, just as one relying upon one's body to carry one's mind around poses no inherent threat (except for the threat of illness and death).

163. *Two Treatises,* 1:53 (p. 179).

164. *The Reasonableness of Christianity,* p. 71.

165. Even the most reasonable person in Locke's world is still only an approximation of the sort of certainty that was present with Jephtha, who slew his own daughter in a deal that he made with God which she herself acquiesced to. In the Bible she told her father that she would sacrifice herself for him, because Jephtha had to fulfill a bargain that he made. The sacrifice isn't easy—she asks for two months to bewail her virginity in the mountains—but she does it. But imagine if Jephtha only told his daughter, "I'm pretty sure that I have to sacrifice you." In the Bible, Jephtha and his daughter love each other; her sacrifice is as much for him as it is for God. And he can ask for her sacrifice without undermining either his love for her or God. Under conditions of doubt, could they do the same? Would they act with as much certainty? Wouldn't knowing that there was a right answer but they couldn't be sure what it was only make things worse? Hence the uncertainty and tension in Locke's subjects.

CHAPTER 3

1. Tracy Strong, *Jean-Jacques Rousseau: The Politics of the Ordinary* (Thousand Oaks, Calif.: Sage Publications, 1994), p. 3.

2. Ibid., p. 41.

3. Ibid., p. 45.

4. Ibid., p. 47.

5. Ibid. p. 146.

6. Ibid.

7. Ibid., p. 147.

8. Strong doesn't directly contend with Derrida but he does write, "I fly a bit in the face here of the magisterial work of Jean Starobinski" in his own treatment of transparency. Ibid.

9. Dunn, *Locke,* p. 11. The first time any part of his *Essay concerning Human Understanding* appeared in print, it was in French. Ibid., p. 19.

10. Tully, pp. 5–7.

11. Jean Starobinski writes of Rousseau's connection to Buffon and hence to Locke, for example arguing that "even where Rousseau is not in Buffon's debt, both men drew on the same sources; both were adherents of Cartesianism as modified by Locke." Starobinski, p. 326.

As for the other philosophers, we have this from Voltaire, for example: "So many philosophers have written the romance of the soul, a sage has arrived who has modestly written its history. Locke has set forth human reason just as an excellent anatomist explains the parts of the human body." Quoted in Cassirer, p. 94.

In the work of Voltaire especially, but also in Diderot and D'Alembert, one finds strong traces of a Lockean influence that is often quite explicit.

12. Ibid., 100–1.
13. Mark Hulliung makes this argument in *The Autocritique of the Enlightenment* (Cambridge, Mass.: Harvard University Press, 1994), pp. 62–103.
14. *Of Grammatology,* p. 283.
15. Ibid., p. 145.
16. Ibid.
17. Ibid.
18. Ibid., p. 147.
19. Ibid., pp. 147–48.
20. Jean-Jacques Rousseau, *Du contrat social,* in *Oeuvres Choisis de Jean-Jacques Rousseau* (Paris: Garnier Frères, 1928), p. 307. [Henceforth *Contrat*]
21. Ibid.
22. Ibid., p. 240.
23. Jean-Jacques Rousseau, *Émile* (London: J.M. Dent and Sons, 1974), p. 47. In conjunction with Jean-Jacques Rousseau, *Émile,* from *Oeuvres Complètes,* vol. IV (Paris: Bibliothèque de la Pléiade, 1969).
24. There is at least one voice that argues that the notion of the state of nature is overused by Rousseau scholars: A. O. Lovejoy, in "The Supposed Primitivism of Rousseau's 'Discourse on Inequality,'" in *Essays in the History of Ideas* (New York: Quartet, 1979), argues that Rousseau's use of the state of nature is merely a device to reflect on his contemporary period, and all talk of him romanticizing "primitive man" is suspect. I agree in the sense that what is important for Rousseau about the state of nature is how it reflects on his contemporary times, but I think that it is telling that in using the state of nature as a device by which to educate his own times, he nonetheless fails to be able to conjure up the very ideal of freedom that he is promoting.
25. This Appendix does not appear in my French edition so I have used a quote from Jean-Jacques Rousseau, *The Social Contract and Discourses* (London: J.M. Dent and Sons, 1973), p. 112. We will see almost exactly the same sentiment echoed a century later with Emerson.
26. Jean-Jacques Rousseau, *Discours sur l'origine de l'inégalité,* in *Oeuvres Choisis,* p. 67. [Henceforth *Discours*] Here Rousseau distinguishes himself somewhat from Locke, who seems to be unable to imagine natural man without a family.
27. Ibid., p. 69.
28. To say that "his female" is only a reference to his "female of the moment" must contend with the fact that this passage shows a developing relationship over time.
29. Rousseau takes Hobbes to task for ignoring the human capacity for compassion. Ibid., p. 59. Hobbes's own description of the state of natural man is much more radically isolated than it is for Rousseau. Although Hobbes's depiction of love in the state of nature is far more autarkic than Rousseau's as a rule, at one point he does allow for families among the pre-Leviathan Native Americans. He called these a "government of small families the concord whereof dependeth on natural lust." *Leviathan,* p. 187. To be fair to Rousseau, Hobbes generally begs the question of why mothers would bother to raise their children in the state of nature. Whereas on the whole, Hobbes does not shrink from the full implications of this vision, Rousseau's model backpedals quite a bit. His introduction of compassion serves as a harbinger of what is "positive" about society, and reveals that rad-

ical freedom, if it were to be extended to its logical conclusion, as Hobbes does, would be something that Rousseau might actually find repugnant rather than ideal.

30. *Discours,* p. 52–53.
31. Ibid.
32. Ibid., p. 70.
33. Ibid.
34. Jean-Jacques Rousseau, *Essays on the Origin of Language* (Chicago: Chicago University Press, 1966), p. 45.
35. As Judith Shklar describes it:

> Self-sufficient and self-contained, they need no one but each other. Theirs is the only relationship free from amour propre. Only within the family is perfect, uncompetitive affection possible. Here alone self love and love for others are one. Shklar, p. 23.

36. Rousseau writes: "In the family, it is clear for several reasons which lie in its very nature, that the father ought to command. In the first place, the authority ought not to be equally divided between father and mother; the government must be single.... Besides the husband ought to be able to superintend his wives' conduct because it is of importance for him to be assured that the children who he is obliged to acknowledge and maintain belong to no one but themselves." "Political Economy," in *The Social Contract and Discourses,* p. 119.
37. Ibid. And here, Rousseau sounds very much like Locke, albeit in regard to a different period of time.
38. Shklar, p. 25.
39. Ibid., p. 58.
40. "Young people of both sexes lived in neighboring houses; interactive commerce required by nature soon led to another no less sweet sentiment and a more permanent one." *Discours,* p. 72.
41. Ibid.
42. Ibid. Even at the height of the Golden Age, when families are fully autonomous, we see the steady enervation of that diffuseness and generality which made this period "free." As the age developed, the sameness of its members deteriorated, with the women changing first. Ibid., p. 71. This sexual division of labor, however, ended up enervating both sexes. Ibid. Men, always Rousseau's primary concern, become "soft," "effeminate," and "cringing." Rousseau writes, "In becoming sociable and a slave, man becomes feeble, fearful and cringing; his soft and effeminate life saps both his strength and his courage." Ibid., p. 46. In other words, the gender system, in sustaining and producing the identity of the patriarch, also serves to undermine that identity. Hierarchy both sustains and threatens the patriarchal subject.
43. *Contrat,* p. 251.
44. Ibid., p. 248.
45. Ibid; his emphasis. Even this harmonious vision is undermined when Rousseau considers actual societies which organized themselves in this way. As we have already seen with the ancient Greeks, although they lived according to the general will, they yet had slaves, dependency, and other social trappings that Rousseau fears.
46. Ibid., p. 251.

47. Jean-Jacques Rousseau, *The Confessions* (New York: Penguin Books, 1953), p. 17. Henceforth *Confessions*. In conjunction with Jean-Jacques Rousseau, *Les Confessions* (Paris: Chez Jean-Jacques Pauvert, 1961).

48. Jean-Jacques Rousseau, *Rousseau, Judge of Jean-Jacques* (Dartmouth: University of New England Press, 1990), p. 13.

49. *Confessions*, p. 19.

50. This fact alone provides a rich ground for possible psychological metaphors; his childhood moving from the Golden Age to the harsh brutality of society where real love is not to be found. Three books which are especially useful for their psychological analysis of Rousseau are Starobinski's *Transparency and Obstruction*, Burgelin's *La Philosophie de L'Existence de Jean-Jacques Rousseau* (Paris: Presses Universitaires de France, 1952), and Ronald Grimsley's *Jean-Jacques Rousseau: A Study in Self Awareness* (Cardiff: University of Wales Press, 1969).

51. *Confessions*, p. 25. According to Paul Jury, Rousseau's affinity for beatings was a result of the guilt that he felt at having "killed his own mother" (in childhood). From Grimsley, p. 28.

52. *Confessions*, p. 26.

53. Ibid., p. 27.

54. An idea which is replicated in various texts, including *Émile,* by the notion that Emile's own "worst enemy" is himself, his own mind.

55. Ibid., p. 107.

56. Ibid.

57. Ibid.

58. At one point, Rousseau got her to spit out some food that she was chewing (by claiming that he had spotted a hair on it) so that he could devour it himself. Ibid., p. 108.

59. Ibid., p. 188.

60. Ibid., p. 189.

61. Ibid. Burgelin writes that Mme. de Warens, despite her "fall from grace" with Rousseau, remained for him the exemplar of womanhood. Their relationship remained his ideal of unity, and further relationships were attempts to substitute for this (second) original one. The relationship with Mme. de Warens (whom Rousseau does after all call "*Maman*") is the closest he comes to a manifestation of the Golden Age in his life. Alluding to Rousseau's play *Pygmalion*, Burgelin calls Mme. de Warens Rousseau's Galatea.

62. Shklar, p. 46.

63. Ibid. See also Burgelin. He quotes Rousseau as saying, "To do nothing is man's first and strongest passion after that of self preservation." Burgelin, p. 130. He goes on to say, "the ethic of Jean-Jacques is based on a metaphysic of laziness...which makes inaction the most basic and stable of man's joys." Ibid., p. 131. Note though that Rousseau distinguishes between idleness in nature and idleness in society; whereas the former sort is to be highly prized, the latter is a great evil which leads to degeneracy. *Confessions*, p. 591.

64. Ibid., pp. 396–97. As we will see, Thoreau makes an almost identical statement.

65. Ibid., p. 385.

66. Ibid., p. 386–87.

67. Ibid.

68. Starobinski, p. 79. Starobinksi also writes that for Rousseau, sexual relations with Thérèse are indistinguishable from masturbation. Rousseau uses the same word, "sup-

plément," to describe both. For further discussion of this point, see Joel Schwartz, *The Sexual Politics of Jean-Jacques Rousseau* (Chicago: University of Chicago Press, 1984) pp. 105, 112. Schwartz writes: "Thérèse provides no obstacle to Rousseau's solitude." And Derrida's *Of Grammatology* details this same relationship in the section entitled ". . . That Dangerous Supplement."

69. Rousseau's sexual relationship with Thérèse supposedly led to the birth of five children, all of whom Rousseau sent to an orphanage. If this is true it might be surmised that, unlike their mother, the children of their relationship could pose a threat to Rousseau's autonomy and so had to be gotten rid of. In terms of the void in Rousseau's heart left unfilled by his unloving relationship with Thérèse he writes:

> Children came who might have filled [the void] but that made things even worse. I trembled at the thought of entrusting them to [our] badly brought up family, to be brought up even more badly. The risks of their upbringing by the Foundling Hospital were considerably less. *Confessions*, p. 387.

70. "Fifth Reverie," *Reveries of a Solitary Walker* (New York: Burt Franklin, 1971).
71. *Confessions*, p. 589.
72. And furthermore in *Émile et Sophie,* we will see that Emile too winds up on a desert island with his own wife, Sophie.
73. Ibid., p. 385.
74. Ibid., p. 396.
75. Ibid., p. 591.
76. Ibid., p. 592.
77. Eventually Rousseau is forced to leave St. Pierre by local authorities. Although he makes it sound like this is the reason that his peace was disturbed, he provides enough evidence that his idyll on this island would not have been what he was looking for in any case, because his traffic here, "far from mortal men," is anything but. Undeterred, he prepares to make for Corsica, the one place left in Europe that he considers has any hope for freedom. At the last minute, this plan too is foiled.
78. Introduction to *Émile,* P. D. Jimack, *Émile,* p. vi.
79. Ibid., p. 16.
80. Ibid., p. 5.
81. Ibid.
82. Ibid.
83. Ibid., p. 14.
84. Ibid., p. 28.
85. Ibid., p. 6.
86. Shklar, p. 148. Shklar is paraphrasing Rousseau's own claim, "The education of the earliest years should be merely negative." *Émile,* p. 57. For Shklar, this education is actually expanded far beyond the early years of one's education.
87. Ibid., pp. 170–71.
88. Ibid., p. 147.
89. Ibid.
90. Ibid., p. 167.
91. Ibid., p. 148. Rousseau describes Crusoe as being "deprived of the help of his fellow men." But here he recognizes that Crusoe wasn't alone; Friday was there too. As with Thérèse, Friday is both an obstacle to and a source of Crusoe's freedom.
92. Ibid., p. 10.

93. Ibid., p. 20.
94. Ibid., p. 59. At times, Rousseau is quite candid about the subterfuge he is putting over Emile. When Emile is a late adolescent, the tutor brags about the fact that compared to other boys his age, he is very docile:

> "[Emile] recognizes the voice of friendship and he knows how to obey reason. It is true I allow him a show of freedom but he was never more completely under control because he obeys of his own free will. So long as I could not get the master over his will, I retained my control over his person; I never left him for a moment. Now I sometimes leave him to himself because I control him continually." Ibid., p. 298.

95. Ibid., p. 20.
96. Ibid., p. 13. Elsewhere in *Émile,* Rousseau advocates a return to the Golden Age for contemporary families. Noting that modern mothers do not "deign" to nurse their children, Rousseau writes that "every evil follows the train of this first sin." Without family affection, and maternal love:

> Nature is quenched in every breast, the home becomes gloomy, the spectacle of a young family no longer stirs the husband's love and the stranger's reverence... there is no home life, the ties of nature are not strengthened by habit; fathers, mothers, brothers, and sisters cease to exist, they are almost strangers; how should they love one another? Each thinks of himself first. Ibid.

97. Ibid., p. 369.
98. Ibid., p. 59.
99. Ibid., p. 409.
100. Perhaps seeking to justify his chastity, the tutor writes: "I would not go and offer my grey beard to the scornful jests of young girls; I could never bear to sicken them with my disgusting caresses, to furnish them at my expense with the most absurd stories, to imagine them describing the vile pleasures of the old ape, so as to avenge themselves for what they have endured." Ibid., p. 316. He does speculate that if he could not have overcome his urges, however: "I would find a suitable mistress and would keep to her." Ibid.
101. Ibid., p. 328. Also, like women, the tutor safely channels Emile's sexuality (at first teaching him how to be free from desire, by controlling his early sexual urges, taking him to VD clinics, and later by supplying him with Sophie).
102. Ibid., p. 20.
103. Ibid., p. 194.
104. Ibid., p. 281. It is in sentiments such as these that I see Rousseau as being as subversive as he is constitutive of the doctrine of love. Here he exposes its ruse even while he enlists it.
105. Ibid., p. 49.
106. Ibid., pp. 83–84.
107. Ibid., p. 396.
108. Ibid., p. 298.
109. Ibid.
110. Ibid., p. 324.
111. Ibid. p. 323.
112. Just as with Locke, sons cannot be free with or without patriarchy.
113. For Rousseau, once in society, men's dependency on women goes a step further. As society is marked by a swirl of opinion and intrigue, men must defer to women to protect

them in an arena in which women have always had more practice. For Rousseau, because they have had long experience in living vicariously through their husbands, women are more adept at the nuance and byzantine manipulations from behind the scenes of life and power in society. Thus chastity is not only a matter of helping men to control their desires, it also becomes a way to control and deflect the desires of society itself:

> [I]t is not enough that a woman should be chaste. She must preserve her reputation and her good name. From these principles there arises not only a moral difference between the sexes, but also a fresh motive for duty and propriety, which prescribes to women in particular the most scrupulous attention to their conduct their manners, their behavior. Ibid., p. 325.

114. Ibid., p. 299.

115. Is it possible that this name, Sophie, comes from one of Rousseau's great romantic crushes: on the Comtesse d'Houdetot, one of whose given names was Sophie? While at La Chevrette, a country resort where he experienced one of his periodic rejuvenations, he met and fell in love with her. *Confessions*, p. 416.

116. Her own lusts have been safely directed at the hero of a book, Telemachus, and so flesh-and-blood men have not interested her until she met the one she was destined for: Emile himself.

117. Ibid., p. 378.

118. Ibid., p. 394. On some level, the tutor is mystified by Emile's infatuation. As a sexless person himself, the tutor's vicarious experience of love doesn't offer him an explanation as to how such an autonomous young man could surrender his liberty so readily to someone else.

119. Ibid., p. 408.

120. Ibid., p. 438.

121. At the same time, Rousseau ironically seeks to resolve Sophie's "otherness" by recourse to traditional gender roles. Throughout *Émile*, Rousseau worried that men were becoming increasingly emasculated by women and that "it is almost a miracle to belong to one's sex." Ibid., p. 356. Also, he frequently combats the notion that Emile might be growing effeminate.

122. Ibid., p. 438.

123. Ibid., p. 437.

124. Ibid., p. 444.

125. *Emile et Sophie ou les Solitaires* in *Oeuvres Complètes,* vol. 2, p. 723.

126. Ibid.

127. Ibid., p. 741.

128. Ibid.

129. Ibid., p. 745.

130. Joel Schwartz presents a slightly different version of this story in his book *The Sexual Politics of Jean-Jacques Rousseau.*

131. Judith Shklar writes that he is "god-like." Shklar, p. 90.

132. Jean-Jacques Rousseau, *Julie, ou La Nouvelle Héloïse* (Wolfeboro, N.H.: Grant and Cutler, 1986), p. 301.

133. Ibid., p. 303; my emphasis.

134. Ibid., p. 405.

135. Ibid., p.407.
136. "The General Society of the Human Race," in *The Social Contract and Discourses*, p. 161. This quote gets at what Rousseau might have in mind in the published version of *The Social Contract* when he says that he can show us how the chains which enslave us can themselves be legitimized. *Contrat*, p. 240.
137. "Political Economy," *The Social Contract and Discourses*, p. 133.
138. Shklar, p. 160.
139. *Discours*, pp. 42–43.
140. *Émile*, p. 8.
141. There is, I feel, no small amount of irony in Rousseau's attempt to transcend the power and draw of women in the family and the Golden Age by usurping the very institution which their presence makes necessary and attempting to turn it into a hyper-masculine one. Contrasting the Spartan and Golden Age style of "family," Shklar writes: "As with the family in the Golden Age, Sparta is a highly hierarchical society, but unified as it is in the name of collective public good, the power of the Spartan kings is benign." Shklar, p. 200.
142. Joel Schwartz points this out in *The Sexual Politics of Jean-Jacques Rousseau*, p. 49.
143. *Émile*, p. 326.
144. Perhaps he still holds out the hope that she still loves her sons, despite her public spiritedness.
145. Ibid., pp. 355–356.
146. *Contrat*, p. 301.
147. Ibid., p. 268.
148. Jean-Jacques Rousseau, *The Government of Poland* (New York: The Bobbs-Merrill Co., Inc., 1972), p. 12.
149. *Contrat*, p. 269.
150. Ibid., p. 265.
151. Although he explicitly argues that he is not in a position to make such arguments, giving the credit to Count Wielhorski, saying, "The Outsider can hardly contribute more than general observations" and saying that his mind is no longer at its "best." *The Government of Poland*, p. 1.
152. *Contrat*, p. 265.
153. *The Government of Poland*, p. 19. Elsewhere he speaks of Poland's "second birth." Ibid., p. 23.
154. *Contrat*, p. 269. Since *Émile* and *The Social Contract* appeared in the same year (1762), it seems reasonable to surmise that he is directly referring to it here.
155. In the case of both romantic and public love, Rousseau uses the same term, "yoke" (we have already "the yoke of manhood," in public terms he speaks of the "yoke of public happiness" (*le joug de la félicité publique*) Ibid., p. 267.
156. Ibid., p. 266.
157. "The General Society of the Human Race," in *The Social Contract and Discourses*, p. 157.
158. Judith Butler, *Gender Trouble* (New York: Routledge, 1990), p. 141.
159. In a sense, like so many of Rousseau's ideas, a different idea of love might be derived, not from either *amour propre* or *amour de soi* alone, but exactly in the tension and distinction between them. Between self- and other-regarding, between enmity and friendship, between what love has been and what it could yet be.

CHAPTER 4

1. Ralph Waldo Emerson, "Nature" (first series), in *Selected Writings of Emerson,* Dennis McQuade, ed., (New York: Modern Library College Editions, 1981), pp. 6–7. [Henceforth *Writings*]

2. Ibid., pp. 6–7.

3. Depicting his "self" as an eyeball has a great deal of meaning for Emerson. This imagery of eyes and sight is fundamental to his work, and an analysis of his use of eye as metaphor unlocks much of what is fundamentally true about and important to his work. For Emerson, the eye and questions of sight were of great personal significance. Temporarily losing his sight in 1825, possibly due to side effects from tuberculosis, he had a terror of going blind. Robert D. Richardson Jr., *Emerson: The Mind on Fire* (Berkeley: University of California Press, 1995), p. 63. [Henceforth Richardson] For Emerson, his eyes were his livelihood, his connection to ideas, in a sense the embodiment of his self (eye/I), and hence, in his own mind, the truth. Amid the passage about crossing the bare common, quoted above, Emerson writes:

   > In the woods, we return to reason and faith. There I feel that nothing can befall me in life—no disgrace, no calamity (*leaving me my eyes*) which nature cannot repair. From "Nature " (first series), in *Writings,* p. 6. (my emphasis)

   Thus it is instructive perhaps that Emerson has reduced his subjectivity in this passage to the one aspect of his self that he cannot bear to do without.

4. Ibid., p. 4.

5. Ibid., pp. 6–7. For Emerson, the term "somewhat" means what "something" means to us today.

6. "Friendship," in *Emerson's Essays,* introduction by Irwin Edman (New York: Thomas Y. Crowell Co., 1926), pp. 151–52 [Henceforth *Essays*] There are occasional small differences between the texts in the Edman and McQuade editions. I have preferred to use the Edman edition for "Love" and "Friendship," as well as for "Manners" and "The Over Soul," the McQuade for everything else.

7. *Groundwork of the Metaphysic of Morals,* p. 130.

8. Stanley Cavell, *The Senses of Walden: An Expanded Edition* (Chicago: University of Chicago Press, 1981), p. 129.

9. Ibid., p. 128.

10. Ibid.

11. Ibid., p. 127.

12. In this sense, Cavell sees Emerson as participating in a philosophical inquiry leading on to Nietzsche himself. Ibid., p. 138. This is another version of Nietzsche's claim in *Ecce Homo* that "only *when you have all denied me* will I return to you." Friedrich Nietzsche, *Ecce Homo* (New York: Penguin Books, 1992), p. 6.

13. Quoted in Cavell, *Senses,* p. 153.

14. Ibid., p. 154. In speaking of "hard" sayings, he is speaking specifically about Jesus's sermons.

15. Ibid., p. 138.

16. Ibid., p. 147.

17. Ibid., p. 146.

18. Ibid., p. 153. Cavell himself recognizes the religious origins of much of this argument:

    > What Jesus required of one who would follow him Emerson requires of himself in follow-ing his genius—to hate his father, and mother, and wife, and children, and brethren, and sisters, yea and his own life (Luke 14:26). Ibid.

    At the same time, Cavell recognizes that "the time for such prophesyzing is absolutely over." Ibid., p. 30.

19. Ibid., p. 128.

20. "Nature" (second series), in *Writings*, p. 391. Note that this was published a year before Thoreau went to Walden. Compare these sentiments with those of Rousseau, already cited in the previous chapter:

    > Must societies be abolished? Must we return to the forest to live among bears?... You... who think man destined only to live this little life and die in peace... your corrupt hearts and endless desires, resume... your ancient and primitive innocence. Retire to the woods.... For men like me, whose passions have destroyed their original simplicity, who can no longer subsist on plants or acorns, or live without laws and magistrates... they will respect the sacred bonds of their respective communities, they will love their fellow crea-tures. Appendix, *The Social Contract and the Discourses*, p. 113.

21. "Nature" (first series), in *Writings*, p. 22; my emphasis.

22. This is not so different from Locke's desire to realize reason in the world through the improvement of land and property, not for the sake of greed and power, but to manifest Godliness or "the all" in the world.

23. Ibid., p. 7.

24. Ibid., "Nature" (second series), p. 387.

25. Ibid., "Nature," (first series), p. 28.

26. Ibid.

27. Ibid. Just as with Locke, reasoning is a learned practice for Emerson; the practice of deducing truth from the world around us leads us to develop and maintain a rational eye up from its animal origins.

28. Ibid., p. 14. The "final cause of nature" is, of course, humanity itself.

29. Ibid., "Self-Reliance," p. 139.

30. Ibid., p. 131.

31. Ibid.

32. Of course, at this point we are not talking about a relationship between persons but between aspects of the self. A discussion of political relationships is yet to come. But we already see a troubling template here, suggesting future difficulties.

33. Ibid., "Nature" (first series), p. 40.

34. Ibid., p. 18.

35. In "The Poet," Emerson writes:

    > For it is that dislocation and detachment from the life of God that makes things ugly. The poet who reattaches things to nature and the whole, reattaching even artificial things and violations to nature, by deeper insight.... Readers of poetry see the factory-village and the railway, and fancy that the poetry of the landscape is broken up by these; for these works of art are not yet consecrated in their readings; but the poet sees them fall within the great order not less than the bee-hive or the spider's geometrical web. Nature adopts them very fast into her vital circles and the gliding train of cars she loves like her own. Ibid., "The Poet," p. 312.

36. "Nature" (first series), pp. 28–29.
37. Ibid., p. 33.
38. Ibid., p. 313.
39. Ibid., p. 316
40. Ibid., p. 317.
41. Ibid.
42. In seeking a firm distinction between the "me" and the "not me," Emerson muddies his own waters by arguing that under the right circumstances, anything can be "natural." As such, the very concept of "nature" proves to be as it has been for Locke and Rousseau, an unstable category, alternately encompassing the "animal" as well as much of technology and art that has been constructed by human beings. Here we come to a familiar-sounding irony: The "me" is defined oppositionally against the "not me," which in turn is defined as that which is not "me." "Authenticity" is not so much a state of solidity as much as a dynamic and emerging relationship between unknown parts. Once again, we are left searching for unity without the right tools.
43. Ibid., "Experience," p. 338.
44. Ibid., p. 335.
45. Ibid. "Nature" (first series), p. 33.
46. Ibid., "Intellect," p. 285.
47. Ibid., "Experience," p. 346.
48. Ralph Waldo Emerson, *Society and Solitude,* in *The Complete Writings of Ralph Waldo Emerson* (New York: Wm. H. Wise & Co., 1878), pp. 625–26 [Henceforth *Complete*]
49. Ibid., p. 626.
50. Emerson lost his first and beloved wife, Ellen, in 1831, his brother Edward in 1834, his brother Charles in 1836, his first son, Waldo (from his second marriage to Lydian Emerson), in 1842, his mother in 1853, his brother Bulkley in 1859, his disciple Henry Thoreau in 1862, and his brother William in 1868. Emerson himself confounded the odds; although suffering from bouts of consumption, he lived to be 78 years old. Richardson, pp. 577–78.
51. Ibid., p. 110.
52. Richardson describes his second marriage to Lydia (or as she was normally known, Lydian) as being much more sober and intellectual. It was a loving and successful marriage but one lacking the tremendous passion and investment that the younger Emerson had for Ellen.
53. "Experience," in *Writings,* p. 328.
54. Ibid., p. 346.
55. "Love," in *Essays,* p. 123.
56. Ibid., p. 130.
57. Ibid., p. 127; first emphasis is mine, following are his.
58. Ibid., p. 128.
59. Ibid.
60. Ibid.
61. Ibid., p. 131.
62. "Experience," in *Writings,* p. 344.
63. Ibid., "Character," p. 361.
64. Richardson, p. 191.

65. Ibid., pp. 9, 33–34
66. "Friendship," in *Essays,* pp. 146–47.
67. Ibid., 152.
68. George Kateb, *Emerson and Self-Reliance* (Thousand Oaks, Calif.: Sage Publications, 1995), p. 119.
69. "Friendship," in *Essays,* p. 154.
70. Ibid., p. 142.
71. Ibid., p. 153.
72. Ibid., pp. 154–55.
73. In the same way that he is unwilling to completely give up his subjectivity during a transcendent moment.
74. Ibid., p. 155. Emerson consoles himself by going on to say:

> But if you come, perhaps you will fill my mind only with new visions; not with yourself but with your lustres, and I shall not be able any more than now to converse with you. So I will owe to my friends this evanescent intercourse. I will receive from them not what they have but what they are. Ibid., p.156.

75. "Experience," in *Writings,* p. 344.
76. "Friendship," in *Essays,* p. 150.
77. "Character," in *Writings,* p. 355.
78. Ibid., "Self-Reliance," p. 132.
79. Ibid., p. 135; my emphasis.
80. Ibid., "Character," pp. 353–54.
81. Kateb, p. 123.
82. Ibid., p. 120.
83. Ibid., p. 121 (quoted from Emerson's *Conduct of Life*); his emphasis.
84. Ibid., p. 125.
85. Ibid.
86. It is true that one can be surprised at times to observe Emerson include women like his contemporary Margaret Fuller in his ideas about great and self-reliant souls—just as he occasionally surprises us by insisting that other societies besides European ones have been great. But if these great women are simply "men in drag," and if in fact Emerson's true interest is (as Kateb admits) mainly or only (biological) men with the masculine pole dominant, then this hermaphroditic system really perpetuates an order in which the few exceptions that it allows are exceptions that would de facto have been allowed under any gendered system (witness the image of the "virago" in earlier times, a woman who was great—and manly—*despite* her female form).
87. "Manners," in *Essays,* p. 352.
88. Ibid., p. 354.
89. Ibid., pp. 354–55. There are shades here of John Stuart Mill.
90. Ibid., p. 366.
91. "Character," in *Writings,* pp. 352–53.
92. Ibid., "The Poet," p. 304; my emphasis. Here again, I am reminded of John Stuart Mill.
93. "Manners," in *Essays,* p. 355.
94. Indeed there are times when Emerson sounds not just undemocratic but anti-democratic. Such as when he writes: "[The people] acquire democratic manners, they foam at the mouth, they hate and deny." "Experience," in *Writings,* p. 348. Or:

nature advertises me in such persons that, in democratic America, she will not be democratized. How cloistered and constitutionally sequestered from the market and from scandal. Ibid., "Character," p. 358.

95. Kateb, pp. 62–63.

96. Ibid., p. 23; my emphasis.

97. Ibid., p. 24.

98. This, Kateb tells us, is for several reasons. First of all, mental self-reliance is above choice—the intellect can try on different ideas and leave them behind without consequence since it is above the fray, but activity implies what might be called "sunk costs"; choices become meaningful, in need of rationalization, and tend to influence future decision making. Then too, active self-reliance is also itself dependent on mental processes, so it is derivative and not an original approach to self-reliance.

99. Ibid., p. 167.

100. Ibid., pp. 145–46.

101. For example, he quotes Emerson as writing that there is some unknowable "inner power in each of us" which " shoots a ray of beauty even into trivial and impure actions, if the least mark of independence appear." Ibid., p. 24.

102. "Nature" (first series), *in writings* p. 36.

103. Kateb himself brings up the specter of active self-reliance becoming corrupted, as it is wont to do in Emerson's work. He writes: "Beyond the will to be economically self-supporting there is inevitably the will to get rich." Kateb, p. 146.

104. Judith Shklar, "Emerson and the Inhibition of Democracy, *Political Theory,* Nov. 1990, p. 602–3.

105. Ibid., p. 604.

106. Ibid., p. 603.

107. A further argument could be made that even these great people would still require those urban masses to know their own greatness by.

108. "Society and Solitude," in *Complete,* p. 667.

109. Ibid., pp. 666–67.

110. Ibid., "Civilization," p. 627. Suggesting yet again that the eye is not without an agenda, not seeing only harmony.

111. Ibid., "Farming," p. 662. Emerson praises the yeomen farmers in much the same way that he does non-European heroes. When he writes in "Manners," "the chief of savage tribes have distinguished themselves in London and Paris, by the purity of their tournure," he probably meant in part to shock his readers from their complacency, but he also evinces a wistfulness for a purer time, before "the masses" existed, when mankind was economically and hence spiritually less dependent. "Manners," in *Essays,* p. 354.

112. Not to mention that to have a democratic vision that writes off "the masses" is politically problematic in the extreme, if not useless. This last point is perhaps unfair to Kateb, whose ironically titled concept of deindividualization is precisely meant to turn us from a mass to a nation of individuals. But even to start with Emerson's premise that we are a "mass" is, I feel, to betray a strong ambivalence toward the very subjects that democratic theory purports to serve.

113. Quoted in Kateb, p. 191.

114. Shklar, p. 612.

115. "Experience," in *Writings,* p. 348. Read in one way, this statement is almost the perfect manifesto of the doctrine of love.

116. Shklar, p. 603.

117. "The Over Soul," in *Essays,* p. 191.

118. Ibid., p. 197.

119. Ibid., p. 204.

120. "Society and Solitude," in *Complete,* p. 625.

121. Kateb, p. 81.

122. Ibid., pp. 81, 94–95.

123 Stanley Cavell, *Conditions Handsome and Unhandsome: The Constitution of Emersonian Perfectionism* (Chicago: University of Chicago Press, 1990), p. 10.

124. Ibid., p. 27.

125. Kateb, p. 168.

126. Cavell, *Senses,* p. 138.

127. Friedrich Nietzsche, *The Genealogy of Morals* (New York: Anchor Books, 1956), p. 159.

128. Nietzsche has above all democratized the notion of the soul, making us not one coherent self but a democratic rabble that can still fall to the tyranny of a theory of a unified soul, offered by Platonism and Christianity. He writes, "One must above all give the finishing stroke to that other and more portentous atomism which Christianity has taught best and longest, the *soul-atomism.* Let it be permitted to designate by this expression the belief which regards the soul as something indestructible, eternal, indivisible, as a monad, as an *atomon.*" Friedrich Nietzsche, *Beyond Good and Evil* (Amherst, N.Y.: Prometheus Books, 1989), p. 19.

129. Cavell, *Conditions,* p. 59.

130. "Friendship," in *Essays,* p. 149.

131. Ibid.

132. The question of number is one that Derrida pursues in *Politics of Friendship.* He asks, "How many of us are there?... How can you count?" *Politics of Friendship,* p. 1.

CHAPTER 5

1. Henry David Thoreau, "Walking," in *Henry David Thoreau: The Natural History Essays* (Salt Lake City: Peregrine Smith Inc., 1980), p. 94.

2. Ibid., p. 116.

3. Ibid.

4. Ibid., p. 130.

5. "We have a wild savage in us, and a savage name is perchance somewhere recorded as ours." Ibid., p. 125.

6. Ibid., p. 114.

7. Ibid., pp. 107–8.

8. Ibid., p.118.

9. Ibid., p.118–19.

10. Ibid., p. 117.

11. Ibid.

12. Ibid., p. 109. In "Walking," Thoreau derives the word "saunterer" from *Sainte-terre,* the Holy Land; clearly he is referring here to America. Ibid., p. 93.

13. Ibid., p. 122.

14. Ibid., p. 126.

15. A solution that is quite different from Emerson's.

16. Ibid., p. 120.

17. Ibid., p. 125.

18. Ibid., p. 133.

19. Ibid., p. 135.

20. Ibid., p. 104.

21. Henry David Thoreau, *Walden and Civil Disobedience* (New York: W.W. Norton & Co., 1966), pp. 209–10.

22. "Walking," p. 122.

23. *Walden,* p. 71.

24. Cavell, *The Senses of Walden Pond,* p. 102.

25. Ibid. Cavell does seem to come to appreciate Emerson more and more in subsequent books and editions of *The Senses of Walden.* He too gives us an idea of nextness. But for Cavell, Thoreau may remain the thinker who spells this out most clearly.

26. Ibid., p. 103.

27. Ibid., p. 108.

28. Ibid., pp. 108–9.

29. Ibid., p. 50.

30. Ibid., pp. 85–86.

31. *Walden,* p. 66.

32. Ibid., p. 71.

33. This is the name given to the piece when it is extracted from *A Week* itself. "Friendship" was written before either *Walden* or *The Maine Woods.* Had it been written after them, Thoreau might have been able to apply what he learned in his other books to this centrally important text. But perhaps we have this backwards: Having written "Friendship" and aware of the pitfalls of this task, Thoreau then set out to explore the boundaries and interior of nature itself in order to find there what he could not find at home.

34. William Howarth writes, "Since John's death that trip [on the river] had achieved an elegiac significance; now Thoreau seemed ready to prepare a deliberate memorial. *The Book of Concord* (New York: Viking Press, 1982), p. 30.

35. Henry Seidel Canby, *Thoreau* (Boston: Houghton Mifflin Company, 1939), pp. 111–13.

36. Ibid., p. 110.

37. Ibid., p. 111.

38. Ibid., p. 117. There is more evidence in poetry that Canby cites that even enlists imagery of the closet, such as: "I cannot make a disclosure—you should see my secret—Let me open any door never so wide, still within and behind them, where it is unobserved.—no fruit will ripen on the common." And "Love is the profoundest to secrets. Divulged, even to the beloved, it is no longer Love." Ibid. Canby thinks the "secret" is Thoreau's love for Ellen. But unless he was pathologically shy, why would Thoreau go to such an extreme to hide such a fully sanctioned love, particularly when he was so terribly lonely?

39. Ibid., p. 121.

40. Echoing Cavell, although in a very different context, Michael Warner tells us in "Thoreau's Bottom," Thoreau too is in search of a "solid bottom," in the other, but for Thoreau this yearning is experienced in much more explicitly sexual (and hence compromised) terms than for Emerson. Michael Warner, "Thoreau's Bottom," in *Raritan,* 11:3 (Winter 1992), pp. 53–79.

41. Another scholar who discusses Thoreau's same-sex yearnings is Henry Abelove. See his article "From Thoreau to Queer Politics," *Yale Journal of Criticism* 6:2 (Fall 1993), pp. 17–29. See also Morris Kaplan's chapter 6, "Queer Citizenship" in *Sexual Justice: Democratic Citizenship and the Politics of Desire*, (New York: Routledge, 1997).

42. Henry David Thoreau, *Journal Volume 1: 1837–1844*, John C. Broderick, general ed. (Princeton: Princeton University Press, 1981), p. 288.

43. Warner quotes Thoreau as considering same-sex lovers as a "third sex." Warner, p. 53.

44. Henry David Thoreau, *A Week on the Concord and Merrimack Rivers* (Orleans, Mass.: Parnassus Imprints, 1987), p. 337. Henceforth "*A Week*".

45. Ibid., pp. 356–57.

46. Ibid., p. 325. This is the same poem that Canby quotes from where he says, "I might have loved him had I loved him less."

47. Ibid., p. 326.

48. Ibid., p. 327.

49. In a short essay entitled "Marriage" Thoreau makes the theme of sublimation even more explicit. For him, true marriage is chaste: "If it is the result of true love, there can be nothing sensual in marriage. Chastity is something positive, not negative. It is the virtue of the married especially. All lusts or base pleasures must give place to loftier delights." Henry David Thoreau, *Friendship, Love, and Marriage* (East Aurora, N.Y.: Roycrafters, 1910), p. 52.

50. *A Week,* p. 327.

51. Harmon Smith suggests that the actual friendship between Thoreau and Emerson was central to both writers' philosophical concepts of friendship (especially in the case of Thoreau), and that Thoreau's vision was necessarily more tragic. Harmon Smith, *My Friend, My Friend* (Amherst: University of Massachusetts Press, 1999), p. 122.

52. *A Week*, p. 336.

53. Ibid.

54. Ibid., p. 342.

55. Sayre makes this point, for example. p. 45.

56. *A Week*, p. 343. An intercourse akin to the trip that Henry and John took together on the Concord and Merrimack Rivers.

57. Ibid., p. 344.

58. Ibid., p. 346. Contrast this with Thoreau's claim in "Walking" that the white man is a non-native plant without strong roots in the soil.

59. Ibid., p. 355. In the version presented in *Friendship, Love, and Marriage,* it adds, "It says, in the Vishnu parana 'Seven paces together is sufficient for the friendship of the virtuous, but thou and I have dwelt together.'" p. 77.

60. *A Week,* p. 338.

61. Ibid., p. 350.

62. Ibid., p. 342.

63. Ibid., p. 344.

64. Ibid., pp. 344–45.

65. *Walden*, p. 1.

66. Smith, p. 100.

67. Canby, p. 216.

68. Canby himself notes that "Emerson surely never thought of him as a dependent or a parasite. Yet he says, 'It is difficult to be a benefactor of a man [i.e., Thoreau] with the independence of a woodchuck and the sensitiveness of a thoroughbred horse.'" Ibid., p. 215. Note Emerson's repeated use of the term "woodchucks" to allude to Thoreau.

69. Ibid., pp. 207–8.

70. *Walden,* p. 7.

71. Ibid., p. 146.

72. Ibid.

73. Ibid.

74. Ibid., p. 147.

75. Ibid., p. 140. At least one kind of Emersonian mood.

76. Ibid.

77. Ibid., p. 144.

78. Robert F. Sayre, *Thoreau and the American Indians* (Princeton: Princeton University Press, 1977), p. 69.

79. For what it's worth, it is reported that his last word was "Indian." Edward Wagenknecht, *Henry David Thoreau* (Amherst: University of Massachusetts Press, 1981), p. 137.

80. Thoreau derives the very name of Walden Pond from a Native American legend (although "Walden" sounds suspiciously Anglo-Saxon to me). According to Thoreau, a group of Native Americans were having a ceremony on a tall hill that stretched up into the heavens. During the "pow-wow," they used profanity ("though this vice is one of which the Indians were never guilty"). As a result, the hill suddenly sank into the ground, becoming the lake we see today. Only one woman escaped: Walden. Whether this story is apocryphal or made up by Thoreau himself seems to be unclear. But the destruction of the phallic hill and the emergence of the maternal from this act of punishment is redolent with mythopoetic as well as psychosexual imagery—harking back once again to Derrida's makeshift and the search for the original mother. (I am indebted to Kateri Carmola for pointing out the myriad possibilities in this story.) *Walden,* p. 122.

81. Ibid., p. 101.

82. Ibid.

83. Ibid., p. 139.

84. Ibid. The reference to *talaria,* the wings that appear at Hermes' heels, suggests the possibility of redemption even for this lowest and most unsuitable of human subjects.

85. Ibid., p. 141. As so often with Thoreau, we note the near complete absence of women in his writings.

86. Ibid., p. 142.

87. Ibid., p. 141.

88. Ibid.

89. Ibid., p. 141.

90. Ibid., pp. 141–42.

91. Ibid., p. 141.

92. Henry David Thoreau, "Chesuncook," in *The Maine Woods* (New York: Thomas Y. Crowell & Co., 1906), Ibid., p. 170.

93. *Walden,* p. 177.

94. Ibid., pp. 142–43.

95. Ibid., p. 140.

96. Sayre himself is forced to admit that Thoreau mainly refers even to Joe Polis, his most important guide, as "the Indian." Howarth suggests that this might have been a way to protect Polis's identity (a more cynical read would be to argue that this allows Thoreau more credit from what he learned from Polis). In general, Howarth sees the work as more fictionalized than most other critics seem to.
97. Sayre, p. 8.
98. Henry David Thoreau, "Ktaadn," in *The Maine Woods,* p. 7.
99. Ibid.
100. Ibid.
101. Henry David Thoreau, "The Allegash and East Branch," in *The Maine Woods,* p. 173.
102. The irony of the name "Polis" speaks for itself.
103. "Ktaadn," p. 85.
104. Ibid., p. 86.
105. Ibid.
106. Henry David Thoreau, "Chesuncook," p. 103.
107. Although he seemed to get along fine without a guide, in other parts of "Ktaadn" Thoreau marvels at how, despite the advances of European science, a good understanding of the woods evades white society:

    though the sailors of Europe are familiar with the soundings of [the] Hudson, and Fulton long since invented the steamboat on its waters, an Indian is still necessary to guide her scientific men to its headwaters in the Adirondac country. "Ktaadn," p. 89.

108. "Chesuncook," p. 116.
109. Ibid., p. 117.
110. Ibid., p. 143.
111. Ibid., p. 145.
112. Ibid., p. 149.
113. Ibid.
114. Sayre, p. 119. Here, Howarth takes exception to this oft-cited claim, saying that this is a "flimsy pretext":

    Polis' literacy and civilized values were important issues in "Allegash" and surely Thoreau had not built a rationale for suppression upon one of the story's main features. No, the reasons for delay were probably less generous: Thoreau trusted neither his portrayal of "the Indian" nor the editor who had solicited his work. Howarth, p. 147.

115. "The Allegash and East Branch," p. 257. At times Thoreau contrasts Polis, a modern Native American with limited skills, to his ancestors. At one point, while commenting that the contemporary Native Americans cannot make arrowheads, he depicts Polis picking up a stone transformed by his ancestors for that purpose, not realizing what it is. Ibid., p. 294.
116. Ibid., p. 185.
117. Ibid., p. 196.
118. Ibid., p. 226.
119. Ibid., p. 200.
120. Ibid., p. 216. Polis actually is a landowner who is worth $6,000, probably a good deal more than Thoreau himself was worth!
121. Ibid., p. 203.
122. Ibid., p. 237.

123. Ibid., p. 258.

124. Ibid., p. 284.

125. Sayre interprets this adventure as an "initiation ceremony" into a social bond with Polis. I don't see much evidence for this. This event occurs late in "The Allegash and East Branch," and the relationship between Thoreau and Polis doesn't alter much before or after this incident.

126. Ibid., p. 324.

127. "Chesuncook," p. 122.

128. Ibid., pp. 129–30. Here, Thoreau uses "next to" in a sense that I find speaks to Cavell's concept of "nextness." Hunting is next to philosophy—it precedes it and is presupposed by it.

129. Ibid., p. 130.

130. Ibid.

131. Ibid., p. 131. Recall that in *Walden* Thoreau calls for overcoming nature and killing the beast within.

132. Ibid. And yet even the moose becomes a possible object of transcendence:

> The moose will perhaps one day become extinct; but how naturally then, when it exists only as a fossil relic, and unseen as that, may the poet or sculptor invent a fabulous animal with similar branching and leafy horns...to be the inhabitant of such a forest as this! Ibid., p. 126.

133. "The Allegash and East Branch," p. 267.

134. "Chesuncook," p. 133.

135. "The Allegash and East Branch," p. 169.

136. Cavell, *Senses of Walden*, p. 110.

137. Ibid., p. 60.

138. Ibid., p. 56.

139. Ibid., p. 61.

140. Ibid., p. 86.

141. *A Week*, p. 334. Obviously this idea of neighborliness is not what Cavell has in mind with "nextness," but it suggests that models of community generated from within the doctrine of love will tend to reproduce the same problems.

142. Ibid., p. 332.

143. Ibid., p. 328. He also writes, "This [friendship] is a plant which thrives best in a temperate zone." Ibid., p. 342.

144. Ibid., p. 332.

145. Ibid., pp. 331–32.

146. Ibid., p. 358.

CHAPTER 6

1. An earlier version of parts of this chapter appeared in *Theory and Event* 4:2 (2000).

2. *Politics of Friendship*, p. 305.

3. *Beyond Good and Evil*, p. 3.

4. *The Genealogy of Morals*, p. 166.

5. Nietzsche argues, for example, that Kant's notion of the disinterested viewer, who views even nude statues with an aloof appreciation, has "smuggled the spectator," preserved a

desiring agent in the heart of his ascetic philosophy. These preserved desires are challenged and complicated in their inclusion in the pursuit of the higher. Ibid., p. 238.

6. Ibid., p. 246, among other examples.

7. Ibid., p. 243.

8. Nietzsche writes that in the Judeo-Christian tradition, "Love grew out of hatred . . . spreading triumphantly in the purest sunlight, yet having in its high and sunny realm the same aims—victory, aggrandization, temptation,—which hatred pursues by digging its roots ever deeper into all that was profound and evil." Ibid., p. 168.

9. Ibid., pp. 177–78.

10. Ibid., p. 173. In *Ecce Homo,* Nietzsche writes, "The man of knowledge must be able not only to love his enemies but also to hate his friends." *Ecce Homo,* p. 6.

11. Friedrich Nietzsche, *The Gay Science* (New York: Vantage Books, 1974), p. 88.

12. Ibid.

13. Ibid.

14. Ibid., pp. 88–89.

15. Ibid., p. 89.

16. *Politics of Friendship,* p. 65.

17. Ibid., p.64.

18. Ibid.

19. Ibid.

20. Although, to be fair, for Aristophanes the humans started the war that led to their "halving."

21. This is certainly the argument of C. B. MacPherson, Alisdair MacIntyre, and Leo Strauss, among others.

22. As Richard Flathman has noted, "Contemporary liberals are at once attracted to and fearful of the diversity and unpredictability that Hobbes theorized; they are both in quest of and wary concerning institutions that promise the order he promoted." Richard Flathman, *Willful Liberalism: Voluntarism and Individuality in Political Theory and Practice* (Ithaca, N.Y.: Cornell University Press, 1992), p. 4.

23. In varying degrees I have in mind works that at the very least see Hobbes as offering a kind of individualist ethos that belies his darker tone. This includes works such as Richard Flathman, *Thomas Hobbes: Skepticism, Individuality, and Chastened Politics* (Newbury Park, Calif.: Sage Press, 1993) and *Willful Liberalism*; Michael Oakeshott, *Hobbes on Civil Association* (Berkeley: University of California Press, 1975); George Kateb, "Hobbes and the Irrationality of Politics," *Political Theory* 17:3 (August 1989); Alan Ryan, "Hobbes on Individualism," in G. A. J. Rogers and Alan Ryan, eds., *Perspectives on Thomas Hobbes* (Oxford: Clarendon Press, 1988); Gregory S. Kavka, *Hobbesian Moral and Political Theory* (Princeton: Princeton University Press, 1986); and Richard Tuck, *Hobbes* (New York: Oxford University Press, 1961).

24. Quoted in Arnold A. Rogow, *Thomas Hobbes: Radical in the Service of Reaction* (New York, W.W. Norton & Co., 1986), p. 44.

25. See for example David Gauthier, *The Logic of Leviathan* (Oxford: Clarendon Press, 1977). Kirstie M. McClure, as we have seen, makes a similar point, as does David Wootton, albeit for different reasons.

26. Tuck, p. 34.

27. See J. G. A. Pocock, "Time, History, and Eschatology in the Thought of Thomas Hobbes," in *Politics, Language, and Time* (Chicago: University of Chicago Press, 1989),

pp. 148–201; or A. P. Martinich, *The Two Gods of Leviathan* (Cambridge: Cambridge University Press, 1992).

28. Other texts such as *Behemoth* are, if anything, even bolder.

29. Tuck, pp. 27–31, and *Leviathan*, p. 711.

30. A. P. Martinich, *Thomas Hobbes* (New York: St. Martin's Press, 1997), pp. 84–85.

31. However, Hobbes has few kind words for these thinkers. And some of those who defend Hobbes as admiring the Puritans might overreach at times. For example, Christopher Hill cites Hobbes as having written: "If in time as in place, there were degrees of high and low, I verily believe the highest of times would be that which passed betwixt 1640 and 1660." Hill, *The World Turned Upside Down*, p. 313. But this sentence is the first passage of *Behemoth*, the very next sentence of which is "For he that thence, as from the Devil's Mountain, should have looked upon the world and observed the actions of men . . . might have had a prospect of all kinds of injustice, and of all kinds of folly, that the world could afford." *Behemoth* (Chicago: University of Chicago Press, 1990), p. 1. This is hardly the stuff of praise, perhaps not even the "grudging respect" that Hill claims it to be. If we do not try to make Hobbes into a Leveller, the paradox that he is so similar to those whom he critiques is all the richer.

32. Andrew Sharp, ed., *The English Levellers* (Cambridge, U.K.: Cambridge University Press, 1998), p. 208.

33. *The World Turned Upside Down*, pp. 141–42. As Hobbes puts it himself, "I can find no where that any man shall live in torments Everlastingly." *Leviathan*, p. 646; see also p. 661.

34. *The World Turned Upside Down*, p. 314.

35. Ibid., p. 113. There is ample evidence in the literature on Hobbes's own "human-centered" politics. For example, Arlene Saxenhouse writes about "Hobbes' human-centered world where political order is imposed against, rather than in conformity with, nature." Thomas Hobbes, *Three Discourses*, Arlene Saxonhouse, ed. (Chicago: University of Chicago Press, 1995), p. 125. See also Richard Flathman, Christopher Hill, Stephen Holmes. Martinich would disagree with this interpretation wholeheartedly.

36. Flathman, *Thomas Hobbes*, p. 1.

37. *Leviathan*, p. 131. Locke says something similar, but as we will see, he does not stick to his convictions with nearly the rigor of Hobbes.

38. Ibid., p. 498–99.

39. *Behemoth*, p. 52.

40. *Leviathan*, p. 499.

41. This is certainly Tuck's take on this. Tuck, p. 30.

42. This needs to be qualified somewhat: Hobbes does care when the overriding religion is one, such as Catholicism or Presbyterianism, in which the absolutism of the religion precludes the possibility of internal thought.

43. *Leviathan*, p. 331.

44. Ibid., p. 332.

45. Ibid.

46. Locke, *The Reasonableness of Christianity* ("A Discourse on Miracles"), p. 80.

47. *Leviathan*, p. 332. Accordingly, I don't think that the difference between "true religion," "natural religion," and false religion, which Flathman writes about, is as clearly defined as he seems to find. Even when God is present, there is doubt and the need for interpretation. Flathman, pp. 22–23. Hobbes does not preclude revelation itself. He writes that

God's commandments are "not a duty that we exhibit to God, but a gift which God freely giveth to whom he pleaseth." Leviathan, p. 332. But this does not amount to a political doctrine.

48. Hobbes's own arguments against rules punishing heresy point to the fact that there must always be a limit to the church's power when it comes to matters of individual conscience.

49. *Leviathan,* p. 586.

50. Norberto Bobbio, *Thomas Hobbes and the Natural Law Tradition* (Chicago: University of Chicago Press, 1989).

51. Thomas Hobbes, *De Cive,* in *Thomas Hobbes: Man and Citizen* (Indianapolis: Hackett Publishing, 1993), p. 100.

52. *Leviathan,* p. 187.

53. *De Cive,* p. 114.

54. Prior to the fall, Locke considers Adam and Eve to have been "a state of perfect obedience." *The Reasonableness of Christianity,* p. 25.

55. *Leviathan,* p. 260. This is further interesting insofar as obedience seemed to be the *only* thing we owed to God in the case of revelation. If we don't even owe God that, what is left?

56. Ibid.

57. And indeed Giorgio Agamben, among others, tells us that this has become the case.

58. I see Hobbes as an early practitioner of strategic essentialism—choosing the "fact" of the body as the basis upon which he will build his new subject and ascribing to that body those qualities which best lead to a desirable outcome.

59. Stephen Holmes, in Introduction to *Behemoth,* p. xl. As when Holmes cites Hobbes's report that in ancient Ethiopia kings would commit suicide upon the demand of the high priests even though the priests were unarmed (and not even present). Hobbes lists the "Feare of Death" as one of the many passions which "encline men to Peace." But there are others, such as "Desire of such things as are necessary to commodious living; and a Hope by their Industry to attain them." *Leviathan,* p. 188.

60. It is true that much of Calvinist-influenced theology at the time also argued that one was never sure of one's status in the afterlife and thus one's attitude to death ought indeed to be marked by a great deal of anxiety. Hobbes's connections to Calvinism are worth noting. He professes admiration for Calvin and William Perkins, among others. Thomas Hobbes, "The Questions concerning Liberty, Necessity, and Chance," in *The English Works of Thomas Hobbes* (London: Scientia Aalen, 1962), p. 266. Yet again the political salience which he derives from his understanding of death and the afterlife is different. For Calvinism, the doubt of election was meant to inscribe the subject all the more forcefully into an obedience to higher laws. For Hobbes, the inability to know of the afterlife from this "grosse, and corruptible" perspective requires that we turn to our own ethical and moral devices.

61. *Leviathan,* p. 262.

62. Ibid., p. 625.

63. Once again, to reiterate Holmes's point, this is not to say that for Hobbes people never will give up their bodies for various reasons. But Hobbes will never *require* them to do so. If they do, it is out of their own choice.

64. Tuck, p. 27.

65. She speaks of him, for example, as advocating "a society relentlessly engaged in a process of acquisition," and thus she participates in a C. B. MacPherson–style "possessive individual" reading of him. *The Human Condition*, p. 31. Hobbes is also attacked by Locke and Rousseau, even while both of them borrow heavily from him. This may, however, attest mainly to the fact that Hobbes is more subversive to the doctrine of love than either of them are.

66. Hannah Arendt, "What Is Freedom?" in *Between Past and Future* (New York: Penguin Books, 1968), pp. 160–65.

67. Ibid., p. 164.

68. *Leviathan*, p. 128.

69. Ibid., p. 127.

70. Ibid., p. 129; my emphasis. Earlier Hobbes tells us that the terms "good" and "evil" as he uses them are not absolute but relative to a situation, to a person or collectivities. Ibid., p. 120.

71. This is quite possibly why Hobbes chose to have his chapter "Of Speech" precede his chapter "Of Reason and Science." Before one can use reason, one must fix things with names, articulate and communicate its existence.

72. Ibid., p. 137.

73. Ibid., p. 132.

74. Ibid., p. 133.

75. "Truth and Politics," in *Between Past and Future*, p. 235. I also find that Arendt's harsh attacks on Hobbes for advocating lying misunderstand him. Hobbes does not advocate lying but rather forging new truths collectively. Arendt is especially vituperative when she argues that Hobbes suggests that Aristotle writes lies to preserve his own life (Ibid., p. 293), but Hobbes is clearly no fan of Aristotle, and saw all of his work as lies. At any rate, in the larger matter of "truth," I don't think that even here Hobbes deserves the kind of attack he sustains from Arendt. Arendt herself is an advocate of narratives and reality being forged out of collective speech and action. So the truth for her is not necessarily some Platonic constant (although at times, such as in "Truth and Politics," it begins to look more like that) but could well be in line with Hobbes's own empiricism.

76. *Leviathan*, p. 239.

77. Locke, *Essay*, p. 344.

78. Ibid., p. 345.

79. Although it is really "without," in natural law itself.

80. It is worth noting that to some extent both Hobbes and Locke downplay the will's primacy—Hobbes by seeing the will as the beginning of a conversation, Locke by subsuming the will to other mental faculties and ultimately to reason. But this difference is critical, for it only reinforces what I've been saying about the two divergent social visions which are produced by these thinkers' respective epistemologies—the one cooperative and the other hierarchical.

81. As Arendt tells us, this notion of sovereignty extends not only to states but to persons and has tragic results. "It is as though the I-will paralyzed the I-can, as though the moment men *willed* freedom, they lost their capacity to *be* free.... Because of the will's impotence, its incapacity to generate genuine power, its constant defeat in the struggle with the self...the will-to-power turned at once into a will-to-oppression." "What Is Freedom?" p. 162.

At the same time, it must be noted that Arendt is not against sovereignty per se, only this particular variant of it. She writes in *The Human Condition* that "The sovereignty of a body of people bound and kept together, not by an identical will which somehow magically inspires them all, but by an agreed purpose for which alone the promises are valid and binding, shows itself quite clearly in its unquestioned superiority over those who are completely free, unbound by any promises and unkept by any purpose." *The Human Condition*, p. 245. It is worth considering further why Arendt needs to hold on to the notion of sovereignty itself at all.

82. "That he which is made Sovereign maketh no covenant with his Subjects beforehand, is manifest; because either he must make it with the whole multitude as one party to the Covenant; or he must make a severall Covenant with every man." *Leviathan*, p. 230.

83. Ibid., p. 238. As Richard Flathman writes of Hobbes's attempts to demand good government, "Although presented in a confident tone of advice readily followed, these remarks are less than encouraging concerning the prospects of good law." Flatham, *Willful Liberalism*, p. 43.

84. Obviously, Hobbes is not offering us a tutorial vision of democracy. The sovereign has absolutely nothing to teach the people—they are the ones engaged in collective judgment.

85. *Leviathan*, p. 271.

86. That Hobbes never alludes to such a possibility is not in and of itself fatal to my argument. Given that he was writing at the beginning of this process, for him to declare that the sovereign would become unnecessary would be to lessen its value at the outset—to lessen the perception of the sovereign's power that is necessary to creating a public space of self-creation in the first place.

87. Hobbes himself, as Flathman points out, dedicates a great deal of effort to ensuring that the sovereign will act justly and, to the degree possible, in accordance with the public felicity.

88. *Willful Liberalism*, p. 36.

89. Ibid., p. 20.

90. Ibid., p. 37.

91. An insight that Marx makes quite brilliantly in "On the Jewish Question." See *The Marx-Engels Reader*, Robert C. Tucker, ed. (New York: W.W. Norton & Co,, 1978).

92. *The Human Condition*, p. 243.

93. "Truth and Politics," p. 241.

94. We see Emerson and Thoreau shared a dislike for philanthropy and critiqued the notion that one can know the good of another person, that one can know that person at all.

95. Quoted in *Politics of Friendship*, p. 254.

96. *De Cive*, p. 111.

97. Ibid., p. 113.

98. Ibid.

99. Here again, I am reminded of Marx. He writes that in capitalist (and liberal) society, we receive love as a reflection of our material worth. But under conditions of communism: "If you love without evoking love in return—that is, if your loving as loving does not produce reciprocal love; if through a *living expression* of yourself as a loving person you do not make yourself a loved person, then your love is impotent—a misfortune." "Economic and Philosophical Manuscripts of 1844," in *The Marx-Engels Reader*, p. 105.

100. Of course, giving without the expectation of receiving is highly reminiscent of Christian ethics and, as I will argue further, is not unrelated. Without seeking to impugn Christian religious ethics, I simply want to point out that the kind of rupture that Derrida is calling for is quite different, precisely because it does not stem from *agape*. Such giving does not so much as receive as establish our love. The differences between these two ideas of giving can be clearly seen in Levinas's attacks on Simone Weil (see below).

101. Jacques Derrida, *The Gift of Death* (Chicago: University of Chicago Press, 1995), p. 41.

102. Ibid., p. 45.

103. Emmanuel Levinas, *Of God Who Comes to Mind* (Stanford, Calif.: Stanford University Press, 1998), pp. 37–38.

104. Ibid. Levinas sees in the doctrine of love itself, in *caritas,* the paralysis that prevents such a possibility. In *Difficult Freedom,* critiquing Simone Weil's own notion of charity, he writes:

> [I]t is precisely this inanity of charity—this resignation at the base of the most active charity, to the misfortune of the innocent—which is a contradiction. Love cannot overcome it, since it feeds off it. To overcome it we must act—and here the place of action and its irreducibilty in the economy of being. Emmanuel Levinas, *Difficult Freedom: Essays on Judaism,* (Baltimore: Johns Hopkins University Press, 1990). pp. 139–40.

105. *Love and Saint Augustine,* p. 56.

106. *The Human Condition,* p. 244.

107. In this way, she does not so much repudiate Heidegger as contend with and "respond" to him.

108. Ibid., p. 247.

109. *Love and Saint Augustine,* p. 75.

110. *De Cive,* p. 100.

111. *Difficult Freedom,* p. 144.

112. Ibid.

113. Ibid., p. 145.

114. Ibid., p. 141.

115. *The Gift of Death,* pp. 50–51.

116. Derrida offers that Heidegger and even Levinas might be considered to engage in "religion without religion," that is to say, have an idea of God that does not rely on the actual existence of God himself (or, as Derrida puts it himself, "think[ing] the possibility of such an event but not the event itself"). Ibid., p. 49; my emphasis.

117. Jacques Derrida, "Violence and Metaphysics: An Essay on the Thought of Emmanuel Levinas," in *Writing and Difference* (Chicago: University of Chicago Press, 1978), p. 114.

118. A sentiment that we see even with Thoreau when he writes, "Can God afford that I should forget him?" Quoted in Canby, p. 178.

119. Giorgio Agamben, *The Coming Community* (Minneapolis: University of Minnesota Press, 1993), pp. 5–6.

120. Ibid., p. 32.

121. Maybe "forgetting" God means in part forgetting the transparent patriarch that we imagine in God's place.

122. Of course, Hobbes clearly believes in a very real God (but then again, so does Levinas in his own way). But the nature of his belief is such that it does not preclude or contradict

the notion of forgetting God. Hobbes too might offer "religion without religion," an idea of an outside that provides a context within which responsibility can take shape.

123. "Violence and Metaphysics," p. 151.

124. Ibid., p. 152.

125. Ibid.

126. Ibid.

127. He is a Jew, of course, but as we have seen, Derrida portrays him almost as a Christian *malgré lui* in "Violence and Metaphysics." But perhaps these terms are not helpful since in *The Gift of Death* Levinas seems more "Jewish," and anyway even the "Christianity" of Patočka is heretical and redolent of "religion without religion."

128. Ibid., p. 153.

129. Ibid.

130. Ibid.

131. This question is redolent of an earlier one: What kind of "Christian" is Hobbes? The role of Christianity itself seems precluded in this dichotomy, but it seems to me that this suspension between Greek and Jew in part describes the realm of Christian thought itself.

132. *The Coming Community,* p. 53.

133. *Politics of Friendship,* p. 306.

134. E. M. Forster, *A Passage to India* (New York, Harcourt, Brace & Co., 1984), p. 362.

INDEX